Dedicated to

W. W. Kulski

My professor of International Relations at the
Maxwell Graduate School of Citizenship and Public Affairs,
Syracuse University, New York, U.S.A.,
To whom the students of the 1950s owe so much

Kashmir and Neighbours

Tale, Terror, Truce

TÜRKKAYA ATAÖV

Ashgate

Aldershot • Burlington USA • Singapore • Sydney

#49001699

© Türkkaya Ataöv 2001

Published by
Ashgate Publishing Limited
Gower House
Croft Road
Aldershot
Hants GU11 3HR
England

Ashgate Publishing Company
131 Main Street
Burlington, VT 05401-5600 USA

Ashgate website: http://www.ashgate.com

British Library Cataloguing in Publication Data
Ataöv, Türkkaya
   Kashmir and neighbours : tale, terror, truce
   1.Jammu and Kashmir (India) - Relations
   I.Title
   954.6

Library of Congress Control Number: 2001091323

ISBN 0 7546 2246 0 (Hbk)
ISBN 0 7546 2252 5 (Pbk)

Printed and bound in Great Britain by MPG Books Ltd, Bodmin, Cornwall

The Essence

Come, come again, whoever, whatever you may be, come;
Heathen, fire-worshiper, sinner of idolatry, come;
Come even if you have broken your vows a hundred times,
Ours is not the portal of despair or misery, come.

—Maulana Jalal-ud Din Rumi (1207-73), tr. Talât S. Halman

&

I beseech my Hindu brothers to rise to the height of their
traditional tolerance which is the basic glory of our Vedic faith.

—I.N.C. President, Sarojani Naidu, 1925

&

[I]n course of time, Hindus would cease to be Hindus, and
Muslims would cease to be Muslims, not in the religious sense,
because that is the personal faith of each individual, but in the
political sense as citizens of the State.

—Quaid-e Azam Muhammad Ali Jinnah, 1947

&

Contents

List of Illustrations

Maps

1. Kashmir and neighbours.

2. Jammu and Kashmir.

3. India: states and union territories.

4. Pakistan's deployment in Batalik.

Photographs

1. The author with Mrs. Gandhi.

2. Morarji Desai, Prime Minister of India, 1977–1979.

3. Rajiv Gandhi and the author, 1988.

4. Atal Bihari Vajpayee, Prime Minister of India, 1996, 1998–.

5. Benazir Bhutto.

6. Kashmiri lake—photo taken by the author.

7. Bunkers on Kashmiri city streets.

8. The author (middle) is shown with Dr. Mustafa Kamaal Pasha (right). Currently a member of the Kashmiri Cabinet, Dr. M. Kamaal was named by his secular-minded father, Sheikh Abdullah, after modern Turkey's founder.

9. The author interviewed by Mrs. Nayeema Ahmad at All India Radio, Srinagar.

10. Hazratbal Mosque on Lake Dal.

Preface

I started taking notes for this book after observing Indian soldiers in Srinagar, Kashmir's summer capital, gazing through the gun-slits of their sand-bagged bunkers. They were trying to coexist with the state's natural beauty, its greatest resource. The panorama from Hotel Welcome, where I stayed, was a glimpse of so much more to delight in. But the bunkers draped in camouflage netting and dotting street corners were also contrasting sights of more to come.

A multi-religious political entity based on *Kashmiriyat*, a common culture shared by the country's Muslims, Hindus, Sikhs, and even Buddhists, gave way to a bloody wedge between various groups of these communities. Insurgencies, kept up by foreign entities, attracted mercenaries who apparently needed a job and a mission. Attacks on Hindus, most of whom were Brahmins belonging to the Pandit caste, and Muslims, both of whom lived, by and large, as *bhai-bhai* (like brothers) for generations, not only relocated virtually the entire Hindu population of the Valley (equally called Vale) of Kashmir, but also made insufficiently supportive Muslims targets. This dangerous episode presented itself in constitutionally secular India whose founding father, Jawaharlal Nehru, was a Kashmiri Pandit himself and where *Sufi* (mystical) Islam as an undogmatic faith with components from sources outside Muslim teaching, moved closer to Hinduism.

Although Article 370 of the Constitution of India recognizes the special position of the State of Jammu and Kashmir (J&K), the latter is a part of India. Hence, the word "neighbours" in the title of the book refers mainly to Pakistan and the export of mercenaries from another neighbour Afghanistan. J&K faces a dilemma. After the grassroots violence, that emerged in 1988, and with Pakistan throwing its lot in with it, terrorism discouraged tourism, on which the state's economy substantially depended, and economic stagnation pushed the unemployed youth towards guerilla activity that pays dividends in more ways than one. The armed rebels are now motivated less by Kashmiri nationalism than "fundamentalism", partially sponsored by neighbouring Pakistani groups and Afghanistan's Taliban and other imported aliens, most of whom are strangers to that land and its peoples. Some called them "guests", who would be more accurately defined as uninvited intruders. More depressingly, during the Summer of 1999, the forces of India and Pakistan, both now possessing a nuclear capability, clashed at Kargil, giving chills to all those who fear the future may be decided by an atomic contest. India may be acclaimed favourably for self-restraint after rebuffing Pakistan's incursion.

Blood-soaked episodes compel me to probe the Kashmir issue, especially in the light of terrorism, not unmindful of the role played by the infamous Taliban-at-arms. Hoping for the triumph of eventual stability in J&K, this book finds it worthwhile, by way of comparison, to offer a description of the fascinating land, manifold people, far-reaching past, and the nation-building experiences of India and Pakistan, which seemingly march to different drummers. Since no issue can be addressed in isolation, the chapters below serve, in my opinion, the main purpose of this research, which is terrorism in J&K as it is the instrument of the foreign policy of the two north-western neighbours of India. There can be no understanding of the issue without some essential background of these closely interrelated factors. The present militants carried out violent actions, partly but consequentially assisted by the Pakistani intelligence services. The Afghan experience was momentous for this neighbouring country for providing it with an infrastructure of trained manpower, camps and weapons as much as a centre of indoctrination of *Mujahideen* (fighters) for Islamic *jehad* (literally "struggle", holy war or ardent effort to spread Islam). This book's sections on violence in the "Seven Sisters" of India's North-East and in Punjab aim to evince the parallelism between all extremist activities in different parts of India.

There is no security either for India and Pakistan, both nuclear states now, or for the whole of the Sub-continent, without peace and stability in J&K. While the road to truce and reconciliation passes through bilateral talks and mutual accommodation, realistic and far-reaching enough to deserve the support of the Kashmiris, the success of the Central Government in New Delhi in regaining the loyalty of the Sikhs of Punjab raises hopes that the alienation in the Valley of Kashmir may well be a nightmare of the past. Just as Pakistan's long-enduring vision that the Kashmiris wish to join their Islamic neighbour lacks sufficiently convincing basis, India needs to pursue policies of more human rights and more jobs, in addition to the need to crush terrorism.

I hope that I have been able to offer more than mere *khali batchit* (empty chatter).

A note on spelling: Some units of language such as names, frequently seen in printed works, may be spelled differently in each case. Among the most repeatedly used words are the Qur'an (Koran), Muhammad (Mohammed), Moghul (Mughal), Abdullah (Abdalla), and the like. For example, a very prominent Muslim thinker (Sir Syed Ahmad Khan) spelled an oft-repeated word even in the titles of his own books in different ways: Mahomedan, Muhammedan, Mohomedan. The controversy stems from the fact that the original term is not an English one, thereby rendered into the Latin script in different ways by various writers. I employ the most frequent or the most likely correct form, if not the choice of the original source itself.

Türkkaya Ataöv
New York-New Delhi-Srinagar-Ankara

Chapter 1

Introduction

Who has not heard of the Vale of Cashmere
With its roses, the highest that earth ever gave,
Its temples, and grottos, and fountains: as clear
As the love-lighted eyes that hang over their wave?
—from *Lalla Rookh* by Thomas Moore.[1]

François Bernier (1620–88), a French physician attached to the Turco-Moghul court (1526–1858) at Delhi in the 17th century, was one of the first Europeans to travel to Kashmir, on which he conferred the title "Paradise of the Indies".[2] The whole ground enamelled with flowers wore the appearance of a fertile garden filled with water, canals, lakes and rivulets. That description is still valid today. Ringed by the snows of the Himalayan range, that jewel on the northern rim of India, has attracted the pens of many travellers since then. As recorded by another European traveller, Ippolito Desideri (1684–1733), a Jesuit priest who hailed from the environs of Florence,[3] the Kashmiris called their land "*Bahisht*" meaning terrestrial paradise. Some have claimed that Kashmir excels even the much-adored Switzerland.[4]

The land itself is still a "paradise" to the eye. But the Kashmir issue, which has become a highly emotive subject interwoven with terrorism, foreign interference and mercenaries, continues to arouse, even after more than half a century following Britain's exit, considerable anxiety, particularly as the immense military potential of India and Pakistan may tempt some quarters to resort to another war. The Prussian Clausewitz had construed it to mean an extension of "politics by other means". Kashmir is a part of India, but the two neighbours, India and Pakistan, have continued their contest over it in the diplomatic arena, and also on the battlefield in the years 1947–48, 1965, 1971, and most recently in 1999. A succession of India's leaders perpetuated the belief that the Kashmiris ought to be accorded a "special status", and Kashmir remains a valuable asset for Pakistani politicians for domestic competition. Kashmiri involvement for Pakistan, which also inherited the "burden" of the North-West Frontier Province (NWFP), causes a dangerous drain of manpower and financial means much beyond the dictates of security, and for India it means the deployment of military strength on a tenuous front line where superiority of numbers and armour can hardly be capitalized. The insurgency in Kashmir and partial foreign involvement behind it constitute a classic low-intensity conflict. The threat of the next armed clash escalating into a major war, even an unforeseen nuclear one, is now a matter of international concern. South Asia stands today at a crossroads. One is the promise of peace, and the other is the threat of another major conflict. The Kashmir issue, among others, holds the key to both of these alternatives.

I had published my first article on Kashmir in the year 1953. "The Kashmir issue" was the topic of my first academic research when I became, a couple of years later, a student of international relations at the Maxwell Graduate School of Citizenship and Public Affairs of Syracuse University in the State of New York. Four decades passed before I had the good fortune to visit the Valley of Kashmir[5] which has inspired countless people by its beauty. I reached Srinagar, the summer capital of the State of Jammu and Kashmir,[6] from New Delhi in a little over two hours by air and looked down on the tortuous country through which Bernier had exasperatingly travelled with the army of the Moghul Emperor Aurangzeb (1618–1707).

Jammu and Kashmir, called by the shorter term "Kashmir", which also comprises Baltistan, Gilgit, Hunza, Ladakh, and Nagar[7] is one of the largest states in the Indian Union.[8] It is also one of the highest habitations in the world. Srinagar is said to be one of the oldest cities of India, presumably founded by Emperor Asoka (Ashoka, c.269–232 B.C.). Kashmir possesses an uninterrupted series of written records of its history since ancient times. Anchored on the extreme north of India, Kashmir experiences, in unlucky times as well as in happier circumstances, a variable climate, including the temperate cool of the Valley, the tropical heat of the winter capital Jammu, and the arctic cold of Ladakh. Not only the nomadic Gujjars, but also the government today moves from the warm regions of Jammu to the cool of Srinagar in summer time.

Almost all the wonderful phenomena of nature may be found in the State of J&K from mountain peaks like the K2[9] or Mt. Goodwin Austin on the Karakoram range, the second highest in the world, to glaciers of great size such as Baltoro. A number of gigantic glaciers are only exceeded in size by the great Humboldt of Greenland.[10] Every morning in Srinagar, sunlight touches the grey waters of the lakes and turns them into a shimmering gold. Its meadows carpeted with wild graceful flowers of rainbow colours, the Valley, thousands of feet above sea-level, is surrounded, even during seedtime and midsummer, by snow-capped mountains and watered by the Jhelum and its tributaries. The Valley is, indeed, "an emerald set with pearls".[11] It is also "unique as an excursion ground"[12] for students of geology. The forests, the green gold of Kashmir, are still preserved. They were a regular haunt of lovers of sports and adventure who could find ibex or wild goats with very long horns, musk deer with slender legs and beautiful eyes, and snow leopards roaming at high altitudes. There are beautiful meadows, frequented for centuries, by shepherds and their flocks, amid forests of silver fir, majestic oak, blue pine, and graceful birch trees.[13] Irrigation canals having previously turned barren tracts into rich fields of rice and wheat, most of the Kashmiris are still dependent on the land for their livelihood. Meadows, alive with crocuses, daffodils and irises, soon give way to juicy peaches, pears and plums. It is the flora of Kashmir that make it the "Happy Valley".[14] Gulmarg, at an altitude of 2,650 metres above sea level, is a "meadow of flowers" with groves of pines and mountains in the background.[15] Kashmir is the only area where saffron (or *kesar*) grows. This is a land of countless springs often with medicinal effects and of waterfalls pouring down.

The country boasts many lakes, the one called the Dal Lake being spanned by wooden bridges that connect the two sides of the capital city. Picturesque and self-contained houseboats, some of which have their own floating gardens, are the homes of many Kashmiris. *Shikaras*, or small flat-bottomed boats that glide between the houseboats, provide other provisions. The Moghul gardens,[16] some commanding a superb view of lakes, were built long before those in Versailles were patronaged by Louis XIV. The rulers of India are believed to have laid "777 gardens" (perhaps to mean "many") only in the neighbourhood of the Dal Lake. It was they who introduced the *chenar* (plane) trees which now symbolize the whole Valley. The name of the small island in the centre of the Dal Lake, or "*Char Chenar*", is derived from the four symmetrical trees on it. All gardens were arranged in a number of terraces, one above the other, spread with flower beds and with rows of fountains in between. The Moghuls watched the fountains and the multicoloured flowers from the exquisitely decorated pavilions.

The monuments, temples and mosques reflect the various long epochs of Kashmir's history and illustrate its diversity. Often a Hindu temple lies next to a tomb of a Muslim saint. Some localities are therefore sacred to the followers of both religions. The Shankaracharya temple (which I visited) was built on the crest of a high hill overlooking Srinagar, and is considered sacred by Muslims and Buddhists alike. The Hazratbal Mosque (that I have seen) is believed to house the hair of the Muslim Prophet Muhammad. Scattered around are also prayer-walls inscribed with "*Om mani padme hum*".[17] Sir Walter Lawrence, an early traveller, states that crime was almost unknown, the sight of blood was abhorrent, and property was absolutely safe. Joshua Duke,[18] a surgeon resident, wrote in 1904 that one felt in the presence of the "Maker of the Universe". All travellers sought to describe the beauties of the scenery. No one left Kashmir unaffected by its peaceful atmosphere. All Kashmiris, whether Muhammadan, Hindu, Sikh, Buddhist or Christian, wanted to return to this tranquil region.

Some of the descriptions above that fit most of Kashmir's long history are, at best, partially true now. To be exact, India, frequently described as "the world's largest democracy", has been battling terrorism for decades, and efforts to move along the path of sustained development are held hostage to violence. Still evolving democratic institutions, elaborated by the founding fathers of developing countries like India, are under threat from militant groups which reject democratic norms. Such networks, whose origins lie in the creation of an environment in the pursuit of objectives defined in religious terms, are leaving their imprint on a number of other countries as well. The Afghan war against Soviet military intervention had attracted volunteers to camps in Pakistan, where they were further indoctrinated in the so-called "Islamic" tenets and received weapons training as well. After the Soviet withdrawal, these volunteers, who constituted a formidable force with expertise in arms and belief in the legitimacy of their cause, sought new battlefields. The same "holy warriors", whose prowess the West once hailed, are in the forefront of today's terrorists, in common cause with the small group of indigenous militants of Kashmir. India, which has suffered from terrorism in various parts of the land, is now their victim.

Hinduism predominated in the very early ages of Kashmir. Buddhism began to prevail at the time of Asoka. A thousand years later, Shaivism became an important cult. The Valley came under the influence of Islam only in the 13th century. The Muslim ruler Zain-ul Abidin (1420–70) should be praised for his exceptional tolerance towards other religions. This early Islamic rule was followed by a rather long Moghul administration with short reigns of Afghanis and Sikhs. Raja Gulab Singh (1792–1857) purchased (1846) all the lands between the Indus and the Ravi from the East India Company. All of this territory remained under his successors until 1947 when Kashmir acceded to India.

The unexpected attack on Kashmir from the Pakistani side in late 1947 raised the vital issue of the defence of the state. It left the formerly hesitant Maharaja Hari Singh (1895–1961) of Kashmir with no choice but that of accession to India and to seek military assistance to defend the country. The Instrument of Accession, put forward by the Maharaja and accepted by Lord Mountbatten, the first Governor-General of an independent India, is a unique document in many respects. On the other hand, the invasion had territorial, constitutional and human consequences. Although Pakistan occupied a part of Kashmir, variously called "Pak-Occupied Kashmir (POK)", or "Azad (Free) Kashmir", and part of it ceded to the People's Republic of China (Aksai Chin), there is clearly the much larger original territory of the erstwhile Dogra Kingdom. Sheikh Muhammad Abdullah (1905–1982), the renowned former Prime Minister of Kashmir, who had been spearheading a movement to end the autocratic rule of the Maharaja since the early 1930s, had raised the pitch of the Kashmiri ethnic identity, or *Kashmiriyat*, to such heights that its religious facet had been undermined. Nevertheless, his secular approach in a country where the majority of the inhabitants happened to be Muslims was a cardinal point. Pakistan's founder Muhammad Ali Jinnah (1876–1948), who lived only about a year as the new Governor-General, also had a secular vision for the future after 1947, but the pursuits of his successors virtually destroyed his dreams. The tribal attack from Pakistan created yet another human problem. Many Kashmiri families, who worked and lived in the cities that fell within Pakistan, could not return to Kashmir, and the ceasefire (1949) cut them off from their original land.

This book aspires to review terrorist activity carried out ceaselessly and systematically in one of the most otherwise alluring spots on our planet. The rise of militancy, not only in Kashmir, but also in Punjab and in India's North-East, is related also to analogous belligerency in and around the borders of Pakistan and Afghanistan. Following preliminary information on the land, people, the past and the constitutional history of Kashmir, this book will focus on the rise of political violence and its consequences, following the evolution of democracy from the period of the provisional government. There might have been a degree of mishandling of the Centre-State relations *vis-a-vis* J&K and the Government of India, but the Congress Party treatment of the former was not much different from what was meted out to other non-

Congress State administrations. The rule of law and democracy in the Indian part of J&K is more than in Pak-controlled Kashmir, Azad Kashmir and the area ceded to China. Evidence also suggests that foreign hands seemed alert and available to capitalize. The internal dynamics and external linkages of terrorism have made it a formidable challenge to world peace as well as national security. While dwelling mostly on the example of J&K, this book endeavours to underline once more the need for an anti-terrorist international regime. While the precedent of the Simla (now, Shimla) Agreement (1972) between India and Pakistan proved the utility of bilateral talks in terms of the Kashmir issue, the drive for anti-terrorism calls instead for international efforts including agreements to standardize legislation, extradition, penalties and cooperation among law enforcement organizations.

Notes

1   Thomas Moore (1779–1852) is an Irish poet, and not Sir Thomas More who wrote *Utopia* (1516). "Lalla Rookh" (1817), a narrative poem set (on Lord Byron's advice) in an atmosphere of Oriental splendour, gave Moore a reputation rivalling that of Byron and Sir Walter Scott. The poem earned what was then the highest paid price (£3,000).

2   François Bernier, *Voyages; contenant la description des États du Grand Mogol, del'Hindoustan, du royaume de Kachemire,* etc…(originally published as: *Histoire de la dernière revolution des États du Grand Mogol,* etc.), 2 vols., Amsterdam, P. Marret, 1709–10; _____, *The History of the Late Revolution of the Great Mogul,* etc., London, M. Pitt, 1676; _____, *Travels in the Mughal Empire,* London, Oxford University Press, 1914; _____, *Reise des Herrn Bernier in das Königreich Kachemir in Allgemeine Historie der Reisen zu Wasser und Lande,* Vol. 2 (1753), pp. 99–128. Also see: The American Library Association, *The National Union Catalogue: Pre-1956 Imprints,* Vol. 698, Supplement, Mansell, 1980, p. 48.

3   Ippolito Desideri, *Reisen nach Tibet, im Jahre 1714,…aus dem Französischen überzetzt in Allgemeine Historie der Reisen zu Wasser und Lande,* Vol. 7 (1950), pp. 562–567.

4   *Keys to Kashmir,* Srinagar, Lalla Rookh Publications, 1953, p. 100.

5   A 478-pp. book with map and illustrations on the Valley: Walter Roper Lawrence, *The Valley of Kashmir,* London, Henry Frowde, 1895.

6   An early account: Frederic Drew, *The Jummoo and Kashmir Territories: A Geographical Account,* London, E. Stanford, 1875, xiii+568 pp. "Jammu" was, then, spelled as such.

7   An early work on the last two regions: Gottlieb William Leitner, *The Hunza-Nagar Handbook,* London, 1889.

8   According to the Constitution, adopted by the Constituent Assembly on 26 November 1949 and which came into force on 26 January 1950, India, a "Sovereign Socialist Secular Democratic Republic", is described as a Union of States. Federal in structure with unitary features, India comprises 25 states, including Jammu and Kashmir, and seven union territories. Government of India, Ministry of Information and Broadcasting, *India 1999, a Reference Annual,* New Delhi, Research, Reference and Training Division, 1999.

9   The peaks on the Karakoram range were designated by the capital letter "K", after Karakoram, and by a number such as K1, K2 or K3. Thus, what proved to be the second highest mountain in the world became known, not by a name, but by merely a letter and

a number. In 1867, however, the name of Goodwin Austin, after the British officer who made the topographical survey of the southern portion of the Karakoram range, was proposed and adopted by the Geographical Society in London. Shafi Shauq, Qazi Zahoor and Shoukat Farooqi, *Europeans on Kashmir,* Srinagar, Summit, 1997, pp. 59–60. An early work on the Karakorams: Oscar Eckenstein, *The Karakorams and Kashmir,* London, published probably by the author, 1896.

10   D. N. Wadia, *Geology of India,* London, Macmillan, 1949, p. 389.

11   Florence Parbury, *The Emerald Set with Pearls and Thomas Moore's Lalla Rookh,* London, Simpkin, Marshall, Hamilton, Kent and Co., 1902.

12   Wadia, *op. cit.,* p. 382.

13   S. Early-Wilmot, *Notes on a Tour in the Forests of Jammu and Kashmir,* Calcutta, 1906.

14   Ethelbert Blatter, *Beautiful Flowers of Kashmir,* Vol. I, London, Staples and Staples Limited, n. d., p. v.

15   Prabha Chopra, *A Panorama of Indian Culture,* New Delhi, Government of India, Ministry of Information and Broadcasting, 1983, p. 113.

16   Charmed by the ambience of Kashmir, Emperor Jahangir (1605–27) initially planned four magnificent outdoor gardens (Achabal, Nishat Bagh, Shalimar Bagh, Vernag). Sylvia Crave *et al., The Gardens of Moghul India,* New Delhi, Vikas Publishing House, 1972, pp. 90–120. An older source: C. M. Villiers-Stuart, *The Gardens of the Great Mughals,* London, A. and C. Black, 1913; Allahabad, India, R. S. Publishing House,1979. Other new sources: Elizabeth B. Moynihan, *Paradise as a Garden: in Persia and in Mughal India,* New York, G. Braziller, 1979; James L. Westcoat, Jr. and Joachim Wolschke-Bulmahn, eds., *Moghal Gardens: Sources, Places, Representations, and Prospects,* Washington, D.C., Dumbarton Oaks Research Library and Collection, 1996.

17   These six syllables mean that through an invisible method and wisdom, one can transform one's impure body, speech and mind into the pure exalted body, speech and mind of a Buddha.

18   Joshua Duke, *Kashmir Handbook,* London, 1904.

Chapter 2

The Wonderland

A striking feature of the origin of the land and the people of Kashmir is the legends with which they are enfolded. Moreover, some conclusions drawn from them now concur with scientific interpretations treating some of those legends as facts. For instance, the narratives about the origins of the Valley almost invariably refer to its having been a vast lake formed from the waters of melting snow on the mountains encircling it. The oldest legend known as the "Nilamatpurana" describes how the "demon" Jalodhbhava, meaning "water-borne" and dwelling in the lake, caused misfortunes to neighbouring areas by devastations and how the lake was drained on Brahma's command and the demon slain after a fierce combat, the tribes then settling on the land. Geological surveys support the legend that Kashmir was at least mostly occupied by a vast lake. The legend goes further that the drainer was called Kashyapa, and hence the reclaimed land was named Kash-yap-mar and eventually Kashmir. The Kashmiris, in their own tongue, frequently call it "Kashir".

The Extent of the Homeland

The State of Jammu and Kashmir, whose full frontiers were founded by Maharaja Gulab Singh, is a component part of the Indian Union. After the First Anglo-Sikh War (1845–46), the East India Company concluded the Treaty of Amritsar (1846) with Gulab Singh according to which the land was sold for cash payment in return for the recognition of the Raja as the ruler of Kashmir. In addition to the genuinely Indian kingdoms of Jammu and Kashmir, the area included part of Tibet and the Pamirs. The country had never been effectively united under one ruler before that treaty. Although the figures are not consistent and identical in all the reliable primary sources,[1] it is well-known that part of Kashmir's original area (probably of 222,713 sq. km.) suffered occupations and annexations. At the cease-fire (1949) after the first Indo-Pakistan War (1947–48), Pakistan held 78,932 sq. km. of the state's territory and ceded 5,180 of it to the People's Republic of China. The latter occupied (1962) 37,555 sq. km. of Ladakh territory, which was a part of undivided Kashmir. According to the "Line of Control" (LOC), agreed (1972) by both sides, 83,806 sq. km. remained under Pakistan's governance, and 138,992 sq. km. under India's authority. This hybrid of aggression, occupation and detaching left at least 101,387 sq. km. with the Kashmiri people, whose ruler had acceded to India during the partition of the Sub-continent between India and Pakistan. Kashmir could not have become completely independent because, not only there was no strong unifying factor to overcome the differences then felt among the various parts, but also it could not maintain an adequate defence of its long (about 1,500 miles) borders and protect its core areas from the incursions of tribesmen. The present state of J&K consists of the Kashmir division, the Jammu portion and the Ladakh area. Apart from India and Pakistan, the state has common borders with Afghanistan, China and Tadjikistan. Standing on the old Central Asian trade route, most of Kashmir is united with India, and part of it is associated with Pakistan, while it touches Afghanistan and borders Chinese Turkistan.

J&K is mostly mountainous, frequently rising to peaks and to narrow high-altitude valleys. The land joining the northern-most extremity of Punjab, the eastern and the western parts of it respectively partitioned by India and Pakistan, is the "Region of Outer Hills" in the south. In the east flows the river Ravi, and in the west the river Jhelum. The Chenab originates near the town Akhnur, and Jammu, the winter capital, commands a view of the river Tawi. The rivers Indus and Sutlej take their origin in Tibet. The next topographical division of the country lies between these "Outer Hills" and the mountains separating the Valley of Kashmir from Jammu. The famous Pir Panjal Range detaches, in a topographic sense, the provinces of Jammu and Kashmir. Appropriately called the "Middle Mountains", this halfway region has some more valleys and rich forests abundant in snow, approaching the heights which embrace the acclaimed Valley of Kashmir of the gigantesque Himalayas. The main axis of the Himalayas or the central range is called the Great Himalayan Range[2] running from the Karakorams (or the Krishna Giri Mountains) in the west to the river Brahmaputra in the east. In popular parlance, Kashmir is often used as synonymous with the Valley of Kashmir which occupies but a very small part of the otherwise bare, mountainous state. While this Valley has a population density of over 200, that of the Indus Valley is about 10.[3] The Karakoram range, which completely shuts off the bleak Tibetan plateau, is the biggest of the difficult mountain passes.[4]

With melting snow streaming down high altitudes, Kashmir in general and the environs of the Valley in particular have to be an amalgam of cliffs, rivers, lakes, and floods. The Manasbal Lake is the deepest, the Wular is the largest, and the Gangabal is the most "sacred". In all the surrounding valleys there are lakelets, varying in size from ponds to sheets of waters some miles long. As melted ice and snow pour down in torrents, floods destroy life and crops causing short-lived famines. Beyond the Valley are Ladakh and Baltistan, virtually cut off by steep cliffs. The great peak K1 (28,265 feet or 8,697 metres) is somewhere there on the mighty Karakoram range, which is the watershed between India and Turkestan. Ladakh is one of the loftiest inhabited regions of the world at 12,000–15,000 feet, with a climate of fierce extremes, from the burning heat in the day to several degrees below freezing-point at night. Leh, a centre of trade, is the capital of Ladakh, and the river Indus flows right through Skardu, the capital of Baltistan.

Several routes, nevertheless, lead out of the Valley, one going to Ladakh, and through it to Tibet and Central Asia and the Banihal road still being the main road to the rest of India. There are many passes to Punjab, some still being referred to as the

Imperial (meaning Moghul) Road. Another one goes to Poonch, used several times by invaders in the past. Some former means of communication and transportation are blocked with the birth of Pakistan and its control of part of Kashmir.

Since geography intended the land south of the Himalayas to be "a political and economic unit",[5] the creation of two sovereign states, India and Pakistan, raised unique questions. As it will be discussed briefly further ahead in this book, the idea of a separate state for the Muslims of the Sub-continent was scarcely given serious consideration prior to 1940. It later evolved into a "nationalistic" expression of a sizable religious minority. One of the problems was the Kashmir issue. Many commentators underline that India's principal claim to Kashmir is based on Mountbatten's acceptance for India, of the Maharaja's accession.[6] On the other hand, India has two important geographical characteristics: the Himalayas in the north and the Indian Ocean in the south. Both of them gave India a distinct identity. This does not mean, however, that both these regions played an identical role in the formulation of New Delhi's foreign policy perceptions.[7] The centuries-old image of the Himalayas as the warden on the lookout in the north conditioned the founding fathers of independent India to be somewhat heedless of threats from other quarters.[8] It is true that the entire Himalayan region comprised a wide range from eastern Afghanistan to parts of north Bengal.

The ocean in the south, that bore the name of the country, occupied, however, a dominant position for India, which has a maritime boundary as large as (about 4,000 miles) its land frontiers, in addition to a number of islands. Apart from several minerals and natural resources lying in the sea bed along the coast, the protection of the Andaman, Nicobar, Lakshwadeep and Minicoy Islands called for a strong navy. It was mainly on account of the Kashmir issue in the north that India neglected, for a time, to look southward where other interests were involved. India's absorption in conflicts first and foremost with Pakistan and later with China, both in the north, forced the country's leadership, largely recruited from the Indian heartland, to concentrate more on that region. Thus land-oriented, India allocated a larger share of the budget to the army and the air force, as if the extension of India was from Kashmir only to Kanya Kumari (formerly Cape Comorin) at the very southern tip. It was only after the Anglo-U.S. Agreement on Diego Garcia (1969) which brought, not only the American Polaris A-3 missiles to the region, but also sharp Soviet response that India moved to declare a regional opinion that the Ocean should be a "Zone of Peace".[9]

The Geopolitics of the Terrain

Concentrating mainly, until then, on the northern borders,[10] India endeavoured to undermine Pakistan's advantages by improving its own communication lines into Kashmir, offered the help of its "complementary" industrial centres, established craft cooperatives to sell their products in the emporiums at advantageous prices, and sought the support of the non-Muslim majority areas such as Ladakh. The products of the cottage industries and most of the food surplus originated in the Valley of Kashmir, where the overwhelming Muslim population congregated, and the markets of India was thought to be more appealing to them than the call to brotherhood in Islam.

The Hindu majority in Jammu as well as the Buddhist people of Ladakh lent active support to India. The Hindu quest for better integration with New Delhi is understandable. While Ladakh, which saw the growth of Buddhism since A.D.400, enjoyed some spiritual relationship with its Tibetan neighbours, its monasteries retained their lands precariously in the face of Prime Minister Sheikh Abdullah's egalitarian agrarian reforms.[11] In addition to these considerations, even the Moghul interest in Ladakh arose from the latter's strategic position with respect to the defence of Kashmir. During the 1947–48 War, the Indian forces arrived just in time to save Leh, the capital, from the contingents that came from Pakistan. The cease-fire line, established by a United Nations Commission, left Ladakh to India. The Indian defence system would be "gravely weakened" by the loss of Ladakh.[12] China claimed, however, that Ladakh was part of Tibet till the middle of the 19th century. China also laid claim virtually to the whole area of the present Arunachal Pradesh, north of the Brahmaputra River, involving 83,743 sq. km. inhabited by nearly 800,000 tribesmen.[13] The full extent of China's views were disclosed (1960) at a conference between the officials of China and India. Chinese assertions were coupled with hints of mutual accommodation including the area of Aksai Chin at the north-western end of Tibet but a part of pre-partition India.

As may be easily envisaged, many Indian writers contend that Chinese claims are contradicted by the "facts of history".[14] The Indian analysts in general judge a tenth century division of an independent kingdom there as the first known document which laid down a boundary between Ladakh and Guge in West Tibet.[15] It may be amplified that later agreements referred to this old, established or traditional frontier. The Indian interpretation conforms with these ancient chronicles, in so far as the main identifications are concerned.[16] Although Ladakh was independent for some centuries, it fell prey intermittently to foreign attacks and invasions, one of them prompting the Ladakhis to bring the Moghul emperor into play. When Akbar (1556–1605) conquered (1586) Kashmir and the Ladakhi king embraced Islam, striking all his coins in the name of the Delhi sultan, that country's fate was well-knit with that of the Moghul Empire and Kashmir. Some European travellers, though not all, who have also visited Ladakh, seem to share the same view about the boundary.[17] The borders now defended by India do not seem to be different from what it apparently used to be some two hundred years ago. Further, the Treaty of Amritsar (1846) contained some significant clauses (Articles 2 and 4) that laid down, once more, the eastern frontier of the Kashmir state. Lieutenant Henry Strachey's maps (1847–48), reproduced by the Government of India, confirm the evidence disclosed above.[18] In 1855, Lieutenant Montgomerie, to be aided by Colonel W. H. Johnson, Goodwin Austin and others, was put in charge of a survey to map the territories of Maharaja Gulab Singh. The completed survey, extensively collaborated by W. H. Johnson, included the northern and the north-eastern border regions, which showed that the Maharaja's territories were found to extend up to the Kuenlun Mountains or the Chinese border. Frederic Drew, who travelled to every corner of Jammu and Kashmir and was also made (1871) the Governor of Ladakh, not only found the Montgomerie-Johnson survey the foundation of every map of the region constructed since, but he himself attached to his own book a series of maps none of which support the Chinese claims.[19] Other official Indian maps of later dates show that Aksai Chin and the Lingzitang plains belong to Kashmir.[20] There is also the possibility that the Chinese, in the 1890s and now, may be confusing the Aksai Chin north of the Lingzitang plains with another Aksai Chin to the east of these plains, the latter apparently never included in Kashmir. British Indian strategic interests demanded that there should be some Chinese and Afghani (the Wakhan Corridor) territories between expanding Tsarist Russia and the northern frontier of India. There seems to be no convincing evidence supporting the contention that the frontier between Chinese Turkistan (Sinkiang) and Ladakh in Kashmir ran along the entire length of the Karakoram Range.

Sir Muhammad Zafrullah Khan, Pakistan's distinguished former Foreign Minister, had said in the early 1950s that every factor on the basis of which the question of accession of Kashmir should be determined, namely, the geographical position, strategic considerations, population, religious bonds, communications, the economic situation, and the flow of trade, all pointed in the direction of its union with Pakistan.[21] Although geography seems more to necessitate a political and economic unit between Kashmir, on the one hand, and both the two neighbours in the south, on the other, it may be asserted to have more physical bonds with Pakistan if considered as the upper part of the Indus basin. The waters of the Valley of Kashmir, the country's most densely settled area, join the Indus as its tributaries. The rivers Ravi, Chenab, Jhelum and Shyok, the latter the main tributary of the Indus, all pour into Pakistan's Punjab or the North-West Frontier Province. It may also be pointed out that there exist much less mountainous barriers between Kashmir and Pakistan compared to those connected with India. But the bulky territory of Ladakh, together with its Buddhist population, on the eastern edge opens towards India, instead. It is difficult to find a unifying factor between this territorially extensive part of Kashmir and Pakistan.

Although Pakistan has since partition, frequently brought up strategic reasons, stating that the country is militarily vulnerable without Kashmir and that India may invade its territory from south-western Jammu, reshaping and adapting the existing international borders in accordance with the security needs of one or the other party will only introduce more anarchy into this part of the world. Furthermore, an Indian invasion by way of Kashmir has not materialized in the last half century. Even Pakistan's repeated assertions that India has been shutting off its neighbour's water supply is difficult to concede. India, which built major installations after partition on the Sutlej River with no Kashmir tributaries, cannot cope with canals or dams simply to wear out an adversary. Moreover, the long-term objectives of India's irrigation projects reveal no concern to exhaust Pakistan. While a country's irrigation problems might serve as tools for shaping an international opinion on an issue with much larger dimensions, Pakistan's customary contention that control of Kashmir is vital for mere economic existence seems to be an exaggeration.

Although Pakistan was asked to shoulder responsibility for Kashmir's communications during partition, India outdid much of the original advantages of its neighbour on account of the rivers and the 16-mile railroad between Jammu and Sialkot by constructing new all-weather roads and tunnels based on detailed plans for improving the internal communication system. While the Jhelum River had traditionally served as the main artery of transport of Kashmir's timber, the post-partition markets for major exports such as cottage industries, fruits and vegetables are now mainly in India.[22] Pakistan's earlier promises of land reforms in those Kashmiri areas under its control have not materialized. Popular support on the basis of religion may, at times, prove to be very scanty as the Bangladesh case expensively demonstrated. In respect to the distribution of population, one may emphasize that the overwhelming Muslim majority resides almost totally in the Valley of Kashmir which is about a tenth of the whole territory, and that various non-Muslim communities, although they constitute small minorities, live on vast patches of lands. The make-up of the people of Kashmir constitutes the theme of the next section.

Notes

1   For instance, although Bamzai gives the total J&K area as 222,713 sq. km. (P. N. K. Bamzai, *Culture and Political History of Kashmir: Vol. l, Ancient Kashmir*, New Delhi, M. D. Publications, 1994, p. l), another source (Verinder Grover, ed., *The Story of Kashmir: Yesterday and Today*, Vol. l, New Delhi, Deep and Deep Publications, 1995, p. ix) quotes the total area as 222,236 sq. km.

2   Man Mohan Sharma,*Through the Valley of Gods: Travels in the Central Himalayas*, New Delhi, Vision Books, 1978, *passim.*

3   L. Dudley Stamp, *Asia: a Regional and Economic Geography*, London, Methuen; New York, E. P. Dutton, 1957, p. 3ll.

4   *Ibid.*, p. 309.

5   George B. Cressey, *Asia's Lands and Peoples*, 2nd ed., London, McGraw-Hill, 1955, p. 417.

6   An early detailed account: Taraknath Das, "The Kashmir Issue and the United Nations", *Political Science Quarterly*, New York, 65 (1950), pp. 264–282.

7   Manorama Kohli, "Indian Foreign Policy: A Geo-Political Perspective", *India Quarterly*, New Delhi, XLVI/4 (October–December 1990), pp. 33–40.

8   Kavalam Madhava Panikkar, *Geographical Factors in Indian History*, Bombay, Bharatiya Vidya Bhavan, 1959. An examination of some early texts in support of the importance of the Khyber Pass in the history of this region: Annetta S. Beveridge, "The Khyber Pass as the Invaders' Road to India", *Journal of the Central Asian Society*, 13/3; 13/4 (1926), pp. 250–268, 368–378.

9   Devendra Kaushik, *The Indian Ocean: Towards a Peace Zone*, Delhi, Vikas Publishing House, 1972; K. M. Pannikar, *India and the Indian Ocean: an Essay on the Influence of Sea Power on India's Foreign Policy*, London, G. Allen and Unwin, 1945; Ranjan Gupta,

The Indian Ocean: a Political Geography, New Delhi, Marwah, 1979; Maharaj K. Chopra, *India and the Indian Ocean: New Horizons*, New Delhi, Sterling, 1982.

10 Robert C. Mayfield, "A Geographic Study of the Kashmir Issue", *The Geographical Review*, New York, 45 (April 1955), pp. 181–196.

11 Lord Birdwood, "The Asian Frontiers of Kashmir", *Asian Affairs,* London, July–September 1952, pp. 241–245.

12 Margaret W. Fisher, Leo E. Rose and Robert A. Huttenback, *Himalayan Battleground: Sino-Indian Rivalry in Ladakh,* New York, Praeger, 1963, p. 143.

13 Sahdev Vohra, "The North-Eastern Frontier of India and China's Claim", *Strategic Analysis*, New Delhi, XII/9 (December 1989), p. 941.

14 F.C. Chakravarti, *The Evolution of India's Northern Borders*, Bombay, etc., Asia Publishing House, 1971, p. 109f.

15 When Tibet's military greatness was over by the 10th century, Kyi-de Nyi-ma-gon, a descendant of one branch of the old Tibetan dynasty, who had established an independent kingdom for himself comprising West Tibet and Ladakh as well, divided his state among his three sons. Also: Zahiruddin Ahmad, "The Ancient Frontier of Ladakh", *World Today*, London, XVI (July 1960), pp. 314–315.

16 One exception may be Ra-ba-dmar-po which favours Tibet rather than Ladakh.

17 For instance: Filippo de Filippi, *An Account of Tibet: the Travels of Ippolite Desideri of Pistoria*, London, 1937.

18 Government of India, *Atlas of the Northern Frontier of India*, New Delhi, Ministry of External Affairs, 1960.

19 Drew, *op. cit.,* p. 332.

20 Such maps were attached to the *Gazetteer of Kashmir and Ladakh (1890) and the Imperial Gazetteer of India* (1887, 1907).

21 Statement made during the United Nations Security Council on 6 March 1951, as reprinted in: Pakistan Delegation, *Verdict on Kashmir*, New York, 1951.

22 P. N. Dhar, "The Kashmir Problem: Political and Economic Background", *India Quarterly*, New Delhi, 7 (1951), pp. 143–162.

Chapter 3

The Kashmiris

Nearly every sixth human being in the world is an Indian. The People's Republic of China alone has a bigger population. Even a cursory look at this Titan reveals the survival of different peoples. Rabindranath Tagore called India "the seashore of humanity".[1] Many came, but few returned. One sees, nevertheless, an unbroken development of civilization from remote antiquity right up to our times. India is a mosaic of many races and cultures. So many centuries of known history brought into being a remarkable amalgam on this Sub-continent. A glance at the people of India may be based on many possible classifications—regional, linguistic, or religious. Although India experienced periods of decline as well, the stream of its culture was always large and comprehensive. While the orthodox elements fought against what was new, the progressive intelligentsia was often busy assimilating the accumulative culture which was never monolithic. It is no exaggeration to say that while entire populations in Europe indulged, for centuries, in orgies of wholesale destruction unparalleled in ferocity, India made constant adjustments with peoples who came wave after wave. With a long history of nearly five-thousand years, its population presents many strains in diverse stages of admixture. As Tagore noted, life moves in the cadence of constant adjustment of opposites; it is a perpetual process of reconciliation of contradictions.[2] Although assimilation does not always amount to integration, the assimilative genius of India has been unique.

Change and Adjustment

The settlements of Mohenjo-daro in Sindh, Harappa and Rupar in Punjab, Lothal in Gujarat, Jaisalmer in Rajasthan, and Maheswar in central India developed a remarkably high degree of civilization.[3] The Negrito, the Proto-Australoid, the Mongoloid, the Mediterranean, the Western Brachycephals and the Nordic Aryans mixed up in India until a 'pure race' became very difficult to find now except in a few secluded pockets. Once having entered India, these various strains lost their alien character. The culture of the people, the descendants of settlers like the Aryans, the Macedonians, the Scythians, the Muslims and the British, has been enriched by a constant process of give-and-take, change and adjustment. Willingness to respect diversity has been a persistent feature of the Indian consciousness. The Aryan conquerors did not wipe out the traditions of the indigenous Dravidian people. Traditionally, Hinduism did not define itself in terms of rigid dogmas. There was no organized attempt by one group to exterminate the other. The assimilative genius of India asserted itself over the differences between Hinduism and Islam which appeared to be too fundamental to admit integration. The great administrators of India—the ancient emperors Chandragupta and Asoka, the Moghul sultans Babur and Akbar or the founding father Nehru—grasped the fact that the people could be held together only through a tolerance of their differences. The British, on the other hand, created artificial divisions and fanned rather than calmed conflicts based on religion, caste and tribe.[4]

Like every other old people, the Indians, living on their vast and diverse land, are certainly influenced by the variegated past, but a closer look will reveal progressive trends. Some of the past traditions are giving ground to preferable humanistic values. For instance, India no longer recognizes the caste system among the Hindus which divides people into hereditary groups of unequal rights. Untouchability is a penal offence. State policies are based, on the whole, on secularism, which befits the culture of a people of many faiths living together for centuries. So long as intolerance is shunned, the more the merrier. Such has been India's dominant attitude. This does not mean, however, that there has never been a national question. It is, moreover, one of the social and political problems facing contemporary India. But the trend is more towards a synthesis involving a corrective of its own inherent contradictions yielding perhaps to a new balance. There are certain residual values, some bad habits and acceptance of good and bad elements from the West. It is this heterogeneity and the recent fractious behaviour that cause some writers to pose the following question: "Whither India?"

The Indian population is a blend of many original stocks supplemented by waves of newcomers. There were several minor aboriginal stocks. A Negroid people, originally from Africa and food-gatherers rather than food-producers with a culture not of a high order, first established themselves and their language on the soil of India. Negroid tribes may still be found in parts of the Tamil country in the south-east and in the Andaman Islands. The Sino-Tibetans, who belong to the Mongoloid type with medium height, yellow skin, high cheek-bones, oblique eyes, and comparative absence of hair, penetrated deep into the heart of the Sub-continent. Only two of the Sino-Tibetan languages are found in India. The Austrics, a very old offshoot of the Mediterranean people, spread east over the whole of the country. When the Dravidians and after them the Aryans came, they mingled with the earliest dwellers, and a new people was formed. The city civilization of Punjab and Sindh appears to be the work of the Dravidians, believed to have migrated from Asia Minor and the Eastern Mediterranean. The people of Mohenjo-daro and Harappa, who fell before the first waves of the Aryan invaders, lived in cities, built of brick with a well-thought out system of plumbing, baths and similar civic amenities. Whether or not the people of Mohenjo-daro and Harappa came from Sumer in Mesopotamia or some of them spread westwards from the Indus basin, they had attained a high degree of maturity around 3,000 B.C. The pacifist temper of the Indian people is traced to them, who are believed to have developed the same attitude. The more important Dravidian languages, fully established as the tongues of well-organized communities, had no relations outside the Sub-continent.

The main body of the Aryans, a wandering pastoral people with superior weapons, descended after 1,500 B.C. somewhere from the Asian steppes to make Punjab their first home. The relics, beginning from Vedic Sanskrit, stand high at the altar of the great heritage of India. It is not certain whether or not the Aryans brought the Vedas with them or composed the Vedic hymns after their arrival. Although they were culturally behind the Dravidians whom they subdued, the synthesis of these two strains produced, in the Sanskrit language,[5] the epics *Mahabharata*[6] and *Ramayana*,[7] the Vedic and Upanishadic metaphysical thought and later classical literature in vernacular tongues such as Bengali, Gujarati, Marathi, Punjabi, and the like. The human history of the Aryan wars is recorded in these two epics, dominated by Rama and Krishna. The modern Indo-Aryan languages of the country are cousins of the other Indo-European languages. The Aryan influence is also seen in the occupational division of the people into four rigid castes.[8] The male alien conquerors, who brought few spouses with them, married Dravidian women, and through them were better influenced by their beliefs, the main stream of their evolving religion centring around the forces of nature.[9]

Hinduism

Hinduism, thus formed, is the oldest living organized religion in the world.[10] Some writers[11] assert that calling Hinduism, the 3000-year old living faith of 80% of the world's largest democracy, a religion is a "philological error" and that the term 'Hindu' is a corrupt form of Sindhu used for the Indus River with a topographical connotation, in this sense not being a name for a religion as Christianity or Islam is. It is a spiritual fraternity, a view of life accepted essentially as an otherworldly progression with a code of conduct called *Dharmashastra* and dedicated to four essential ends involving duties, wealth, pleasures and freedom. Although few of the beliefs of the earliest Hindus are accepted in their original forms today, this fourfold order of life later became the basis of Indian culture.[12]

Some writers trace the historical basis of secularism in India to the Vedic times.[13] This evolution was not the same as secularization in the Western world, which indicates the emancipation of various spheres of society, social groups, the individual's consciousness, human activity and behaviour, social relations and institutions from the influence of religion. The fall in the influence of the church in Western Europe came particularly clearly to the fore during the Renaissance, the Reformation and in the years leading up to the bourgeois revolutions. For instance, the French Revolution of 1789, not only served to accelerate the transfer of the landed property in the hands of the church, but also helped, to some extent, the principles of freedom of conscience to take root, separated the church and the state, and partially removed education from the jurisdiction of the church. The separation of church and state was implemented by the latter on the basis of non-intervention in internal church affairs, removal of acts concerning civic status from the control of the church, and refusal on the part of the state from obliging citizens to profess a particular religion.

Hindu society, on the other hand, was instituted as "a loose constellation of values and beliefs articulated in a social order characterized by a distinctive structural identity".[14] Although the seminal constituents of this religion may be found in a few texts, the intellectual notions are reflected in a wide range of folk cults in different sectors of the social set-up. The unifying compulsion may be observed not in a doctrinal identity, but in that social structure, or a large number of units called *jatis*. While each of the latter rested upon rules of conduct and all were related to each other through a kind of hierarchical organization (*varna*), the Rig-Veda proclaims that "the Reality is one, the wise call by many names" (*Ekam sat, vipra bahudha vadanti*). Hinduism is not based on a particular book and has no organized church. It may be asserted therefore that people belonging to this faith have been comparatively free to subscribe to their own way of thinking based on personal experience and reason. The Hindu rulers in the ancient Indian state allowed religious and philosophical schools to profess and propagate their views freely, and also ensured freedom to government employees.

There were revolts against Hinduism, which was dominated, in its earlier phases, by unalterable caste distinctions, animal sacrifice, and other primitive practices. These conventions offended a great many people who sought for reforms, Jainism[15] being the first organized effort to effect a change. It held out the first clear warning against superstition such as attaching sanctifying power to pilgrimages, bathing in sacred rivers or believing in tribal deities. Epictetus and Marcus Aurelius would fully agree with the formulation that non-violence, love of truth, purity of thought and deed, and renunciation of materialistic obsessions would make freedom a reality. With the coming of Buddhism, Jainism gradually lost its hold over eastern India.

Founded by Lord Siddhartha Gautama (c.563–c.483 B.C.), son of a rich Hindu raja, Buddhism became a system of morality and philosophy based on the belief that life was too full of suffering to be worth living.[16] During the period of Confucius in China, Jeremiah in Judea, and the pre-Socratic philosophers in Greece, Prince Gautama was born in India, who was gradually deified as the Buddha or the "Enlightened One". He broke away from the rigours of caste which had become characteristics of the Indian society. When he referred to the pervasiveness of pain, he was perhaps diagnosing *angst* which the Existentialists of the 1950s would also find to be universal. His affirmation of the authenticity of the earth, of "being-in-the-world",[17] to use a Martin Heidegger (1889–1976) phrase, would not put him in the category of an irredeemable pessimist. "May those who revile me, afflict me, beat me, cut me in pieces with their swords, or take my life—may they all obtain the joy of complete enlightenment".[18] He established a monastic order, to which he welcomed the lowest castes. Buddha aiming at social equality, his creed first obtained a dominant position in India under the patronage of Emperor Asoka (c. 269–232 B.C.), the grandson of Chandragupta. It was the mighty dynasty of the Mauryas that absorbed the Asiatic part of the empire left by Alexander the Great of Macedonia (356–323

B.C.). The first empire in Indian history was established almost immediately after Alexander's withdrawal. Chandragupta, the founder of the empire, with his minister, Kautilya,[19] established international contacts. Asoka, who further unified the greater part of India, adopted Buddha's humanist gospel.[20] He declared that a truly religious person would have regard for all faiths. Just as Protestant criticism had created a reformed St. Ignatius Loyola and the Jesuits, the influence of Jainism and Buddhism stimulated Hinduism towards a process of self-cleansing.

Thus, during the next few centuries, one sees in northern India the formation of an "Indian" people based on the intermixture of the Austric, Mongoloid, Dravidian and Aryan, taking up the language of the last-mentioned as its speech. The modern (new) Indo-Aryan languages may be traced to the same genetic origin. The Aryan languages may be classified into the northern (or Himalayan), north-western, southern, eastern, east-central, and central groups. It includes Iranian, the modern standard form of which came to India with the Turkic and Iranian conquerors after A.D. 1000. The Dardic tongues in the central group embrace three branches, one being Kashmiri. Most scholars consider the Kashmiri language to be basically a Dardic-Aryan dialect influenced by Sanskrit.

After Asoka's death, the Mauryan Empire gradually broke up, encouraging fresh invasions from the north-west. The foreign Saka (or Sakha, a group of Turkic-speaking peoples from around the region of Lake Baikal in the north)[21] invasion, not only gave India its classical Sanskrit style, but also established the five important principalities of Sindh, Taxila, Maharashtra, Malwa and Mathura. Patronizing astronomy, the Sakas made Ujjain the Greenwich of that age. The Kushans, the Scythians, the Huns and the Jats came down in waves. Buddhism also having suffered a setback after the fall of the Mauryan Empire, it was no longer the predominant religion of the land. The Guptas, the patrons of Hinduism, did not persecute the Buddhists, however.

Muslim Incursions

As with the Aryans, the Muslim incursions into India were also spread over centuries.[22] Even during the times when Hindu society was crystallising, the alien worldviews brought by the new warrior communities pouring into the region were absorbed within the Hindu fold. Islam, which fostered a sense of belonging conveyed through the concept of *umma* (universal Muslim society), was different from the others previously absorbed in the Hindu amorphous matrix. The Muslim faith first came to Malabar with the traders of southern Arabia, then reached Tamil Nadu. The young Muhammad bin Qasim's expedition (A.D.712) was a brief Umayyad raid into Sindh aimed to safeguard the Arab trade routes with south India and Ceylon, but it resulted with the borrowing of mathematics and medicine from India leaving in the process the name of Islam there. The large majority of Muslims who came to India in different times were the Turks, Afghans and Persians. The Ilbari Turks stabilized the first Sultanate in Delhi (1206), followed by five other dynasties that lasted till the establishment of the Turco-Moghul Empire. The Muslim wave of conquests came under Subuktagin, Mahmud Gaznavi and Muhammad Ghori, the last one setting up permanent sovereignty over northern India. Although Mahmud claimed to be a champion of Islam by smashing idols, along with him came Abu Raihan Muhammad ibn-Al Beruni (973–1048),[23] who was eager for inter-cultural understanding. Familiar with Hindu literature, Beruni mentions the four *Vedas,* the eighteen *Puranas,* the *Mahabharata* and the *Ramayana.* He enriched Sanskrit by translating Euclid and Ptolemy into that language, and rendered the word *Nabi* (Prophet) into Sanskrit as *Jina,* which he used both for Muhammad and the Buddha. Timur[24] tried another invasion repeated by his descendant Babur, who captured Delhi (1526).

The most significant contribution of Muslims was in the north-western region of the country. The proselytizing activity of the *Sufi* saints (mystical lovers) played an important part in attracting substantial numbers to Islam. The contribution of the so-called Moghuls and their Islam to Indian culture was immense. India became united after so many centuries; there was a heightened consciousness of India's oneness. Although some present-day Hindu extremists would rather consider Muslims as conquerors and therefore as outsiders, and attribute the growth of Islam to forcible conversion, the majority of the Indian Muslims are indigenous people who embraced Islam for a variety of reasons. Some rulers resorted to force, but Islam's aversion to caste distinctions should explain the voluntary conversions by the masses. An (Hindu) Indian writer of the 19th century (1894) records that Islam "did not place any insuperable barrier between man and man such as Hinduism interposed by its caste system".[25] Not only the Muslims in most cases were fighting men who had not brought their women and took local wives, but also those who were low in the social scale deemed Islam an opportunity to assert their dignity. The dominant class in Muslim society was the aristocracy in alliance with the gentry. But Islam was able to transform, not only the consciousness of urban groups, but the indigenous peasant communities as well. Especially the rural people were drawn to Islam through the *Sufi* saints, whose outlook was quite different from the *ulama* (Muslim clergy) and whose hospices dotted the settlements with significant social activity. The possibility of a spiritual synthesis between Hinduism and Islam was explored at the popular as well as the elite level.

The Moghul court became the nucleus for a many-sided culture. There had always been two trends, the orthodox and the humanist, in the long history of the Muslims in India. The Hindu *Bhakti* (selfless, intense devotion to God) and the Muslim *Sufi* movements brought together men on a common platform of humanism.[26] Hindu and Islamic mysticisms were blended and written in Hindi. There is a galaxy of names of enlightened rulers such as Skandar Lodi of Delhi (1489–1517), Zain-ul Abidin of Kashmir or Moghul Emperor Akbar and writers like Malik Muhammad Jaisi (1493–1538), Abd-ur Rahim Khan-e Khanan (1556–1627) or Faizi (1547–95) whose lives were devoted to the values of composite culture. Emperor Akbar commissioned the translations of the Hindu classics, on whose illustrations the Hindu and Muslim artists worked together in the royal atelier. The greatest contribution of Akbar, a conscious integrator, was his undermining of differences in religion and his offer of equal opportunity of advancement to all Indians. Toleration was forced on these Turkic rulers by force of circumstances. Akbar's religious eclecticism may have formulated an unsophisticated probing for some sort of a 'secular' approach[27] fitting the Indian milieu. The *Din-e Ilahi* (the Religion of God), a new worldview, was his attempt at syncretism. The semblance of so-called 'secularism' under the Moghuls varied in nature and depth according to circumstances. Free or forced conversions put aside, the spiritual dialogue between the Hindu and Muslim elites did not achieve the kind of community of sentiment that would bring the lowly classes of these two religions together, but it did not prevent secular cooperation between the ruling groups of the two communities. The Moghul rule might have reached almost the maximum through which individuals and groups in pre-capitalist societies could interact with each other. It should also be added that Moghul achievements in architecture, other arts and literature were immeasurable. Especially in architecture, the Moghuls left a great legacy, and it is an Indian legacy now. The imperial workshops created very high standards in production whose excellence may be gauged from the impressive monuments in the whole Sub-continent and also the scattered specimens in world museums.[28]

While Emperor Akbar repudiated the theocratic conception of the state, Nanak and Kabir founded two new religions to end communal discord. From Guru Nanak (1469–1539), who established a community of the followers, called Sikhs or 'disciples', came the cryptic words that there was "no Hindu and no Muslim" but a new faith transcending both. The initial Sikh belief was integrative to the core. Not only the noble Brahmin and the miserable Pariah, but also the *kafir* (infidel) and the *mlechha* (foreigner) ate together in the *langar* or the community kitchen. Likewise, the first planned city of India at Fatehpur Sikri, under Akbar, expressed a synthetic philosophy of life. The Red Fort in Delhi bore this couplet: *Agar Firdaus bar ruy-e zamin ast,/ Hamin ast-o hamin ast-o hamin ast* (If there be a Heaven on earth, it is here, it is here, it is here).[29] The majority of the Zoroastrians[30] of today are also Indian citizens. While the Parsis (previously spelled as Parsees) now number about 150,000, theirs is a very ancient tradition, absorbed by the Old Testament. Indian pluralism had areas of tension as well as accommodation, but it represented an integral whole with a slow development, throughout centuries, towards a pattern of coexistence.

Hindi, which the Constitution of India gives the status of the country's official language (side by side with English), includes all the dialects in India to the east of the Punjab and Sindh, to the west of Bengal and Orissa, to the north of Gujarat and Maharashtra, and to the south of Nepal. Many dialects may be found in the orbit of Hindi. "Hindustani", derived from Persian, means the language that belongs to Hindustan (India). Urdu, which took its present form only in the 18th century as the standard speech of the Moghul court in Delhi (*Zaban-e Urdu-e Mu'alla* or the Language of the Exalted Court), is mostly of foreign (Persian, Arabic and Turkic) origin but is now a truly Indian language. Urdu poetry is the most eloquent expression of the heritage of Islam in India. But not only Muslim writers cultivated a literary garden out of these foreign words on the soil of India, but also Hindu intellectuals took to Urdu.

Understandably, India is one of the world's biggest centres of Muslim life and culture.[31] Although it is impossible for a foreign observer to distinguish between a Bengali or a Punjabi Muslim and a Bengali or a Punjabi non-Muslim, the forces of history have also created great centres of Muslim life in Hyderabad, Locknow and Srinagar, and in metropolitan areas like Delhi and Bombay. The Muslims constitute the second biggest religious group in India and surpass in numbers all the other groups put together. It was in the name of the last Muslim Emperor Bahadur Shah (*imperabat*: 1837–58) that the first war of Indian independence, which the British called the "Mutiny", was fought (1857–58).[32]

British Contribution

The British brought with them a completely alien culture, that of Protestant Europe, communicated through an alien language—English, superimposed on India, initially through the conquest of Bengal in the 17th century. The Christians can pride themselves on having added no small enrichment to the same cultural heritage.[33] There are as many Christians in India as the entire population of Belgium or as many Catholics as in Britain. Christianity is as much a part of the country as the temples that the West has been reading of in the renowned British writer Rudyard Kipling. Moreover, in a country as ancient and vast as India, it is only natural that the Christian scene should not be uniform as well. There are Anglo-Indian, Goan, Naga, Kerala or Tamil Christians. Christianity in India never knew the kind of persecution it experienced during the early centuries of its existence elsewhere. Dr. Rajendra Prasad, a former President of India (1950–62) repeated the contention that St. Thomas the Apostle had come (A.D.52) to India when many of the countries of Europe had not yet become Christian.[34] It was the Portuguese, however, who brought the initial Christian missionary effort—in a crude and ruthless way. Kerala is the region where Christianity has the longest tradition. One of the first acts of St. Francis Xavier who arrived (1542) from Europe, was to throw the Jesuit College of St. Paul at Goa open to Indian students. Deeply concerned to find a solution to the religious division of his country, the Moghul Emperor Akbar sent to Goa for Christian priests to instruct him in the doctrines of their faith. It was not until the British entry that the great age of evangelisation dawned. The Christian community in India has been outstanding for its efficacious social conscience. The founder of the Missionaries of Charity was a simple-looking contemporary woman better known as Mother Teresa.[35] The genius of Mohandas Karamchand Gandhi (1869–1948) found in Christ's recommmendation to turn the other cheek a promising weapon.

The British, an alien race, dominated Indian life for two centuries. Their rule led to a number of new developments. They brought their language which eventually became an official one. Some other groups, long migrated into India, had

3. The Kashmiris 23

adopted local languages. For instance, the Syrian Christians in Kerala spoke Malayalam, the Beni-Israel Jews in Maratha used Marathi, and the Parsis employed Gujarati. The tribes of India speak languages which are different, not only from those of non-tribal India, but also from each other.[36] The British emerged as the dominant power, ruling first through the East India Company and finally directly (1857–1947) under the Crown. As heirs to the Magna Carta, the Cromwellian puritanical revolt, the Glorious Revolution of 1688, and the Industrial Revolution, they established a rigorous law and order, introduced the railway system, improved the postal service, and opened schools and hospitals, but superimposed the class set-up of Europe on the caste structure of India. By the time they became dominant in India, the Industrial Revolution was already in full swing in the British Isles. To extract tribute from a vast colony, the British introduced an altogether new corpus of laws and institutions of administration, just as they transformed the values of the new subjects. They eliminated the aristocracy and the gentry and established contact with the peasant-proprietors as well as the rural small landlords for purposes of surplus extraction. While rail and road networks reached the interior from the great ports of Bombay, Calcutta, Karachi and Madras, market linkages broke down the isolation of the rural communities. Growing industrialization of Britain was bound to disrupt India's unsophisticated rural economy. Britain exported cotton goods, opened up factories and created industrial towns. While the latter attracted workers from villages, the joint family and the caste system began to crack, women workers gained some self-confidence, and Western education shattered the walls of dogma.[37] The vast colony was tied to the economy of the metropolitan heart of the British Empire, industrial products and technology flowing into India and serving the traditionally affluent and the newly-enriched classes.

In spite of a host of rationalizations such as the civilizing mission of Christianity, Jeremy Bentham's view of utility as the most rational basis or order[38] and Social Darwinism[39] sanctioning the domination of the stronger, the British rule was established to extract material resources from the subordinate Indian community for the benefit of the dominant economy. In spite of such justifications for conquest and exploitation, the British rule, without any plan, accelerated the democratic process. The rule of law developed while personal law decayed, the break up of the joint family and the emergence of new industrial centres increased the sense of equality, and the people challenged the position in which they found themselves instead of accepting it as fate. While Sir Syed Ahmad Khan (1817–98) led his co-religionists to accept Western education and Raja Ram Mohan Roy (1774–1833) started a Hindu reform movement, the Indians, who tried to add some tenderness to the imported capitalist civilization, later challenged the morality of the latter which considered socialism as the only source of dictatorship. Sir Muhammad Iqbal (1875–1938) tried to reconstruct religious thought in Islam, and Sir Sarvepalli Radhakrishnan (1888–1975) formulated a Hindu faith more intelligible and acceptable to the Western mind. The British impact had, indeed, changed the traditional Indian outlook almost in every sphere of life.

For the benefit of their imperial rule, the British administrators exploited the tensions between feudal principalities and religious communities. Apart from dividing India into directly administered "British India" and indirectly governed "Princely States", they basically perceived the people as members of religious communities. When the latter became the outstanding consideration for representation in local bodies or recruitment for public service, religious distinctions were transformed in time into political cleavages. While the British classified the people as Hindus or Muslims, not only rallying them around religion to express basic demands, but also for voting, candidacy, election or appointment, politics was turned into 'communalism', which opposed secular politics and fractured national unity.

It was this process of imperial rule, later reinforced by the Hindu and Muslim extremists, that eventually led to the partition of India. The Muslim League and Hindu extremism as well as the colonial authority pushed aside the time-honoured heritage of inter-communal coexistence, thereby rupturing a *sui generis* composite culture that had evolved through centuries of synthesis. The indefensible supposition that religion alone would suffice to identify a nation and build a state lost sight of other realities concerning regional and linguistic variations in both the Hindu and the Muslim communities, hard facts felt in coming decades. The first consequence of the British legacy of communalist rule was the creation of Pakistan, where the theologians, the military, high bureaucracy and the commercial sub-class turned their backs to Muhammad Ali Jinnah's statements after independence favouring a secular society. While the hard-core religious groups sought to satisfy their political ambitions under the garb of Islam, often disguising themselves as 'Muslim nationalists', other members of Pakistan's elite had difficulty in creating a consensus on a far-reaching and all-inclusive identity for the country.

The second consequence of the British legacy may be the evolving drive to make communal politics, albeit as a repercussion, legitimate in basically secular India. Militancy in Kashmir, India's North-East and in Punjab have much to do with the spill-over from Muslim communalism as well as the promotion of terrorism from Pakistan. Partition has divided British India, first in terms of territory, and also in the idiom of politics. When British colonialism set foot on India, there had been cultural diversity but unity, sufficient to erect a pan-Indian national identity. Indian philosophy, described as *darshan* (vision), is inevitably a fascinating story.[40] Long British rule ground down much of that unique legacy.

J and K: A Melting Pot?

Jammu and Kashmir as well may be termed a melting pot of many ancient cultures. The continual process of the amalgam of old and new cultures is also a fact of this northern-western portion of India. With important centres of various languages and religions, the land nurtured thinkers like Shankaracharya and Sarfi, historians including Pandit Kalhana and Hasan Shah Koihami, poets of the calibre of Gani and

Fani, and monarchs such as Lalita Ditya, Avanti Warman, Qutub-ud Din and Zain-ul Abidin who patronized learning and art. The land has been a home of various races and sects. During its long and chequered history, the people came into contact with the Persian, Central Asian, Indian, Macedonian, Tibetan and other civilizations resulting, as in the history of whole India, in a tolerant blending of cultures. These differences are reflected in folklore or fantastic but beautiful stories on which inhabitants divided with beliefs and traditions fall back.[41] The population of J and K is heterogeneous. The Kashmiris live in the Valley and in Kishtwar, the Punjabis predominate in the western districts, the Dogras and the Gujjars live in Jammu, and the Ladakhis form the main part of the people in Ladakh.

The Brahmins, popularly called the "Kashmiri Pandits" (teacher), and divided into 133 exogamous *gotras* (caste affiliation) whose social position is determined by the nature of occupation, are considered to be specimens of the ancient Aryan settlers in the Valley.[42] Eating meat in contrast to the strict vegetarianism of the Brahmins elsewhere in India, this small community in Kashmir is well educated with a traditional occupation of government service. Jawaharlal Nehru (1889–1964) is the best known among the Kashmiri Pandit administrators and statesmen. The Sikhs, who were chiefly concentrated in the Muzaffarabad district before partition, were later forced to migrate to other parts of the state.

The overwhelming majority of the people in the Valley professes Islam. At the advent of the Muslim religion in Kashmir, the culture of the indigenous people was neither purely Hindu nor Buddhist. "Kashmir Shavaism", also known with the simple but distinctive name of *Trika,* is a type of idealistic monism or a system of philosophy, different from Shavaism in general.[43] Opposed to the caste-oriented social system, Islam evolved there as a "vehicle of social protest" against the Brahmanic culture.[44] The "intrusive Islam", which, in the process of a journey from Arabia to Persia and Central Asia had already made compromises with various local cultures, sustained many Hindu beliefs. Except a minority who immigrated from the neighbouring Muslim lands and who could not bring their families with them, the Muslims of Kashmir were largely converts and did not completely abandon age-old traditions. Even the Muslim *ulama* of "great accomplishments" (*sahib-e karamat)* visited Hindu places of worship, and the *tawa'af* of a Hindu temple was replaced by visits to the shrines of the *Sufi* saints. The imprint of a foot on a stone is *Kadam-e Rasul* (Prophet Muhammad's foot) for the Muslims and *Vishna Pad* (Vishna's foot) for the Hindus.[45] Although the Muslims were divided among themselves as the Sunni and the Shi'a sects,[46] the Muslim sheikh simultaneously projected Arjuna[47] as well as Caliph Omar (*imperebat*: 634–44) and Caliph Ali (*imperebat*: 656–61) as symbols of bravery and valour. A typical example of the mutual impact of Hinduism and Islam is represented by the Sufism of Kashmir known as the *Rishi* movement,[48] whose adherents rejected family life, inflicted bodily sufferings upon themselves and retired to jungles. The Muslims played a prominent part, nevertheless, in the development of Kashmiri culture. The glorious Moghul Gardens, the Hari Parbat Fort and the Jumma and Pathar Masjids are artistic testimonies to this outstanding contribution.[49]

The hilly tracts extending to the plains of Punjab in the south is called Dugar, the home of the Dogras, divided into Hindus and Muslims. They speak Dogri, a mixture of Sanskrit, Punjabi and Persian. The Gujjars, rearing cattle and sheep, migrated from Rajasthan and adopted Islam. Their language is a form of Rajasthani. The Bombas and Khakhas, who were once a source of terror until Maharaja Gulab Singh subdued them, are the inhabitants of the Jhelum Valley. Kashmir has been a stronghold of Buddhism for many centuries.[50] Before conversion to Islam, the Dards, living in the barren land to the north of the Valley called Dardistan, were followers of Buddhism. Even today traces of Buddhist influences may be found in some of their rituals. Although the preponderant majority of the Baltis inhabiting Baltistan, situated between Dardistan and Ladakh, profess the Shi'a sect of Islam, there are still some villages practising Buddhism. Further to the east is Ladakh, the land of the religious followers of the Dalai Lama of Lhasa. The *gompas* or monasteries, which own much of the cultivable land, are temporal as well as religious institutions.[51]

Kashmir very early came to be affiliated to the cultural world of Sanskritic India. The Kashmiri language as well as Sanskrit were formerly written in the *Sarada* (*Sharada*) character, an Indian writing now surviving in the Gurumukhi of Punjab.[52] The Kashmiri language, previously treated as the language of the Brahmins, and therefore, as having grown out of Sanskrit, is now placed in the Dardic branch of the non-Sanskritic languages. Arabic/Persian script has been adapted for its use. Kashmiri, one of the recognized national languages of the Indian Union, appears to be in its bases a Dardic-Aryan dialect, profoundly influenced by Sanskrit.

Throughout the changes in Indian history, one may safely assert that there has been a spirit of underlying unity. Prolonged intercourse brought about a remarkable cultural unity. The idealism of Gandhi[53] was a blend of the *Bhagavadgita*,[54] Jainism, Christianity and Islamic teaching. Nehru, born to an aristocratic Kashmiri Brahmin family and privileged to study at Harrow and Cambridge, was an eclectic. He wrote a series of letters to his daughter, Indira Gandhi, on aspects of man's story on the globe, later printed as *Glimpses of World History,* attempted a *Discovery of India,* and proclaimed his own faith in socialism. That unity needs to be nurtured in the whole of India as well as in Kashmir. While Gandhi emphasized unity, Rabindranath Tagore (1861–1941)[55] saw the need to preserve diversity. Like the red corpuscles in blood, they should neither rise above nor fall below a certain proportion. Being the second largest nation in the world after China, India is a "mini-world". With such a large population, governed by one Constitution and federally ruled by one set of ministers, unity cannot mean dull uniformity. Perhaps, there is no other instance of free elections in which hundreds of millions of people vote at once. But differences should not destroy the fundamental unity that this chapter tried to encapsulate. While the feeling of regionalism gets the better of every other feeling in some regions, every child is born to a tradition of being an Indian, and one may look upon Hindi and Urdu basically as one language. The process of synthesis may not have been completed yet, but as a former President of India stated decades ago, "whether it is a question of religion or language or of any other aspect of life or activity, resorting to violence is indefensible".[56]

Notes

1   Vijaya Lakshmi Pandit, *The Evolution of India,* London, Oxford University Press, 1958, pp. 4–5.
2   Rabindranath Tagore, *A Vision of India's History*, Calcutta, Visha-Bharati Bookshop, 1951, p. 13.
3   Robert L. Raikes, "The End of the Ancient Cities of the Indus", *American Anthropologist*, Washington, D.C., 62/2 (April 1964), pp. 248–299. The author suggests that Mohenjo-daro and Harappa declined on account of geomorphological changes and consequent flooding and not because of social factors. An earlier classic: Mortimer Wheeler, *The Indus Civilization*, London, Cambridge University Press, 1968. A recent perspective on Harappa: Gregory L. Possehl, ed., *Harappan Civilization*, Warminster, U.K., Aris and Philips, 1982.
4   *The Cambridge History of India* wrote: "The Indian empire is the abode of a vast collection of peoples who differ from one another in physical characteristics, in language and in culture more widely than the peoples of Europe". Vol. I, Cambridge, Cambridge University Press, 1922, p. 37.
5   C. Kunhan Raja, *Sanskrit,* New Delhi, Indian Council for Cultural Relations, n.d.; Sunuti Kumar Chatterji, ed., *The Cultural Heritage of India, Vol. V, Languages and Literatures*, Calcutta, Institute of Culture, 1978, pp. 4, 79–88.
6   The two epics of India were related to a "social revolution" or the conflict of the new and the old within the Aryan community. The *Mahabharata*, probably the longest poem ever written (with roughly 200,000 lines, most of them sixteen syllables each), is generally referred to as the Great Epic of India (as opposed to the other major pan-Indian epic *Ramayana*, the story of the hero Rama Dasharathi). It was composed of the ancient Sanskrit language, in northern India, over a period extending from 400 B.C. to A.D. 200. The title literally means the great story of the rivalry and war of the descendants of Bharata, the two families of cousins, the Pandavas and the Kauravas. Bharata is the name for India in the modern Indian languages. The *Mahabharata* is about eight times the size of Homer's *Iliad* and *Odyssey* combined. In addition to stories, prayers and hymns are recited, and advice on ethics and on royal administration is given. Bibliographies: P. Lal, *An Annotated Mahabharata Bibliography*, Calcutta, Writers Workshop, 1967; J. Bruce Long, *The Mahabharata: a Select Annotated Bibliography*, Ithaca, Cornell University, 1974. *Mahabharata* texts: J. A. B. van Buitenen, tr. and ed., *The Mahabharata*, Books I–V, 3 vols., Chicago, University of Chicago Press, 1973–78; Manmatha Nath Dutt, *A Prose English Translation of the Mahabharata*, 18 books, Calcutta, Elysium Press, 1895–1905. Other works: R. N. Dandekar, "The Mahabharata: Origin and Growth", *University of Ceylon Review*, Colombo, 12 (1954), pp. 65–85; Upendra Nath Ghosal, "On Some Recent Interpretations of the Mahabharata Theories of Kingship", *Indian Historical Review*, New Delhi, 31 (1955), pp. 323–329; Manorama Jauhari, *Politics and Ethics in Ancient India: a Study Based on the Mahabharata*, Varanasi, Bharatya Vidya Prakashan, 1968; Promatha Nath Mullick, *The Mahabharata as It Was, Is, and Ever Shall Be: a Critical Study*, Calcutta, Pioneer Press, 1934; Brajdeo Prasad Roy, *Political Ideas and Institutions in the Mahabharata*, Calcutta, Punthi Pustak, 1975; Mary Carroll Smith, "The Mahabharata's Core", *Journal of the Oriental Society*, New Haven, Conn., 95 (1975), pp. 479–482; Chintamar Vinayak Vaidya, *The Mahabharata: a Criticism*, Delhi, Mehar Chand Lachhman Das, 1966.
7   The *Ramayana,* composed at approximately the same time, features Vishnu incarnate in Rama. Dhairyabala P. Vora, *Evolution of Morals in the Epics (Mahabharata and*

Ramayana), Bombay, Popular Book Depot, 1959; Benjamin Khan, *The Concept of Dharma in Valmiki Ramayana*, Delhi, Munshiram Manoharlal, 1965.

8   The four castes are the Brahmins (priests and scholars), Kshatriyas (kings and warriors), Vaisyas (traders), and Sudras (artisans and tillers of the soil).

9   An early (1879) sketch of the religions of India (the Vedic religions, Brahmanism, Buddhism, Jainism and Hinduism) in the *Encyclopédie des Sciences Religieuses* (Paris) later (1882) appeared in book form: A. Barth, *The Religions of India*, tr. Rev. J. Wood, 2nd ed., Delhi, Low Price Publications, 1990.

10   An understanding of the "fundamental unity" underlying the great living religions of the world: O. P. Ghai, *Unity in Diversity*, New Delhi, Institute of Personal Development, 1986. For a description of all the states in India: T. K. Suman Kumar, *India: Unity in Diversity*, New Delhi, Anmol Publications, 1992.

11   For instance: P. N. Oak, "Ancient Hinduism is Tailored to Become Modern U.N. Religion", *Hinduism*, Sussex, 28 (September–October 1968), pp. 13–15.

12   Vijaya Ghose, ed., *Tirtha: the Treasury of Indian Expressions*, New Delhi, CMC Ltd., 1992, pp. 229–254.

13   For instance: B. N. Puri, "Secularism-Western and Eastern-a Study", *World Affairs*, New Delhi, I (December 1990), p. 110.

14   Ravinder Kumar, *The Making of a Nation: Essays in Indian History and Politics*, New Delhi, Manohar, 1989, p. 176.

15   Ghose, *op. cit.,* pp. 254–257.

16   For a clear explanation of the basic Buddhist teachings: Walpole Rahula, *What the Budha Taught?* London, Fraser, 1978. An earlier (original German in 1905) source by one who lived in the Buddhist countries for nearly ten years: H. Hackmann, *Buddhism as a Religion*, Delhi, Low Price Publications, 1993.

17   Martin Heidegger, *Existence and Being*, Chicago, H. Regnery Co., 1949.

18   Krishna Chaitanya, *A Profile of Indian Culture*, New Delhi, Indian Book Company, 1975, p. 85.

19   A celebrated Brahmin (4th century B. C.) who achieved the enthronement of Chandragupta Maurya. Also called Chanakya or Vishnugupta, he wrote the political treatise *Arthasastra*, often compared to Machiavelli's *The Prince*. A recent translation: R. P. Kangle, *The Kautilya Arthasastra*, Delhi, Motilal Banarsidass, 1992. On this unique treatise on 'the science of polity' and the great Maurya era: Somnath Dar, *Kautilya and the Arthasastra*, New Delhi, Marwah Publications, 1981.

20   Haridas Bhattacharyya, ed., *The Cultural Heritage of India: Vol. IV, The Religions*, Calcutta, Institute of Culture, 1953–62, pp. 44f.

21   Ronald Wixman, *The Peoples of the USSR: an Ethnographic Handbook*, Armonk, N.Y., M. E. Sharpe, Inc., 1984, pp. 219–220.

22   A John Briggs translation from the original Persian (1829) of Mahomed Kasim Ferishtas: *History of the Rise of the Mahomedan Power in India*, Vols. I–IV, Delhi, Low Price Publications, 1990.

23   Al-Biruni, *Alberuni's India*, tr. Edward C. Sachau, 2 vols., Lahore, Government of West Pakistan, 1962. Also: Najibullah Khan, "Abouraihan Al-Beirani and His Time", *Afghanistan*, Kabul, 6/1 (1951), pp. 17–27.

24   Timur (also called Timur Lenk, Turkish for 'Lame'; English Tamerlane or Tamburlaine) (1336–1405).

25   Pramatha Nath Bose, *A History of Hindu Civilisation during British Rule*, Indian reprint, Delhi, Low Price Publications, 1993, p. 48.

26 Indian Council for Cultural Relations, *Towards Understanding India*, New Delhi, Bhatkal Books International, 1965, p. 18.
27 Humayun Kabir, "Unity in Diversity", *Readings from India*, ed., G. N. S. Raghavan, New Delhi, Indian Council for Cultural Relations, 1996, p. 8.
28 Ishtiaq Husain Qureshi, *The Administration of the Moghul Empire*, Delhi, Low Price Publications, 1973, p. 61.
29 R. Nath, *Islamic Architecture and Culture in India*, Delhi, B. R. Publishing Corporation, 1982, p. 103.
30 The descendants of people in Persia during the first millennium B.C., who worshipped a supreme God (Ahura Mazda) and who were forced out of that country on account of Islam's expansion in the 8th century. They are known as the Parsis in contemporary India.
31 Government of India, *Muslims in India*, New Delhi, Ministry of Information and Broadcasting, 1966. By a prominent member of the Church of South India: Stephen Neill, *A History of Christianity in India*, 2 vols., Cambridge, Cambridge University Press, 1984–85.
32 Bahadur Shah, more an aesthete (as a poet, musician and calligrapher) than a political leader, seemed like a client of the British and without real authority. He figured briefly in the "Indian Mutiny". After the rebellion was put down by the British, he was exiled to (then) Burma.
33 Frederick V. Moore, *Christians in India*, Government of India, Ministry of Information and Broadcasting, 1964.
34 From his speech at the St. Thomas' Day Celebrations in New Delhi on 18 December 1955.
35 Ethnic Albanian and born in Yugoslavia, Mother Teresa of Calcutta, the Roman Catholic missionary: Navin Chawla, *Mother Teresa*, New Delhi, Gulmohar Press; London, Sinclair-Stevenson, 1992.
36 Government of India, *The Tribal People of India*, New Delhi, Ministry of Information and Broadcasting, 1973.
37 Humayun Kabir, "The Impact of the West on Indian Traditions", *The Emerging World: Jawaharlal Nehru Memorial Volume*, Bombay, Asia Publishing House, 1964, pp. 81–92.
38 Graham Wallas, "Bentham as Political Inventor", *Contemporary Review*, London, CXXIX (1926), pp. 308–319; Leslie Stephen, *The English Utilitarians*, 3 vols., New York, G. P. Putnam's Sons; London, Duckworth and Co., 1900. For a critical evaluation: Élie Hallévy, *La Formation du radicalisme philosophique: la révolution , et la doctrine de l'utilité (1789–1815)*, Paris, F. Alcan, 1900.
39 G. Spiller, "Darwinism and Sociology", *Sociological Review*, University of Keele, VII (1914), pp. 232–253; Lucius Moody Bristol, *Social Adaptation*, Cambridge, Mass., Harvard University Press, 1915, pp. 58–68.
40 An exposition of ideas which moulded the Indian mind during the last two centuries: V. S. Naravane, *Modern Indian Thought*, Bombay, Asia Publishing House, 1964.
41 Bani Roy Chaudhury, *Folk Tales of Kashmir*, New Delhi, Sterling Publishers, 1983.
42 *Keys to Kashmir, op. cit.*, p. 31.
43 J. C. Chatterji, *Kashmir Shaivaism*, New Delhi, Indological Bank Corporation, 1978, pp. 1–2; Grover, *op.cit.*, Vol. I, pp. 82–91; S. L. Shali, *Kashmir: History and Archaeology Through the Ages*, New Delhi, Indus Publication Co., 1993, pp. 164–174.
44 M. Ishaq Khan, "Kashmiri Culture vis-à-vis Islam", *Cultural Heritage of Kashmir*, ed., S. M. Afzal Qadri, Srinagar, University of Kashmir, 1997, p. 24.
45 Muhammad Ashraf Wani, "Islam in the Kashmir Environment", *ibid.*, p. 57.
46 John Norman Hollister, *The Shi'a of India*, London, Luzac and Company, 1953, p. 141f.

47 Arjuna, the youngest of the three full Pandava brothers, is the hero in the *Mahabharata*. A work of unusual breadth and depth: Ruth Cecily Katz, *Arjuna in the Mahabharata: Where Krishna Is, There Is Victory*, Columbia, South Carolina, University of South Carolina Press, 1989. Also: Kalyan Kumar Dasgupta, "The Arjunayanas: an Ancient Indian Tribe", *Journal of the Oriental Institute*, Baroda (modern name: Vadodra), India, 20 (1970–71), pp. 431–441.

48 Mohammad Ishaq Khan, *Kashmir's Transition to Islam: the Role of Muslim Rishis*, New Delhi, Manohar, 1994.

49 In the Kashmir style of Indo-Islamic architecture, the chief building material of many of the structures is timber, since wood had been used for a long time before the Muslim rule there. A few buildings were constructed of stone during the Moghul rule, however. Ziyaud-din A. Desai, *Indo-Islamic Architecture*, Government of India, Ministry of Information and Broadcasting, 1970, p. 42f.

50 D. C. Ahir, *Heritage of Buddhism*, Delhi, B. R. Publishing Corporation, 1989, p. 47.

51 A physical documentation of the monasteries: Romi Khosla, *Buddhist Monasteries in the Western Himalaya*, Katmandu, Nepal, Ratna Pustak Bhandar, 1979.

52 *The Cultural Heritage of India: Vol. I, The Early Phases*, Calcutta, Institute of Culture, 1953–62, p. 56; K. S. Singh and S. Manoharan, *People of India, National Series, Vol. IX: Languages and Scripts*, New Delhi, Oxford University Press, 1993, p. 26.

53 Also known as Mahatma (Great Soul), 'Bapu', 'Bapuji', and 'Gandhiji'. His best known book: M. K. Gandhi, *An Autobiography or the Story of My Experiments with Truth,* tr. from the Gujarati by Mahadev Desai, Ahmedabad, Navajivan Publishing House, 1996.

54 The *Bhagavadgita* ("The Song of God", in the *Mahabharata*, VI, 23–40) is a lecture delivered by Krishna to Arjuna on the battlefield, before the start of the Kurukshatra War. Throughout the centuries, the *Bhagavadgita* has become, independent of the bigger epic, an important text of Hinduism. For the text: J. A. B. van Buitenen, tr. and ed., *The Bhagavadgita in the Mahabharata: Text and Translation*, Chicago, University of Chicago Press, 1981; Franklin Edgerton, *The Bhagavad Gita*, Cambridge, Mass., Harvard University Press, 1972; Sarvepalli Radhakrishnan, *The Bhagavadgita: with an Introductory Essay, Sanskrit Text, English Translation and Notes*, New York, Harper Torchbooks, 1973; R. C. Zaehner, *The Bhagavad-Gita: with a Commentary Based on the Original Sources*, Oxford, Clarendon Press, 1969. Others: Antonio T. De Nicolás, *Avatara: the Humanization of Philosophy through the Bhagavad Gita*, New York, Nicolas Hays, 1976; Aurobindo Ghose, *Essays on the Gita*, Pondicherry, Sri Aurobindo Ashram, 1966.

55 A man of incredible creativity, he was awarded (1913) the Nobel Prize in Literature for his collection of poems, *Gitanjali*. India and Bangladesh adopted songs by Tagore as their national anthems.

56 Rajendra Prasad, *The Unity of India*, New Delhi, Ministry of Information and Broadcasting, 1970, p. 68.

Chapter 4

Historical Backdrop

Although Kashmir,[1] the seat of the Sanskrit from the earliest times with a script of its own (*Sarada*), seemed to be geographically cut off from its neighbours, it was not immune, unlike the ancient Egyptian civilization around the Nile, to foreign incursions. Kashmir might have briefly come under the sway of the Persian Achaemenid dynasty. When Alexander of Macedonia crossed the Indus, a local king (Anhisartes) had his authority extended over parts of Kashmir. With the death of Alexander, Chandragupta, the founder of the Maurya Empire, got all the satrapies of north-western India as a result of his treaty with General Seleukos. Macedonian artistic influence motivated many local artisans whose centre of learning and work came to be Gandhara. While a synthesis of Indo-Hellenic civilization gave birth to the remarkable Gandhara school of art, Kashmir and Gandhara had close political relations.

From Asoka to the Moghuls

It was probably Asoka of Indian fame (surnamed 'The Pious')[2] or another Asoka of Kashmir who established the city of Srinagar[3] in about 250 B.C. and introduced the Buddhist monks into Kashmir, which became, with temples and statues, a school of teaching of this religion. While the Naga or snake worship was the religion of the original inhabitants of the Valley, at least one great Indian religion, Saivism,[4] found some of the best teachers on the banks of the Vitasta (Jhelum). But starting with Asoka, several local rulers patronized Buddhism. Many Kashmiri missionaries went to Tibet, China and elsewhere as self-exiles to disseminate the religion. A great Kashmiri who converted Java and the neighbouring islands to Buddhism was Gunavarman, and Buddhayasas accomplished a similar mission in China.

After Asoka's death the country was harassed by various *mlechhas* (foreigners), a prominent one being the Kushan dynasty. The latter built up an extensive empire under Kaniska, whose territories covered all land from Central Asia to Bengal. But perhaps the most glorious period of Kashmir's history ended with the reign of Anavtivarman (A.D. 9th century), followed by court intrigues, famines, poverty of the masses, heavy taxation, popular uprisings, civil wars, and destruction. Rinchin, a fugitive prince from Tibet, who came to Kashmir with a few hundred armed men, and who embraced Islam, became the first Muslim ruler (Rinchin Shah or the assumed title of Sadr-ud Din, 1325–27) of the land. His wife, Kota Rani, ascended the throne after him and is acknowledged as the last Hindu ruler. After pitiless misrule, the harassed people seemed ready to accept Islam, which did not meet with violent opposition.

Although the Kashmiris during the reign of Lalita Ditya (699–736), had clashed with the Arab armies, young Bin Qasim's rule in India was short-lived. Islam came to the Sub-continent and to Kashmir, not from the west, but from the north. The so-called Moghuls who established their glorious empire in India were actually the descendants of Timur, the Central Asian Turkish sultan. The portraits of the Turkish sultans, painted in India, has no trace in their features of a Mongoloid race. Islamic influence was felt in Kashmir, however, long before the land had Muslim rulers. To a people wearied of feuds, famines and unfavourable deals Islam offered a more or less equitable treatment. Mahmud Gaznavi,[5] a former Turkish slave, invaded India and swept upon Kashmir over the Pir Panchal Pass in 1015 and 1021, but was compelled to withdraw. Zulfi Kadir Khan, a descendant of the mighty Genghis Khan, entered Kashmir with a force of 70,000 cavalry.

Islamic influence was initially carried to the Valley by missionaries and military men who found a yielding climate on account of misrule by Hindu kings. Although the country seemed sealed up behind its mountains, especially after the failure of the repeated expeditions of Mahmud Gaznavi, the *Sufi* dervishes and military power brought Islamic teachings to the Valley.[6] Having embraced an existence of meditation, the disciples of Abu Sayyid of Persia wore a garment of wool (*suf*) throughout their monastic life as Islamic mystics, and hence were called "*Sufis*". There were common attitudes and beliefs between the Pantheist Sufism and the Saiva philosophy. Islam entered Kashmir from Central Asia, the original home of the Turkic peoples. Although four great *Sufi* orders (Suharwardi, Kubravi, Naqshbandi and Qadiri) reached the Valley, an indigenous order, known as *Rishi*, developed there.[7] The first name associated with Islam was Bulbul Shah, who converted Rinchin and several others to Islam and acquired some influence in the Valley. The first mosque built, near the fifth bridge in Srinagar, is now known as Bulbul Lankar. The most prominent *Sufi* after him was Sayyid Ali Hamadani, who widely disseminated Islamic teaching and practice in Kashmir. Most of the Kashmiri saints dabbled in politics and established matrimonial relations with members of the royal court. The *Rishi* saints of Kashmir, on the other hand, kept aloof of the ruling circles and preached love of mankind. Sheikh Nuruddin, also known as Nund Resh, popularized this version of *Sufism*. India, with its multi-racial, multi-religious and multi-lingual pattern of society, was always attracted to men who could narrow these differences. The Muslim *Sufis* were that kind of men.

Bulbul Shah was not a military or a political figure, but a saintly *Sufi* who propagated Islam in Kashmir. It was he who converted Rinchin, originally a prince of Ladakh, but later the first Muslim king in Kashmir, into Islam. Shah Mir, who had accompanied Rinchin, ascended the throne (1339–42) under the name of Sultan Shams-ud Din, and became the founder of the Sultan dynasty which ruled Kashmir for 222 years. Although Sultan Skandar (1389–1413) and Ali Shah (1413–20) carried forced conversions of low-caste Hindus and destroyed some temples, religious tolerance was the norm. It was through *Sufism* that Islam could absorb the pre-Islamic practices.[8] Islam adapted itself to different cultures in India as well.

The benevolent Shahi Khan, better known as Zain-ul Abidin (1423–74), among them, who reigned peacefully and moreover led a saintly life, is known for his high sense of toleration, reforms to protect the tillers of the soil against the revenue officers, patronage of scholars, education and craftsmen, and his reconquest of Punjab and western Tibet. First and foremost, he exercised freedom of conscience for all and maintained, as a patron of learning, a good many Muslim and Hindu scholars at his court. He got some books translated from Sanskrit and Arabic into Persian and Kashmiri, and built a library that included copies of rare works extinct elsewhere in India. Sheikh Noor-ud Din Wali, "Alamdar-e Kashmir" (The Standard-bearer of Kashmir), commonly known as Nund (Pious) Rishi, was a saint, patriot and poet of Zain-ul Abidin's time, whose thoughts moulded the minds of generations. Zain-ul Abidin was among the pallbearers in the huge procession of mourners when Nund Rishi passed away (1438).[9] Also as a supporter of public works, Zain-ul Abidin built a dam from Anderkot to Sopor and ordered the Nalla-Mar canal to be dug. Judging by the great number of Hindus who gained favour under this Muslim *Badshah* (ruler), the tradition says that "a Hindu spirit had entered into his body which moved his feelings towards the Hindus".[10]

Kashmir was threatened by invasions during the reigns of the Turco-Moghul[11] sultans Babur (Babar), Humayun and Akbar. Having brought Delhi under his sway, Zahir-ud Din Muhammad Babur (1526–30)[12] planned to occupy the strategic land of Kashmir. His armies, which had defeated the last of the Afghan rulers, Ibrahim Lodi, in the battle of Panipat (1526), also subdued the forces of Ghazi Khan of the Chak dynasty and entered Kashmiri territory. Babur's son Humayun (1530–56)[13] took Srinagar without a fight, but withdrew a month and a half later. Finally, the invasion of Srinagar by Akbar's (1556–1605)[14] general Qasim Khan on 14 October 1556, and the flight of the last Chak sultan made Kashmir a province of the mighty Moghul Empire. Akbar's conquest marking the beginning of the country's modern history, the Moghul rule lasted close to two centuries. Akbar encouraged religious debate and cultural exchange in Srinagar as well as in Delhi. He tried to win loyalty to the *Din-e Ilahi*, an eclectic belief of his own drawing ideas from all the current religions.

When Akbar had breathed his last (1605), he had already occupied Baltistan and Ladakh. Jahangir (1605–27),[15] who succeeded his father, and his resourceful queen visited Kashmir several times. Not only did he utilize the many hills coming down to a spring to plant a pleasure garden, including the legendary Shalimar, he was also moved by the suffering of human beings, and therefore prevented a number of inhuman practices such as burying women along with their dead husbands or killing girl babies at birth. It was Jahangir who systematically planted *Char Chinar* or a plane tree at each of the cardinal points in order to produce shade wherever the sun may be. When Jahangir was dying, he was asked whether he wanted anything; his reply was: "Only Kashmir!"[16] His son, Shah Jahan (1627–58),[17] as an eminent builder among the Muslim emperors, constructed a network of roads in the Valley apart from laying gardens such as Gulshan, Hassanabad and Chasma Shahi. The Moghul gardens had remained one of the Valley's tourist attractions until the outbreak of contemporary terrorism in Kashmir. The Hazratbal Mosque on Lake Dal, built by Shah Jahan, has a special sanctity for being the repository of *Moe-e Muqaddas*, i. e., an hair of Prophet Muhammad. It is one of Kashmir's most treasured relics.[18] While Shah Jahan gave his daughters in marriage to Hindus, his governor Zaffar Khan abolished the taxes on saffron, wood, sheep and boatmen.

Although Aurangzeb (1658–89)[19] was scrupulously honest, his practice of communal discrimination signified the beginning of the end. He almost undid what his forefathers had done. While some of his governors gave relief to the suffering people during famine, fire and floods, Iftikar Khan was a tyrant especially over the Brahmins for four years (1671–75). The martyrdom of Tegh Bahadur, a Sikh *guru* (the preceptor who gives life direction),[20] took place then. During Aurangzeb's time and after, Kashmir witnessed outbreaks of religious fanaticism as well as revolts. The *Sheikh-ul Islam* of Kashmir gave instructions (1720) for hostile, even slaughterous measures against the Hindus. The Bomba and the Gujjar tribes revolted, and there were times when anarchy reigned in Kashmir. The religious intolerance of those who propagated a pure faith was generally "the product of competing factions of the nobility seeking to promote their self-interest".[21] The population of the Valley grew to be predominantly Sunni Muslim while the Hindus moved southwards, and the Buddhists retreated to Ladakh. But Abd-ul Samad, a governor who came (1722) from Lahore with a huge army, put the fanatical *Sheikh-ul Islam* (Mulla Sharaf-ud Din) to death and removed all the restrictions formerly placed on the Hindus.

The early Muslim sultans had not tampered with the religious beliefs of the people. Zain-ul Abidin was a monument of toleration and equity. But the spread of Islam was not always peaceful. The society being basically a feudal one, there were frequent clashes for power among the princes and others, their conflict encouraging feuds between the Sunni and the Shi'a Muslims. For instance, during the long-drawn struggle (1484–1516) for the throne between Muhammad Shah and Fath Shah, the former captured power three times and the latter as many as five times. Such unstable administration and recurrent chaos were accompanied by heavy taxation and misery.

From the Afghanis to the Dogras

Kashmir easily fell into the hands of the Afghani king. Some Kashmiri leaders actually invited Ahmed Shah Abdali[22] to invade Kashmir. The force under Abdullah Khan Iskh Aqasi thus brought to end (1752) the Moghul rule in Kashmir. Ahmad Shah, who previously enjoyed governmental prerogatives in the eastern portion of the large monarchy of Nadir Shah of Persia, originally a Turk (Nadir Quli), assumed the title of "*Dur-e Duran*" (Pearl of the Age), and hence his clan came to be known as Durrani. Although Ahmad Shah was invited to Kashmir to rid the country of the last cruel Moghul governor, not only his general Abdullah Khan tolerated a reign of terror as soon as he entered the Valley, the Afghan rule of 67 years almost reduced Kashmir to the degree of slavery.[23] Kashmir fell from the frying pan into the fire. When Ahmad Shah died (1771) in Kandahar, the economy of the Valley was in ruins, and there was lawlessness in the whole country. A certain Azad Khan tied up the Hindus two and two in sacks and sank them in the Dal Lake. When he was succeeded by Madad Khan, the latter's performance created now a well-known proverb: "*Zulm-e Azad ra rasid Madad*" (Madad out-Heroded Azad). More Hindus fled from the Valley. The cruelty of the Afghani rulers on non-Muslims did not win the support of the Muslims either. A Persian line described the Afghan rule as the worst kind of despotism that the Kashmiris had suffered: "*Sar buridan pesh in sangin dilan gul chidan ast*" (These stone-hearted people thought no more of cutting of heads than of plucking a flower).[24]

The local leaders, whether Muslim or Hindu, joined hands in inviting Ranjit Singh to invade Kashmir. Not only Raja Ranjit Dev of Jammu in the south had gathered enough strength to plan the conquest of the Valley, the Sikhs, who had beaten back the Afghanis, were also rising in the Punjab. While the earlier attempts of the Sikh contingents were unsuccessful, Kashmir eventually fell into Sikh hands, whose army, 30,000 strong, fought at Shupayan (1819).[25] After a period of about five centuries, the country once more came under Hindu rule.

Islam influenced Hinduism in Kashmir and vice versa to a greater extent than generally accepted. Not only the lower castes embraced it through the *Sufi* missionaries, and even the Brahmins, who held to Hinduism, were influenced by it, and adjusted themselves in terms of certain beliefs and practices. A distinguished writer of the Muslim period who personified Kashmir's compound culture was Mulla Mohammad Mohsin Fani, who in his *Dabistan-e Mazahib* (1645) examined the mythologies and the philosophies of all religions but expressed his liking of some aspects of faiths other than Islam to which he belonged. While even the Muslim rulers wed Hindu women and were influenced by their religion, the new converts continued to observe the old rituals from which they could not break easily. Muslims gave refuge to innumerable Hindus under distress, and the Pandit nobles opposed the Sikh attempt to demolish the sacred shrine of Khanqah-e Moualla, one of the grand edifices of the Muslim period. While Kashmir was too deeply rooted in its traditions to wither away under the Muslim storm, Islam there was necessarily fraternized with local components, perhaps with the exception of the Moghul style of architecture. Even after so many centuries, "one comes across people named Muhammad Ali Pandit, Iftikhar Raina or Rafiq Rishi" who retain their Hindu surnames.[26]

The Sikhs, originally a religious sect, transformed themselves, in due course, into a military force. The British, who were soon to face Tsarist Russian expansion in Central Asia and the extension of the Chinese border to Sinkiang (Chinese Turkistan), concluded (1806) a treaty of friendship with Raja Ranjit Singh which secured the latter from interference in his plans to annex the north of the Sutlej River. When Ranjit Singh crossed to the south of the river, some Sikh chiefs sought the protection of the British who induced the Raja to sign (1809) another treaty once the Napoleonic threat of an alliance with Persia subdued. These moves did not prevent Ranjit Singh, however, from taking (1819) Kashmir out of Afghani hands. The life of the Kashmiris under the new Sikh government did not improve. In fact, while the aristocratic Sikh *sirdars* (commanders) lived lavishly in magnificent palaces, the average men and women on the streets strolled in rags. This state of affairs did not prevent the British, after Ranjit Singh's death (1839), from granting to his successor Gulab Singh the hilly district of Jammu together with Kashmir and making him outwardly an independent ruler but actually a British vassal. From the Sikh annexation of Kashmir to Ranjit Singh's death the British felt concern over Afghani and Sikh power. The first Anglo-Afghan war[27] was a calamity for the British, and the campaigns against the Sikhs were victorious yet enfeebling. The British chose to assist Gulab Singh, the master of Jammu, to establish himself in Srinagar with a new role that would promote the interests of the Imperial Government as well.

The inhabitants of Jammu get their name "*Dogra*", a corruption from the Sanskrit "*Dogirath*", meaning "two lakes", from Mansar and Siroinsar, situated to the east of the city. The province of Jammu was given (1820) to Gulab Singh, a Dogra Rajput, and his successors with the hereditary title of Raja. Jammu and Doggar, the land of the Dogras, are often but wrongly considered to be synonymous. Doggar extends to three Indian states, namely, Jammu and Kashmir, Punjab and Himachal. Jammu was the "nerve center and most well-known part of Doggar".[28] "Dogri" is one of the major languages of Jammu and Kashmir, with an alphabet of its own and spoken by a larger number of people than any other language of the state.[29]

The British

Gulab Singh, one of the most trusted military aids of Ranjit Singh, subjugated Ladakh and Baltistan. With the conquest of the last two pieces of land, Gulab Singh's possessions more-or-less encircled Kashmir from the south and the east. The First Anglo-Sikh War (1845–46)[30] ended with the Treaty of Lahore which brought to the British the hilly territories between the rivers Bias and Indus including Kashmir. The British, in their turn, sold the latter to Gulab Singh for the paltry sum of 75 lacks of rupees (or £750,000 sterling) through the Treaty of Amritsar (16 March 1846),[31] which also meant that the British henceforth recognized the independence of the "Dogra regime" in Jammu and Kashmir, and honoured the ruler with the title of the Maharaja, who entered Srinagar the same year. Already the master of Jammu, Ladakh (up to the Drass River) and Baltistan, the Maharaja, who later occupied Gilgit as well, thus founded the modern State of Jammu and Kashmir, which assumed its undivided shape, including part of the Pamirs and of Tibet besides the Indian kingdoms of Jammu and Kashmir. This whole area had never been effectively united under one administration before. The Kashmir Valley was now returned to a Hindu ruler, but the overwhelming majority of the Valley's population had become Muslim since the time of Queen Kota Rani. Gulab Singh was to rule over a Muslim majority, just as the Muslim Nizam of Hyderabad and the Muslim ruler of Junagadh were ruling over predominantly Hindu populations. The British 'gift', the result of a well-planned policy, "was not for the sake of money, but for a major political reason, i.e., to weaken the Sikh power".[32]

The Gulab Singh regime had to subdue the warlike Bomba and Khakha tribes of the Valley and resist the British to control its frontier policy, as well as searching for solutions to the economic chaos especially in the rural areas. The Maharaja eradicated some of the worst aspects of the *begar* (forced labour) system. He ordered the rationing of rice for the city population and removed part of the tyrannical practice imposed on the shawl-weavers by requiring them to pay only for the actual work done by them on the loom and recognizing their right to change their employers and to minimum salaries. He was not a saint, and his methods might have been primeval, but he took some pains to govern justly. He punished corrupt officials in a rude manner, but he considered great expenditure on palaces a waste of resources. He remained an orthodox Hindu, but having started his career as a petty official in the Court, he conquered kingdoms and eventually became one of the most remarkable Indians of the 19th century. With the revolt of the Indian army at Meerut in mid-1857, the old regime had made, in Nehru's words, "its last despairing effort" to drive out the British.[33] After the death (1858) of Gulab Singh, Maharaja Ranbir Singh promoted trade by constructing a few roads and establishing a postal service. He introduced experimental tea gardens, allocated money for the silk industry and wine-making, and abolished the tax for the ailing shawl business.

While the British seemed more occupied by the expansion of Russia, which stormed Chimkent (1864), Tashkent (1865), Samarkand (1868) and Khiva (1873),[34] famine, raging in Kashmir, took away three-fifths of the total population of the Valley on account of the continuous rains that destroyed (1877–78) the crops. The shawl industry was even more depressed when the French market was lost after the Franco-German War (1871). A year later, the Sunni weavers looted the property of the Shi'a manufacturers and traders. On the other hand, in response to recurring revolts, Gilgit was permanently annexed to Jammu and Kashmir, and agreements were made with the rulers of Hunza and Nagar to guarantee trade safety.

Pratap Singh's long reign (1885–1925) was marked by more British interference mainly on account of tensions on the northern frontiers of India. Although popular complaints multiplied while the treasury remained empty, the tangible rationale behind the British curtailing of the new Maharaja's power was not the grievances of the people, but the craving for control over that vital border region. As the Russian military appeared more frequently on the Pamirs, effective rulership passed from the hands of the Maharaja to those of a Council of Regency, subject to the supervision of the British Resident who was to become the final referee in all matters. He was the spokesman of the Central Government with the duty of keeping a close watch on the administration. Enjoying even some judicial powers not mentioned in official documents, his office was a veiled dictatorship, and his advice was a command. Encouraged by the Russian début and the latter's hunger for branching out, the Hunza-Nagar forces revolted but were suppressed by none other than Colonel A. G. Durand, the British Political Agent in Gilgit. The Kashmir State contributed men and money for all these expeditions. Having obtained the control of the frontier posts, the British saw no harm in appointing (1891) the Maharaja as the new President of the Council, even if only as a figurehead. As the Imperial Government further consolidated its positions in the northern frontier and as relations with Afghanistan improved, the State Council was abolished (1905), but the Maharaja's orders had to be approved by the British Resident. The Maharaja placed the resources of his state at the disposal of the British Government during the First World War. Even then, he would act in accordance with the advice of the Resident regarding frontier problems and keynote administrative reorganizations. Full powers were restored to Maharaja Pratap Singh only in 1921. When he was succeeded by his nephew, Raja Hari Singh, groups of young Kashmiri men, mostly non-Muslims educated in the state and the missionary schools (first established in 1874 and 1881 respectively) or in the colleges in Srinagar (1905) and Jammu (1908), were imbued with notions of equality and freedom.

Indian Nationalism and the Muslims

These circumstances nourished ideas of Indian nationalism and independence as well as providing for the seeds of problems connected with some nationalities and minorities.[35] The nationalist movement in the pre-partition Indian Sub-continent had its own peculiarities. The fact that nationalism there grew under British colonial rule had an impact on that transformation in more ways than one. Britain set foot in India when its capitalist formation had reached the stage of expansion abroad. It was British assets, supported by financial means, that encountered and paralysed Indian feudalism, and thereby economically unified India through capitalist economic forms, including a network of communications so vital for colonial rule and also helpful to convert a medieval people into a modern nation. Just as this evolution was motivated by the interests of foreign capital, the blossoming of local nationalism under colonial rule had to be, in some ways, dissimilar to the evolution of British or French nationalism. While this transformation, stimulated by foreign interests, provided the objective basis for the rise of the Indian nation, not only its special features prevented the forging of the whole Indian peoples into a coherent nation, but British capitalism, which fought against feudalism at home, perpetrated some local feudal relics in that "most precious jewel in the crown", again for its own sake. While British capitalism inevitably helped the consolidation of economic forms that contributed to the creation of nationalism in India, subjectively it sought to rely on forces that retarded the process of national consolidation.

      Indian nationalism, on the other hand, grew unevenly in terms of time and momentum. Different communities and regions joined it at different times and in various tempi. The Muslims in the north or the Hindu Bengalis in ports, the peasantry or the urban dwellers, the depressed classes or the traditionally wealthy reacted differently and at different times. Those who were galvanized early and those who joined the wagon late thought of themselves as separate groups. The differences were on account of a number of factors such as the proximity to the great cities, the level of economic development or the size of the educated sub-class. Under the circumstances, various groups, with personalities of their own, seemed to develop separately. But all initially believed in a single Indian state, none favouring partition. The future independent state had to be based on some kind of federalism, with the provinces enjoying autonomy.

When various nationalities in India wanted to unite the territories inhabited by their own people and develop their own culture, this longing was only a quest for self-expression, not in conflict with the general union of the whole country. There were several commercial or industrial groups in a number of awakened nationalities, however, which incited hatred against their rivals in other national or religious groups by trying to incite the consciousness of the masses and presenting their economic interests under different garbs. Made up of conflicting groups with different interests, the Hindus and the Muslims had common religion as far as their respective communities were concerned. Otherwise, both the Hindus and the Muslims had a class structure with their own landlords, moneylenders, professionals, shopkeepers, peasants and workers. The adherents of these two leading religions were dispersed all over India.

But it was inevitable in this growth of nationalism that the Muslims, the depressed classes, and some other socio-religious groups also developed movements of some identity. None of them spoke the same language, however; nor did they inhabit a definite territory or have a common economic life. In many places, as in Bengal, one could not differentiate a Muslim from a Hindu except for one differential—religion. Hinduism or Islam was an important bond.

With no common territory, language or economic life, the Indian Muslims shared no monolithic interests encompassing all. There were Muslims in Punjab, Sindh, Baluchistan, the North-West Frontier Province, Kashmir and in East Bengal, all reflecting different identities, in addition to a common religion. Similarly, there were Hindu Bengalis, Hindu Biharis or Hindu Marathas. Using a different tongue and living at a particular place, all of them represented a different nationality. But in religious terms, the Indian Muslims of the time, constituting a 90 million group within the 400 million Indian population, was the biggest minority.

It is relevant to remember that the Muslim masses, everywhere in India including Kashmir, were economically weak. The British conquest of India brought down the Moghul Empire and its Muslim aristocracy. While the latter lost its political power and economic positions, a new landlord class was made up of Hindu merchants and money-lenders, who became the mainstay of foreign rule. The Hindus had started to interact with the British much earlier than the Muslims. The first contacts had necessarily been in the ports like Bengal, Bombay and Madras, which were predominantly Hindu, and not in northern India, where the dominant segment of the Muslims lived. It was first in the Hindu areas that the new economic system was created by the British, supported with roads, new cities and educational facilities. When the British brought their educational system to India, it was the Hindus, rather some of them, who benefited from this new opportunity, while the Muslims stuck to traditional learning.

The ripening political concept of "Muslim nationalism" reflected the desire of the feudal upper crust of that religious community to regain its privileges, long denied by the colonizing British. Conditions of extremely weak capital formations in most of northern India were conducive to channeling local frustrations into the mainstream of religious identity. Although the feudal elements seemed to spearhead this identity, large non-feudal economic classes or groups such as the peasants, small landowners, and artisans, for whom Islam symbolized former power, united in their rivalry or even hatred of the Hindu occupancy in the middle and lower levels of the country's trade, industry and civil service. The landlord upper crust found in Islam a ready instrumentality that could go to the heart of the masses with whose support they could, above all, protect their own interests. Much later did they rally to the call for the creation of an Indian Muslim state.

The foundations of a Muslim state in parts of India were laid some time before the formation of "Pakistan". Being late comers in national awakening in India, the Muslim thinkers sought for ways to overcome their limits. One should bear in mind the names of Shah Waliullah (1703–62),[36] Syed Ahmad Khan (1817–98)[37] and Muhammad Iqbal (1873–1938),[38] among the outstanding Indian Muslim thinkers, as precursors of the reconstruction of Islam from which the content of Pakistan's philosophical roots were developed. Waliullah, whom Iqbal defined as "perhaps the first Muslim"[39] who refuted the former interpretations of the Islamic dogma and searched for a "purification", or a reversion to early Islam. This negation of obsolete forms and the desire to return to essentials blended to cause contradictions in Waliullah's philosophy allowing two opposite trends in later Muslim thought to quote him for different purposes.

Syed Ahmad Khan was the first to suggest the principles and the application of a new orientation. Although he personally belonged to the upper stratum of the Indian Muslim feudal society, his recommendations and achievements aimed to serve a much larger community. After the failure of the so-called "Indian Mutiny" (1857),[40] a popular uprising that further strengthened the anti-Muslim trend of British policy, he suggested a programme for political collaboration with the British and also educational measures to restore the former status of the Muslim community. While the latter sought, in general terms, for new ways to change the attitude of the British authorities towards them, Syed Ahmad Khan started a movement of Western education amalgamated with Islam. The Muslims had to abandon their antiquated religious dogmas as well as their repugnance towards contemporary Western civilization. The result was the Mahomedan Anglo-Oriental College (1877), now the Aligarh Muslim University.[41] Religion was a means to preserve the community's indigenous culture, but a new centre had to spread secular education through which the regeneration of the Indian Muslims could be accomplished. Even some verses in the Qur'an, whose form was allegorical, needed new interpretations to be based upon reason. Syed Ahmad Khan's new criterion of truth, or his quest for a rational interpretation of religious dogma, earned him the title of a (British) knight, but the *ulama* insisted that religious faith ought to be over and above man's reasoning.

As expressed in Sir Syed Ahmad's book,[42] the newly educated Muslims were expected to remain loyal to the British. While urging faithfulness to the latter, Sir Syed opposed the Indian National Congress, some of whose early leaders like the Ghose brothers, Pal, Rai and Tilak, stressed the "Hindu ideology" as a weapon against the foreigners. But it hardly appealed to the Muslims; neither did the Congress decision to boycott the British goods, which would promote the Indian industrialists, not the Muslims who did not yet own any mills. It raised the price of the local products, manufactured and sold by Hindus.

Indian Muslims of later generations honour Muhammad Iqbal[43] as a great poet, philosopher and a religious reformer. There are journals, societies and an academy that bear his name. Although his impact was felt in the decades after the First World War, the Muslims of the Sub-continent regarded him as their spiritual father because he was, in contrast to Syed Ahmad Khan, anti-colonial, echoed the disposition of the younger generation by bringing the Islamic teaching closer to the norms of Western thinking, and expressed his ideas in beautiful and impressive verse. While influenced by the Medieval *Sufis*, and especially (the Turkish) Maulana Jalal-ud Din Rumi (1207–73),[44] Islam needed, in Iqbal's view, to have its principles expressed in the ideas of modern times. He found some ideas of Henri Bergson (1859–1941) similar to those of Rumi, and was attracted by Friedrich W. Nietzsche's (1844–1900) ideal of a superman with a strong will.[45]

The divergence of Hindu-Muslim interests provided the colonial power with the opportunities to stimulate different religious groups to follow divergent currents. Devices like separate representation, the central theme of the so-called "reforms" known after the viceroys (Minto-Morley, 1909; Montague-Chelmsford, 1919),[46] were parts of the communal principle in the constitutional machinery of the remodelled Indian state. The Indian nationalists criticized the system of separate electorates as a deliberate strategy of Britain to weaken the unity of the Indian peoples. Bengal, for instance, was divided into East and West on the basis of religion and ostensibly for convenience in administration.

Political consciousness thus gathering momentum among the Islamic circles, the Muslim League,[47] a political party, was formed (1906) signifying an important turning point in the history of the country. The British started taking strong measures against them, as the Muslims developed political maturity before, during and after the First World War. They banned Muslim publications and interned their leaders such as Muhammad and Shaukat Ali and Maulana Azad.[48] When the Muslims protested against the dismemberment of the Ottoman Empire and the Greek invasion of Anatolia, the Indian National Congress enthusiastically supported them. What was then called the "*Khilafat* Movement" united the Hindus and the Muslims to a degree unparalleled before.[49] Sindhi and Pathan Muslims organized a "*Hijrat* Movement" (migration) to Afghanistan as a reaction to the Treaty of Sèvres (1920) that the victors of the First World War wanted to dictate to the Turks. However, the

Republican Turks themselves soon abolished the *Khilafat* and secularized their state and when the Afghan Government refused admission to the Indian Muslims, the wind was taken out of the agitators' sails, and Hindu-Muslim unity began to shatter. The nationalist leaders failed to offer a programme of principles and actions after the non-cooperation movement against the British. When some leaders, like Gandhi, injected Hindu religious ideas into the nationalist movement, this created the wrong impression in some minds that the Congress was actually a Hindu movement. Cooperation gave place to communal riots, behind which there were the vested interests of groups belonging to different faiths who gave a communal form to their struggle.

Both the Muslim communal tradition and the *Hindutva* (literally 'Hinduness') tradition propounded the "two-nations theory". As early as 1927, M. A. Ansari saw communalist tendencies not only in some pronouncements of Jayakar, but also of Jinnah.[50] There was a "strange agreement" in both attitudes.[51] The Hindu Mahasabha (Great Hindu Association) had no quarrel with Jinnah's two-nations theory. Gandhi was anathema to both Muslim and Hindu communalists. The British backed the Muslim League in preference to other Muslims who joined hands with the Congress.

The masses, on the other hand, whether Hindu or Muslim, had identical interests. They were not the ones who got the seats in the legislatures or in the bureaucracy. A programme of principles and action to emanate from either side could unite them. The Hindu money-lender oppressed the Muslim debtor, and the Hindu Bengali landlord exploited the backward Muslim Bengali peasant. This relationship was presented as a communal conflict. The money-lender and the landlord suppressed the debtor and the tenant, whether a Hindu or Muslim.

When the Viceroy, Lord Linlithgow, proclaimed India's entry into the Second World War without prior consultation with the main political parties, the Congress and the Muslim League were equally desirous to attain independence or at least an immediate transfer of as much power as possible. The British Government looked forward to the cooperation of the Indians in the prosecution of the war, at the end of which they could enter into consultations with several interested parties to bring the benefits of parliamentary democracy to the peoples of India. The Hindus, who formed three-fourths of the population and were far ahead of the Muslims in terms of wealth, cohesion and education, perhaps inevitably identified their communal interests with Indian nationalism. They built the Indian National Congress, founded in 1885,[52] as a strong political instrument with which neither the moderate Liberal Federation nor the extremist Hindu Mahasabha could compete for authority or representation. Its "mahatmaic" leader, Gandhi, a sincere humanitarian, was nevertheless the very quintessence of Hinduism for the masses.

The Muslims, who were only one-fourth of the total population and a minority everywhere, except in the north-west and the north-east, wanted freedom from British rule as much as the Hindus but considered their lesser status in education, adminis-tration, trade and industry not befitting their traditions of greatness and also feared possible Hindu domination in the new social fabric after independence. Jinnah never posed as a man of religion but equalled Gandhi in single-mindedness of purpose. The Muslim League leadership, which had already interpreted the formation of the Congress-led governments after the 1937 elections as hostile acts against their interests, stood in awe of a Hindu-dominated future Constituent Assembly. At the Lahore session of the Muslim League, a decision (23 March 1940),[53] moved by the Bengal Chief Minister A. K. Fazl-ul Haq and which came to be known as the "Pakistan Resolution",[54] stated that no plan would be acceptable to the Muslims unless designed on the principle that "geographically contiguous units are demarcated into regions which should be constituted, with such territorial readjustments as may be necessary, that the areas in which the Muslims are numerically in a majority as in the north-western and eastern zones of India should be grouped to constitute independent States".[55] Jinnah's complementary statement[56] on this occasion describing the Hindus and Muslims as belonging to "two different civilizations" based mainly on "conflicting ideas and conceptions" is generally acknowledged as the beginning of the well-known two-nations theory. However, while the Congress leadership rejected it with anger more than displeasure, some extremist circles such as the Hindu Mahasabha had previously referred to the two communities as "two nations",[57] and some Muslim organizations were against the idea of a separate sovereign state for the Muslims of India. For instance, the All-India Momin Conference, the Jama'at-ul Ulama, the Azad Muslim Conference, and the Ahrar Party were all against the Muslim League, and the Khuda-e Khidmatgar of the North-West Frontier Province, the Watan Party of Baluchistan, and the All-India Shi'a Political Conference were pro-Congress. Apart from the Muslim League, only the Communist Party of India, among the significant political parties, recognized the Muslim right to secession. The Pakistan Resolution also implied the partition of Punjab and Bengal.

Sheikh Abdullah

When the new Maharaja in Kashmir ascended the *gaddi,*[58] the newly-forming elite had gathered some experience in political agitation, and the local government had developed some apprehension on how to suppress it. The freedom struggle, led by the Indian Congress Party, found echoes in several princely states, including J&K where especially the youth was influenced by the anti-imperialist movement. The Non-cooperation and the Salt *Satyagraha* movements (1930), launched by the Indian National Congress under Mahatma Gandhi's leadership, had repercussions there too. Srinagar could not stay out of the team of leading cities in India where huge processions were organised when people heard of Gandhi's arrest. The British encouraged such movements, provided they possessed a potential to break up the country along communal lines. Stormy campaigns against the Maharaja's rule, if supported by the Muslims, could help pay a dividend for the all-inclusive British interests in India. The All-Kashmir Muslim Conference, founded earlier, held (1930) its annual meeting in Lahore, one of the centres where the feeling that Islam was "in danger" could be indisputably felt. The anti-Dogra sentiment had struck solid roots with Kashmiri leaders such as Sheikh Muhammad Abdullah and the *Mirwaiz* (the chief Muslim preacher) in the Valley. The return home of Muslim young men, among them Sheikh Abdullah, educated at different Indian universities, was like a spark near explosive material. When the *Mirwaiz* died, his funeral was attended by the whole Muslim population of Srinagar.

As a young teacher who quit his post protesting Hindu resistance to the entry of Muslims into state service, Sheikh Abdullah organized one enormous meeting after another, one of which led the police to resort to arms and 21 dead. Muslim fury aimed at the Maharaja's government as well as fellow Hindus, whose shops were looted. It was on 13 July 1931 that almost the entire Muslim population rose in rebellion against "Hindu rule". The latter was now interwoven with shootings, imprisonments and public floggings. But it was under popular pressure that the Maharaja announced amnesties for all political prisoners, handed back the confiscated mosques, and promised the formation of a commission to explore the grievances of the people. When the Jammu and Kashmir Muslim Conference came into existence in late 1932, Sheikh Abdullah was elected its first president. A Legislative Assembly, called *Praja Sabha*, was set up on a limited franchise and with powers of recommendation only. While it consisted of 75 members, 33 of whom were to be elected by a little more than 3% of the population, it could only ask questions, introduce bills, and discuss the budget. When the British Indian Government got (1935) Gilgit on a 60-year "lease", the Resident let the Maharaja enjoy freedom in dealing with the political agitators.

Popular Kashmiri leadership drew closer to the Indian National Congress, Sheikh Abdullah and others moving to a secular base forming the National Conference, comprising Muslims, Hindus and Sikhs. As soon as Sheikh Abdullah was released (28 February 1939) from the Muzaffarabad jail, he started to urge re-naming the organization as a non-communal united front.[59] According to a resolution of the special session (10–11 June 1939) of the Jammu and Kashmir Muslim Conference in Srinagar, that organization was henceforth named the All-Jammu and Kashmir National Conference, and every adult person, man or woman, irrespective of religion, creed, caste, or colour, could become a member. The resolution was "a landmark in the history of the freedom movement in Kashmir".[60]

Chaudri Ghulam Abbas Khan explained in the special session that whatever has been done since 1931 had been for the rights of the Muslims from a communal platform. The attitude of the Kashmiri Government towards the Muslims had been merciless, and during the past eight years the Muslim Conference had tried to relieve them of difficulties, but it was necessary now to bring all the communities onto a common platform.[61] The large majority of the Hindus and the Sikhs were also oppressed. Moreover, the majority should gain the confidence of the minority. Mirza Muhammad Afzal Beg added that, since one could name Muslim members of the Assembly who opposed laws designed to benefit the peasants or give Muslims due representation in services, the real division was "economic, not religious".[62] Maulana

Muhammad Sayeed Masoodi argued that Islam permitted Muslims to enter into alliance with non-Muslims and that there was no way of success other than a united struggle under a common political organization.[63] Pandit Prem Nath Bazaz, the first non-Muslim leader to speak, stated that it had been his longing to bring all the communities onto a common platform.[64] The resolution was opposed by some delegates who stressed that the Muslim masses were backward and less organized and that there could be no unity between the weak and the strong. Some of the educated Muslims did not favour the national secular policies of the leadership. All seemed to feel that it would be harmful to bring the Kashmir freedom movement under the influence of the Indian National Congress, the Muslim League or the Hindu Mahasabha. Pandit Jia Lal Kilam criticized both the Muslim and the Hindu communal organizations on the grounds that they were detrimental to the causes of nationalism and secularism, and that they should not accept assistance from the Muslim League which demanded the partition of India and the Hindu Mahasabha which sought to establish the *Hindu Raj*.[65] Of the 178 delegates who attended the meeting, only three voted against the change of the name of the organization. The first session of the newly-formed National Conference was held at Anantnag, and Sheikh Abdullah was elected President. The green flag with the crescent at the centre, which was the party flag of the Muslim Conference, was replaced by a red flag with a plough in the middle.

Some delegates wanted the new National Conference to be established without disbanding the parent organization. The old Muslim Conference continued to receive support from the Muslim League and its leader Jinnah, who had come back from England in 1935. With many members in its ranks (and Muslim Presidents in the past), the Congress was the only "national" party. But when the Congress formed coalition governments in the provinces right after the elections of 1937, it created in the minds of some Muslim leaders that it ultimately aimed at a monopoly of power. Disregarding some sensitivities, the Congress governments adopted *Bande Mataram,* a song taken from a Bengali novel (*Anandamath*), which the Muslims considered to be "anti-Muslim", apart from discarding the Urdu script in favour of Hindu letters.[66] When the League met (1937) in conference at Lucknow, Jinnah declared that the Muslims could expect "neither justice, nor fair-play under Congress government".[67] The old contention that the Muslims were unfairly treated, i.e., under-represented on local bodies, starved of educational opportunities, restricted in their use of Urdu, and the like, gained new force. Every communal trouble was scrutinized, put on record and published as a formal indictment of the Congress governments.[68]

While the Hindu Mahasabha, founded in 1915 as a cultural organization for the preservation of Hinduism, had now become primarily political, and its president, Veer V. D. Savarkar, previously sentenced for murderous terrorist crimes, attacked the Congress for pursuing a non-communal policy and thus betraying the cause of Hinduism, some Muslim minds had begun to contemplate the division of India into Hindu and Muslim compartments. In the 1930s, they were talking about "Muslim self-determination".[69] Some Muslim intellectuals, not members of the Congress, also combatted this downright policy of partition.[70] It was the drastic, not the moderate, policy that ultimately prevailed with Jinnah and the Muslim League. The Congress vehemently opposed the demand for Pakistan, and some Muslims suggested an alternative formula to resolve the conflict.[71] While Gandhi condemned the proceedings at Lahore, and an All-India Independent Muslim Conference, organized in Delhi with Khan Bahadur Allah Baksh, a past Premier of Sindh, and Maulana Abul Kalam Azad, just elected the Congress President in the background, denounced partition, Jinnah was now the most popular and powerful Muslim in India.

These occurrences affected Kashmir less than expected. While the Maharaja put all his resources at the disposal of the British Government for the purposes of the Second World War and was appointed to the Imperial War Cabinet for such cooperation, the National Conference adopted (1944) a programme of social activity for the benefit of the whole people based on a more democratic platform. Of all the people's movements in the various states in India, the Kashmir National Conference was far the most popular. The real background of this popularity and also that of its President, around whose name songs and legends grew up, was basically economic. Sheikh Abdullah, who contrasted the terrible poverty of the people with the enormous riches of the few and the potential resources of Kashmir, demanded political reforms and responsible government.[72] This movement allied itself with the All-India States Peoples' Conference, which was an independent body but working in line with the National Congress. Sheikh Abdullah became a Vice-President of the All-India body and was also elected its President while in prison.

While Jinnah's visit to Kashmir (1944) to create sympathy for the two-nations theory won little following,[73] the National Conference moved closer to the Indian National Congress, led by Gandhi and Nehru, as may be gauged by the attendance of Maulana Azad, Khan Abdul Gaffar Khan and other Congress leaders in the latter's unique session (1945) in Srinagar. Sheikh Abdullah's "Quit Kashmir" movement (1946) aiming to transfer power from the Maharaja to the people drew Nehru to Kashmir, who was arrested as he moved into the state. Gandhi, who also visited Kashmir about a year later, seemed impressed by the low level of communal strife. The Muslim League there had no particular following. Sheikh Abdullah was so popular that even the communal Hindu and Sikh organizations demanded his release when he was put in prison. It was mainly on account of the policy of the National Conference and its President that Kashmir kept out of communal strife during the period when the rest of India had been engulfed in it. Sheikh Abdullah cut the image of a saviour to his people.[74]

The Princely States

On 17 June 1947, the British Government announced the Indian Independence Act which stated that they would waive their authority over India on 15 of August of the same year. The territories with Muslim majorities were to be independent Pakistan, and the rest would constitute India. The question arose as to the future of the

Princely States, which were not directly ruled by the Government of India. The British would cease to exercise the power of "Paramountcy" over 562 of them,[75] including Jammu and Kashmir, meaning that their rights flowing from their relationship to the Crown would no longer exist, and all rights surrendered by them to the paramount power would return to them. The Princely States could enter into a federal relationship with the successor governments in British India on the basis of the Indian Act of 1935 and the Indian Independence Act of 1947. Both of these Acts of the British Parliament provided that a state could join the Dominion of India by an Instrument of Accession. During the period between 17 June 1947, when the Government of India Act was passed, and 15 August 1947, when India became independent, the ruler of a Princely State could reach a Standstill Agreement with either or both of the independent Dominions with respect to customs, transit and communications, posts and tele-graphs, or other like matters.

When Pandit Nehru sent (17 June 1947) a note on Kashmir[76] to Rear-Admiral Viscount Mountbatten of Burma, the Governor General of undivided India,[77] the state consisted of roughly three parts: Kashmir proper; Jammu; Ladakh, Baltistan, Skardu and Kargil. The Muslims, who formed 92% of the population in Kashmir proper, were 77.11% (3,101,247) in the whole state. The Muslims of Jammu also constituted the majority there (61%). The total percentage of the Hindus was 21% (809,165), the others being chiefly Sikhs (65,903) and Buddhists (40,696). The total, then, stood at 4,021,616.

The Maharaja, believed to envisage an independent Kashmir State, delayed his decision regarding accession and sought from both the Dominions a Standstill Agreement to come into effect on 15 August 1947. While the Muslims of Kashmir celebrated 15 August as "Pakistan Day", the Maharaja, as V. P. Menon put it, was "in a Micawberish state of mind, hoping for the best while doing nothing".[78] While the Kashmiri authorities were simultaneously (12 August 1947) trying to conclude such agreements regarding communications, supplies and postal arrangements with the two countries, Kashmir was invaded by Pakistani tribals, partially aided by the Pakistani Army.

Notes

1   Two leading Indian sources on the history of Kashmir: P. N. K. Bamzai, *Culture and Political History of Kashmir*, 3 vols., New Delhi, M. D. Publications, 1994; Verinder Grover, ed., *The Story of Kashmir: Yesterday and Today*, 3 vols., New Delhi, Deep and Deep Publications, 1995.
2   A biographical account drawing upon the ancient Asokavadana: John S. Strong, *The Legend of King Asoka*, Princeton, New Jersey, Princeton University Press, 1983.
3   A much earlier king, Pravarsen, is also mentioned as the one to have founded the city of Srinagar. P. Gwasha Lal, "A Short History of Kashmir: from the Earliest Times to the Present Day", Grover, *op. cit.*, Vol. I, p. 11.

4   R. G. Bhandarkar, *Vaisnavism, Saivism and Minor Religious Systems*, Varanasi, Indological Book House, 1965.

5   On Sultan Mahmud, whose capital remained at Gazna but whose empire stretched into the heart of India: Muhammed Nazim, *The Life and Times of Sultan Mahmud of Ghazna*, Cambridge, Cambridge University Press, 1931; Mohammad Habib, *Sultan Mahmud of Ghaznin*, New Delhi, S. Chaud, 1951.

6   Sayyid Athar Abbas Rizvi, *A History of Sufism in India*, New Delhi, Munshiram Manoharlal, 1983. On Hindu mystics and Muslim *Sufis* of India: S. A. H. Abidi, *Sufism in India*, New Delhi, Wishwa Prakashan, 1992, pp. 99–121.

7   A. Q. Rafiqi, "Sufism in Kashmir", *Contemporary Relevance of Sufism*, ed., Syeda Saiyidain Hameed, New Delhi, Indian Council for Cultural Relations, 1993, pp. 321–322.

8   Hiro, *op. cit.*, p. 2.

9   G. N. Gauhar, *Sheikh Noor-ud-Din Wali*, New Delhi, Sahitya Akademi, 1995, p. 8.

10   Grover, *op. cit.*, p. 23.

11   Two short accounts of the Moghuls: Vincent Arthur Smith, *The Oxford History of India*, Oxford, Clarendon Press, 1858; John F. Richards, *The New Cambridge History of India, I/5, The Mughal Empire*, Cambridge, Cambridge University Press, 1993. Two popular narratives: Bamber Gascoigne, *The Great Moghuls*, London, Jonathan Cape, 1971; Waldemar Hansen, *The Peacock Throne*, New York, 1972. A scholarly undertaking based on original material but internationally little used (Turkish) source: Hikmet Bayur, *Hindistan Tarihi*, 3 vols., Ankara, Türk Tarih Kurumu, 1946–1950.

12   Babur's own memoirs: *Babar-Nama (Baburnamah)*, tr. Wheeler M. Thackston, Washington, D.C., Freer Gallery of Art, 1995. Also: *Babur-Nama (Memoirs of Babur)*, tr. from the original Turki text by Annette Susannah Beveridge, Delhi, Low Price Publications, 1995. On the memoirs: Stephen Dale, "Steppe Humanism: the Autobiographical Writings of Zahir-al-Din Muhammad Babur, 1483–1530", *International Journal of Middle East Studies*, 22 (1990), pp. 37–58.

13   Ishwari Prasad, *The Life and Times of Humayun*, Allahabad, Central Book Depot, 1976; Muni Lal, *Humayun*, New Delhi, Vicas, 1978.

14   The official history of Akbar's reign: Abul Fazl, *Akbar-Nama*, tr. H. Beveridge, 3 vols., Calcutta, Asiatic Society of Bengal, 1907–39. A new source: S. M. Burke, *Akbar: the Greatest Mogul*, New Delhi, Munshiram Manoharlal, 1989.

15   Jahangir's own account: *Tuzuk-i Jahangiri*, tr. Alexander Rogers and Henry Beveridge, Delhi, Munshiram Manoharlal, 1968; Muni Lal, *Jahangir*, New Delhi, Vikas, 1983.

16   Grover, *op. cit.*, p. 25.

17   An abridgement of the official chronicles of Shah Jahan's reign: W. E. Bedley and Z. A. Desai, eds., *The Shah Jahan Nama of 'Inayat Khan*, Delhi; New York, Oxford University Press, 1990; Muni Lal, *Shah Jahan*, New Delhi, Vikas, 1986.

18   Ajit Bhattacharjea, *Kashmir: the Wounded Valley*, New Delhi, etc., UBS Publishers, 1994, pp. 214–215.

19   Aurangzeb's biography: Jadunath Sarkar, *History of Aurangzib*, 5 vols., Bombay, Orient Longman, 1972–74; Muni Lal, *Aurangzeb*, New Delhi, Vikas, 1988.

20   From Sanskrit, *gu* means ignorance and *ru*, to remove or destroy. A Sikh *guru* directs the lives of *guru-bhai* and *guru-behen* (brother and sister), whose relationship is as important as that of actual siblings.

21   Vernon Hewitt, *Reclaiming the Past? The Search for Political and Cultural Unity in Contemporary Jammu and Kashmir*, London, Portland Books, 1995, p. 39.

22   An historical account of the Abdalis, derived from Pushto manuscripts: Aminullah
      Stanakzai, "The Abdalis: a Study of the Dynasty", *Afghanistan*, Kabul, 19/1, 2 (1964), pp.
      37–39, 26–33. On Ahmad Shah Baba, the founder of the Durrani Empire and the father
      of the Afghan nation: Ganda Singh, "Ahmad Shah: the Man and His Achievements",
      Afghanistan, Kabul, 8/1 (1953), pp. 1–19.

23   I. H. Siddiqi, *Afghan Despotism in India*, Aligarh, Three Men Publication, 1969.

24   Prem Nath Bazaz, "Kashmir and Its Peoples", Grover, *op. cit.*, Vol. I, p. 159.

25   Ranjit Singh led three campaigns for the annexation of Kashmir, which he finally
      captured in 1819. For the impact of Sikh rule: R. K. Parmu, *A History of Sikh Rule in
      Kashmir: 1819–1846*, Srinagar, Department of Education, Jammu and Kashmir Govern-
      ment, 1977. Also: Charles von Hugel, *Kashmir under Maharaja Ranjit Singh*, New Delhi,
      Atlantic, 1984. For the life of the ordinary people under Sikh rule: Dewan Chand Sharma,
      Kashmir under the Sikhs, Delhi, Seema Publisher, 1983.

26   Rema Devi R. Tondaiman, "Vignettes of Kashmir", *The Hindu*, New Delhi, Magazine
      section, 26 July 1998, p. xi.

27   J. A. Norris, *First Anglo-Afghan War: 1838–1842*, Cambridge, 1967.

28   H. Raj Sharma, "Through Corridors of Jammu's Past", Grover, *op. cit.*, Vol. I, p. 67.

29   H. Raj Sharma, "The Origin of Dogri", *ibid.*, pp. 73–76.

30   Hugh Cook, *The Sikh Wars*, Delhi, Thomson Press, 1975. Also: Patrick Turnbull,
      "Ferozeshehr and the Sikh War: December 1845", *History Today*, London, XXVII/1
      (January 1977), pp. 31–40.

31   K. M. Panikkar, "Treaty of Amritsar and the Foundation of the Kashmir State", Grover,
      op. cit., Vol. I, pp. 92–113.

32   M. L. Kapur, "Kashmir Sold", *ibid.*, p. 60.

33   Jawaharlal Nehru, *The Discovery of India*, New Delhi, Indian Council for Cultural
      Relations, 1976, p. 201. For the response of the British to the shock of the 1857 revolt:
      Thomas R. Matcalf, *The Aftermath of Revolt: India, 1857–1870,* New Delhi, Manohar,
      1990.

34   Hugh Seton-Watson, *The Decline of Imperial Russia: 1855–1914*, New York, Frederick
      A. Praeger, 1952, pp. 82–89.

35   Hugh Seton-Watson, *Nations and States: an Enquiry into the Origin of Nations and the
      Politics of Nationalism*, London, Methuen, 1977, pp. 290–297.

36   On the religious rather than political views of this key figure in the South Asian Islamic
      tradition: J. M. S. Baljon, *Religion and Thought of Shah Wali Allah Dihlawi: 1703–1762*,
      Leiden, The Netherlands, E. J. Brill, 1986.

37   On Syed Ahmad's reconciliation of human reason and divine omnipotence: Bashir
      Ahmad Dar, *Religious Thought of Sayyid Ahmad Khan*, Lahore, Institute of Islamic
      Culture, 1957; Christian W. Troll, *Sayyid Ahmad Khan: a Reinterpretation of Muslim
      Theology*, New Delhi, Vikas, 1978; Hafeez Malik, *Sir Sayyid Ahmad Khan and Muslim
      Modernization in India and Pakistan*, New York, Columbia University Press, 1980.

38   Some of Iqbal's works: *Asrar-e Khudi* (The Secrets of the Self), *Shikwa—Jawab-e
      Shikwa* (Complaint and Answer), *Zabur-e Ajam* (Persian Psalms) and *Javid-nama* ... The
      Iqbal Academy in Lahore brings out the *Bazm-e Iqbal*, a review devoted to a critical study
      of his thought and those branches of learning in which he was interested.

39   Muhammad Iqbal, *The Reconstruction of Religious Thought in Islam*, London, Oxford
      University Press, 1934, p. 97.

40 For a review of recent historiography of 1857 in a broad social and economic framework, some new trends and a few gaps in research: Kalyan Kumar Sengupta, *Recent Writings on the Revolt of 1857: a Survey*, New Delhi, Indian Council of Historical Research, 1975, especially pp. 56–61.

41 By Aligarh's Vice-Chancellor when the school entered its second century: A. M. Khusro, *Aligarh: a Century Ends and a Century Begins*, Aligarh, Aligarh Muslim University, 1977.

42 *An Account of the Loyal Mahomedans of India*, Meerut, J. A. Gibbons, 1860. Also by Sir Syed Ahmad Khan: *The Causes of the Indian Revolt*, Benares, Medical Hill Press, 1873; *Essay on the Question Whether Islam Has Been Beneficial or Injurious to Human Society in General*, Lahore, Orientalia, 1870; *The Mohomedan Commentary on the Holy Bible*, Ghazeeporo, the author, 1882; *On the Present State of Indian Politics, Consisting of Speeches, and Letters Reprinted from the "Pioneer"*, Allahabad, the Pioneer Press, 1888; *Report of the Members of the Select Committee for the Better Diffusion and Advancement of Learning among Muhammedans of India*, Benares, Medical Hall Press, 1872; *Review on Dr. Hunter's Indian Musalmans: Are They Bound in Conscience to Rebel against the Queen?* Benares, Medical Hall Press, 1872.

43 The origin of the idea of a separate Muslim state is controversial among the writers of this movement. Sir Muhammad Iqbal's presidential address at the Allahabad session of the All-India Muslim League in late-1930 is often considered as the starting point. (For instance: Muhammad Munawwar, *Dimensions of Pakistan Movement*, Rawalpindi, Services Book Club, 1989, p. 120.) However, Iqbal probably envisaged only the union of the Muslim-dominated north-western territories of the Sub-continent within a large federation af all India and not an independent Muslim state (Shamloo, ed., *Speeches and Statements of Iqbal*, Lahore, 1948, pp. 10–35). Recent research indicates that this idea was presented from time to time even in the 19th century. The first group was made up of British administrators and writers, who were interested in dividing and ruling India on communal lines. (Wilfred Scaven Blunt, *Ripon-a Private Diary*, London, 1909, pp. 107–108.) The second group was made up of some extremist Hindus who organized militant revivalist movements, such as the *suddhi* (purification) designed to convert Muslims into Hinduism and the *sangathan* (consolidation) aiming at greater unity among the Hindus. (For the views of Lala Hardayal, the chief spokesman of Hindu extremism, in the 1920s, see: *The Times of India*, New Delhi, 25 July 1925; *The Comrade*, 22 May and 5 June 1925. For similar views: Indra Prakash, *A Review of the History and Work of the Hindu Mahasabha*, New Delhi, 1938.) The third group was the Muslim protagonists of the same idea, who could neither reconcile themselves to the loss of power in India and were also influenced by the Pan-Islamic movement of the time. (Ishtiaq Husain Qureshi, *The Muslim Community of the Indo-Pakistan Subcontinent, 610–1947: A Brief Historical Analysis*, The Hague, 1962.) For more detail: M. Rafique Afzal, ed., *The Case for Pakistan*, Islamabad, National Commission on Historical and Cultural Research, 1979, pp. xi–xxxiv. Also: Syed Sharifuddin Pirzada, *Evolution of Pakistan*, Lahore, 1963.

44 Harendrechandra Paul, *Jalalu'd-Din Rumi and His Tasawwuf*, Calcutta, Sobharani Paul, 1985. Also: Nazir Qaiser, *Rumi's Impact on Iqbal's Religious Thought*, Lahore, Iqbal Academy, 1989.

45 Ulrick Enemark Petersen, "Breathing Nietzsche's Air: New Reflections on Morgenthau's Concepts of Power and Human Nature", *Alternatives*, 24/1 (January-March 1999), pp. 83–118; Alex J. Bellamy, "Introducing Nietzsche to the Study of Nations", *Nationalism and Ethnic Politics*, London, 5/1 (Spring 1999), pp. 118–143.

46   Arthur Berriedale Keith, *A Constitutional History of India: 1600–1935*, Delhi, Low Price Publications, 1930; 1990, pp. 226–273. For the operation of the reforms and the report of the Simon Commission: *ibid.*, pp. 274–318.

47   A biography of the Karachi-born Muslim League leader and creator of Pakistan: Stanley A. Wolpert, *Jinnah of Pakistan*, Oxford; New York, Oxford University Press, 1984. A reassessment of Jinnah's aims: Ayasha Jalal, *The Sole Spokesman Jinnah: the Muslim League and the Demand for Pakistan*, Cambridge, Cambridge University Press, 1985. The author suggests, a position strongly criticized by Pakistan, that Jinnah's demand for an independent state for the Indian Muslims was not really the goal he wanted, and that he favoured instead a loose union between the two entities joined in defence and foreign policy.

48   A comprehensive study on a remarkable intellectual, Maulana Abul Kalam Azad, whose life was dominated by three passions: Hindu-Muslim unity, freedom of India, and love of learning: Tributes, appraisals and selected writings on the occasion of his Centenary: Syeda Saiyidain Hameed, ed., *India's Maulana: Abul Kalam Azad*, 2 vols., New Delhi, Indian Council for Cultural Relations, 1990.

49   Gandhi lent his strong support to the Khilafat cause. All-India Khilafat Committee was formed with Seth Chhotani of Bombay as President and Maulana Shaukat Ali as Secretary. Parshotam Mehra, *A Dictionary of Modern Indian History: 1707-1947*, Delhi, Oxford University Press, 1985, p. 377; M. Naeem Qureshi, "The Indian *Khilafat* Movement (1918–24)", *Journal of Asian History*, Wiesbaden, 12/2 (1978), pp. 152–168; Sukhbir Choudhary, *Indian People's Fight for National Liberation: Non-Cooperation, Khilafat and Revivalist Movements*, New Delhi, Srijanee Prakashar, 1972, pp. 213–386. English translation of a leading Turkish source on the Khilafat Movement: M. Kemâl Öke, *The South Asian Muslims' Freedom Movement and the Turkish National Struggle*, Ankara, Ministry of Culture, 1986.

50   Mushirul Hasan, ed., *Muslims and the Congress: Select Correspondence of Dr. M. A. Ansari, 1912–1935,* Delhi, Manohar, 1979, p. 20.

51   Humayun Kabir, *Muslim Politics: 1906–47 and Other Essays*, Calcutta, K. L. Mukhopadhyay, 1969, p. 51.

52   Fourteen studies by the Congress Party during the century long (1885–1985) history: Ram Joshi and R. K. Hebsur, eds., *Congress in Indian Politics: a Centenary Perspective*, Riverdale, Maryland, The Riverdale Co.; New Delhi and London, Sangham Books, 1988. Another centenary collection: Paul R. Brass and Francis Robinson, eds., *Indian National Congress and Indian Society: 1885–1985, Ideology, Social Structure, and Political Dominance*, New Delhi, Chanakya, 1987.

53   The Islamic Republic of Pakistan now officially celebrates the anniversaries of this particular date as the Republic Day.

54   For full proceedings of the session: Syed Sharifuddin Pirzada, *Pakistan Resolution and the Historic Lahore Session*, Karachi, Pakistan Publications, 1968. It was originally referred to as the Lahore Resolution, but came to be known in popular parlance as the Pakistan Resolution, so dubbed by the Hindu press.

55   Chaudri Muhammad Ali, *The Emergence of Pakistan*, Lahore, Services Book Club, 1988, p. 38; Syed Sharifuddin Pirzada, *Foundations of Pakistan: All-India Muslim League Documents, 1906–1947*, Vol. II, Dacca, 1969, p. 341.

56   Jamil-ud-din Ahmad, ed., *Some Recent Speeches and Writings of Mr. Jinnah*, 5th ed., Vol. I, Lahore, Muhammad Ashraf, 1952, pp. 172–178.

57 Richard Symond, *The Making of Pakistan*, London, Faber and Faber, 1949, p. 59.
58 Hindi term for the (low cushioned) seat of a ruler.
59 Ram Krishan Kaul Bhatt, *Political and Constitutional Development of the Jammu and Kashmir State*, Delhi, Seema Publications, 1984, pp. 82–87.
60 Gulam Hasan Khan, *Freedom Movement in Kashmir: 1931–40*, New Delhi, Light and Life Publishers, 1980, p. 385.
61 Muhammed Yusuf Saraf, *Kashmiri Fight for Freedom*, Vol. I, Lahore, Feroze Sons Ltd., 1977, pp. 531–533.
62 *Ibid.*, p. 534.
63 Khan, *op. cit.*, pp. 378–379.
64 *Ibid.*, pp. 384–385; Saraf, *op. cit.*, pp. 534–535. Four later books by Prem Nath Bazaz: *Dispute about Kashmir*, Delhi, Kashmir Democratic Union, 1950; *Azad Kashmir: a Democratic Socialist Conception*, Lahore, Feroze Sons, 1951; *Inside Kashmir*, Srinagar, Kashmir Publishing Company, 1941; *Struggle for Freedom in Kashmir*, New Delhi, Kashmir Publishing Company, 1954.
65 Khan, *op. cit.*, p. 385.
66 *Indian Annual Register*, ii (1937), p. 143 in R. Coupland, *Indian Politics: 1936–1942*, Madras, Oxford University Press, 1944, p. 182; _____, *The Indian Problem: Report on the Constitutional Problem in India, 1932–1942*, Part II, London, 1944, pp. 103, 322–323.
67 *Ibid.*, p. 182.
68 The "Pirpur Report" (Delhi, 1938), which argued the Muslim case, did not resort to sensational or provocative language. The "Shareef Report" (Patna, 1939), which gave repulsive details of "atrocities", nevertheless, maintained the temperate style of the previous report. A third formal indictment (Fazl-ul Haq, *Muslim Sufferings under Congress Rule*, Calcutta, 1939) bitterly complained that, in some Hindu quarters, the *azan* (Muslim call to prayer) was forbidden, there were attacks on worshippers in mosques, noisy processions prevented prayers, pigs were thrown into mosques, Muslim shops were boycotted, and the like. The Bihar Government's reasoned reply answered some of these charges point by point.
69 A new phase in the history of the idea of a separate Muslim state started with Choudhary Rahmat Ali, who published on 28 January 1933 a four-page leaflet, entitled *Now or Never: Are We to Live or Perish for Ever?*, signed by some other Muslims and circulated from Cambridge, using the word "Pakstan" (spelled without an "i") perhaps for the first time, the letter "k" standing for Kashmir. Although Rahmat Ali founded the Pakistan National Movement, his propaganda for "Pakistan" was confined to Britain. There is little evidence to prove that the Muslims showed any interest in the scheme before the 1936–37 elections. During 1938–39, however, *Majalis-e Pakistan* (Pakistan Societies) were formed in a number of cities.
70 Syed Abd-ul Latif from the Osmania University in Hyderabad, for instance, published three booklets (*The Cultural Future of India*, Bombay, 1938; *A Federation of Cultural Zones for India*, Secunderabad, 1938; *The Muslim Problem in India*, Bombay, 1939) in which he argued that India was not a single "composite nation" but partition was not desirable or necessary. The author's chief criticism of the Pakistan proposals was that the creation of an independent Muslim state would not solve the communal problem since there would still be huge minorities on both sides. However, in 1939, Sayyid Zafarul Hassan and Muhammad Afzal Husain, both from the Aligarh Muslim University,

published a scheme *(The Problem of Indian Muslims)* proposing three independent states. Mian Kifayat Ali suggested five different "countries" *(The Confederacy of India*, Lahore, 1939), and Sir Skandar Hayat Khan seven "zones" *(The Outlines of a Scheme of Indian Federation).*

71   B. R. Ambedkar, *Pakistan or the Partition of India*, Bombay, 1946, pp. 192–193.

72   Sheikh Mohammad Abdullah, *New Kashmir*, New Delhi, Kashmir Bureau of Information, 1950, *passim.*

73   For Sheikh Abdullah's rejoinder to Jinnah's criticism of the J&K National Conference, see: A. Moin Zaidi, ed., *Evolution of Muslim Political Thought in India: Vol. VI, Freedom at Last*, New Delhi, Indian Institute of Applied Political Research, 1975–79, pp. 613–615.

74   Somnath Tikku, *Sheikh Abdulla: the Saviour of Kashmir*, Srinagar, Kashmir, Mercantile Press, 1947.

75   On the rulers of the 562 states of Princely India: Charles Allen and Sharada Dwivedi, *Lives of the Indian Princes*, London, Arena, 1986.

76   Great Britain, *The Transfer of Power, 1942–1947: Constitutional Relations Between Britain and India*, Vol. XI, London, Her Majesty's Stationary Office, 1982, pp. 442–448.

77   P. Kodanda Rao, "Mountbatten and Kashmir", *Indian Review*, Madras, 52/12 (December 1951), pp. 573–576. The first biographer to have access to the Mountbatten (1900–79) archive: Philip Ziegler, *Mountbatten: the Official Biography*, London, Fontana; New York, Alfred A. Knopf, 1985.

78   Anthony Read and David Fisher, *The Proudest Day: India's Long Road to Independence*, London, Jonathan Cape, 1997, p. 503.

Chapter 5

Accession and After

The Muslim community in India before partition stood in the ratio of one to four of the whole population. In almost every state they were a considerable number. They constituted then, as now, the majority in Jammu and Kashmir, and in certain areas their proportion is today much larger than even the national average, for instance in Laccadive, Minicoy and Amindivi Islands (94.37%).[1] Scattered throughout the length and the breadth of the country, the Muslims are more than a protected minority; they are a significant community. In 1947, there was no longer a possibility of preserving a united India, and the British Labour Government took the bold decision of proclaiming the transfer of power into Indian hands. The only course left open was that of negotiations for the clear-cut demarcation of frontiers between the future state of Pakistan and the rest of the country.

Despite the advent of independence, rejoicing soon left its place to chaos and bloodshed between groups of Hindus, Muslims and Sikhs. A revolt broke out in Western Kashmir, followed by invasion of tribesmen from the Pakistan side, not necessarily helping their co-religionists, but indulging in pillage and plunder. These events led to the first Kashmir War and the accession of this princely state to India. The issue was brought to the United Nations, which heard the arguments of India and Pakistan, formed a special commission, passed several resolutions, established a cease-fire, and appointed several mediators. Bilateral relations took place off and on, and the two neighbours fought four wars over Kashmir, which even now stays as cut in two along the Line of Control.

Partition and Accession

As Independence Day (15 August 1947) came closer, however, the two neighbouring states found themselves in bloody chaos. There was not much point in investigating who started the carnage, but both the Hindus and the Muslims accused each other of taking the first step. Riots flared up everywhere, especially in Punjab, Bengal, Bihar and Assam. Gandhi, an unbending opponent of violence, an "incarnation of Rousseau and Tolstoy"[2] who attempted to stop the outbreaks in some of the worst-affected areas, had almost no influence on the threatening monster of communalism poised to destroy freedom at birth. Perhaps it was Gandhi's finest hour when this rallying point of sanity tortured his frail body with fasts of atonement. That spiritual giant with a national perspective fell to an assassin's bullets. His martyrdom (30 January 1948) in the hands of a communalist group (hired trigger: Nathu Ram Godse), who turned on the one man at that hour with the humane consciousness of the Indian people, was the final atonement.[3] Partition, which was an economic absurdity, was justified as a process to steer clear of a full-fledged civil war. The Muslim League seemed "to anticipate with pleasure a collapse of India".[4] While Hindus and Sikhs were fleeing from Pakistan, and Muslims from India, millions of refugees were in the process of being exchanged.

Both Nehru and Jinnah[5] well knew that the Princely States like Jammu and Kashmir would be independent and sovereign entities on the termination of British Paramountcy and that they were free to decide to join India or Pakistan or remain independent. It is generally accepted that the falterings of Sir Hari Singh, the Maharaja of Kashmir, abruptly came to an end by the invasion of desperados and groups of the newly-formed Pakistan Army, some posing as volunteers, and that such soldiers wearing plain clothes, but equipped with modern arms, and *lashkars* (bands of tribesmen) were allowed to infiltrate into Kashmir territory raiding, burning and looting parts of the border area from Gurdaspur up to Gilgit, threatening invasion which had actually begun in Poonch, then spread to Sialkot and finally to Hazara. The Indian version, substantiated by General Akbar Khan in his book, was that this infiltration was planned and actively carried out by the Government of Pakistan, that the latter let loose the tribal people on Kashmir holding out to these newly-acquired poor citizens the alluring promise of land and plenty there, and also to kill the Pathanistan movement, thereby securing its own safety in an expanded Muslim society.[6] Major General Akbar Khan was the officer charged with the responsibility of organizing the raids.

Communal riots and clashes in neighbouring Punjab inevitably incited some Kashmiris, especially the predominantly Muslim inhabitants of Poonch, who had never resigned themselves to the Maharaja's rule. Hindu and Sikh attacks on Muslim villages in Jammu, where there was a large non-Muslim population, easily aroused irritable opinion both in Poonch and in Pakistan. Those Muslims who escaped to Pakistan related dreadful stories of the numerous outrages of some Hindus and Muslims. Even by the beginning of September, Poonch men, joined by "volunteers"[7] from the west bank of the Jhelum, had started standing up to the Kashmiri security forces. A certain Muhammad Ibrahim Khan, an elected Poonch representative in the J&K Legislative Assembly who had slipped away to Pakistan, established a command post at Murree near the Poonch border.[8] The Pathan tribesmen, who had been converging on the borders of J&K since early September, began infiltrating Kashmir proper, bolstered by modern equipment and transport facilities which only Pakistan could spare. Khan Abdul Qayyum Khan, later a Chief Minister of the North-West Frontier Province (NWFP), rallied tribes to pass to the Kashmir side.[9] Lamb states that the Poonch rebels sought Pakistani assistance while the Maharaja was probing for Indian help. He adds that only after accession, could the Indians be defending their own land against invaders.[10] The infiltrators, moreover, murdered and looted their own co-religionists as well as the Hindus and Sikhs in many places.

On 22 October 1947, a large force of armed raiders, probably still under the unofficial command of some Pakistani officers, entered Muzaffarabad in lorries, continuing their invasion and looting towards Baramula and eventually with their eye on Srinagar.[11] Colonel (later Major-General) Akbar Khan destined to be a leading commander in this first Kashmir War,[12] apparently had consultations with some Pakistani leaders, possibly including Prime Minister Liaquat Ali Khan.[13] Nehru probably knew nothing about the infantry battalion and the mountain artillery battery that the Sikh Maharaja of Patiala put at the disposal of Hari Singh. When Jinnah heard about the Sikh detachment, he asked General Sir Douglas Gracey, the acting Commander-in-Chief of the Pakistan Army, to send his own troops but was told that all British officers would have to resign from the Pakistan Army in order to discourage such a move, tantamount to an inter-Dominion war.[14]

Pakistan cut off food supplies, oil and some other essential commodities to Kashmir, whose government interpreted these moves as economic blockade. The Government of Pakistan, which officially explained the reduction in supplies to the reluctance of traders disturbed by violence, might have also hoped to show the significance of economic links with the southern centres like Karachi. The government in New Delhi, likewise, accentuated the economic benefits of union with India as well when the Nizam of Hyderabad[15] and the Nawab of Junagadh,[16] both Muslims ruling over predominantly non-Muslim inhabitants, personally opted for Pakistan. Indian troops intervened (1 November 1947) in Mangrol, causing no bloodshed however, and a plebiscite in Junagadh (20 February 1948) showed an overwhelming support for India.[17] Those voting for Pakistan in Junagadh, with a population of nearly 700,000, mostly Hindus, were only a handful.[18] One has to agree with the analogy that while in the cases of Hyderabad and Junagadh, the Government of Pakistan supported the Muslim rulers, when Junagadh held out against accession to India, on the ground that under the Mounbatten Plan, it was for the rulers to opt to join either Dominion, the same government seemed to deny the ruler his option in the case of J&K.

The attack on Kashmir appears to have raised the vital issue of defence. Alarmed by the outspreading invasion and the prospect of repeated devastation, the Maharaja appealed to India on 24 October for military help. Losing control over parts of Kashmir, he entertained the idea of either eventually acceding to India or remaining independent. His new Prime Minister, Justice Mehr Chand Mahajan, supported by *Sirdar* Vallabhbhai Patel, the Indian Deputy Prime Minister also in charge of the States Department, had informed Nehru of the Maharaja's intention.[19] Sheikh Abdullah writes in his autobiography[20] that he was staying with Nehru at the latter's York Road residence when the Maharaja's Prime Minister arrived along with V. P. Menon, referring to the accession and requesting troops right away, otherwise he would go to Jinnah for reconciliation. Seeing Nehru furious, Sheikh Abdullah told him that the National Conference also supported the accession decision. What looked like the Maharaja's previous indecisiveness may also have been his 'castle in the air', or his vision of the 'Switzerland of the East', also shared by Sheikh Abdullah. It is quite possible that there were some plans on the Indian side, at least in Patel's mind,[21] in the eventuality of an armed clash in or for Kashmir.

When the Poonch insurgents declared (24 October) the formation of a secessionist Azad (Free) Kashmir,[22] R. L. Batra, the Deputy Prime Minister of the J&K Government, was sent to the Indian capital with a plea for military aid and an offer of accession, if need be.[23] A meeting of the Defence Committee took place in New Delhi under Mountbatten's chairmanship. No troops could be sent "unless Kashmir had first offered to accede".[24] While Sheikh Abdullah, released from jail on 29 September, flew to New Delhi to personally appeal to the Indian Cabinet to despatch armed forces to repel the invaders, V. P. Menon, the Secretary of the States Ministry and Patel's right-hand man in accession matters,[25] went twice to Srinagar, returning with a signed accession and a request for troops.[26]

In an official letter dated 26 October 1947, the Maharaja saw "no option but to ask for help from the Indian Dominion" and also decided to accede to the latter attaching "the Instrument of Accession for acceptance".[27] The matters with respect to which the Dominion Legislature might make laws for Kashmir were listed as defence, external affairs, and communications. Mounbatten replied (27 October 1947) accepting the Instrument and stating that as soon as law and order were restored in Kashmir, the question of accession ought to be settled "by a reference to the people".[28] He seemed convinced that Kashmir now being legally Indian territory, the appearance of Pakistani troops there would be an act of aggression. He mentioned to Jinnah that the issue could be settled with a plebiscite, but after the restoration of order. Beginning with the morning of 27 October, initially two infantry battalions and eventually some 35,000 Indian troops were airlifted within a matter of a few days, seemingly a difficult process without previous preparation for such an eventuality.[29]

For Nehru, Kashmir was not merely an ancestral home. It symbolized India's succession to the British *Raj* no less than the legal justification of accession; it was of strategic importance for the defence of the Sub-continent; it was also a "powerful lever for secular sentiment".[30] Nehru viewed an independent but weak Kashmir an invitation to trouble from all sides. For Jinnah its adherence to Pakistan would have been a sanction of the two-nations theory. The idea of an "Islamic state" would be greatly imperiled if Kashmir remained Indian. It would even challenge the legitimacy of the very idea of Pakistan. Jinnah's dream of Kashmir as a "bridge" more or less connecting the two halves of the new country was the most vital link. But the existence of the Hindu and Buddhist majorities in large parts of the country, if they too would join Pakistan, was nothing more than a violation of the two-nations theory. The two approaches clashing, there ensued in Kashmir a desultory warfare for a little over a year (October 1947–January 1948).

Kashmir was one of the first disputes brought to the United Nations.[31] While Pakistan denied involvement in the unfolding imbroglio, the representative of India to the United Nations stated (1 January 1948) that a situation coming under Article 35 of the U.N. Charter, continuation of which was likely to endanger international peace and security, existed between India and Pakistan resulting from the aid that the invaders were drawing from Pakistan for operations against Kashmir. He requested the Security Council to call on Pakistan immediately to stop giving such assistance, and if that country did not desist from such action, India might be compelled in self-defence to enter its neighbour's territory to take military action against the invaders.[32] Sir Zafrullah Khan, the Foreign Minister of Pakistan, replied by levelling counter-charges and calling upon the Council to take action. The main points concerned India's undertakings in Kashmir, the occupation of Junagadh and other states by Indian forces, mass destruction of Muslims, and failure to implement agreements between the two countries. He related the situation in Kashmir as a popular revolt against the Maharaja's oppression.

The resolution of the Council (17 January 1948) called upon India and Pakistan to take all measures to improve the situation and requested the Council be informed of "any material change" which occurred. When a United Nations Commission on India and Pakistan (UNCIP) was dispatched to those countries, Sir Zafrullah Khan informed (5 July 1948) them in Karachi that three Pakistani brigades had been on Kashmir territory since May. The UNCIP noted (13 August) that the presence of Pakistani troops in Kashmir constituted a "material change" in the situation. Part I of this basic resolution required a cease-fire. Under Part II, Pakistan had to withdraw all its forces while India was required to keep sufficient troops for the security of the state including the observance of law and order. Part III stated that India and Pakistan wished that Kashmir's future be determined in accordance with the will of the people and to that end, both governments agreed to create the conditions whereby such free expression would be assured. When supplementary resolutions were accepted both by India and Pakistan, a cease-fire was ordered.

The Security Council or the Commission never having questioned the legality of Kashmir's accession to India, the state was practically cut in two, and the military situation reached a stalemate. The United Nations avoided any consideration of the juridical aspect of the accession, which was, according to Joseph Korbel, a member of the UNCIP, "a perfectly plausible procedure under Article 96 of the Charter", authorizing the Security Council with the right to request the International Court of Justice to give an advisory opinion on any legal question.[33] Although neither party asked for an advisory opinion, it was perhaps more striking that Pakistan also did not raise the issue. India held the bulk of Kashmir Province, Jammu and a part of Poonch while Pakistan took Baltistan, Gilgit, a narrow strip of Kashmir Province, and parts of Poonch and Mirpur in Jammu along the West Punjab border. The lines upon which the Cease-fire Agreement (27 July 1949) took effect remained unchanged until the outbreak of the 1965 War. The UNCIP created a United Nations military presence, which still continues on both sides of the cease-fire line.

According to a prominent Indian Muslim, the Instrument of Accession formed "the cornerstone of the ambiguities on Kashmir".[34] No matter how and exactly on which date it was signed, it did not discontinue, however, the Maharaja's sovereignty or the validity of any Kashmiri law save as provided by the same document. It stipulated a minimal transfer of power to the Indian Government. What would be the constitutional relationship between that state and the Indian Union? Patel seems to have considered the Instrument as adequate and final. Nehru reflected that an acceptable sort of people's ratification was indispensable. The J&K National Conference leadership also judged the Instrument only as a "formal act". First and foremost, the existing 1939 Constitution being extinct, the state needed a new administrative form to serve as a vehicle as the voice of the people. In the eyes of the National Conference, the state that they represented was a Muslim majority one, the existing arrangements between the Maharaja and India could not form the basis of the constitutional organization of Kashmir, and its future Constitution ought to be determined by fresh agreements.

Sheikh Abdullah, who had first become the head of the J&K Emergency Government and appointed four months later (5 March 1948) Prime Minister as head of the Interim Government, informed Nehru that if the proposals of the Kashmiri Government were not accepted, his party, now engaged with frontal attacks on the Maharaja, would be unable to secure the support of the Muslims for accession to India. Although Nehru, during a long meeting with Sheikh Abdullah, conveyed his disagreements with many of the outrageous accusations against the Maharaja,[35] Patel, who invited Hari Singh to New Delhi, disclosed to him that they would like to see him leave Kashmir temporarily appointing his son, Yuvraj Karan Singh as Regent during his absence.[36] Abdullah's first priority was a land reform, which every member of the ruling Dogra dynasty would find to be extreme. On Martyrs' Day (13 July 1950), the government declared its policy of liquidating the big landed estates and transferring land to the tillers. The Act (17 October 1950) itself limited the right of ownership with 22 acres excluding orchards, grass and fodder farms. He accentuated governmental role in the development of industry and established a planning bureau, recalling in the minds of some commentators the Soviet five-year plans.

Article 370

A Constituent Assembly of Kashmir was to determine the future constitutional organization of the state. An agreement seemed to have been reached by the National Conference leaders and the Central Government, envisaging, *inter alia*, that the provisions of the Indian Constitution regarding the governments in states would not apply to J&K, that Kashmir's Constitution would be framed by the state's Constituent Assembly, and that the control of the Kashmiri Army would remain vested with India. While the Interim Government nominated four members to represent J&K in the Constituent Assembly of India (eventually in the *Lok Sabha*), Sheikh Abdullah, in a press statement to an influential English paper,[37] had pleaded for the independence of Kashmir, and the National Conference leaders evolved fresh proposals, one being that the administrative control over the Kashmiri forces would be restored to the state. The earlier agreement was already enshrined, however, in the Constitution of India as draft Article 306-A. The Kashmiri leaders told Gopalaswami Ayangar, the Minister of States in the Central Government, that Kashmir had acceded to India in regard to only three subjects: foreign affairs, defence and communications, and retained its independence in all other matters. A revised draft was also rejected, and a final one, renumbered as Article 370 of the Indian Constitution, giving a special status to Jammu and Kashmir, came into force.[38] The powers to amend its provisions were vested with the Indian Parliament.[39]

In late 1951, a Constituent Assembly, which the Kashmiri leadership deemed to be a constitutional sequel to the freedom struggle, was convened with seventy-five members, all from the National Conference or other sympathetic supporters, and twenty-five more seats reserved for those to represent the Pakistani-controlled territories. The Muzaffarabad regime, dominated in the early years by some of Abdullah's opponents in the Muslim Conference and unable to survive without Pakistan's blessing and patronage, wavered politically in accordance with the change of power in Karachi or Islamabad. While it may be deemed not unnatural for a number of Indian Muslim organizations to be overtly critical of Pakistan's rule in parts of Kashmiri land,[40] some Pakistani sources also disapproved of the lack of a simple election, over so many years, to let those Kashmiris choose a representative government of their own.[41] The J&K election, however, was boycotted by the Praja Parishad, which represented the Hindu middle class and was therefore against any land reform. But, in a way, the people had spoken although only less than 5% of the electorate had gone to the polls. In mid-1952, a Kashmiri delegation went to the Indian capital to sign the Delhi Agreement (24 July), which recognized the unconvential prerogatives of the State Legislature.[42]

Abdullah's perception was that a unitary system, coupled with communalism, would submerge the identity of the Kashmiri people. There was no difference of opinions as far as Kashmir's accession to India was concerned. He had differences, however, on the limits of that accession. The citizens of Kashmir, which was to have its own flag and be vested with all the "residuary powers", would enjoy land ownership rights denied to Indians from other states. While the other Indian States would have premiers too, their designation being "Chief Minister", Kashmir's head of government was going to be the only one in India with that title outside of the Prime Minister of the Indian Republic. Sheikh Abdullah announced the end of the Dogra-Hindu dynasty, founded in the past by Gulab Singh. A constitutional Head of State, the *Sadar-e Riyasat*, was to be elected by the Legislative Assembly. The choice was Y. K. Singh for a period of five years. To respect the sentiments of the local people, the medium of instruction in the public schools and the official language throughout the state was to be Urdu, and Hindi, recognized as *lingua franca* by the Indian Constitution, was not to enjoy that prominence in J&K. Although the recruitment of the Kashmiris in the army had been stopped by successive foreign rulers for so many centuries, the new leadership established a National Militia to vindicate the pride of the people. Education became free in the new schools opened in big towns. The children of the poor now had the opportunity, for the first time, to reach high levels. The big landed estates were abolished, old debts of the poor liquidated, cottage industries subsidized, factories set up, all towns and many villages electrified, inexpensive transport systems established, and entrepreneurs financially helped. It seemed that after a long period of poverty, the Kashmiris were going to witness the dawn of a new era.

Beginning with the first Security Council resolution, India insisted that a plebiscite could be held only following the restoration of order in Kashmir, meaning the withdrawal of the tribal invaders and the Pakistani forces. As Hewitt observes, it was never considered necessary, however, to hold a plebiscite in the princely states. The plebiscite in Junagadh (1948) was not a consistent policy.[43] Although conscious of his leadership of a predominantly Muslim community, Sheikh Abdullah seemed to have been deeply attached to secular philosophy. He strove against complete absorption by anyone of his powerful neighbours, but he was more inclined towards India than Pakistan. Apart from the sad memories of the tribal invasion, the people would vote for India, if need be, as long as the popular *Sheer-e Kashmir* (The Lion of Kashmir) was at the helm of the administration. Pakistan realized that a plebiscite at this stage would probably mean the total loss of Azad Kashmir and the rest, especially when some Indian troops would still be there. With the feeling in the Valley on account of arson, looting and rape by the invaders, an early plebiscite would probably go against Pakistan.

The UNCIP, nevertheless, proposed a Plebiscite Administrator, the U.S. Fleet Admiral Chester W. Nimitz (22 March 1949), to take over some sovereign powers over the disputed territory for the duration of the plebiscite. India declined the offer. The Security Council, then, appointed one mediator after another, who proposed plans for consideration. General A. G. L. McNaughton (Canada) suggested the withdrawal of all Pakistani regulars but only the reduction of the Azad Kashmir forces. Sir Owen Dixon (Australia) recommended "regional plebiscites", that is, the awarding of each area according to the outcome of the vote therein. Liaquat Ali Khan insisted on a single plebiscite over the entire state. India would then agree to a plebiscite if the hand of Pakistan, branded as "aggressor", was excluded. Pakistan would accept it if the influence of India and Sheikh Abdullah was greatly diminished. Dr. Frank P. Graham (U.S.A.) could not accomplish any headway either.[44] Consequently, the Kashmir issue did not appear in the Security Council agenda until the beginning of 1957. In the meantime, however, the J&K Constituent Assembly declared (17 November 1956) the state to be an integral part of the Union of India. When Gunnar Jarring's (Sweden) attempt to mediate was equally unsuccessful, the Security Council lost all initiative until the mid-1960s.[45] Pakistan raised the issue when (1963) some Indian politicians called for the "liberation" of Azad Kashmir and when a hair of Islam's Prophet Mohammed disappeared (1964) from the Hazratbal Mosque in Srinagar. Under the circumstances then, Nehru, a believer in secularism, abhorred the idea of a partition of J&K either by plebiscite or negotiations, basically resting on communal criteria. By the same principle, he also opposed the independence or secession of any part of India.

Sheikh Abdullah, who strove for a semi-independent status for his own state to realize extensive land reforms and benefit from the plentiful tourist possibilities of the land, sometimes gave indications, alarming for India, that he may be steering towards a further change in Kashmir's association with that country. But his leadership gravitated towards secularism, which was also the goal of the Indian Constitution. Although there were some tendencies even in India standing for a degree of religious intolerance at some future date, the presence of Kashmir in the Union of India, in Sheikh Abdullah's view, would be a major factor in stabilizing relations between the Muslims and the Hindus of that country. Further, in association with the landlord-ridden Pakistan, with so many feudal privileges intact, he could not possibly realize any of his economic reforms. Kashmir's traditional markets were also centred in India. It was India, not Pakistan, that could give Kashmir technical services and material for industrialization. Although an all-weather road-link for trade then existed only with Pakistan, a stable system of communication with India was also feasible. Pakistan was a Muslim state, but a feudal one. The appeal to religion constituted a wrong approach, however sentimental. Pakistan did not represent the organic unity of all the Muslims in the Sub-continent either. As one Muslim was as good as another, the Kashmiri Muslims, in Abdullah's opinion, should choose the Muslims living in India. Religious affinity alone, on the other hand, did not determine the political alliance of a state. There was no Buddhist, Christian or even a Muslim bloc. What would be the fate of the non-Muslims of Kashmir? The third course of keeping aloof from both India and Pakistan, but having friendly relations with both of them, seemed attractive but it was not easy to protect the independence of a small country with insufficient strength to defend itself. A neighbour had invaded Kashmir in spite of a valid Standstill Agreement. Sheikh Abdullah had no difference of opinion on the fact of Kashmir's accession with India; he had differences on the limits of that accession.

The probings of the Working Committee of the Constituent Assembly into the future of the state, including a variety of risks and probabilities, none yet considered to be conclusive, scared circles who would rather have closer union with India. For instance, the majority of the Ladakhis felt threatened by Abdullah's land reforms which limited the wealth of the traditionally dominant Buddhist monasteries. The total cultivated area in the state was about 2,200,000 acres,[46] most of which was owned by the Maharaja, his *Jagirdars* and the landlord class of *Chakdars*. In their eyes, Sheikh Abdullah seemed bent towards additional powers—some admittedly authoritarian, but probably to withstand such vested interests. A disinformation campaign, aided by communal forces, created suspicion against him. For instance, the influential Ladakhis declared that in the event of the state drifting away from India, they would rather severe their relations with Kashmir and merge directly with the Indian Union.[47]

In Jammu the opposition was spearheaded by the Praja Parishad, which was against a separate flag and a separate Constitution for J&K. Prem Nath Dogra, its leader, associated with the Bharatiya Jana Sangh in India and who advocated the abolition of Article 370, was detained on Abdullah's orders. Dr. Syana Prasad

Mookerjee, Jana Sangh's President arrested at the state border, was pronounced dead of heart attack while under detention. Closely watched by the Intelligence Bureau,[48] more accountable to the Central Government, Sheikh Abdullah was dismissed on the night of 8–9 August 1953, and replaced by his lieutenant, Bakshi Ghulam Muhammad.[49] Abdullah, arrested almost instantly and charged with conspiracy, remained in prison until 8 April 1964, was discharged by a special court, rearrested about a year later, and remained under detention until 1968. For most of the detention period, the Sheikh turned from a 'quisling' to a 'patriot' in Pakistan.

The customs barrier was removed (13 April 1954), and the state became economically an integral part of India. When elections were held in early 1957 under the new Constitution (26 January 1957), patterned on the Indian Constitution, the bulk of the seats again went to the National Conference, only seven being won by the Hindu parties. The performance of the National Conference was even better in the 1962 elections. The government in New Delhi identified such confirmations as late but popular endorsements of the 1947 accession. There had been, however, some measure of manipulation almost in all the phases of the electioneering process, easy to judge from the way Bakshi Ghulam Muhammad's rotten reign (1953–63) came to an end. Succeeded by Khwaja Shamsuddin, the title of *Sadar-e Riyasat* was changed to Governor, and the Prime Minister would henceforth be referred to as Chief Minister. While Sheikh Abdullah, now (temporarily) out of jail, was visiting Muzaffarabad, Nehru passed away (27 May 1964). When the new Indian Government allowed Abdullah to attend the Afro-Asian Conference in Algiers, his private discussions with China's Chou En-lai caused the cancellation of his passport and subsequent arrest. Although some civil disturbances occurred in Kashmir in reaction to the renewal of arrest, Sheikh Abdullah's formal successors relied increasingly more on India.

Direct Talks

Correctly assuming that international opinion expects Indo-Pakistani disputes to be settled by peaceful means, it is appropriate to remember, with an echo for future action, that there is a long and renewed process of bilateral discussions between the two countries. It was India that initiated the first phase of direct talks right after the first Kashmir War. The Nehru-Liaquat Ali meeting in New Delhi (20–24 July 1950) and the correspondence between the two (until 28 November 1950) underlined peaceful solution through negotiations. India was not prepared to accept the intrusion of any 'foreign' entity, not even the United Nations. Although the possibility of direct talks came up during the Commonwealth Prime Ministers Conference in London (8–15 January 1951), Nehru's stand was that Kashmir was basically a domestic Indian matter. A plebiscite was unnecessary, he reasoned, because the people had voted in a way through the Kashmiri Constituent and the Legislative Assemblies. If there had to be a plebiscite, there was no need for a Plebiscite Administrator with full powers or troops from other countries, no matter how neutral they might be; it could be conducted following the withdrawal of the Pakistani forces and in the presence of the Indian troops.

The uncomplimentary posture of the Hindus of Jammu and the Buddhists of Ladakh of the Abdullah regime prompted Nehru to discuss with Pakistan's new Prime Minister Muhammad Ali Bogra, during the Commonwealth Prime Ministers meeting in London and in Karachi (25–27 June 1953) the idea of regional plebiscites. Bogra requested a new round of talks after Sheikh Abdullah's dismissal. Although the two premiers came together in New Delhi (17–20 August 1953), Nehru soon became less and less interested in overall voting.

Approaching the mid-1950s, Pakistan opted for a foreign policy accepting American military bases on its territory in return for military aid, the main motive for this radical change of course being the Kashmir issue. Becoming an alliance partner with the United States in the South East Asia Treaty Organization (SEATO, 8 September 1954), Pakistan's agreements with Turkey, a NATO member, provided the first steps for the evolution of the Baghdad Pact (24 February 1955), later (19 August 1959) called CENTO. Pakistan joined (17 September 1955) both the Baghdad Pact and SEATO, India standing clearly aloof from both. Pakistan and Turkey, on the other hand, became links between these three Western-sponsored alliances, embracing the whole gamut of nations from Canada to the Philippines that contained the Eastern bloc. Following the *coup d'état* (1958) in Iraq, Pakistan accommodated itself (5 March 1959), along with Iran and Turkey, with a bilateral defence agreement with the United States. Apparently, Pakistan endeavoured to secure from the United States as much military aid as possible to bring its armed potential on par with India. In contrast, Nehru, believing in non-alignment, emerged as a champion of the causes of the Afro-Asian countries, initially in the Bandung Conference in Indonesia (1955).[50] Nehru's visit to the Soviet Union was followed by the Bulganin-Khrushchev tour of India including Srinagar. The Soviet Union, not only guarded India's interests during the Security Council meetings, but also extended military aid to India.[51]

A Chinese involvement was added to the American and Soviet preoccupation with the Kashmir issue. The armed clashes (1959) between the Chinese and the Indian patrols along the Assam and Ladakh borders proved to be the forerunners of the much more serious confrontation in 1962.[52] Nehru reached an agreement (19 September 1960) with General (later Field Marshal) Mohammad Ayub Khan, Pakistan's President since 1958,[53] on the waters of the Indus basin, some (the Beas, Ravi and Sutlej) going to India, and others (the Chenab, Indus and Jhelum) going to Pakistan. Perhaps this *modus vivendi*, Beijing's inclusion of Hunza as part of China and India's cession (1958) of the small Berubari enclave to East Pakistan inspired Ayub Khan to suggest a joint defence of the Sub-continent. Nehru's suspicion of Ayub's proposal, the meagre dividends of the American connection, and the Indian action in Goa[54] played some role in Pakistan's quest for better relations with mainland China.[55] India's 'dispute' with China concerned the boundary in Kashmir, the frontier where Uttar Pradesh, Himachal Pradesh and Punjab came up to the Chinese border, and the

MacMahon line or the eastern part of the dividing line from Bhutan to Burma (now Myanmar). The boundary with China included a large piece of territory known as the Aksai Chin projecting out to the east. In spite of the Sino-Indian armed conflict, there were short but renewed talks (27 December 1962–16 May 1963) between Pakistan's new Foreign Minister Zulfikar Ali Bhutto and Sardar Swaran Singh in Rawalpindi, New Delhi, Karachi and Calcutta. The Indian Government greatly resented Pakistan's Border Agreement with China (2 March 1963). It looked to New Delhi that Pakistan had given away a small portion of Kashmir to a third party in order to gain its support in the overall issue.

Lal Bahadur Shastri, a Union Minister, took on Nehru's mantle when this founding father died. Sheikh Abdullah had made some preparation for a meeting between the Indian and Pakistani leaders. The short discourse between Ayub Khan and Shastri at the Karachi airport (12 October 1964) did not exceed the phraseology of reciprocal goodwill. Ayub Khan was soon (3 January 1965) to face a presidential election against Fatima Jinnah,[56] the sister of Pakistan's founder, and Shastri had to weigh properly the public antipathy towards Pakistan. Following his victory at the polls, Ayub Khan continued to cope with the increasing influence of a hawkish trend, which the Foreign Minister Bhutto perhaps personified more than anyone else. India, whose economy was encountering hardships, had exhibited a poor performance during the armed clash with China. The disappearance of Prophet Muhammad's hair from the Hazratbal Mosque in Srinagar caused serious outcries, and the announcement that Hindu was to be (26 January 1965) an official language of the Union led to similar disapprovals in Madras State (later Tamil Nadu). During the month of Ayub Khan's visit to China (2–9 March 1965) there were border incidents between East Pakistan and West Bengal as well as on the Rann of Kutch that separated Sindh from India.[57] A prominent geographer describes it as "a vast expanse of naked tidal mudflats, a black desolation flecked with saline efflorescences".[58] Ayub Khan and Shastri signed (30 June 1965) an agreement, however, restoring the *status quo ante* in the Gujarat-Pakistan border.[59] Such an accord fell short of preventing non-violent civil disobedience movements spreading in reaction to Sheikh Abdullah's arrest after his return from Algiers. In the opinion of the determined portion of the decision-makers, Pakistan could well seek and experiment with new avenues to hold on to the Kashmir issue. The end-product of this transforming atmosphere, which took it for granted that Kashmir was ready for revolt against Indian hold, was "Operation Gibraltar".

Pakistan officially trained and encouraged *Mujahideen* to infiltrate into Indian-controlled territories.[60] To stop infiltration, the Indian Army thought it to be duty bound to occupy (25 August) certain passes in the Kargil sector, turning then to Uri and Poonch. The Azad Kashmir troops, supported by Pakistan's regular units, attacked the Chhamb district at the end of the cease-fire line, coming very close to the City of Jammu. When Indian columns moved towards Lahore and Sialkot, a full-fledged Indo-Pakistani War had begun.[61] The raiders from outside banked on getting wide local support, but the bulk of the Kashmiri people gave the lie to the lurid expectations of 'popular uprising' put out by the Pakistani means of mass communication. Having reached a stalemate or a course more against Pakistan, Ayub Khan sent an appeal to President Lyndon B. Johnson to intervene personally while U Thant, the U.N. Secretary-General, continued his efforts for a cease-fire. Both sides agreed to stop fighting (26 September 1965), especially when the Security Council *demanded* it. Aleksei Kosygin, the Soviet Prime Minister, offered his good offices and the Uzbek capital of Tashkent for a negotiated settlement, which Ayub Khan and Shastri accepted. According to the Tashkent Declaration (10 January 1966), the armies withdrew, diplomatic relations were re-established, and they agreed to continue bilateral discussions.

While Indira Gandhi, Nehru's daughter, upon becoming Prime Minister after Shastri's unexpected death, endeavoured to rouse active Soviet support, Bhutto, finding faults with Pakistan's military command, left the administration and established (1967) his own organization, the Pakistan People's Party (PPP). Contrary to the expectations of the hawkish politicians in Islamabad, the *Mujahideen* movement, openly sponsored by Pakistan, had failed to transform itself into a nation-wide rebellion. Moreover, violence, now described as "terrorism", was being recognized as an international hazard. While New Delhi partitioned Eastern Punjab and honoured the Sikhs for their loyalty to India by giving them the portion overwhelmingly inhabited by their people, the J&K Government arrested some Islamic leaders, including Mirwaiz Muhammad Farooq and Maulana Muhammad Sayeed Masoodi. Some Sikhs took this award as an acknowledgement of a political structure meant for themselves. Meanwhile, the government in Srinagar was becoming more servile to New Delhi. Sheikh Abdullah being in detention, the party in power had changed its name to 'Pradesh (State) Congress' and won the majority of seats, through an election boycotted by the Plebiscite Front. The latter was formed by Mirza Afzal Beg to represent the views of the Abdullah group. One of the first undertakings of Sheikh Abdullah after his release from jail was to go to Rawalpindi and tell Ayub Khan that the solution should be such that neither country ought to have the feeling of being outmatched nor should it weaken the foundations of Indian secularism.[62]

Ayub Khan's place was taken (25 March 1968) by General Yahya Khan as Martial Law Administrator and later as the head of a military junta. In the next (1970) elections, Bhutto's PPP won 81 seats out of 183 in West Pakistan, but Mujibur Rahman's Awami League got 160 out of 162 seats in East Pakistan. The Awami League scored a landslide victory in the first general elections in Pakistan.[63] Swooping down (25 March 1971) on the people of East Pakistan with aerial bombing, artillery and tanks instead of conceding the office of the Prime Minister to Mujibur Rahman signalled a fatal armed encounter between the forces of Pakistan's two wings.

It also led to the Third Indo-Pakistani War and the creation of the independent state of Bangladesh. On account of the hijacking of an Indian plane,[64] New Delhi banned Pakistani overflights across the long Indian territory. While some ten million refugees streaming into West Bengal gave India, which signed (9 August 1971) a Treaty of Peace, Friendship and Cooperation with the Soviet Union, a reason for getting involved in the crisis, Pakistan, which arranged a secret visit of Henry Kissinger, President Nixon's National Security Adviser to China,[65] found itself in a "Fourteen Days' War" (December 1971) that it could not win. Pakistan could not even secure a few advantages that it could use in the Kashmir issue.[66] It lost its eastern wing, the discredited military rule, which had brought so much suffering to both wings of the country, had to wind itself up, and Bhutto, the well-off landlord of Sindh and the former hawk in foreign relations, met Indira Gandhi in Simla to salvage some of what seemed wrecked.[67] The Simla Agreement (3 July 1972) stated that the two neighbours were resolved to settle their differences by peaceful bilateral negotiations or by other peaceful means, that neither side should unilaterally alter the situation, that they should always respect each other's national unity and territorial integrity, that they would refrain from the threat or use of force against each other, and that the Line of Control (LOC) in J&K resulting from the cease-fire (17 December 1971) should be respected by both sides. Designated military commanders of both sides delineated the LOC, indicating the position of the two armies on the day of the cease-fire. Commanders signed the maps showing the LOC to endorse the agreement on it. Both governments accorded approval to the joint recommendations submitted by the commanders. The cease-fire line, later referred to as the LOC or the LOAC (Line of Actual Control), became the *de facto* border between the Indian and the Pakistani controlled areas. A joint statement by India and Pakistan paved the way for withdrawal of troops to their sides of the international border.

The Kashmir Accord

The Muslims of the Valley were inclined to stand their ground on Article 370, no matter how diminished it was by now, but the Hindus and Sikhs of Jammu as well as the Buddhists of Ladakh would have liked to see it abolished. Indira Gandhi would also have preferred a contracted *modus operandi* not to shatter a precarious balance by encouraging some other Indian states to seek the same exemptions. The pro-Pakistan Jamaat-e Islami had won five seats in the 1972 elections against the majority of the Pradesh Congress Party, led by Syed Mir Qasim, who now filled the deceased Sadiq's place. Under the changing circumstances, the Central Government, hoping to achieve a more stable government under Sheikh Abdullah, who had remained in the political wilderness for more than two decades, announced (24 February 1975) a "Kashmir Accord", which stated that J&K, still governed by Article 370, was a "constituent unit" of the Indian Union and while residuary powers of legislation would remain with the state, the Union Parliament would continue to have the power to make laws relating to the prevention of activities towards disrupting the "territorial integrity of India or secession of a part of the territory from the Union".

While the State Congress Party unanimously elected Sheikh Abdullah as its leader, Pakistan, which protested to the United Nations, and Mirwaiz Muhammad Farooq's circle denounced him for having "sold out" Kasmir's interests. While the

Islamic forces in the Valley, supported by sections of the unemployed educated young generation, were attaining far greater strength than ever before, Sheikh Abdullah reconstituted the National Conference and persuaded the State Governor (L. K. Jha) to order fresh elections. Indira Gandhi and her party were defeated in the 1977 general elections,[68] and Morarji Desai's Janata Government[69] in New Delhi approved the J&K elections (30 June–3 July 1977) which gave Abdullah's National Conference forty-seven out of seventy-six seats. Backed by the Muslim vote but unable to restrain the disgruntled, Sheikh Abdullah's administration, in the opinion of some commentators, more and more unfolded towards personal iron sway. Immediately after assuming power on 6 July, he "proceeded audaciously to consolidate his dictatorial regime".[70] While explaining some of his actions, such as governmental authority of detention up to two years as a compelling measure against Pakistani infiltrators, some of his closest friends, like Mirza Afzal Beg, had to give up and leave him in the lurch. After Indira Gandhi's return to power (1980) and almost on the heels of her meeting (22 July) with Abdullah, the aged *Sheer-e Kashmir* handed the reins of power to his son Dr. Farooq Abdullah.

Violence Anew

A new wave of Islamic fundamentalism was sweeping over the Valley when Sheikh Abdullah died (8 September 1982). Having led a non-violent struggle against the feudal and autocratic rule of the Maharaja and having stood fast to the ideal of secularism in the dark days of the holocaust of partition, Sheikh Abdullah had remained at the centre of the political and social life of the state for more than half a century. During his long and controversial career, he persistently fought against the forces of communalism and upheld the values of religious tolerance befitting a leader of a composite culture. First as the leading figure in the freedom struggle, and then as the patron of *Kashmiriyat* he earned the epithet of *Sheer-e Kashmir*. He survived the jails of Hari Parbat, Bahu, Badarwah and others, which could only imprison his body but could not crush his spirit. About a million people joined his funeral procession, bidding him a tearful farewell. Sheikh Nooriddeen Noorani had laid the foundations of a composite culture, Zain-ul Abidin enriched the secular traditions of the country, and Sheikh Abdullah strengthened the time-honoured heritage.[71]

The influence of the Iranian Revolution, the Muslim reactions to the Soviet military presence in Afghanistan, the beginnings of Sikh secessionism, and the echo of Hindu antagonism fed rising susceptibility to dissent in Kashmir. Official reports as well as news items in the Indian press on frequent Pakistani infiltrators and cases of Indian soldiers whose loyalty was questioned, whether exaggerated or not, intensified. The Jamaat-e Islami teachers opened dozens of schools, and preachers, some from Pakistan, addressed the *Jum'a* (Friday) congregations in mosques. Frustrated young Muslims were getting prepared to join movements promising a *Nizam-e Mustafa* (Prophet's Order).[72] The traditionally tolerant Rishi-Sufi cult was giving way before an Islamic fundamentalism. To compel India to part with the Valley required armed strength. Only a whispering campaign of *Azadi* (freedom) being 'around the corner' was insufficient. From where would the arms come?

More questions were posed as to how much of the foreign aid for the Afghan *Mujahideen* actually stayed in the hands of the Pakistani military. It was in the midst of this rise in the political barometer that both India and Pakistan, misemploying the loophole in the 1972 Simla Agreement, moved up their forces to the imperfectly defined terminus of the cease-fire line, particularly the Siachen glacier. Indira Gandhi's meetings with Farooq Abdullah within the framework of these lively confrontations coalesced with riots and strikes. The appointment of Jagmohan Malhotra, a former Lieutenant-Governor of New Delhi who had ably suppressed communal disorders in the past, not only removed Farooq Abdullah from the government as well as from the presidency of the National Conference, but perhaps inflated the tension in the Valley.[73] G. M. Shah, Dr. Farooq Abdullah's brother-in-law and his political rival who succeeded him, could not curb the growing violence. The entire scenario came to be dominated by militancy, and terrorist activities started to take a heavy toll of life. It was feared that the Valley would go the 'Beirut way'. His resignation brought the governor's rule, with the suspension of the Legislative Assembly, and more control of the Central Government. The return of Farooq Abdullah to power, the renewal of the elections (1987), and Jagmohan's resignation (1990) could bring neither administrative stability, nor freedom from terrorism.

In the 1990s, there were no longer scarce, insignificant and moderate demonstrations. Police stations were now bombed, western tourists attacked, high officials kidnapped, victims killed, and public figures assassinated. The Jamaat-e Islami produced a youth movement called the Jamiat-e Tulba, supported from abroad including some oil-rich Middle Eastern states. Khomeini's name ("Hindi"), originally from India, was a halo of respect, as was the popular Palestinian *intifada*. The end of the Soviet participation in the Afghani War let loose quite a number of militants as well as weapons. The State of J&K found itself in a rising level of terrorist violence, to which neighbouring Pakistan was not a spectator.

Notes

1   Kamlesh Kumar Wadhwa, *Minority Safeguards in India: Constitutional Provisions and Their Implementation*, New Delhi, Thomson Press Limited, 1975, p. 14.
2   Georges Fischer, "Romain Rolland and India", *World Affairs*, New Delhi, I (December 1990), p. 22.
3   Romesh Thapar, *India in Transition*, Bombay, Current Book House, 1956, pp. 18–19.
4   Amaury de Riencourt, *The Soul of India*, London, Jonathan Cape, 1961, p. 345.
5   P. N. S. Mansergh *et al.*, eds., *Constitutional Relations between Britain and India: the Transfer of Power: 1942–47, Vol. XI, the Mountbatten Viceroyalty, Announcement and Reception of the 3 June Plan, 31 May–7 July 1947*, London, H.M.S.O., 1982, p. 438.
6   Bamzai, *op. cit.*, Vol. III, p. 755.

7   A process had developed by which "generous leave was granted without much worry as to how and where the applicant took his holiday". Small sub-units took their leave together and were of use in the "Azad" forces. Lord Birdwood, *A Continent Decides*, London, Robert Hale, 1953, pp. 229–230.

8   Alastair Lamb, *Kashmir, a Disputed Legacy: 1846–1990*, Karachi, Oxford University Press, 1992, pp. 124–125. Also: Sardar Muhammad Ibrahim Khan, *The Kashmir Saga*, Lahore, Ripon Printing Press, 1965.

9   Hewitt, *op. cit.*, p. 74.

10   Lamb, *op. cit.*, p. 155. Lamb states later (p. 258), however, that the Government of Pakistan "was innocent of the charges made against it by India" in 1947. Hewitt records, on the other hand, that "Pakistan first denied any presence in Jammu and Kashmir, then refused to vacate areas occupied by its army, and demanded Indian withdrawal". Hewitt, *op. cit.*, p. 78. Although in Alastair Lamb's judgement his second telling of the Kashmir story, after the earlier (1966) book, blows away many cobwebs, this promise is not sustained in the eyes of the following prominent Indian writer: B. G. Verghese, "Lamb's Tales from Kashmir", *The Kashmir Issue*, London, High Commission of India, 1993, pp. 153–163. Also in: *Sunday Mail*, 14–20 June 1992.

11   An amazing tale of horror and misery of a woman, the wife of the District Officer in Srinagar, in the "Azad Kashmir" area after the raiders invaded Kashmir in 1947: Krishna Mehda, *Chaos in Kashmir*, Calcutta, Signet Press, n.d.

12   Akbar Khan fought under the pseudonym of "Tariq", after the Muslim leader who had crossed the Gibraltar into Spain in the year 711.

13   Akbar Khan, *Raiders in Kashmir: Story of the Kashmir War, 1947–48*, Karachi; Islamabad, National Book Foundation, 1970; 1975, p. 17.

14   General Gracey reversed his decision when the Indian troops approached the Poonch-West Punjab border. Lamb, *op. cit.*, p. 162.

15   On the development of imperial policy towards Indian princely states, especially Hyderabad: Bharati Ray, *Hyderabad and British Paramountcy, 1858–1883*, New Delhi, Oxford University Press, 1988; Phillips Talbot, "Kashmir and Hyderabad", *World Politics*, Baltimore, I/3 (April 1949), pp. 321–322; "Kashmir and Hyderabad", *The Economist*, London, 155/5476 (7 August 1948), pp. 211–212; Krishna Das, "Kashmir and Hyderabad", *The Organiser*, New Delhi, I/23 (4 December 1947), pp. 5, 14.

16   "Kashmir, Hyderabad, Junagadh", *India Today*, New Delhi, October 1947, pp. 1–2.

17   G. N. S. Raghavan, *Introducing India*, New Delhi, Indian Council for Cultural Relations, p. 76.

18   Only 91 votes out of an electorate of 201,719 favoured Pakistan.

19   Lamb, *op. cit.*, pp. 128–129. Also: Mehr Chand Mahajan, *Accession of Kashmir to India: the Inside Story*, Sholapur, Institute of Public Administration, 1950; _____, *Looking Back*, London, 1963.

20   The original in Urdu: *Aatesh-e Chinar*, Srinagar, Ali Mohammad and Sons, 1988. A short English version: *Flames of the Chinar: an Autobiography*, abridged, translated from the Urdu and introduced by Khustwant Singh, London, Penguin Books, 1995, pp. 83–101.

21   Sardar Vallabhbhai Patel, *Sardar Patel's Correspondence: 1945–50, Vol. I, New Light on Kashmir*, ed., Durga Das, Ahmedabad, Navajivan Publishing House, 1971.

22   M. Hafizullah, *Towards Azad Kashmir*, Lahore, Baram-i-Frogh-i-Adab, 1948.

23   Mahajan, *op. cit.*, p. 150. Lamb states that Batra "almost certainly did not show" the accession document to the Indian leaders: *op. cit.*, pp. 134–135.

24   Alan Campbell-Johnson, *Mission with Mountbatten*, London, Robert Hale, 1951, p. 224.

25   From the pen of a leading architect of integration: Vapal Pangunni Menon, *The Story of the Integration of the Indian States*, Calcutta, Orient Longmans, 1956; New York, Arna, 1972.

26   On the military climax of October 1947: Lieut.-General L. P. Sen, *Slender Was the Thread: Kashmir Confrontations, 1947–48*, Bombay, Orient Longmans, 1969; Major-General D. K. Palit, *Jammu and Kashmir Arms: History of the J&K Rifles*, Dehra Dun, Palit and Dutt, 1972.

27   These documents are available in a number of official and unofficial sources. For instance: Grover, *op. cit.,* Vol. III, pp. 107–111; P. L. Lakhanpal, ed., *Essential Documents and Notes on Kashmir Dispute*, New Delhi, International Books, 1965, p. 57; *J K Newsline*, February 1994, pp. 9–12.

28   A noteworthy source on the validity of accession: Hari Om Agarwal, *Kashmir Problem— Its Legal Aspects*, Allahabad, Kitab Mahal, 1979. Although the official communications concerning military aid and accession and their dates have been accepted as true by virtually all observers, be they sympathetic or hostile to the Indian case, Lamb maintains in a brochure (*The Myth of Indian Claim to Jammu and Kashmir: a Reappraisal*, with no publisher and date indicated) that "these documents could only have been signed *after* the overt Indian intervention" (p. 2). He argues in his book entitled *Kashmir* (*op. cit.*, pp. 150–152) that accession was legally invalid (because it violated the Standstill Agreement with Pakistan and disturbed an established understanding), that the Maharaja (overthrown by his own subjects and a ruler only in Jammu and Ladakh) was no longer competent to sign the Instrument, that it was conditional (committing him to consult his people) and that India annexed much of Kashmir by force (in consequence of conspiracy with the British).

29   The total number of tribesmen were probably between 2000 and 5000. Mohinder Bahl, *Whither Kashmir*, New Delhi, n.d., p. 41; Wolpert, *op. cit.*, p. 348.

30   Thapar, *op. cit.*, p. 21.

31   Rahmatullah Khan, *Kashmir and the United Nations*, Delhi, Vikas, 1969; H. S. Gururaj Rao, *Legal Aspects of the Kashmir Problem*, Bombay; New York, Asia Publishing House, 1967; Surendra Chopra, *Mediation in Kashmir: a Study in Power Politics*, Kurukshetra, Vishal Publications, 1971.

32   United Nations, *The Yearbook of the United Nations: 1947–48*, New York, 1949, pp. 387ff. Since it was quite monstrous to Nehru's mind that the "invader" should be treated as equal to the "defender", author Sheean maintains that India's original appeal under the "Pacific Settlement of Disputes" (Article 35) rather than "Acts of Aggression" (Article 39) of the U.N. Charter may be "due to a technical error". Vincent Sheean, *Nehru: the Years of Power*, London, Victor Gollancz Ltd., 1960, pp. 100–101. Lamb upholds the view that the Indian side then took care not to call Pakistan an "aggressor", at least in the United Nations. Lamb, *op. cit.*, p. 165.

33   Josef Korbel, *Danger in Kashmir*, Princeton, New Jersey, Princeton University Press, 1954, pp. 114–115.

34   Riyaz Punjabi, "Kashmir Imbroglio: the Socio-Political Roots", *Contemporary South Asia*, London, 4/1 (1995), pp. 39–53.

35   Nehru's letter, dated 20 May 1948, to his daughter Indira: "[Sheikh Abdullah] came to see me. He was very depressed about everything ... According to the Sheikh, the only solution is that H. H. should abdicate in favour of his son ..." Sonia Gandhi, ed., *Two Alone, Two*

Together: Letters between Indira Gandhi and Jawaharlal Nehru, 1940–1964, London, Hodder and Stoughton, 1992, p. 555.

36 Karan Singh, *Autobiography*, Delhi, Oxford University Press, 1997, pp. 100–101.

37 Interview to Michael Davidson in the *The Scotsman*, Edinburgh, 14 April 1949.

38 Mohan Krishan Teng, *Kashmir: Article 370*, New Delhi, Anmol Publications, 1990, pp. 44–78.

39 While Article 1 of the Indian Constitution conceived J&K to be an integral part of the Indian Union, Article 370 was so different from the "Mysore model" which accepted a Constitution, proclaimed on 25 November 1949, framed by India. Menon, *op. cit.*, p. 295. Also: Mahendra P. Singh, *V. N. Shukla's Constitution of India*, 9th ed., Lucknow, Eastern Book Company, 1996, pp. 905–909. The continued application of Article 370 was questioned in *Sampat Prakash v. State of J&K* (1969).

40 Government of India, *Kashmir: Indian Muslims' Challenge*, New Delhi, Information Service of India, 1965.

41 *The Civil and Military Gazette* of Lahore (5 June 1955) and *Khyber Mail* (27 August 1964) quoted in: Government of India, *Occupied Kashmir: a Pakistan Colony*, New Delhi, External Publicity Division, 1965, pp. 2 and 4.

42 On the unconventional prerogatives: M. K. Teng and Santosh Kaul, *Kashmir's Special Status*, New Delhi, Oriental Publishers, 1975; Ram Krishen Kaul Bhatt, *Political and Constitutional Development of the Jammu and Kashmir State*, New Delhi, Seema, 1984; Krishan Mohar Teng, *State Government and Politics: Jammu and Kashmir*, New Delhi, Sterling, 1985. These three studies provide analysis of the political institutions and operatives that the Constitution of J&K envisaged. That state was accorded a special position in the Indian constitutional system. A prominent Kashmiri recorded about three decades later, however, that developments, unforeseen by the Constitution-makers, occurred, and worse, ugliness overshadowed beauty when state politicians, especially the Muslim leaders, used Article 370 to exploit the gullible masses. Prem Nath Bazaz, *Democracy Through Intimidation and Terror: the Untold Story of Kashmir Politics*, New Delhi, Heritage, 1978, pp. 1–7.

43 Hewitt, *op. cit.*, p. 78.

44 The reports of McNaughton, Dixon, Graham and Jarring in: Government of Pakistan, *Reports on Kashmir by United Nations Representatives*, Karachi, 1958; 1962.

45 Sisir Gupta, *Kashmir: a Study in India-Pakistan Relations*, Bombay, Asia Publishing House, 1966; Rahmatullah Khan, *Kashmir in the United Nations*, Delhi, Vikas, 1966; Surendra Chopra, *U.N. Mediation in Kashmir: a Study in Power Politics*, Kurukshetra, Vishal Publications, 1971.

46 Bamzai, *op. cit.*, Vol. III, p. 802.

47 *Ibid.*, p. 808.

48 The account of the Bureau's Director: B. N. Mullik, *My Years with Nehru: 1948–1964*, Bombay, etc., Allied Publishers, 1972.

49 Both men had similar (humble) origins, but diverse talents. While both seemed physically strong, Abdullah was a self-confident speechmaker with inflammatory gestures, "Bakshi Sahib" was a realist with a widespread reputation that he would attend to all wrongs. Sheean, *op. cit.*, pp. 108–115.

50 The foreign policy performance of India's first prime minister: Bal Ram Nanda, ed., *Indian Foreign Policy: the Nehru Years*, New Delhi; London, Sangam Books, 1989. Written at the time of the 1983 New Delhi Non-Aligned Summit, attended by 97

members: Hari Jaisingh, *India and the Non-Aligned World: Search for a New Order*, New Delhi, Vikas, 1983. The evolution of India's foreign policy: Harish Kapur, *India's Foreign Policy, 1947–92: Shadows and Substance*, New Delhi; London, Sage Publications, 1994.

51   Indo-Soviet relations based on Russian sources: Robert H. Donaldson, *Soviet Policy Toward India: Ideology and Strategy*, Cambridge, Mass., Harvard University Press, 1974.

52   Two opposing studies on the border dispute: Alastair Lamb, *The China-India Border: the Origins of the Disputed Territories*, London, Royal Institute of International Affairs, 1964; Gondker Narayana Rao, *The India-China Border: a Reappraisal*, Bombay, Asia Publishing House, 1968.

53   W. A. Wilcox, "The Pakistan Coup d'Etat of 1958", *Pacific Affairs*, Vancouver, 38/2 (Summer 1965), pp. 142–163; Khalid Bin Sayeed, "Collapse of Parliamentary Democracy in Pakistan", *The Middle East Journal*, Washington, D.C., 13/4 (Autumn 1959), pp. 389–406.

54   Amarendra Nath Roy, "Kashmir and Goa", *Vigil*, 5/33 (16 October 1954), pp. 16–17.

55   Mohammad Ayub Khan, *Friends Not Masters: a Political Autobiography*, London, Oxford University Press, 1967, pp. 117–119, 164–166.

56   Fatima Jinnah (1893–1967), known as *Madar-e Millat* (Mother of the Nation), was the first leader of the All-India Muslim Women's Committee. She toured India campaigning on behalf of women's welfare, education and training, and also founded a medical college in Lahore.

57   On the clashes between the Indian and the Pakistani forces in the Rann of Kutch area as a prelude to the 1965 War: Saeed Ahmad, *The Indo-Pak Clash in the Rann of Kutch*, Rawalpindi, Army Education Press, 1973. Also: Mujtaba Razvi, *The Frontiers of Pakistan: a Study of Frontier Problems in Pakistan's Foreign Policy*, Karachi, National Publishing House, 1971, pp. 80–92.

58   O. H. K. Spate, *India and Pakistan: a Regional Geography*, London, Methuen, 1967, p. 64.

59   The author of the following book, who was the C-in-C of the Pakistani Air Force until mid-1965, is critical of Ayub Khan for agreeing to a ceasefire and states, in the introduction, that the war was fought for no purpose. Mohammed Asghar Khan, *The First Round: Indo-Pakistan War, 1965*, London, Islamic Information Services, 1979.

60   In addition to other writers, this fact is also accepted by Lamb, *Kashmir, op. cit.*, p. 258.

61   Indian view: Hari Ram Gupta, *India-Pakistan War: 1965*, Vols. I–II, New Delhi, Hariyana Prakashan, 1967–68; Pakistani view: M. Asghar Khan, *op. cit.*

62   Sheikh Abdullah, *op. cit.*, pp. 153–155. He asserts that Ayub Khan misrepresented S. Abdullah's views in his book: Ayub Khan, *op. cit.*, p. 128.

63   G. W. Choudhury, *The Last Days of United Pakistan*, Bloomington, IN., Indiana University Press, 1974; Herbert Feldman, *The End and the Beginning: Pakistan, 1969–1971*, London, Oxford University Press, 1975; M. Rafiqul Islam, *A Tale of Millions: Bangladesh Liberation War, 1971*, Dacca, Bangladesh Books International, 1981.

64   One of the two Kashmiris, who brought (30 January 1971) an old type Indian aircraft to Lahore, initially welcomed as partisans of the Pakistani cause, set fire to the plane. The event was pulled to every conceivable direction, i. e., as a plan of the Indian Intelligence to "substantiate" a connection between Pakistan and terrorism through a certain (perhaps non-existing) Kashmir National Liberation Front (Lamb, *Kashmir, op. cit.*, pp. 287–293)

or as a plot devised by Pakistan Intelligence to divert attention from the East Bengal crisis. For an Indian view: B. L. Sharma, *Kashmir Awakes*, Delhi, 1971.

65 Walter Isaacson, *Kissinger: a Biography*, New York, etc., Simon and Schuster, 1992, pp. 710, 750–751.

66 Sunanda K. Datta Ray, "The Offered Hand: Kashmir for Bangladesh", *The Statesman*, New Delhi, 2 June 1991.

67 A retired general on the weaknesses of Pakistan's defence in the light of the 1971 defeat: M. Attiqur Rahman, *Our Defence Cause: an Analysis of Pakistan's Past and Future Military Role*, London, White Lion, 1976.

68 For some commentators, India has been a "one-party democracy" for decades since independence: Stanley A. Kochanek, *The Congress Party of India: the Dynamics of One-Party Democracy*, Princeton, New Jersey, Princeton University Press, 1968.

69 For some other writers, the alternative to the Congress Party was Hindu nationalism: Yogandra K. Malik and Vijay Bahadur Singh, *Hindu Nationalism in India: Rise of the Bharatiya Janata Party*, Boulder, Colorado, Westview Press, 1994. Also: Bruce Desmond Graham, *Hindu Nationalism and Indian Politics: the Origins and the Development of the Bharatiya Jana Sangh*, Cambridge, Cambridge University Press, 1990.

70 Bazaz, *op. cit.*, p. 146.

71 A short but enlightening homage to the Kashmiri leader: Riyaz Punjabi, "Kashmir: Abdullah Era (1931–82)", *Journal of Peace Studies*, New Delhi, II/11 (July–August 1995), pp. 8–24.

72 Tanzil-ur Rahman, *Islamization in Pakistan*, Islamabad, Council of Islamic Ideology, 1984; Manzooruddin Ahmed, ed., *Contemporary Pakistan: Politics, Economy, and Society*, Karachi, Royal Book Company, 1982, pp. 27f. ; Charles H. Kennedy, "Islamization and Legal Reform in Pakistan: 1979–1989", *Pacific Affairs*, Vancouver, 63/1 (Spring 1990), pp. 62–77; S. S. Bindra, "Imperatives of Islamization in Pakistan", *New Quest*, Bombay, 76 (July–August 1989), pp. 223–227.

73 Farooq Abdullah, *My Dismissal*, Delhi, Vikas, 1985, especially pp. 7–16.

Chapter 6

Nation-Building

Although the minutiae of the past do not necessarily guide the solutions for the future, no debate on current affairs may go far enough without some references to them. In the case of Indo-Pakistani relations, the central event of partition still casts a long shadow over the politics of the Sub-continent. The combined efforts of the departing imperialist power and the Muslim aristocracy, which resented the loss of an empire to a European country and which chose to believe in the formation of nation-states on the basis of religion, brought about the partition of the Sub-continent. The British contributed their Machiavellian share to the sequel of the Lahore Resolution (1940). While the Muslim League positions showed similarities with the *Hindutva* ideologies, the votaries of the two-nations theory came to power in the newly-carved state of Pakistan, but their counterparts among the Hindus failed to create a similar structure in the rest of India. However, the institutions of both countries are now under stress and need renewal. The Quaid-e Azam's wise forethought that the Muslims and the Hindus ought to cease to be so in the political sense as citizens of the state has been buried with him. While the centralizing drive of successive Indian governments since the 1970s marginalized some minorities and caused the eruption of religious or ethnic tensions, the question for Pakistan is whether nationhood may be built on religion alone. The recurring crises suggest, as in India, that the trend should be towards federalism. Both countries still seem to be going through the process of nation-building.

The year 1947, which marks the sunset of British colonialism, transmitted a legacy of ideas, practices and institutions to both India and Pakistan. After partition and independence, India, where nationalism with secular over-tones triumphed, continued with a competitive and highly participatory parliamentary system and a clearly defined limited role for its military. Pakistan, with Islamic orientation, on the other hand, stifled secular nationalism, and allowed the military to dominate most of its political life. Not only the majority of the Muslims of the Indian Sub-continent stayed back, but Pakistan failed even to absorb the *Mohajirs* who came over, could not prevent the secession of the Muslim Bengalis, and declared (1974) the Ahmadis (Ahmadiyyas) as a non-Muslim minority. The struggle for liberation from foreign rule promoted both nationalism and communalism, and while entrenched Muslim communalism, now referred to as "Islamic fundamentalism", in Pakistan overwhelmed democratic practice as well as secular hopes, India's dominant democratic secular nationalism is under the siege of communalist forces. Although "fundamentalism" has been a recurring phenomenon in the Muslim world, it does not have a uniform pattern[1] because, in addition to the fact that the Sunni-Shi'a divide rules out agreement on some essentials, the fundamentalists do not share common objectives.[2] Apart from the dissimilarities in the function of religion in the two successor states, civil-military relations are also different. The issues of confession of faith and the limits of the military may even be considered as interlinked when one remembers that one of the armed forces received an impetus of Islamization especially during the anti-Soviet struggle against Afghanistan. The Indian army is generally judged as an apolitical force, and Pakistan's politics is largely dominated by the Punjabi military lobby.

The Beginning

From the very beginning, India and Pakistan tried to build their own diverse polities. In spite of its shortcomings, India has been able to build some safeguards into its system, including constitutional and legal provisions covering federalism, secularism and social justice, participatory parliamentary democracy ordaining adult franchise, periodic elections, political parties and representative institutions, and an intellectual milieu embracing a free press. With twenty-five States and seven Union Territories, most of India's federating states are bigger in size and population than about two-thirds of the sovereign entities in the world. Especially after the collapse of the Soviet Union, India stands as the most heterogeneous federal nation. There are eight major religious communities, the Hindus being the largest (82.7%), followed by the Muslims (11.8%), Christians (2.63%), Sikhs (2%), Buddhists (0.7%), Jains (0.4%), Zoroastrians (0.3%) and Jews (0.1%). The Hindus constitute the majority or plurality everywhere except Kashmir and in some southern islands. Nevertheless, there are more Muslims in India than in Iran, Iraq, Saudi Arabia, Sudan and Syria put together. Problems concerning coexistence emerge among the Hindus, Muslims, Sikhs and Christians. While the lists of the total number of languages and dialects vary from one printed source to another, there are 15 major languages, led by Hindi (264.1 million), followed by Telugu (54.2 m.), Bengali (51.5 m.), Marathi (49.6 m.), etc.

Jawaharlal Nehru of India, reflecting the great synthesis, was a leader of national consensus on the values of democracy, secularism, federalism, social justice and independent foreign policy. Educated in those norms, he practised, preached and moulded public opinion, first as one of the central figures of a progressive national movement for more than four decades (from the 1920s) and then as a nation-builder (1947–64). He was no longer alive when the first Indian satellite was put into orbit around the Earth.[3] But when he was no more, modern complexes had transformed the face of ancient India, in a historically short period, placing it among the first ten industrially developed countries.

The circumstances under which Pakistan came into existence forced the country's polity to link national with religious identity. Constituting only a minority in prepartition India, part of the leadership of the Indian Muslims chose to assert the Islamic identity and eventually politicize Islam, rather than keeping religion in the private sphere.[4] Those who propounded Muslim consolidation as a kind of supra-class unity eulogized an Islamic state as a panacea for social ills. Such an appraisal undermines the role of the Muslim landlords who saw in the separation of the Muslim community a means of protecting their own interests against Hindu and Sikh competition.[5] Nevertheless, Pakistan was the only modern state created exclusively in the name of Islam.[6] The demand for a separate homeland based on Islam was a unique event in contemporary history. On 14 August 1947, the last Friday of the holy month of Ramadan, Jinnah assumed the office of Governor-General of Pakistan, and the cabinet was sworn in. One of the most populous Muslim states had come into existence. Only two days before, the Constituent Assembly resolved that he should be addressed as the 'Quaid-e Azam' (the Great Founder).

It had always been known that partition would leave minorities on both sides. Curiously enough, the creator of Pakistan opted for a secular society. The Quaid-e Azam had stated in early 1941 at the Madras session of the Muslim League that no government would succeed without creating security and confidence in the minorities if its policy is tyrannical over them.[7] His Presidential Address at the Constituent Assembly on 11 August 1947 included the following thoughts: "You are free to go to your temples...to your mosques or any other places of worship in the State of Pakistan. You may belong to any religion or caste or creed—that has nothing to do with the business of the State...[W]e are all citizens and equal citizens of one State...[I]n course of time, Hindus would cease to be Hindus, and Muslims would cease to be Muslims, not in the religious sense, because that is the personal faith of each individual, but in the political sense, as citizens of the state".[8] This was "a ray of hope".[9] Although such affirmations might have caused the eyebrows of some of the listeners to be raised, Jinnah meant to begin to work in that spirit and hoped that the alienations between the majority and the minority communities would vanish. A man who had fought for an Islamic state was impressing upon the members of the Constituent Assembly and the citizens the virtues of secularism.

But a great holocaust followed on both sides of the partition line. Had the original date for the transfer of power (1 June 1948) been allowed to stand, both governments could organize their administrative machinery for the maintenance of law and order better, and the terrible massacres, at least in the scale that they did assume, could have been avoided. H. S. Suhrawardy, who happened to be the Chief Minister of Bengal at the time of partition, accepted Gandhi's invitation to resist discord in Calcutta, his stronghold, and left East Bengal to Khwaja Nazimuddin, who came from Dacca. Thanks to the personalities, popular images and the efforts of these two 'sons of the soil', Bengal and Calcutta were spared the horrors of Punjab. When the holocaust was over, there were still minorities in Pakistan: the Hindus, the largest number outside India; Christians,[10] abound in Portuguese surnames; Parsis, the descendants of small bands of refugees who left Persia after the collapse of the Sassanid dynasty; and Buddhists, who constituted the majority in the Chittagong Hill Tracts (now in Bangladesh).[11]

All of Pakistan received 23% of the territory and 19% of the population of colonial India.[12] Pakistan was made up of two wings, the western part divided into Punjab, Sindh, Baluchistan and the North-West Frontier Province (NWFP). The last three had relatively small populations, and the Hindu minority was numerically weak and scattered all over the provinces. But in Punjab, also in the west, and in Bengal in the east, the non-Muslims formed over 40% of the population. While the NWFP in the west was the smallest, the neighbouring Punjab Province, or its western part that fell to Pakistan, was the largest (205,000 sq. km.). The ethnic and cultural population fell roughly into these four geographical units. These provincial groups now spill over the borders so that there are more Pathans in Karachi than in Peshawar or more Baluchis in Sindh than in Baluchistan. Besides these four provincial peoples, there was a fifth group, the *Mohajirs* or the refugees who came over from India in 1947. Arriving mostly from the Urdu-speaking Muslim areas of India such as Delhi, Uttar Pradesh and Bihar or from the Gujarati-speaking parts of Bombay and Kathiawar, the *Mohajirs* had "no provincial bias" and were "more devoted to the Pakistan ideology".[13]

India—Problems of Pluralism

Sometimes characterized as the "world's largest democracy", a "bourgeois republic", "a welfare state" or with some other label, India is committed, in the more than five decades of its existence, to the democratic form of government. In terms of socio-ethnic dimensions, the country is composed of large segments of religion, language and caste, and within the socio-economic context, it oscillated, in the past, between an Indian brand of "socialism" and the preferences of powerful new industrialists. As a compulsion of its cultural heritage, the Indian society has to show a deep sense of commitment to pluralism. Within the Indian context, fundamentalism denotes an attitude to stick to the scriptures in their puritan form, at times accompanied by force to preserve one's ideals.[14] Communalism implies prejudice against another group with the intention to marginalize, subjugate or eliminate it.

The most salient aspect of the social problem in India is communalism, the point at issue between the Hindus and the Muslims. At the base of the socio-economic structure, however, is the caste system, made up of several rigid concentric circles subject to change, however, due to industrialization and urban growth. This subsection aims to evaluate the consequences of the communalist phenomenon on Indian politics.

Communalism[15] is not adherence to a certain religion or an entanglement with a religious group; it does not uphold conservative values, not even an unscientific defence of bigotry. It is not a matter of piety, nor devotion to moral ends. It is a convenient abuse of religion, or perception of other communities as opponents, using a religious community against others to acquire or enhance power and wealth. It is against secularism and democracy. Nehru once described it as an Indian version of fascism. As the Indian Muslim poet Muhammad Iqbal said, *"Juda ho deen siyasat se to reh jaati hai changezi"* (If values be divorced from politics, tyranny is inevitable").[16] Although an open democratic order, as in India, allows all or almost all views to be defended and organized, thereby laying the masses open to undemocratic and segregative forces as well, the invigoration of communalism is likely only with the backing of certain political circles. To prevent a challenge to inter-communal harmony, and therefore to national identity, of which secular culture is a foundation stone, is a worthy ordeal as much as to create a genuine democracy is a great experiment.

Many Indians describe their administration to be *"par excellence* a secular state".[17] For them, secularism is not a concept to which India was a stranger in the course of their long and chequered history. It is in accord with the best traditions of the culture of the soil. The caravan of secularism (and democracy) has made, indeed, progress for quite some time. Asoka was a Buddhist but there was no distinction between Buddhists and others. Akbar was a Muslim but Hindus and Muslims held the highest civil and military offices in the state without distinction. To characterize Asoka and Akbar as strictly secular rulers would be a misnomer, but it would not be wrong to describe them as accommodative of cultural diversities while running the administration of the state.

After independence, the Indian leaders proclaimed that the edifice of the Indian state would be raised on the principle of secularism. There were some differences of perspective among them, however, over what secularism meant in the Indian context. Gandhi equated constitutional phraseology only to *sarva dharma shambhava* (equal treatment of all religions). He was tolerant because of his Hinduism, not in spite of it. He possessed a dauntless courage based on faith in human goodness. Jinnah called him "a Hindu leader", but he fell prey to the bullet of a Hindu while proceeding to the prayer meeting where every evening the song *"Ishwar Allah tere naam, sab ko sammati de Bhagwan"* (Both Ishwar and Allah are your names, may the Lord give auspicious harmony to all) was sung. Nehru wanted secularism to be an ideology for the Constitution and helped to promote the kind of transformation that Europe had undergone.[18] He severely criticized the anti-secular trend in his own party and strongly attacked the Jan Sangh as a reactionary grouping. He wrote several letters to the Chief Ministers not to associate themselves with any religious ritual in their official capacity. But the Jabalpur riots (1961) shook him, and he later associated secularism in India with equal distance from all religions.[19]

Two competing political tendencies, the Hindu Mahasabha on the Hindu side and the Muslim League on the Muslim side, contested the "composite culture" theory of the Indian National Congress leaders. When the Muslim League, which insisted until independence to be the sole spokesman of all the Muslims disappeared from the Indian scene, Maulana Abul Kalam Azad, who believed that there was "no greater hindrance than narrow-mindedness",[20] convened (1948) the Lucknow meeting of the Muslims, which decided that henceforth there would be no exclusive Muslim political party in India.[21] Since then, the Muslims formed various regional and national organizations, none of which was an exclusive Muslim political party only for their own co-religionists. Azad refused to contest from Rampur, a Muslim majority constituency, in the 1952 elections stating that he could not represent the Muslims only. The Indian Muslims have shown great faith in the Constitution of the country.

The Indian Constitution[22] carefully balanced, on paper, the rights of the individual in regard to religion and the authority of the state to exercise its regulatory power in the larger interests of the community. There is no established state religion, and citizenship is unrelated to the faith of the individual (Articles 5–7). Everyone is equally entitled to freedom of conscience and the right to freely profess, practice and propagate his or her religion. Every religious denomination has the right to maintain institutions for religious purposes and to manage its own affairs. No one may be compelled to pay taxes for the promotion of any religion. No religious instruction may be provided wholly out of state funds (Articles 25–28). The 42nd Amendment of the Constitution (1976) includes the word "secular" in the Preamble.[23] According to the Constitution, the state, which is a political association concerned only with the social relations between its citizens, belongs to them all. These provisions enshrined a befitting pledge to India's minorities for which the country's greatest son had laid down his life. The Muslims, who were satisfied with these provisions, made every effort to contribute their share to the development of the society at large.

However, secularism is not so much a matter of state policy; it is more a frame of mind and an attitude in everyday life. Secularism may be a target concept; secularization, on the other hand, is a process. Secularism demands unfaltering belief in the "god of knowledge". It accepts no authority but that of nature, adopts no methods but those of science, and respects no rule but that of conscience.[24] It believes in undivided guidance in the torch of secular truth which provides lasting "illumination in the areas of darkness".[25] The Indian tradition is certainly helpful for the working of democracy and a secular state with a stress on tolerance, separation of political and religious functions, and the absence of an organized church for the majority community. But some members of the present generation find themselves ground between two stones: a famine of faith posing as secularism on the one hand, and communalism masquerading as religion on the other. Indian democracy, even taken with its faults, avoided so far the most blatant abuses of Pakistan. But narcissistic comparisons should not prevent critical self-examination.

The rise of communalism in India necessitates a short reassessment of the working of the political system. Not only communal riots between the Hindus and the Muslims increased rapidly during the recent decades, police atrocities, established by several official inquiry commissions, started to occur beginning with the seventies. Muslim families were burnt alive in their homes or shops. Although Hindus were also assaulted, the main victims were Muslims.[26] Because of its oceanic range, Hinduism is often portrayed as a creed that cannot be communalized. It is described as *anadi* (without foundation), *arupi* (without form), and *nirbandha* (without ties).

The view that Hinduism, in contrast to Islam, is naturally oriented towards secularism overlooks some similarities easily observable in the "Rashtriya Swayamsewak Sangh" (RSS) and the Jamaat-e Islami Hind (JIH), representing some Hindu and Islamic groups respectively.[27] The RSS identifies the nation with the Hindu society and proclaims that only the Hindu has been living there as the child of the soil.[28] The RSS is opposed to a secular state and composite culture. Hindu *rashtra* (nation) embraces all the people whose culture bloomed in greater India from the Himalayas to the southern seas. Its core is *Hindutva*. The rest are aliens, traitors or second-class citizens. The RSS, which places singular emphasis on morality derived from Hindu values, includes the whole Sangh Parivar or all political, cultural, student and labour organizations. It remained passive for a few years after Gandhi's assassination but started (1951) to support Jan Sangh as its political front, and later sided with Janata (1977) and the Bharatiya Janata (1984).

Similarly, the Jamaat-e Islami, founded (1941) by Maulana Maudoodi, believes in the supremacy of Islam and Muslims against all others as well as in the establishment of an Islamic state. After partition, the Jamaat was divided into two organizations, one for Pakistan and the other for India. The headquarters of the Jamaat-e Islami Hind (JIH) was shifted to Delhi. For years, communally inclined publications on both sides built tensions, provocateurs preyed on sensibilities, and the militants of the opposing groups clashed. Forced by circumstances, the RSS and the JIH eventually joined forces to struggle against the common enemy—secular and rational thinking. Communalism, used by the political parties of India to achieve their own political goals, caused alienation in the society. Such trends were bound to generate explosive repercussions in Kashmir.

The Babri Masjid-Ramjanambhoomi episode in Ayodhya[29] and the demolition of the historic mosque (6 December 1992) on "Black Day" (*Swabhiman Divas*) continue to cast a "long, menacing shadow over Indian polity".[30] It was a criminal act, a defiant violation of the court, a tragedy that brought to mind Gandhi's assassination. The Muslims were terribly alienated on this score.[31] "Ayodhya", as the name indicates, was a place of "no war". While the perpetrators felt emboldened to flaunt it as a step towards *Hindutva*[32] and Hindu *rashtra*, the non-communal parties, in contrast to the condemnation of the communal mind in one voice after that "Black Evening" of 30 January 1948, used the crime to abuse their rivals instead of asserting secularism and democracy so vital for India as a nation. It was an attack on the nation itself rather than only on the Muslim community.

Some Hindus believe that the Moghul Emperor Babur, who never visited Ayodhya, raised a Ram or Vishnu temple to the ground to build the Babri Masjid on its place. Ayodhya has about 6,000 temples, whose *pandas* (Hindu priest) claim that theirs is the original Ramjanam temple. There is even doubt that the present Ayodhya is the same city of the Ramayan era. Neither several old classics mention that a temple there was destroyed to build a mosque, nor any Hindu-Muslim dispute occurred over it for so many centuries after the construction of the Babri Masjid, until very recently. No matter what had actually happened in history, all places of worship were to stay intact as India had inherited them on Independence Day.

In a midnight operation in the year 1949, a group of people, silencing the guard, put Hindu idols inside the mosque, which remained closed for thirty-five years (1951–86) under court orders. Guru Golwalkar, whose name as the *Sarsanhchalak* of the RSS came into prominence with the murder of Gandhi, instructed his followers that India was exclusively a Hindu nation, and "Vishwa Hindu Parishad" (VHP), founded in 1964, championed the demand that the lock be opened for use of the building by Hindu worshippers. Several *Dharm Sansads* (Religious Parliament) declared the demolition of the mosque. While some top executives assured the nation that the Babri Masjid would not be destroyed but a Ram Temple would be built at Ayodhya, thousands of Shiv Sena[33] activists arrived, and Sang Parivar organizers divided the city into sectors to plan and supervise the expected operation. While the protest rally of the Babri Masjid Action Committee (BMAC), supposedly to represent Muslim leadership but actually comprised of the equally communal-minded individuals, was fired at by the state police, the Kar Sevak "volunteers" rehearsed the method of breaking on nearby rocks as an exercise for dismantling the mosque. When the demolition commenced, part of the mob was also attacking twenty-three other mosques and Muslim houses killing about 2,000 people. By late afternoon, the Babri Masjid was no more.

The Ayodhya episode, standing at the apex of a hate complex, also assaulted the immemorial Indian legacy, detaching itself from the national consensus and shaking the foundations of the secular democratic motherland. Led astray by bigots and swashbucklers, the power-seekers behind the tragedy wounded India's open society while intimidating its Muslim citizens. The communalist elements, and together with them, the country to a certain extent, are passing through a decade of aggressiveness. While there may be misperceptions in the different segments of any pluralist society, more so in India's extremely complex pattern, enlightened leadership is accountable for correct policies and their appropriate application. The Muslims of India are also expected to play a stabilizing, and not a belligerent, role in bolstering the composite culture, from which millions of Hindus and Muslims will benefit. The Muslim priority should be to help sustain a democratic and secular culture rather than reaching the throats of Hindu communalists for the sake of a non-functioning mosque.

To protect the religious minorities and to make recommendations to ensure effective enforcement of laws and safeguards, the Parliament of India passed (1992) the National Commission for Minorities Act, which reconstituted the Minorities Commission set up a decade and a half ago, both with the mandate to review measures and submit annual reports. The Commission for Linguistic Minorities investigates into matters relating to the safeguards for linguistic groups. A National Minorities Development and Financial Corporation was also set up to provide economic and developmental activities for the benefit of backward sections among the minorities. The Ministry of Welfare shouldered the administration of legislation for the *wakfs* (Muslim pious organizations), the central council of which established the Maulana Azad Education Foundation to promote education for the backward sections of the Muslim minority. What remains is the dedicated implementation of these objectives.

Indian intellectuals frequently call for a deep analysis of secularism, enshrined in the Constitution and united action against communalism and in favour of a reconstruction of an ideology of nation-building and a secular state.[34] It falls on the contemporary Indian compatriots, Hindu and Muslim, to evolve serious strategy to defend and strengthen secularism and complete Nehru's great vision. Narasimha Rao, the Prime Minister during the Ayodhya affair, was not the progenitor of the problem, but the end recipient of the daunting challenge which demands a united approach. Secularism is not something which is good if it delivers the minority vote but something to be shunned if it does not. If India is the largest democracy, it should rest on freedom, equality and rights, all three asserting the sovereignty of the people. Every citizen cannot practice his or her religion unless the society is committed to the norm of freedom. The notion of *sarva dharma sambhava* will not carry much weight if the nation does not uphold equality. The state is also expected not to discriminate against any religious community or bestow privileges on one or the other. A return to the Gandhi-Nehru line should be: "We don't just tolerate other faiths, *hum sweekar kartay hain* (we welcome them)".[35]

India—Social and Economic Transformation

Feudalism persisted in India until the mid-19th century, postponing the challenge of a socio-economic transformation after independence. The Objectives Resolution, conveyed into the gracefully-phrased Preamble of the Constitution, sanctioned development and socio-economic justice as well as liberty. Population, poverty and the future of India were very closely interlinked.[36] Although there has been tremendous increase in production and services since India's independence, per capita growth is far from being impressive. There were millions unemployed, and many more millions under-employed. The state of malnutrition, poor shelter, and insufficient health services were terrifying. Yet, there was no planning to meet the fearful growth of the birth rate or any way to motivate the people to voluntarily accept a smaller family norm.

India, which possessed a railway system spanning the length and breadth of the country as the only silver lining when British rule ended, developed a competitive industrial base in the last half century. The founding fathers immediately proceeded to establish cement, steel, power and heavy engineering plants. Indian economic development came a long way from this beginning. In addition to basic industries, India progressed in computer software, nuclear power and space technology. It looks forward to become the fourth largest economy in the world in two decades.

With only a few private industries, like the Tata steel plant, set up prior to independence, India set off as a planned economy. Consequently, Bharat Heavy Electrical Limited, Indian Oil Corporation, National Thermal Power Corporation, and the Steel Authority of India Limited flourished as state-owned companies. The First 5-Year Plan (1951–56) laid stress on agriculture, with the condition that 44% of total investment allocated to it was used to develop industry in later years. Since Pakistan inherited one-fifth of the population but about a quarter of food supply of the Sub-continent, the result was shortage of food for India. Moreover, while nine-tenths of the acreage under jute and nearly three-quarters of that under cotton went to Pakistan, almost all of the jute and cotton mills remained in India. To supply the necessary raw materials for them, lands in Assam, Bengal and Bihar had to be converted for jute and cotton crops. The First Plan was little more than a collective of ongoing projects, but in terms of achievement, it was the most successful, the country exceeding the target for food production and attaining all the other economic targets. The Second and the Third Plans aimed to develop the basic industries fundamental to furthering economic growth.

Nehru had advocated since the early 1930s the nationalization of services in order to diminish the restraint on the poor. Even prior to independence, a Congress appropriate committee made a timely distinction between enforceable civil rights and socio-economic rights that needed new legislation. Both concepts, which became Fundamental Rights and Directive Principles of State Policy adopted by the Constituent Assembly, covered the right to work, equal pay for equal work to men and women, adequate wages, free and compulsory education, fair distribution of resources, and uplifting of the poorer sections of the population. These principles, while siding with the down-trodden lower orders, were necessarily against the *Jagirdars*,[37] *Mirasdars*,[38] and the *Zamindars*,[39] and the usurers known by different names like the *Banias, Chetties* or *Sahukars*.

Hitherto dispossessed groups, led by newly-emerging leaders, inevitably came face to face with the threatened vested interests, who generally exhibit remarkable capacity to survive by adapting to changing contingencies. Although India seemed well on the way to achieving an economic take-off by the end of the third five-year plan (1965), the momentum of growth was broken within a couple of years. According to some commentators, the decisive cause of economic stagnation after 1966 was political. The stratum consisting of small manufacturers, traders, market-oriented proprietors and similar self-employed groups, which benefited from economic stagnation and therefore had a vested interest in its perpetuation, had risen to dominance.[40] Instead of the "parasitic nature" of these intermediate groups, which held back the "wheel of history", the rise of the middle class would involve a break with the pattern of industrialization. In spite of economic growth, motivated by the "invisible hand" of the free market system balanced with rational central planning, the expected fair distribution did not generate. The nation, getting more and more populous, was still divided into the majority poor primarily consisting of the destitutes, unemployed, lower service men, poor tillers of the soil, and the urban workers on the one hand, and the few rich encompassing the leading capital owners, rural landlords, middle bourgeoisie, well-to-do commercial people and the highest professionals, on the other. In spite of some mobility, the misery of the bulk of the poor still seemed to be an unalterable destiny (*karma*). The removal of poverty, amidst rising population, remains as the number one item on the country's agenda. Rating perhaps sixth in the global count for overall industrial production but figuring well over 100th in terms of per capita income, the contradiction of growth and poverty continued to coexist. Although this fact may be partly due to population explosion, socio-economic inequality in India has a long heritage, sanctified by the rigid caste structure distributing professions by the accident of birth. All responsible Indian leaders revolted against this side of the heritage. While an ancient society is being transformed into a modern polity, the contradiction is nevertheless visible. Every upsurge in national standards continues to offer unequal benefits to the entrenched haves at the expense of the lower castes and classes.

The precarious steering of the political course between the dominant classes, whose support many politicians need for survival, and the promises made to the needy electorate, without whose vote no government can last, has so far failed to bring the socio-economic transformation drive to the level envisaged in the early independence decade. The off-and-on alliances of parts of the upper half of society with the odds and ends of groups such as the communalists only depreciate efforts of nation-building.

Pakistan—Political Pandemonium

Pakistan faced almost insurmountable problems since its very inception. It is often repeated that the new Government of Pakistan began to function in "hastily improvised shacks, without records, without furniture, and even without paper or pencils".[41] The resources of the young country, which lacked an administrative core, were scanty. Karachi, then a little bit more than a fishermen's town, had to house the capital of the new nation, divided into two sections, East Pakistan comprising about one-seventh of the area but four-sevenths of the population while West Pakistan, separated from the former by a distance of close to 1,600 km., embracing six-sevenths of the area on which only three-sevenths of the population lived. Bengal in the east and Punjab in the west, the most populous provinces, were themselves partitioned, the former having lost its chief port Calcutta, and the latter deprived of the water headworks. Not only the entrepreneurial Hindus and Sikhs migrated *en masse*, but also the country, which yet lacked capital and technical know how, had to cope with millions of Muslim refugees from India. Presently, nearly all of Pakistan's 1.5 million Hindus reside in the province of Sindh, where they constitute just over 7% of the total population. In Sindh's south-eastern district of Thar Parkar, the Hindus account for a little over one-third of the local population.[42] A few Hindu *banjas* (mainly traders or trading communities) are to be found in Karachi.

Almost 5% of Pakistan's population are now non-Muslims, the Christians being the largest single group (over 1.5%). Apart from the Hindus and the Ahmadis (1.4–3.2%), a sprinkling of Jews, Sikhs and Parsis form the rest. The Christians, who stayed behind after partition, live in the country's largest province, Punjab. Most of them working as agricultural and construction workers, some of their churches in Pakistan were destroyed after the Babri Masjid affair in India.[43] Fierce riots against the Ahmadis, who get their name from the founder of their sect, do not believe in the finality of the Prophethood of Muhammad.[44] In 1974, Pakistan's Parliament excluded from the fold of Islam all those who do not believe in the absolute and unqualified "Finality of the Prophethood of Muhammad".[45] Under Pakistan's Constitution, the highest administrative posts (of President, Prime Minister, Commander of the Armed Forces, and provincial governors) are reserved for Muslims alone. The laws of witness (*qanoon-e shahadat*) consider the evidence of the non-Muslims (and women of all religions) of less value than that of the Muslim males.

Most of Pakistan's political life was replete with civil disobedience movements, processions, strike calls, accusations of rigged elections, frequent curfews, states of emergencies, military coups, indefinite postponement of elections, bans on political activity, "taming of parties", dismissals of cabinets, reinforcements of martial law, censorship, detentions, house arrests, murder of opponents, executions, farcical referendums, electoral frauds, boycott of elections, and the pursuit of bringing the country into conformity with the *shari'a* law.

In the space of a year, Pakistan had to face some hard facts, such as providing for close to ten million refugees, fighting a war in Kashmir, and trying to go forth without the father of the country. Its very continuance was "something of a miracle".[46] Jinnah, the nation's charismatic leader and the first Governor General, died only a little over a year after independence, and the tenure of the able Prime Minister Liaquat Ali Khan (a *Mohajir*) was cut short by assassination three years later. After their departure there was a vacuum in the Pakistan polity. During the first decade (1947–58), Pakistan had one commander-in-chief but seven prime ministers.[47] No nationwide elections on the basis of universal adult suffrage were held in the first twenty-three years of its existence. Several governments established their legitimacy, but none could maintain it for more than a brief period. Until the year 2000, it had twenty-one executive heads of government, the majority of whom were dismissed from office. By the time the Eighth Amendment to the Constitution (Article 58/b/2), which gave absolute power to the president to dismiss any elected government, was repealed (1997) by Nawaz Sharif, it was already used to throttle four elected governments. Prime Minister Sharif, in his second term as well, could not escape the same fate even after his massive mandate and show of strength for the repeal.

Political instability followed almost until the world reached the threshold of the next century. Pakistan had four constitutions within a quarter of a century, initially creating five provinces, later reduced to two, but rearranged as five again following the secession of the eastern wing. The basic governmental structure oscillated between parliamentary and presidential practices as well as between unicameral and bicameral systems. The parliament was closed down several times, accompanied by frequent martial laws and dictators.[48] There were three wars with India, and a civil war with the Muslim Bengalis. Despite unity during the Pakistan movement (1940–47), "the nascent state could not come to terms with the problems of ethno-nationalism".[49]

Constitution-making was uncommonly delayed. The first Constituent Assembly, outliving its five-year term, failed to produce a constitution, and the second Constituent Assembly's Constitution of 1956 was abrogated (1958) by Governor General Iskandar Mirza, who had just taken the oath of defending it. The 1962 Constitution was likewise shelved by the Sandhurst-trained General Ayub Khan. Only the military defeat that caused the secession of East Bengal discredited the dictatorship of General Agha Muhammad Yahya Khan opening the way to the democratic Constitution of 1973. Pakistan's identity crisis, even after the secession of East Bengal, has been severe. The continuous search for national integration is clearly related to the crisis of identity.

While the first Constituent Assembly amalgamated the four provinces of West Pakistan into a single unit, Yahya Khan revived the old federative pattern, and replaced Ayup Khan's presidential system and indirect elections with a parliamentary form of government and direct elections with seats reserved for provinces on a population basis. The Awami League, led by Mujibur Rahman, having secured nearly all the seats from East Bengal, proved strong enough to form an absolute majority in the central legislature in the first ever general elections of late 1970.[50] The opposition of Zulfikar Ali Bhutto's "socialist-leaning" PPP[51] to this idea led to arrests, border clashes, war and the emergence of independent Bangladesh.[52]

The late 1960s witnessed the birth of the Organization of the Islamic Conference (OIC), and the beginning of the 1970s saw the sudden outburst in crude oil prices. When Bhutto assumed office, the manpower-starved oil-rich countries found a ready source of supply of Muslim workers from Pakistan, the militarily-weak sheikhdoms found sufficiently-trained armed forces, and Colonel M.-al Gaddafi as well as King Faisal thought that Pakistan could build nuclear capability with some financial assistance. The year 1971 was a fateful year for Pakistan. The military government unleashed its well-equipped army, eventually defeated lock, stock and barrel, on the armed forces and the people of East Bengal, causing the death of about three million inhabitants and the migration of about ten million more.[53] The new Constitution (1973), democratic in outlook, declared Islam as the religion of the state, for the first time. The Qur'an and the teachings of Islamiyat became compulsory for the Muslim citizens, and bringing the existing laws in conformity with the injunctions of the Qur'an and the Sunnah an Islamic duty. The learning of Arabic was encouraged while the Islamic Council and an Advisory Council of Islamic Ideology were constituted. Pakistan hosted the second Islamic Summit Conference (Lahore, 1974), which established an international Islamic Bank, a proposal submitted by Pakistan. Friday instead of Sunday became the weekly holiday, and the consumption of alcohol and gambling as well as night shows and horse racing were banned. The hanging of Bhutto, the 'Quaid-e Awam' (or the Popular Leader) as he styled himself, removed from power by a military coup (5 July 1977)), was an event unparalleled in the modern history of the Sub-continent.

While General Muhammad Zia-ul Haq's administration publicized the belief that his *Nizam-e Mustafa* plan of action was different from the Islamization programmes of the previous governments,[54] some commentators seemed convinced that his Islamic legal reforms have had only a minor impact on the corpus of Pakistan's legal system.[55] The thin veneer of westernization, characteristic of the Pakistani elite, wore out, and with the new generations dominating political discourse, the 'nativization' of the country's politics necessarily involved more Islamization.[56] Ayub was a 'brown Englishman', and Zia appeared to be more rooted in his native culture.[57] Perhaps the first measure under Zia toward Islamization was the introduction of separate electorates as the basis of the future elections, expecting voters belonging to different religious persuasions to exercise their franchise only for their own candidates. Soon, *khatt-e Imam* (Khomeini line of thinking) got the upper hand.

Eventually, directives were issued to government departments for *namaz* (prayers) during office hours, to be led by departmental heads. All business centres were obliged to close for Friday prayers. A committee was set to revive the Islamic institutions of *zakat* (poor tax) and *ushr* (agricultural tax).[58] In addition to present courts, *shari'a* benches were created, whose decisions could not be challenged in any other court.[59] *Hudud* punishments were introduced for drinking, theft, dacoity, and adultery.[60] Zia discouraged co-education but encouraged *chadar* (closed garments) for women. A *Shari'a* Faculty was established at the Quaid-e Azam University in Islamabad, the Council of Islamic Ideology was empowered to make recommendations as to the measures for bringing existing laws into conformity with the Qur'an and the *Sunnah* (the sacred tradition in rule or custom), and the Islamic Research Institute was entrusted with the task of conducting research in Islam.[61] Steps were taken to revise textbooks and curricula. The poor flocked to the *madrasas* (religious schools) which gave them food and shelter. The television and radio were ordered to redesign their programmes according to the Islamic teachings. With the echo of the Iranian outcry of *Musalman-e Pakbaz* the unwanted Muslims were eliminated, and persons known for their strong commitment to an Islamic order were appointed to key government positions. Zia promulgated (15 June 1988) an Ordinance which made the *Shari'a* the supreme law of the land.[62] He exhausted all of his political cards, including Islam, to legitimize his rule. Had he lived, he would have been confronted by an "extremely hostile opposition".[63] While some criticized him severely for being antidemocratic, reactionary and discriminatory to women, some *Islampasands* found what he did as too little. The mysterious crash that killed him (17 August 1988) perhaps gave him an "honourable" exit.[64]

General Zia-ul Haq's regime had lasted very long (1977–88) without much challenge to its authority, except the launching (1981) of the Movement for the Restoration of Democracy (MRD). Perhaps more time must elapse before his place in the country's history can be more objectively assessed. He might have moved Pakistan to a prominence desired by some of the earlier leaders, but he is now remembered as the man who illegally seized power, and after more than a decade of repressive rule, left behind unemployment, hunger, discrimination, corruption, drugs, debt and empty Islamic rhetoric.[65] Although the transfer of power to elected representatives put Islamization on a low key, no political party could ignore that concept during the 1988 election. Every leading party had its own "pocket Maulvi" as an ally. Everyone carrying with it an Islamic label, Benazir Bhutto's PPP had Jamiat-ul Ulama-e Islam, and the Muslim League had Jamaat-e Islami.[66] One of the first things that Benazir, the long-time exiled leader of the PPP and who wanted to keep her father's legacy alive, did was to perform *umrah* (the lesser pilgrimage to Mecca). She naturally upheld (January 1989) the governmental ban on Salman Rushdie's *Satanic Verses*. Her administration did neither dismantle the *shari'a* courts, nor rescind the *hudud* ordinances, nor curb the authority of the Council of Islamic Ideology.

No government could take backward steps from the Islamization drive. The end result was the birth of various umbrella organizations for the major sects and groups, namely, the Sipahi-e Sahaba for the Sunnis and the Tahrik-e Jaffria for the Shi'a. When a group of *ulama* had approached Quaid-e Azam asking him to enforce the *shari'a*, he reportedly replied: "Whose *shari'a*? Hanafi's? Hanbali's? Shafaie's? Maliki's?"[67] Pakistan, thus, became a safe haven for many radical Islamic groups in the world, and turned into a violent society. The premises of the *madrasas* are now centres of *jehad* to where arms and ammunition flow freely, and private armies settle scores in the name of Islam.

There were times when armed clashes occurred between supporters of competing political forces, and the country seemed to be on the verge of civil war. Following in the footsteps of the Taliban, students from the religious schools in the tribal areas of the frontier go around raiding houses and burning television sets "to purge the society" of what they brand as un-Islamic practices.[68] The Government of Pakistan succumbed to the demands of the Tahrik-e Nifaz-e Shari'a-e Muhammadi (TNSM) with the enactment of the Shari'a Nizam-e Adl Regulation (1999) in Malakand. The Chief Minister (Sardar Mehtab Ahmad Khan) reportedly said: "This is a historic step with far-reaching significance. The day is not far when *inshallah* the people of the area will achieve the distinction of guiding Pakistan and the whole Islamic world in the enforcement of the *shari'a*".[69]

Benazir Bhutto,[70] the daughter of the executed prime minister, twice (1988–90, 1993–96) served as the chief executive and dismissed on both occasions, was frequently accused of corruption and finally found guilty of embezzlement of funds. While Nawaz Sharif was holding supreme executive authority after the mid-term general election in 1997, which some authors defined as a "smooth transfer of power" the country had never witnessed before,[71] and while Pakistan was looking forward to the next National Assembly and presidential elections in 2002, General Parwaz (Pervez) Musharraf, Chief of Staff, usurped power (1999) but promised a return to civilian rule—without a fixed date, however.[72] Sharif had returned to power with a mandate big enough to strike down the controversal Article 58/2/b and to refuse to revive the Council for Defence and National Security, thereby depriving the armed forces of direct leverage they had thus far enjoyed, the absence of such mechanisms to change corrupt governments increased the danger of extra-constitutional intervention.

Since independence, Pakistan meant Punjab, first and foremost. The Punjabis were in all the key positions, and politicians from that province dominated the country's polity. Benefiting from the line of reasoning that India never reconciled itself to the idea of partition, the leaders of the armed forces, who are also mostly Punjabis or in accord with them, possess the state. They have accumulated more authority in the absence of charismatic civilian leaders, whose public images are often blended with corruption as well as failure. They hanged Zulfikar Ali Bhutto, who had given Pakistan a sort of legitimate government. Many of them argued that democracy did not suit Pakistan, and engineered one *coup d'état* after another. Calling the shots under civilian or military governments, the armed forces formulated the policy towards the neighbours and the great powers. They endorsed the repetition of the Afghan experience in Jammu and Kashmir. Pakistan's social fabric is giving way because of the country's present connection with the Afghan *Mujahideen*, whose camps are training grounds for Islamic zealots. In response to the excessive "Punjabization" of Pakistani politics, and also attracted by the Pathan Taliban, the Pushtu people of Pakistan may encourage the formation of "greater Afghanistan". If their interest is channeled towards an independent state for the Pathans, the issue of "greater Baluchistan" may also come up, as the *Mohajir* demand a separate province.

The Pushtunistan (Pakhtunistan) movement (NWFP) was dormant[73] while the Sindh and the Baluch movements rose over time. Their rise or fall are related to the domestic and international factors. Even when the new Islamic state was to be formed in 1947, the Pushtun, Sindhi and the Baluchi elites pursued the goal of establishing their own autonomous states. Realizing a successful boycott campaign against the special referendum held by the British, the Pathans in the north-west evidently favoured the formation of their own state. The hope of a synthesis between liberal nationalism and the Islamic *umma,* which had characterized the state ideology of Pakistan at the beginning of partition, broke down, to be restructured under Ayub Khan in the form of a new one-unit and one-official language entity called West Pakistan, now to adhere to a "Basic Democracy" system[74] and a pro-Western foreign policy. The elite of the non-Punjabi peoples, who could not find their due share even in this new system, interpreted the nation-building efforts of the military-bureaucratic leadership as domestic colonialism. The traditional landed elite in the north-west was left outside political power, the rich agricultural land of Sindh was partially distributed among the Punjabi senior officials, and Baluchistan's natural gas went to the other provinces as well. Not only the Pushtun, Sindhi and the Baluchi elites, but also Ayub Khan himself eventually based his own political autobiography on the trial-and-error belief that the developing countries needed Western friends, not masters.[75]

Zulfikar Ali Bhutto's policy of "Islamic socialist community"[76] and sharing of power with other ethnic elites, designed to meet the challenge of continuing local grievances, came to an abrupt end. Divergence towards a new non-aligned path in foreign affairs did not help, and the non-Punjabis emphasized their regional nationalism. Sindhi and Baluchi guerilla organizations had already emerged when Bhutto was overthrown by the military. Ethnic alienation persisted while the new administration reverted to the one-unit and one-language policy and closer relations with the Muslim world. Afraid of Soviet military intervention in Afghanistan, the masses once more clustered around the Islamic axis, further bolstered by the Iranian Revolution. In spite of such 'blending' factors, the non-Punjabi nationalities continued off-and-on to resist the melting pot of the Pakistani state. The North-West Frontier Province may be renamed as "Pakhtunkhwa". If the *Mujahideen* ignite a civil war on Pakistan's soil, the long-standing demand for an independent Pathan state may reopen.

The feelings of alienation and separate identity among *Mohajirs*, those Muslim refugees who fled India at the time of partition and came over to Pakistan to settle in Karachi, Hyderabad and Sukkur, occurred as a result of a number of recent events and led to their mobilization under the banner of the MQM. The original idea of Pakistan did not envisage *en masse* transfer of population, but as Muslims from minority provinces came "by train loads, on trucks, lorries, bullock-carts and on foot"[77] to become legitimate citizens of the new state, they were given an initial identity of "*Panahgeers*", also meaning refugees, as the first symptom of their denial of guaranteed status. These refugees, who had come mostly from the urban areas of India, had already broken from rural way of life and also from the feudal mentality, and were therefore closer to the Sindhi *hari* or Punjabi *mazera* (peasant), and not the Baluchi *sirdar* or the Pathan Khan (landlord). In addition to being more devoted to the Pakistan ideology, the *Mohajirs* were, at least initially, more advanced educationally compared to the other four ethnic groups in West Pakistan. One of the outstanding refugees of the country was the first Prime Minister Liaquat Ali Khan, assassinated in 1951. This dramatic event led many among the refugee community to think that those who came from outside were not accepted as the "real sons and daughters of the soil" even though their children might later be born on that land.[78]

The *Mohajir*-Pathan clashes were the first ethnic riots in Karachi. Gohar Ayub Khan, the son of President Ayub Khan, is believed to have engineered the attacks on the *Mohajir* community when the latter supported Fatima Jinnah, the sister of the Quaid-e Azam, against the President during the late-1964 elections. The *Mohajirs*, not only doubted the credibility of the election, but also feared the further erosion of their influence on account of the shift of the federal capital from Karachi to Rawalpindi, Ayub Khan's birth place. The *Mohajirs* felt alienated again when the Sindh Assembly, dominated by the Sindhi-speaking members of Bhutto's PPP, passed (1972) a bill accepting Sindhi, along with Urdu, as the provincial language,[79] and also when the regime, which nationalized big business, introduced an urban-rural quota in Sindh arousing *Mohajir* fears that they were once more losing their status. When the right-wing political parties joined the Punjab-Pathan alliance, and the PPP associated itself more with the rural Sindhis, and when this political balance led (1985) to new ethnic riots in Karachi, the *Mohajirs,* always supportive of "Pakistani" nationalism, were forced to seek and define their own identity. The MQM was formed (1984), on the basis of the All-Pakistan Mohajir Student Organization, a few days after General Zia-ul Haq extended the rural-urban quota system for another ten years. After Altaf Hussain, the MQM leader, announced that he would unite the *Mohajirs* under the banner of their own party, gunmen and the police opened fire on several occasions killing members of the MQM or its sympathizers.[80] Some *Mohajirs* now demand a separate province to be called Jinnahabad or Jinnahpur.

Pakistan—Search for Economic Stability

Pakistan's economy passed from sluggish performance to spectacular changes. Neither of the two wings of Pakistan possessed an industrial base at the time of independence. With the migration of Hindus and Sikhs from Bengal and Punjab, Pakistan lost its businessmen, and hosted Muslim refugees from parts of India. The partition of Punjab led to a water dispute with India with graver consequences for a population dependent mainly on agriculture. The nation's exports are still limited to two primary commodities, namely, raw cotton and rice. While forced to spend large sums on defence, Pakistan earned enough (until 1971) from the export of Bengali-grown jute to pay for imports and the development of an embryonic industry. During the 1950s, agriculture and export earnings from cotton and jute were the mainstay of the economy. Merchants earned more than the manufacturers during the Korean War (1950–53) since purchasers would rather stockpile raw materials. Political instability obstructed the proper application of the first Five-Year Economic Plan (1955–60), but the second one (1960–65) motivated some progress in agriculture and created an initial industrial base. While the war with India (1965) and adverse weather conditions crippled the third Five-Year Plan (1965–70), provinces began to grumble more loudly over regional disparities, and the poorer sections of the population expressed grievances by street violence, which swept away Ayub Khan's "decade of development". The country had embarked, under Ayub Khan's leadership, along the path of economic growth, marked by major infrastructure projects such as the Tarbela and Mangla dams.

Although the fourth Five-Year Plan (1970–75) and the Bhutto regime (1971–77) conceived and projected a socio-economic revolution, the decade of the 1970s was marked by a series of shocks such as the loss of East Bengal, the pouring into Pakistan's treasury of workers' remittances, nationalization, the rise of the oil price, and the devaluation of the Pakistani rupee. Aiming at some regional and economic justice, the plan nationalized a good many industries, medium agro-processing units, banking and insurance, soon to degenerate into inefficient bureaucracies.[81] The marked preference for a public sector-dominated economic model based on capital intensive, heavy industry bred distrust between the state and the entrepreneurial class. While industry was subject to extensive nationalization, the government did not pursue land reforms. Bhutto resorted to religious phrases such as *Musawat-e Muhammadi* (Muhammadan equality) to win mass support. The nationalization drive transferred industrial assets from private *Mohajir* hands to the state dominated by the Sindhi elite led by the Prime Minister. The emerging *Mohajir* bourgeoisie interpreted the PPP "socialism" as a deceptive appearance for conservative Sindhi "feudalism". Despite overall growth mainly on account of the employment opportunities during the oil boom in the Middle East, the economy was vulnerable due to the low productivity of the major commodity-producing sectors, the widening domestic resource gap and the instability of the export sector. The announcement of percentage rates of increase over small beginnings reminded one of the old Soviet trick used to convey the impression of success.[82] In spite of the rhetoric, very little had been done to distribute goods and services more equitably throughout society. The country's balance-of-payments was characterized by an increasing trade gap, rising debts and repayment of external loans.

The economic grievances on the heels of the military adventure in East Bengal were among the causes of the fall of the Bhutto regime, whose economic policies were reversed by the Zia government. The loss of the eastern wing denied a truncated Pakistan revenues from jute. Not only certain economic units were denationalized, Muslim economists sought alternatives to be taken to safeguard equity and the economic interest of the least-privileged classes within the framework of the moral principles of Islam.[83] President Zia ruled over a prosperous-looking Pakistan largely due to Bhutto's industrial legacy, the inflow of workers' remittances, and the Soviet military presence in Afghanistan. However, the structural problems of Pakistan's economy continued to persist. The prime ministers who followed Zia had to adhere to the guidelines prescribed by the international donor agency. The post-Zia period witnessed slow growth rates, increase in inflation, and widening disparity in income distribution. Its economy traditionally being a loan-oriented one, the debt burden kept rising, and exports lagged behind imports. When the IMF approved in the late 1990s the renewal of the lending programme, it was meant to pave the way for a short-term stabilization of the balance-of-payments.[84] Unable to meet even the repayment of earlier domestic debt, the country is in economic decline.

The major characteristics are high population growth, fiscal policy failures, foreign trade deficit, poor domestic savings, inadequate local and foreign investment, excessive defence spending, decaying infrastructure, and rampant corruption. Whatever prosperity there had been, it was due to foreign assistance, not indigenous initiative. Aid was squandered away, and indigenous capabilities, including an entrepreneur business culture, were not encouraged to grow.[85]

Nature has blessed Pakistan, on the other hand, with many ingredients of a vibrant agricultural economy. With four large storage reservoirs, 16 barrages, 12 interriver links, 43 main canals, and three storage dams, Pakistan possesses the largest irrigation network in the world. Accounting directly for one-fourth of Pakistan's GDP and half of total employment, the agricultural sector is, without doubt, the mainstay of the country's economy. Cotton-based products contribute today more than half of Pakistan's total exports. There exists a direct correlation between agricultural performance and the country's overall economy. On the other hand, the vested interests of the Pakistani landlord class, dominant in politics and bureaucracy, withstand all attempts to introduce land reforms. Even more than half a century after independence, the feudal landlords maintain their iron grip on the nation-state. The Daultanas, Khars, Legharis, Mazaris and the Nawabzadas "see their death" in agrarian reforms.[86]

Putting aside two cosmetic changes in 1959 and 1972, one may assert that there has never been a meaningful land reform. In Punjab, 1% of the landowners possess 26% of the total cultivable land.[87] The landed aristocracy blocked the few attempts designed to extend social justice.

Home remittances, the second largest source of foreign exchange earnings about a decade ago, are also declining annually. Oil reserves being modest, the focus shifts to the large coal deposits recently discovered in the Sindh province. Literacy level put at 35% for the overall population, Pakistan's human development indices are among the weakest in the region. The country's technological handicap is in evidence in all fields, including agriculture.

In retrospect, it may even be asserted that Pakistan enjoyed an enviable record as a fast developing country until the 1990s. During most of the years after its economy began its "take off" some three decades ago, Pakistan had the second largest economy in South Asia, in absolute terms after India and in per capita measurement after Sri Lanka. Remembering its pitiful resources and capital endowment at independence, and in comparison with other countries, Pakistan's earlier economic achievements may be termed as uncommon. But as the country approached the next millenium, it became apparent that the economy was suffering from deep-rooted infirmities. Pakistan's economic growth rate in the last decade, compared with 5.4% per annum over the years 1958–68 or 6.5% on the average during 1978–88, was considerably lower or a mere 4%. That country has been living beyond its resources for the last decade or so. Its leadership pursues high defence expenditure while domestic and external debts sharply increase. Despite an overall trend of economic failures, the Pakistani armed forces have made major military acquisitions. Lack of improvement in relations with India necessitates the continuation of high defence expenditure. This situation was the economic setting for the nuclear tests of mid-1998 and the renewal of armed encounters in Kashmir a year later. International sanctions in the post-nuclear weapon test phase adversely affected the economy. Having at times per-formed better than India in terms of basic economic yardsticks such as average growth rate or per capita income, Pakistan is now showing a marked slowdown among the major South Asian economies.

That country may produce 70% of all soccer balls manufactured worldwide or it may be a global supplier of surgical instruments of some quality, but its annual debt-servicing requirements lately amount to 5% of its GDP and 40% of export earnings. While agriculture, which is the very foundation of the economy, is exhibiting signs of plateauing, remittances from the oil-rich Gulf area are nowhere plentiful as they used to be during Bhutto's and Zia's time. Both of these vital components seem to be exhausted. Industry is ill-equipped to be the engine of future growth, and there are no other engines in sight. Abstention from costly foreign skirmishes, such as the ones in Kashmir, will help. One can only agree with a number of Pakistani intellectuals that it is necessary to reduce military spending and other non-productive expenditures in order to release additional resources for the country's economic development on an independent basis.[88]

Notes

1   Dilip Hiro, *Islamic Fundamentalism*, London, HarperCollins Publishers, Paladin Series, 1989. The author rightly observes that the manner in which the fundamentalist movement is conducted varies widely from country to country.

2   Rafiq Zakariya, *The Struggle within Islam: the Conflict between Religion and Politics*, London, Penguin, 1988, pp. 174f. The United States Government dug out the term "fundamentalism" from the history of Western nations as a sort of a "swear word" for the Khomeini revolution in Iran. It means adherence to the letter of the scripture, and denotes intolerance in the name of religion. It carries the danger of lapsing into violence and even terrorism.

3   Türkkaya Ataöv, "Nehru-A Profile", *A. Ü. Siyasal Bilgiler Fakültesi Dergisi*, Ankara, XLIV/3–4 (Temmuz-Aralik 1989), pp. 75–83.

4   Although a *new* Islamic state, Pakistan was, like its older neighbours, a product of historical processes. Hence, it included one of the great civilizations of Asia: R. E. M. Wheeler, *Five Thousand Years of Pakistan*, London, Royal India and Pakistan Society, 1950.

5   Marietta T. Stepanyants, *Pakistan: Philosophy and Sociology (Filosofiia i Sotsiologiia v Pakistane)*, Moscow, Nauka, 1971, p. 13.

6   Shirin Tahir-Kheli, "In Search of an Identity", *Islam in Foreign Policy*, ed. Adeed Dawisha, Cambridge, Cambridge University Press, 1986, pp. 68f.

7   For Jinnah's statements on the minorities: Government of Pakistan, *Quotes from the Quaid*, rev. ed., Islamabad, Ministry of Information and Broadcasting, 1992, pp. 103–107. Also: Latif Ahmed Sherwani, "Quad-i-Azam and the Minorities", *Pakistan Journal of History and Culture*, Islamabad, XII/1–2 (1991), pp. 38–62.

8   *Quotes from the Quaid, op. cit.*, pp. 103–104.

9   "Towards National Consolidation", *Secular Democracy*, New Delhi, XXIV/5 (August 1995), p. 7.

10 A general description: Karl Heinz Pfeffer, "Eine sozio-ethno-religiöse Minderheit: die Christen West-Pakistans", *Sociologus*, 12/2 (1962), pp. 113–127. The Goan Christians in Karachi in the 1970s: Raffat Khan Haward, "An Urban Minority: the Goan Christian Community in Karachi", *The City in South Asia: Premodern and Modern*, eds., Kenneth Ballhatchet and John Harrison, London, Curzon Press; Atlantic Highlands, New Jersey, Humanities Press, 1980, pp. 299–323.

11 Four chapters by S. K. Gupta, Anthony D'Souza, Maki Dhunjibhoy and Shachi N. Barua: *Minorities in Pakistan*, Karachi, Pakistan Publications, n. d.; Robert H. S. Hutchinson, *Chittagong Hill Tracts*, Delhi, Vivek, 1978; R. W. Timm, *The Adivasis of Bangladesh*, London, Minority Rights Group, 1991.

12 Yu. V. Gankovskii, L. R. Gordon-Polonskaya, *Istoriya Pakistana*, Moskva, Izdatel'stvo Vostochnoy Literaturi, 1961, p. 110.

13 S. Amjad Ali, *The Muslim World Today*, Islamabad, National Hijra Council, 1985, p. 144.

14 Z. M. Khan, "Religious Fundamentalism in Indian Context", *World Focus*, New Delhi, 232 (April 1999), pp. 3–5.

15 From a well-known leader of enlightened public opinion in India: Rasheeduddin Khan, *Bewildered India: Identity, Pluralism, Discord*, New Delhi, Har-Anand Publications, 1994, p. 202f.

16 S. N. Mishra, "India's Tragic Impasse", *Secular Democracy*, New Delhi, XXIV/5 (August 1995), p. 13.

17   Sampurnanand, "Secularism in India", *The Emerging World, op. cit.*, p. 197.
18   For the social and intellectual aspects of the declining hold of the Church and its doctrines on European society: Owen Chadwick, *The Secularization of the European Mind in the 19th Century*, Cambridge, Cambridge University Press, 1991.
19   An Indian writer who claims that secularism has deep roots in the Indian society: K. M. Panikkar, *The Foundations of New India*, London, George Allen and Unwin, 1960.
20   Shanker Dayal Sharma, *Aspects of Indian Thought*, New Delhi, Sterling Publishers, 1993, p. 49.
21   On Azad's three passions, namely, India's freedom from British rule, Hindu-Muslim unity, and passion for learning: V. N. Datta, *Maulana Azad*, New Delhi, Manohar, 1990.
22   A comprehensive examination of the Indian Constitution: Moolamattom Varkey Pylee, *India's Constitution*, New Delhi, S. Chand and Co., 1992. An alternative: R. Joshi, *The Indian Constitution and Its Working*, New Delhi, Sangam Books, 1986.
23   For 'some aspects of the Muslim problem of the 1970s': Natalia Giorgevna Prussakova, "O Nyekotorih Aspektah 'Musul'manskoy Problemi' v Sovremennoy Indii (70-e Godi)", *Zarubejniy Vostok: Religiozniye Traditsii i Sovremennost'*, Moskva, Akademii Nauk SSSR, 1983, str. 168–181.
24   Paper submitted to the International Seminar in Commemoration of the Centenary of Maulana Abul Kalam Azad, 14–16 February 1990: Türkkaya Ataöv, "Religion in the Age of Science", *A. Ü. Siyasal Bilgiler Fakültesi Dergisi*, Ankara, XLV/1–4 (Ocak-Aralik 1990), pp. 23–29.
25   B. N. Puri, "Secularism-Western and Eastern-A Study", *World Affairs*, New Delhi, I (December 1990), pp. 109–111.
26   Zafar Ahmad Nizami, "Plight of Minorities in India", *World Focus*, New Delhi, 232 (April 1999), p. 14.
27   Irfan Ahmad, "RSS Versus the Jamaat", *ibid.*, p. 16.
28   Des Raj Goyal, *Rashtriya Swayamsewak Sangh*, New Delhi, Radha Krishna Publications, 1979, pp. 158f. Also see M. S. Golwalkar's following books: *Bunch of Thoughts*, Bangalore, Vikram Prakashan; *Thoughts on Some Current Problems*, Bombay, Hindustan Sahitya Publications, 1957. Some RSS publications: *We or Our Nationhood Defined*, Nagpur, Bharat Publications, 1939; *Why Hindu Rashtra*, Bangalore, Kesari Press; *Not Socialism But Hindu Rashtra*, Karnataka, RSS Publication, 1964.
29   In his analysis of the Moradabad massacre (1980), the slaughter of Uttar Pradesh *harijans* (1981) and the Ayodhya controversy, the following author, with commitment to secularism, rejects religion as a symbol of hate: M. J. Akbar, *Riot after Riot: Reports on Caste and Communal Violence in India*, New Delhi, Penguin India, 1988. Especially on Ayodhya: Sarvepalli Gopal, ed., *Anatomy of a Confrontation: Ayodhya and the Rise of Communal Politics in India*, London, Zed Books, 1993.
30   D. R. Goyal, "Babri Shadow Over India", *Secular Democracy*, New Delhi, XXIV/9 (December 1995), pp. 16–18.
31   Due to that demolition and related developments, India's relations with some OIC states came under strain. A. K. Pasha, *India and OIC Strategy and Diplomacy*, New Delhi, Centre for Peace Studies, n. d., pp. 15–53.
32   Popularized by campaigners exalting Hinduism as India's "true national faith".
33   An analysis of Shiv Sena chauvinists and other terrorist groups: Vidiadhar Surajprasad Naipaul, *India: a Million Mutinies Now*, London, Minerva, 1991. On the preferential treatment in employment opportunities: Mary Fainsod Katzenstein, *Ethnicity and Equal-*

ity: the Shiv Sena Party and Preferential Politics in Bombay, Ithaca, New York, Cornell University Press, 1979.

34   For instance: Subrata Banerjee, *Secularism and Indian Polity*, New Delhi, Joshi-Adhikari Institute of Social Sciences, 1987, p. 10.

35   Bhavdeep Kang, "Born-Again Hinduism", *Outlook*, New Delhi, 1 February 1999, p. 28.

36   Karan Singh, *Population, Poverty and the Future of India*, New Delhi, National Institute of Family Planning, 1975. The author was Head of State in Kashmir for eighteen years (1949–67) and later (1973) Minister of Health and Family Planning in the Central Cabinet.

37   Holder of revenue-producing lands assigned for salary, i.e., a *jagir*.

38   Holders of hereditary lands.

39   Landlords who control the peasants directly.

40   For instance: Prem Shankar Jha, *India: a Political Economy of Stagnation*, Bombay, Oxford University Press, 1980. The author examines the causes of the onset of economic stagnation after 15 years of seemingly healthy growth.

41   Ishtiaq Husain Qureshi, *The Struggle for Pakistan*, Karachi, University of Karachi, 1979, p. 310.

42   Yoginder Sikand, "Hapless Minorities of Pakistan", *Secular Democracy*, New Delhi, XXIV/5 (August 1995), p. 18.

43   A Federal Shari'a Court member in Islamabad considers some foreign suspicions that those who do not believe in an ideological Islamic state may be trampled upon as second rate citizens as unfounded apprehensions. Abdul Ghafur Muslim, "Comment", *Journal*, Kent, U.K., Institute of Muslim Minority Affairs, 9/2 (July 1988), p. 269.

44   A descendant of a Turco-Moghul family from Samarkand, Mirza Ghulam Ahmad (1836–1908) founded (1889) the Ahmadi movement (whose adherents are also sometimes known as Qadianis) and declared himself to be the "Messiah" to demonstrate the truth of Islam. Orthodox Muslims were enraged, however, by his challenge of the fundamental doctrine of *katm-e nabuwwat*, which underlines that Muhammad is the last of all prophets. Some Ahmadis (most notably Sir Muhammad Zafrullah Khan, Pakistan's Foreign Minister in the 1950s, and subsequently a judge of the International Court of Justice) have achieved prominence. See: Muhammad Zafrullah Khan, *Servant of God*, London, Unwin Brothers, 1983. For the teachings of the Ahmadiyyah Movement: Bashir-ud Din Mahmud Ahmad, *Invitation to Ahmadiyyat*, Henley, U.K., Routledge and Kegan Paul, 1980; Spencer Lavan, *The Ahmadiyyah Movement: Past and Present*, Amritsar, India, Guru Nanak Dev University, 1974.

45   The celebrated Indian Muslim poet philosopher Sir Muhammad Iqbal had expressed (1934) his views on the "Qadianis and Orthodox Muslims", which provoked Nehru to write some articles on the same movement in *The Modern Review* (Calcutta). In reply to Nehru's articles, Iqbal wrote a detailed rejoinder published under the title *Islam and Ahmadism* (new printing: Lahore, Sh. Muhammad Ashraf, 1980). Underlining that Islam founded itself on the religious idea alone, Iqbal asserted that the Muslims were naturally much more sensitive to forces which they considered harmful to their integrity, and therefore, any religious society arising from the bosom of Islam, claiming a new prophethood for its basis, had to be regarded "as a danger to the solidarity of Islam". In his words, Islam could not reconcile itself to a movement which threatened its present solidarity and held the promise of further rifts.

46   Wayne Ayres Wilcox, "Nation-Building: the Problem in Pakistan", *World Writers on Pakistan*, Karachi, Pakistan Publications, 1968, p. 28.

47   India had one prime minister and seven commanders-in-chief.

48   Ralph Braibanti, "The Research Potential of Pakistan's Development", eds., Lawrence Ziring, Ralph Braibanti and W. Howard Wriggings, *Pakistan: the Long View*, Durham, N.C., Duke University Press, 1977, pp. 438–440; Norman D. Palmer, "Changing Patterns of Politics in Pakistan: an Overview", ed., Mansooruddin Ahmed, *Contemporary Pakistan: Politics, Economy, and Society*, Karachi, Royal Book Company, 1982, pp. 45–53.

49   Tahir Amin, *Ethno-National Movements of Pakistan: Domestic and International Factors*, Islamabad, Institute of Policy Studies, 1988, p. xxiv.

50   Muhammad Abdul Wadud Bhuiyan, *Emergence of Bangladesh and [the] Role of [the] Awami League*, New Delhi, Vikas, 1982; Rounaq Jahan, *Pakistan: Failure in National Integration*, New York, Columbia University Press, 1972.

51   Shahed Javid Burki, *Pakistan Under Bhutto: 1971–77*, London, Macmillan, 1980.

52   Hasan Askari Rizvi, *Internal Strife and External Intervention: India's Role in the Civil War in East Pakistan (Bangladesh)*, Lahore, Progressive Publishers, 1981; Hasan Zaheer, *The Separation of East Pakistan: the Rise and the Realization of Bengali Muslim Nationalism*, New York, Oxford University Press, 1994; Zulfikar Ali Bhutto, *The Great Tragedy*, Karachi, Pakistan People's Party, 1971.

53   For a chronicle of breathtaking events in the course of nine months: Jahanara Imam, *Of Blood and Fire: the Untold Story of Bangladesh's War of Independence*, New Delhi, Sterling Publishers, 1989. A Pakistani journalist's spine-chilling, eye-witness account of large-scale massacre perpetrated by the militarists on the people of East Bengal: Anthony Mascarenhas, *The Rape of Bangla Desh*, Delhi, Vikas Publications, 1971.

54   Tanzil-ur Rahman, *Islamization in Pakistan*, Islamabad, Council of Islamic Ideology, 1984.

55   Charles H. Kennedy, "Islamization and Legal Reform in Pakistan: 1979–1989", *Pacific Affairs*, Vancouver, 63/1 (Spring 1990), pp. 62–77.

56   Anwar H. Syed, "The Pakistan People's Party: Phases One and Two", *Pakistan: the Long View, op. cit.*, p. 89.

57   Richard F. Nyrop, "Pakistan", *The Middle East Journal*, Washington, D. C., 32/1 (Winter 1978), p. 93.

58   *Islamisation of Banking System in Pakistan*, Islamabad, Pakistan Publications, n.d.

59   Justice Aftab Hussain, *Federal Shariat Court in Pakistan*, Islamabad, Pakistan Publications, n.d.

60   *Introduction of Hudood Laws in Pakistan*, Islamabad, Pakistan Publications, n.d.

61   *Islamic University and Institute of Training in Shari'ah and Legal Profession*, Islamabad, Pakistan Publications, n.d.

62   For a great many Pakistani writers, General Zia took "concrete steps towards the introduction of Islamic order in Pakistan". For instance: Masudul Hasan, *Pakistan: the Call of Islam*, Islamabad, Pakistan Publications, n. d., p. 40. In the eyes of some Muslim commentators, however, even that *Shari'a* Ordinance is "no more than a vicious device to entrench European hegemony in the spheres of legislation and morality and exclude the Islamic values". Ibrahim Sulaiman, "Fallacy of Law Reform in Muslim World", *Islamic Order*, Karachi, X/2 (Second Quarter 1988), p. 24.

63   Rasul B. Rais, "Pakistan in 1988: from Command to Conciliation Politics", *Asian Survey*, Berkeley, XXIX/2 (February 1989), p. 201.

64 *Dawn*, Karachi, 18 August 1988. A book of tribute to him: *Shaheed-ul-Islam Muhammad Zia-ul-Haq*, London, Indus Thames Publishers for the Islamic Council, 1990.
65 Shahid Javed Burki, "Pakistan Under Zia: 1977–1988", *Asian Survey*, Berkeley, XXVIII/10 (October 1988), pp.1082–1100.
66 S. S. Bindra, "Imperatives of Islamization in Pakistan", *New Quest*, Bombay, 76 (July–August 1989), p. 226.
67 "Pakistani Movement: Was It Communal or National Based in the Region", *The News*, 17 April 1997, quoted in Sreedhar and Nilesh Bhagat, *Pakistan: a Withering State?* Delhi, Wordsmiths, 1999, p. 155.
68 Behroz Khan, "Frontier Taliban", *Newsline*, Karachi, 10/8 (February 1999), pp. 44–45.
69 Ismail Khan, "The Politics of Shariah", *ibid.*, pp. 42–43.
70 Benazir Bhutto, *Daughter of the East: an Autobiography*, London, Hamish Hamilton, 1988. Written with a political purpose, much of the book is an account of Z. A. Bhutto's trial, his execution and the daughter's detention.
71 For instance: Z. A., "Making History?" *The Herald*, Karachi, October 1999, p. 28b.
72 In an address to the nation on 17 October 1999, General Musharraf gave a crumbling economy, lost credibility, demolished state institutions, provincial disharmony and "brothers...at each other's throat" as reasons for the military take-over (Government of Pakistan, *Address to the Nation by...General Pervez Musharraf*, Islamabad, Ministry of Information and Media Development, 1999). Some third parties see a connection between Ossama bin Laden, the "guest" of the Taliban in Afghanistan, and the fundamentalist groups operating in Pakistan and consider the military coup as reinforcing that bond (for instance: Mervyn Dymally, "Pakistani Military Coup Reinforces Spreading Threat of Jihad", *San Francisco Chronicle*, 25 October 1999). Also: Yuri Tissovski in *Vek,* Moscow, 41–99 (22 October 1999). Qazi Abdul Wahid, a prominent fundamentalist leader, the Jamaat-e Islami *amir* disclosed in a Lashkar-e Taiba congregation at Muridke near Lahore (3–5 November 1999) that the Nawaz Sharif government "was about to launch a big crackdown on religious groups...but that he was removed". *The Friday Times*, Lahore, 12 November 1999. When Gen. Musharraf expressed that he was impressed by modern Turkey's secularist M. Kemâl Atatürk, Q. H. Ahmad declared that "only an Islamic system could work" in Pakistan. (*Dawn*, the Internet, 21 October 1999.) Although the new military leader called on the *ulama*, the religious clergy, expecting them "to come forth and present Islam in its true light", that is, "tolerance and not hatred, universal brotherhood and not enmity, peace and not violence, progress and not bigotry" (also: Suzanne Goldberg reporting in *The Guardian*, 22 October 1999), some others asserted that Musharraf also had "extreme Islamic contacts" (Ehsan Ahrari's analysis in *Jane's Intelligence Review*, Surrey, U.K., 15, October 1999).
73 Khalid Bin Sayeed, "Pathan Regionalism", *The South Atlantic Quarterly*, Durham, N.C., 63 (1969), pp. 478–504. On the "Afghans" who live on the Pakistan side of the Durand Line: James W. Spain, *The People of the Khyber: the Pathans of Pakistan*, New York, Praeger, 1963. By a British officer who spent "a lifetime among Pathans": Olaf Caroe, *The Pathans: 550 B.C.–A.D. 1957*, London, Macmillan, 1958. Drawing on historical precedent, some authors conclude that the peoples on either side of the Hindu Kush have a common past, and therefore, a common future: Mohammad Haidar, "Pak-Afghan Common Destiny", *WUFA,* quarterly journal of the Writers' Union of Free Afghanistan, Peshawar, 1/3 (1986), pp. 47–51. On the Pakhtunistan Movement: Dorothea Seelye

Franck, "Pakhtunistan-Disputed Disposition of a Tribal Land", *The Middle East Journal*, Washington, D.C., 6/1 (1952), pp. 49–68.

74 Mohammad Ayub Khan, "A New Experiment in Democracy in Pakistan", *Annals*, Philadelphia, 348 (March 1965), pp. 109–113.

75 Ayub Khan, *Friends Not Masters, op. cit., passim.*

76 Bhutto's success at the polls of 1970 was due in large measure to the promise of complete overhaul of institutions, a *Mawashrati Taraqi* or "modernization", not clearly defined. For his followers, the new structure ranged from a Westminster-type of parliamentary democracy to a "dictatorship of the people". See: Burki, *op. cit.,* pp. 79f.

77 Rashid Jamal, *Mohajirs of Pakistan: Plight and Struggle for Survival*, Karachi, Loh-e-Adab Publication, 1998, p. 15.

78 Türkkaya Ataöv, "A Case of Discrimination", *EAFORD Newsletter*, Geneva, December 1997, pp. 16–17. An essay based on the observations of the author, born and raised in the United Provinces of British India: Afak Haydar, "The Mohajirs in Sindh: a Critical Essay", ed., J. Henry Korson, *Contemporary Problems of Pakistan*, Boulder, Westview Press, 1993, pp. 107–124.

79 Tariq Rahman, "Language and Politics in a Pakistan Province: the Sindhi Language Movement", *Asian Survey*, Berkeley, XXXV/11 (November 1995), pp. 1005–1016.

80 See MQM Bulletins released from the International Secretariat in London. Also: *A Petition to Mr. Kofi Annan...by the...MQM on the Terrifyingly Shocking Killing of Ten MQM members by Government Agencies*, London, 16 August 1998.

81 Syed Nawab Haider Naqvi and Khwaja Sarmad, *Pakistan's Economy Through the Seventies*, Islamabad, Pakistan Institute of Development Economics, 1984.

82 W. Eric Gustafson, "A Review of the Pakistani Economy under Bhutto", ed., Manzooruddin Ahmed, *Contemporary Pakistan: Politics, Economy and Society, op. cit.*, pp. 145–162.

83 Sayed Nawab Haider Naqwi and Asghar Qadir, *A Model of a Dynamic Islamic Economy and the Institution of Interest*, Islamabad, Pakistan Institute of Development Economics, n.d.

84 The Economist Intelligence Unit, *Country Report: Pakistan, Afghanistan*, London, 1999, pp. 21–23.

85 Bidanda M. Chengappa, "Pakistan's Economy: Trends and Issues", *Asian Strategic Review: 1998–99*, New Delhi, Institute for Defence Studies and Analyses, 1999, pp. 225–267.

86 Ishtiaq Ahmed, "Feudalism in Pakistan", *The Nation,* Islamabad, 22–23 May 1997.

87 Sreedhar and Bhagat, *op. cit.*, p. 126.

88 For instance: Kaneez Fatima, "The Other Side of U.S. 'Generosity'", *World Marxist Review*, Prague, 11 (November 1988), pp. 112–114.

Chapter 7

Tryst with Terror

Modern democracy, which may be identified with popular sovereignty, majority rule, constitutional liberties, participation in decision-making at all levels, drive for egalitarianism, protection of minorities and much else, is a complicated package. No matter how composite it may look, however, democracy is incompatible with terrorism.[1] Fascist parties excluded, most political groupings and governments have seldom failed to claim a democratic legitimacy. Democracy, which seems to promise a form of government based on the harmony between the rulers and the ruled, is irresistible, at least as a slogan. It is conceivable, on the other hand, only when sectional or public interests are acknowledged and organized for political action.

Another justifiable assumption is that no state is seriously democratic unless opposition is permitted to form and participate in the contest for power. In some countries, opposition rests on tribes or regions, which may not accept a common good in the overall state. In societies where the opposition forces are of this type, democratic institutions lead to clashes more than bringing harmony. In such instances, some kind of unifying principles in the form of an ideology, "guided democracy" and "army above politics" may emerge. Although even such governments are not necessarily without virtue, democracy assumed, during its formative years, the existence and the dominance of rational human beings. Some contemporary analysts believe, however, that the democratic process has its own irrationalities.

A Matter of Definition

Likewise, it is difficult to use the term "terrorism" accurately within a legal context. That word, first used during the French Revolution to portray government by intimidation but later expanded to mean many other things, has no completely accepted definition.[2] The international community acting as the League of Nations (L. of N.) and the United Nations (U.N.) attempted to define the term or the concept.[3] According to Article 1 of a L. of N. Convention (1937), terrorist undertakings are "criminal acts directed against a State and intended or calculated to create a state of terror in the minds of particular persons or the general public". A U.N. General Assembly Resolution (1985) concentrated on "misery, frustration, grievance and despair" engendered by "colonialism, racism and situations involving mass and flagrant violations of human rights and fundamental freedoms".[4] As pinpointed in the U.N. Security Council Resolution (1999), the international community now "[u]nequivocally condemns all acts, methods and practices of *terrorism* as criminal and unjustifiable, regardless of their motivation, in all their forms and manifestations, wherever and by whomever committed, in particular those which could threaten international peace and security".[5]

Some individual authorities spelled out the substance of the same word in various other ways. For instance, Crenshaw indicated that terrorism was the result of both emotional pressures and strategic choice considerations.[6] Post suggested the notion of "terrorist psycho-logic" espousing that political terrorists commit violence in consequence of psychological forces.[7] Pearlstein maintained that terrorists were characterized by narcissistic personality trait disturbances traceable to childhood self-image injuries.[8] Weinberg, who introduced the role of projective identification and developed the function of the defence mechanism of splitting in the paradoxical terrorist personality, underlined that terrorists with personality trait disorders would not necessarily exhibit striking psychopathology.[9]

One needs to be distrustful of sweeping generalizations. For instance, the U.N. Resolution which refers to colonialism, racism and situations involving human rights is a simplistic supposition. Terrorism occurs in democracies perhaps more than in authoritarian regimes. It is discernible in homogeneous as well as in heterogeneous societies. It may grow on the basis of historical grievances or blossom on account of economic and political failures. Even economic prosperity, as in Germany, may lead to its burgeoning. Compromise on the part of the ruling government or even yielding to some demands of the terrorists, as in post-Franco Spain (1975), may not assure the finale of the fury. As Laqueur expresses categorically, terrorism can be best overpowered in root-and-branch totalitarian states which do not permit any discordance.[10]

Although it is clearly difficult to use the term accurately, at least in a legal sense, the man in the street has an image in his mind. For an average person, terrorism implies a defiance of law, a violent conduct against an individual or a group of people or the representatives of an authority, planned to intimidate or coerce the latter to meet the demands underlying the terrorist act. It is violence against civilian targets and others by clandestine or at times by state-inflicted (although not necessarily state-tolerated) groups with the intention of inducing shock. On the other hand, the sprinkling of bullets from the gun of an insane person, a hunger strike, sporadic mob violence or clandestine political opposition, each discomforting to the government and some even criminal in legal terms, are not acts of terrorism. Not all forms of violence, however, are easily distinguishable from terrorism. While it is generally believed that assassins act alone but terrorists operate in teams, the murderers of Anwar-al Sadat and Indira Gandhi were acting on behalf of political groups. Although it is widely assumed that terrorists function in urban areas, some Latin American groups and the Kurdish Workers Party (PKK) have been active in rural regions as well. Describing targeting non-combatants as part of terrorism, some specialists characterized it as wanton attacks on innocent citizens. While those who occupy a building with diplomatic immunity may take anyone who may be there as hostage, the assassinations of Sadat and Indira were the result of carefully selected targets.

Terrorism is customarily considered to be violence from below. Although never a dictator in the modern sense, being checked in the Committee of Public Safety as well as the opposing Hébertist faction, "the Reign of Terror" from above set in (1793–94) as M. I. Robespierre came to dominate the French Revolution. Similarly, the Nazi appeal since 1933 to prejudices widely held in Germany against Jews, intellectuals, liberals, leftists and pacifists, including the Holocaust, constitute terror from above. The outbreak of terror, accompanied by repeated "purges" of the Communist Party and the Soviet administration, both under the undisputed leadership of J. Stalin, also indicated the application of brutal power from above.

An Element of Politics

Although terrorism, on the basis of references above, may be considered as an old form of destructive and cruel behaviour, it has become an increasingly important element of contemporary world politics. In the early post-1945 period, the dominant practice of international terrorism was the so-called "revanchist" violence against the expansion of the Communist bloc in Eastern Europe. Its protagonists were then members of extremist emigrant groups who had found refuge in different Western countries. Although the immediate targets were harassed, events such as the storming of the Romanian diplomatic premises in Bern or the pursuits of the Croatian hijackers in the mid-1950s failed to put the world on its guard. A growing type of international terrorism which emerged in the postwar years was the so-called "radicalism" whose roots were ostensibly to be found in anarchism. This pattern of petit-bourgeois phenomenon embraced some young people who appeared to believe in desperate destruction as an alternative to political methods of opposition to the status quo. Sometimes unemployed and often outcasts in the productive and cultural life of societies, they found themselves in the midst of a crisis of moral values. Usually a small minority, they volunteered to symbolize and talk for greater groups.

The last-mentioned groups have long-term objectives as well as immediate targets. Some of them, like the Jammu and Kashmir Liberation Front, aspire to independence on behalf of a people or nation. Some nurture the limited objective of "removing" someone, obtaining the release of a prisoner, wringing ransom, gaining publicity, provoking reprisal or breaking public order. One reason for the difficulty in offering a definition to suit everyone concerned as well as all cases may stem from the fact that terrorist acts are committed to several specific purposes. On the other hand, all or most of such explicit plans may be designed to serve the same overall ambition.

Clandestine groups are necessarily small in number. It is their isolation from the overwhelming majority that plays a role in inciting them more towards violence. Disregarding the criteria for social development, they are inclined to glorify the subjective factor and play politics and revolution. Like the alchemists of bygone ages, they frequently expect societal miracles from bombs and assassinations. Their opposition hardly promises long-term prospects, but it almost surely discredits the efforts of social forces which could otherwise help achieve desirable goals. In other words, by reducing politics to criminal actions and by accepting violence as the style of struggle, the terrorists of our day, including those in Kashmir, disorganize the authentic forces of change.

Another kind of international terrorism seeks to present itself as a commendable instrument and a component part of a national liberation movement. It tries to derive its justification from the understanding that the struggle for such an end is a form of expression of the lawful right of peoples to self-determination. During the long Cold War period, the two superpowers as leaders of the Eastern and Western bloc of nations considered the encouragement of the "liberation movements" within territories in the other's sphere of influence as a requirement of respective national interests. First V. I. Lenin and later Woodrow Wilson, representing the leadership of the two ideologically-competing societies of the post-1919 world, well publicized the principle of a people's right to self-determination, a criterion still widely conceded as an agreeable dictum. However, if all groups of people which may claim such a right are granted sovereignty and independence, contemplating for a moment that the existing nation-states will consent to their own dismemberment, the membership in the U.N. General Assembly will expand several fold from its present (2000) embrace of 188 countries.

Some brands of terrorism which pretend to be vehicles of "emancipatory" endeavours may well be unconnected with the right of peoples to necessary self-defence. They may be assessed, instead, as dangerous forms of abuse of the anti-colonial and liberatory struggle, or indications of a separate aim, with interests of their own. The so-called "anti-colonial terrorism" cannot be on a level with the goals of peoples struggling for national liberation. Such a movement does not endorse terrorist acts claiming human lives among innocent civilian populations either in the area of conflict or anywhere else.

One of the dominant features of recent terrorism has been the proliferation of groups motivated by religion, giving that kind of violence a "divine imperative".[11] Contrary to the bias of some Western circles, it is not only Muslims who produce groups of religious terrorists. In addition to the "holy terror" in parts of Kashmir, legitimization of violence is also discernible among some radical Sikhs in India, white supremacist American Christians, and some Jewish messianic movements in Israel. Strong sectarian elements may also be observed in Armenian, Irish, Palestinian and Tamil terrorist groups. Consequently, "Hamas" asserts that Israel will exist until Islam will obliterate it, some Jewish fanatics plot the destruction of the Dome of the Rock, a Sikh group seeks to "cleanse" Punjab of foreign influences, and white supremacists lay plans to engage in indiscriminate, mass killings.

While teams which purport to represent one or the other ethnic/religious groups call for independence, not only a few such groups aspire for independence, there are also too many areas all over the world with more than one claimant. For some of them, the blessings of fusion may make up for the gamble of secession. Many groups, however, feel frustrated over the odds of independence, a breeding ground for terrorism, likely to increase rather than diminish in the near future.

Chosen Traumas

According to Montville, ethnic/religious terrorism is based on a feeling of victimhood shared by an identity group caused by some traumatic event in the past, that group continuing to take to heart a conscious or unconscious threat to its present or future well-being.[12] The terrorists build up their interpretation of legitimacy on the perception of an occupying army and a colonizing bureaucracy and seek to legitimize violence against the so-called "foreigner" as "incorporeal" acts of war. There may be open or concealed affinity between the terrorist group and the mass of people that formation claims to represent, and both may fail to appreciate the suffering of the other group.

Vamik Volkan, a prominent professor of psychiatry who gave us, in several of his publications, a *tour de force* for an understanding of the psychodynamics of relations between cultural or national groups, offers the concepts of "chosen traumas" and "chosen glories" as the most potent forces of a group's identity.[13] The former refers to an event that incites in the members of a group feelings of humiliation and victimization by another group. The event may be the Holocaust for the Jews or the assault (1984) on the Sikh's Golden Temple complex. A group does not "choose" to be victimized, but "chooses" to dwell on the event. Since human beings cannot accept change without grief for what has been lost in the past, the mourning process is an inherent response involving shock, sadness and attempts to retain the lost object in memory. But the group that feels victimized may be too angry to mourn, and therefore, find it difficult to make peace. Furthermore, the chosen trauma may be passed from one generation to another in a way, not only that it may or may not have a resemblance to the actual event, but also it may gather a renewed emotional content. The inability to mourn may become a political force and turn into some sort of new power. Pain may reach such an uncontrollable degree that a group may turn into a mob and some of its members into terrorists.

Violence towards some monuments such as the destruction of certain statues in Russia after the fall of the Communist order (1991) or the attack on the Babri Masjid in Ayodhya (1992) is an example of a way to vent anger resulting from pain. While the grievance is passed from the older to the younger generation the original trauma is mythologized, and the description of the event may become entirely one-sided. The "egoism of victimization" no longer allows the acknowledgement of injuries sustained by the other group. A trauma may bring to mind former traumas and thus the more distant ones. The recent (1984) assault on the Golden Temple may remind the Sikhs of the defilement of the same back in 1746, and their massacre by Ahmad Shah Abdali of Afghanistan in 1762. The Sikh leadership refers to these repressions as the "Lesser and the Greater Holocausts".[14] The past plays a very important role in dealing with and accommodating the present. It matters little whether the memory is factual or mythical, ancient or recent.

A "chosen glory", a corresponding phenomenon, is an event that furnishes a group with the memory of a success over another group. While bolstering the group's self-esteem, the chosen glory may also be mythologized. It also refers to a shared mental representation of an event this time perceived as a triumph over the enemy. It is remembered again and again to gather support for a group's self-esteem. Both chosen traumas and glories are taken in by the individual as a growing child, who, in the words of Volkan, wears two layers of clothing, one belonging to the individual, and the other symbolizing a loose covering that shelters many individuals. The latter is like a "large tent" in which chosen traumas and chosen glories are woven.[15] Group leadership represents the column that supports the tent. The individuals lead a routine but regular life if the tent is stable. Governmental insensitivity towards one or more of the groups and a neighbour's interference as well as natural catastrophes and economic vacillations may destabilize the tent. It is of immense importance to perpetuate the stability of the tent and prevent its collapse.

It may shake, however, on account of a number of reasons including domestic stresses and foreign intermingling. Terrorism flourishes and may even gain support under these circumstances. Specific terrorist acts are, nevertheless, carried out by certain individuals, and not by some others who may feel all the more sympathy for the same cause. The reason for this contrast lies in the personal background of the individual blended with group experience. The members of the terrorist leadership core frequently suffer from certain "wounds" which they feel are "cured" as their "enemies" are made to suffer. Some of them may have themselves been victims of terror in the past. Others may not have become direct victims of violence but seasoned in extreme poverty. The decision to join a terrorist group enables the individual to abandon a discredited identity and embrace a new one. The latter sanctions the terrorist to blame an enemy, against whom the individual will canalise, not only all hatred, but also personal unwanted parts. Individuals, peoples and nations sometimes find in others, whether other persons, groups or neighbours, a vulnerable target to project their own bad internal objects. The enemy within becomes the enemy without. If an enemy does not exist, it has to be invented.[16] Enmity as well is an integral part of the lives of human beings. Freud explained this phenomenon in his "narcissism of minor differences".[17] Moreover, to have an enemy outside the group helps strengthen cohesion within. At times, the role of the enemy is inflated and overemphasized. For instance, the bombing (1995) of the Alfred P. Murrah Federal Building in Oklahoma City was immediately tied to various "foreign" groups, rationalizing the diversion of attention from the violence rampant among Americans.[18]

Upswing in Violence

Only fringe phenomena until recently, extreme political movements in Europe became significant, not only on account of violent attacks on minorities and immigrants, but also the power of racist political parties has increased, influencing some mainstream parties to compete for the right-wing vote.[19] Rising unemployment, coupled with waves of refugees from the former Communist bloc, led large portions of the European electorate to search for scapegoats. While foreigners and minorities were maltreated in many parts of Western Europe, the collapse of Communism unleashed ethnocentric feelings mainly in parts of Eastern Europe and then in the whole continent. Consequently, the red light of warning being already on, the future of Europe is unclear. Violent activities and growing electoral support for racist, anti-Semitic and xenophobic reactions may be pale forerunners of more to come.

France's *Front National* is the largest far-right party in Europe, electorally supported on an anti-immigration platform. Racism and violence pose serious questions in Germany as well. The Berlin Wall fell, but "the psychological wall" (*Die psychologische Mauer*) persists. Presently, it is rather perilous to be a foreigner (*Ausländer*) in Germany.[20] Just as Hitler's National Socialists detested the Weimar Republic, contemporary neo-Nazis view German democracy with open contempt.[21] Considering democracy as a degenerate political system inconsistent with Germany's historical tradition, the neo-Nazis aim to establish a totalitarian order. As part of this strategy, foreigners, guest-workers and Jews have been selected as specific targets of violence. With old prejudices being in the foreground, Europe is presently experiencing a resurgence of violence with strong racist overtones.

With the demise of the bipolar structure of international relations, one witnesses the outbreak of old conflicts and animosities among nations and peoples of the Balkans and East Central Europe.[22] The way in which the international community dealt with the aggression, occupation, genocide and ethnic cleansing in the former Federal Yugoslavia will have a profound impact on the attitudes towards Western Europe's own difficulties. It may also have repercussions on Russia, if the latter attempts to unify all or some Russians living in the fourteen former Soviet republics.[23] In Eastern Europe, armed extremist movements such as the *Pamyat* in Russia, the *Chetniks* in Serbia, the *Ustashis* in Croatia and the *Vatra Romaneasca* in Romania grew in size and influence.

India, which is the dominant power in South Asia, has a background of parliamentary democracy.[24] Violence may be defensible in some just causes, but democracy and terrorism are surely incompatible. Democracy tries to settle disputes by peaceful means. Violence, on the other hand, uses the weapons of terror. But paradoxically, some aspects of democracy feed violence. Real or perceived challenges to personal or cultural identity are capable of arousing fanatical activism.[25] The challenge need not be as dramatic as Iraq's policy of denying the separate identity of the Kuwaitis. Even the identity may be a mere fantasy, but, as Freud discovered, fantasies are also "facts".[26]

As sufficiently brought out in the previous sections, India and Kashmir have been melting pots of peoples and cultures. Frequently described as "the largest democracy", India has long been considered a model among developing countries for its success in the implementation of democratic institutions. Moreover, the ideal of non-violence has often been identified with the cultural tradition of India. Apart from Hinduism, other related beliefs such as Buddhism and Jainism, are also identified with the precepts of non-violence. Mahatma Gandhi had turned this unique tradition into a workable passive resistance against British colonialism.

But to survive is the ultimate aim of any organization, above all, the terrorist groups. The total accomplishment of an advocated cause may threaten the goal of survival. A terrorist group should be successful enough to maintain and perpetuate itself, but such ascendancy should not reach the point of putting the terrorist group out of business.[27] The Indian experience in parts of the country indicates that terrorism may increase when an official peace process begins.

Notes

1   Paul Wilkinson, *Terrorism and the Liberal State*, London, Macmillan, 1979; _____, *Terrorism versus Liberal Democracy: the Problem of Response*, London, Institute for the Study of Conflict, 1976.

2   Gaston Bouthoul, "Definitions of Terrorism", *International Terrorism and World Security*, David Carlton and Carlo Schaerf, eds., New York, John Wiley and Sons, 1978, pp. 50–53; John Dugard, "International Terrorism: Problems of Definition", *International Affairs*, London, 50/1 (January 1974), pp. 67–81. Two bibliographical studies: August Norton and Martin Greenberg, *International Terrorism: an Annotated Bibliography and Research Guide*, Boulder, Colorado, Westview, 1980; Edward Mickolus, *The Literature of Terrorism: a Selectively Annotated Bibliography*, Westport, Connecticut, Greenwood, 1980.

3   For conventions on terrorism, see: Jonah Alexander *et al.* eds., *Control of Terrorism: International Documents*, New York, Crane, Russak, 1979.

4   U. N. General Assembly, 40th Session, "Resolution 40/61", (9 December 1985), pp. 301–302 in *Resolutions and Decisions Adopted by the General Assembly during the Fortieth Session*, Supp. No. 53 (A/40/53), Official Record, New York, 1986.

5   U. N., S/RES/1269 (19 October 1999). Emphasis in the original.

6   M. Crenshaw, "The Causes of Terrorism", *Comparative Politics*, New York, 13 (1981), pp. 379–399; _____, "An Organizational Approach to the Analysis of Political Terrorism", *Orbis*, Oxford, 29 (1985), pp. 465–489; _____, "The Logic of Terrorism: Terrorist Behavior as a Product of Strategic Choice", *Origins of Terrorism, Psychologies, Ideologies, Theologies, States of Mind*, ed., W. Reich, Cambridge, Cambridge University Press, 1990, pp. 7–24.

7   J. M. Post, "Terrorist Psycho-logic: Terrorist Behavior as a Product of Psychological Forces", Reich, *op. cit.*, pp. 25–40.

8   R. M. Pearlstein, *The Mind of a Political Terrorist*, Wilmington, DE, Scholarly Resources, 1991.

9 C. A. Weinberg, "Terrorists and Terrorism", *Mind and Human Interaction*, Charlottesville, VA, 3 (1992), pp. 77–82.

10 Walter Laqueur, *The Age of Terrorism*, Boston, Little, Brown, 1987, p. 157.

11 Bruce Hoffman, " 'Holy Terror': the Implications of Terrorism Motivated by a Religious Imperative", *Studies in Conflict and Terrorism*, Bristol, PA, 18 (1995), pp. 271–284.

12 Joseph P. Montville, "The Psychological Roots of Ethnic and Sectarian Terrorism", *The Psychodynamics of International Relationships*, eds., Vamik D. Volkan, Demetrios A. Julius and Joseph V. Montville, Lexington, Mass., Lexington Books, 1990, p. 193.

13 Vamik D. Volkan, *The Need to Have Enemies and Allies: from Clinical Practice to International Relationships*, Northvale, New Jersey, Jason Aronson Inc., 1994, pp. 155f.

14 A study by a Sikh on the Afghan ruler who devastated Punjab: Ganda Singh, *Ahmad Shah Durrani: Father of Modern Afghanistan*, Quetta, Pakistan, Gosha-e Adab, Nisa Traders, 1977. An English translation of a Persian manuscript on the crucial Panipat Battle (1761): Casi Raja Pandit, *An Account of the Last Battle of Panipat and of the Events Leading to It*, tr. Lieut. Col. James Brown, Bombay, Oxford University Press, 1926. "Of every description of people, men, women and children, there were said to be five hundred thousand souls in the Mahratta camp, of whom the greatest part were killed or taken prisoner…" *Ibid.*, p. 40.

15 Vamik Volkan and Max Harris, *Shaking the Tent: the Psychodynamics of Ethnic Terrorism*, Charlottesville, VA, Center for the Study of Mind and Human Interaction, Monograph No. 1, 1993, pp. 19f.

16 Rafael Moses, "The Perception of the Enemy: a Psychological View," *Mind and Human Interaction*, Charlotteville, VA, 7/1 (February 1996), pp. 37–43.

17 D. S. Werman, "Freud's Narcissism of Minor Differences: a Review and a Reassessment", *Journal of the American Academy of Psychoanalysis*, New York, 16 (1988), pp. 451–459.

18 H. F. Stein, "The Rupture of Innocence: Oklahoma City, April 19, 1995", *Clio's Psyche*, 1 (1995), pp. 12f.; _____, "When the Heartland is No Longer Immune: the April 19, 1995 Bombing of the Oklahoma City Federal Building", *Psychohistory News: Newsletter of the International Psychohistorical Association*, Springfield, ILL., 14 (1995), pp. 2–4.

19 Türkkaya Ataöv, "Rising Racism in Europe", *Turkish Daily News*, Ankara, 21 January 1995.

20 Adam M. Weisberger, "German Unification and the Jewish Question", *Mind and Human Interaction*, Charlottesville, VA, 6/1 (February 1995), pp. 8–14.

21 James H. Anderson, "The Neo-Nazi Menace in Germany", *Studies in Conflict and Terrorism*, Bristol, PA, 18 (1995), pp. 39–46.

22 Vesna Pesic, "The Cruel Face of Nationalism", *Journal of Democracy*, Baltimore, 4/4 (October 1993), pp. 101–103; Jenusz Bugajski, "The Fate of Minorities in Eastern Europe", *ibid.*, pp. 85–99.

23 Türkkaya Ataöv, "Russians Outside Russia", *Turkish Daily News*, Ankara, 5 October 1994.

24 Dennis Austin and Anirudha Gupta, *The Politics of Violence in India and South Asia: Is Democracy an Endangered Species?* London, Research Institute for the Study of Conflict and Terrorism, 1990.

25 W. Nathaniel Howell, "Islamic Revivalism: a Cult Phenomenon?", *Mind and Human Interaction*, Charlottesville, VA, 5/3 (1994), pp. 97–103.

26 Peter Loewenberg, "The Psychological Reality of Nationalism: between Community and Fantasy", *Mind and Human Interaction*, Charlottesville, VA, 5/3 (1994), pp. 6–18.

27 Post, *op. cit.*, pp. 37–38.

Chapter 8

The Narco-Link

Terrorism is a general threat to humankind. In spite of occasional decline in the number of incidents in some societies, fresh and supplementary varieties of terrorism also develop. Accompanying this comprehensive and far-reaching peril, ominous links between terrorist and crime groupings come to light. In the words of Boutros Boutros-Ghali, former U.N. Secretary General and professor of international law, we are confronted by "crime multinationals".[1] The "business" of crime accounted for U.S. $1,000 billion a year, twice the size of the global oil dealings, and 4% of the international economy.[2]

As one of the new-fangled variations of terrorist *modus operandi*, drug production and trafficking have, not only "gone global", but the drug trade is caught up with multifarious unlawful activities, including the following: terrorization of the cultivating peasants, illicit trafficking, illegal immigration, abuse of children as carriers and sellers, coercion, kidnapping, theft, extortion, torture, weapons purchases for insurgency, murder, massacre, smuggling of stolen art objects, unlicensed gambling, prostitution, turf wars among the sellers, and the like.[3] Every stage of the "business" involves material and human costs as well as violence. The average terrorist, no matter what the other motives seem to be, may be more aroused by the enormous proceeds and earnings, simply "the fast buck". After all, if car theft, a routine crime, had been a legitimate business, it would have ranked fifth worldwide among the 500 companies on earth.[4] Illicit drug trafficking is designated, after the arms trade, as the second largest international business with an annual turnover estimated at between $300–$500 billion a year.[5] The recognition of the threat of drug trafficking is evident from the decision to declare the years 1991–2000 as the "U.N. Decade Against Drug Abuse".

The "Golden Crescent"

Among the world's largest drug growing areas are the "Golden Crescent" and the "Golden Triangle". Pakistan is located, together with Afghanistan and Iran, in the narcotics-producing region of South-West Asia known as the "Golden Crescent", an area which had been a traditional producer of opium. Eighty percent of heroin consumed in Europe is of South-West Asian origin.[6] In that region, drug usage has long been a "part of the local culture".[7] 'Heroinization' reads like a horror story especially in Pakistan, where the task of the drug traffickers was made easy during the

Afghan war.[8] As noted by a previous U.S. ambassador in Islamabad, Pakistan has a higher rate of heroin addiction than Americans.[9] Afghan opium and heroin began to be diverted to Pakistan's tribal areas in increasing quantities mainly for trafficking to international markets. Long the linchpin of the Golden Crescent, Afghanistan, "may have overtaken Burma (Myanmar) as the world's leading producer of opium".[10] Close to three million people in Pakistan in the age group 15-35 years are using a variety of narcotics; local consumption in that country assumed alarming proportions. According to the American Drug Enforcement Administration (DEA), people in high places in Pakistan were involved in the drug trade.[11] The announced results of the eradication campaign in Pakistan's Dir district, which used to produce more than one-third of the country's opium, do not correspond to the observations made by the United Nations representatives, and only some of the poppy crops in the Nihag Valley were destroyed leaving many opium-producing villages untouched.

The proliferation of illicit drugs in many parts of the country, including Azad Kashmir, brought havoc to that society as the number of addicts reportedly increased. As a chief processing and transit point for the heroin produced in the Golden Crescent and one of the world's largest exporters, Pakistan is in the grip of a severe drug problem, which cannot be resolved merely by checking poppy cultivation in the country. It has a few million drug addicts, and its two neighbours continue sending large quantities of opium to Pakistan refineries for processing. In addition to the mobile laboratories in territories controlled by the Afghan *Mujahideen*, there are more than one-hundred refineries in the tribal areas of Pakistan. Having become possibly the world's largest heroin supplier, mainly to Western Europe and the United States, the credibility and prestige of that country abroad has been seriously eroded.[12]

The Government of Pakistan admits that the country is experiencing an acute drug situation as the vicious circle of demand and supply is getting bigger and bigger affecting all sections of the population. The economic losses to the nation are colossal measured in terms of hundreds of millions of rupees spent on activities like law enforcement and treatment of addicts, all being additional burdens on the limited resources of the country.

Narcotics trafficking involves the production of drugs such as cannabis,[13] heroin,[14] cocaine,[15] mandrax[16] and others, and their trade attracts in the process the active participation of ethnically, religiously or ideologically motivated entities. The Afghanistan-Iran-Pakistan area sends heroin taken from opium gum ends to Europe and to the United States. The heroin from the Yunnan province (China) reaches the international markets via Hong Kong and Taiwan. Even entrepreneurial North Koreans entered the heroin business. Myanmar has long been a major opium producer. In the Golden Triangle, it remains as the "bread basket of the opium trade".[17] The Basque (Spain), Irish (U.K.), Naga (India) and PKK (Turkey) separatists as well as a number of others in all continents partly funded their violent actions through involvement in the illicit drug trade. Powerful new mafias emerged with the radical changes in Eastern Europe, Russia and Central Asia. Criminal organizations in Russia have set up supply routes to the Baltic ports, Hungary, the Czech Republic and Slovakia. The five newly-independent republics in Central Asia are increasingly being referred to as a new "Columbia". The consequences of the corruption of public authorities and the destabilization of the whole economy is most evident in the Latin American country of Columbia, where a cocaine king financed the campaign of a presidential candidate. The impoverished Albanian peasants cultivate cannabis, mostly in plantations established by the Sicilian mafia. Some Nigerians are operating new drug routes from the Caribbean and South America into Britain. That country has become the key to the drug trade from both South-East and South-West Asia. Kenya is playing a key role in the narcotics smuggling networks that blight the region. Southern Africa also developed into an important transport hub for illegal narcotics. As evident in the U.S. invasion (1989) of Panama,[18] drugs may be a stimuli in interventions in other countries.

Although Afghanistan had officially banned opium poppy cultivation as early as 1957, the ban proved to be ineffective on account of the inaccessibility of the remote production areas and their domination by traditionally uncontrolled tribal forces as much as the irresolution and impotence of the central government in Kabul. The armed conflict after the Soviet intervention (1979) speeded up production. Its sale contributed to the funding of the anti-Soviet war effort, intermixed with the support of Pakistan and Iran to the *Mujahideen*. The Soviet adventure in Afghanistan exposed, in addition, large number of soldiers to drugs, in a way not dissimilar to the American experience in Vietnam.[19]

As a consequence of the Soviet intervention in Afghanistan, groups on both sides of the border, armed with modern automatic weapons, indulged in heavy clashes with guards when smugglers were intercepted. The unravelling of the Soviet Union also led to the break-up of the previously centralized anti-narcotics effort. The achievement of independence on the part of a number of non-Russian republics now prevent cross-border cooperation of police and customs officials but proves to be no obstacle to criminal trafficking. Narco-mafia possesses large amounts of money to subvert those who should be combatting them. The establishment of the Commonwealth of Independent States (CIS) has in no way provided a key to the growing problem. The phenomenon is so exceptional that anti-drug activity has been written into the new Russian military doctrine. However, in addition to the lack of knowledge of modern investigative techniques and a chronic shortage of all kinds of equipment, the large sums of money, resulting from the drugs trade, is fuelling the corruption. Further, the opening of the borders since the collapse of the Communist bloc (1989) created new opportunities to ease the smuggling of drugs from far away places in the East.

While Iran became a major transshipment point for illegal opiates from Pakistan and Afghanistan, opium and heroine (not hashish) export from the latter increased even after the control of the country by the Taliban fundamentalist leadership, which imposed a ban on hashish, consumed by the Afghans, but not on poppies from which opium and heroine are made and exported. Islamic guerillas from Afghanistan have been endeavouring to extend their influence in Tajikistan and even beyond.

Owing to Pakistan's vulnerable borders with Afghanistan in the north and its long coastal belt in the south, that country's geographical location is perfect for drug trafficking.[20] For some years now, heroin has become the lifeblood of Pakistan's economy and political system. Those who hold purse strings in production and transport purchase protection, gain access to political circles, and acquire large shares in industries and banking. It is also a major source for groups of local people, including the terrorists absorbed in violence at home and across the border. The profit to drug dealers is over \$8 billion or almost double Pakistan's annual budget. The country provides transit routes for drugs reaching the West via Pakistan International Airways (PIA) or the Karachi port, the main narcotics entrepot in the region. Hyderabad in Sindh is also a leading way station for heroin on its way down to Karachi. Heroin is sold and bought throughout much of Punjab. The underworld of the legendary city of Lahore, whose oriental charm has allured the invader and tourist alike since times immemorial, is now run by various heroin gangs. The PIA routine was so repeatedly used that the Saudi Arabian authorities warned that direct flights between Peshawar and Jeddah could be stopped.[21] The Karachi course passes through Yemen to Southern Europe or the African route via Somalia and Ethiopia to Kenya and onwards. The Balkan journey starts in Afghanistan and advances via Pakistan, Iran, and Turkey.[22]

The ban by the Iranian Revolution on all forms of narcotics production and consumption pressurized dealers to go underground or abroad, principally to Pakistan. Settling in Karachi and Quetta, the latter the capital-city of Pakistani Baluchistan, they helped reconstruct and enlarge covert drug activities. The ban by the Zia-ul Haq regime, especially the Prohibition Order of 1979, further coerced the dealers to go underground and bolstered the hands of the long-standing networks in the North-West Frontier Province and Punjab. In spite of General Zia's Islamization policy, some senior officials around him were reportedly engrossed in drug-related pursuits. The war in Afghanistan disrupted some of the old routes, bringing Pakistan more to the foreground in the illicit drug trade. Such blossoming narco-link, aided by all these circumstances, enabled Pakistan's Inter-Services Intelligence (ISI) as much as the drug smugglers to bring arms to several parts of India including Kashmir.

No policy of containing and uprooting terrorism can be rewarding if it does not fully reflect on and challenge the narco-link. The whole procedure, starting with its cultivation up to weapons purchases for insurgency, seems to be the greatest single breeder of violence and crime all over the world, including the conflict-ridden land of Kashmir. Some other clashes such as the Naga-Kuki violence also had their roots in the lucrative drug transactions. Much of the illicit drug profits are used to finance and arm insurgents and terrorists. The trade is further promoted by intimidating and corrupting some of the law-enforcers. A number of government officials are frequently blamed, although not necessarily indicted, for direct links with drug smuggling. Some key officials even in the security service are thus undermined and neutralized.[23] Not only the insurgents, but also some foreign powers may sponsor terrorism and drug trafficking if the latter seem to serve their short-term interests. Pakistan's role in the case of Kashmir and that of violence in other parts of the Indian Union are no exceptions.

Drug money plays a significant role in Pakistan's domestic politics. Those who dominate the parallel economy based on drugs enterprises may destabilize any administration that threatens their business. Privatization offered vast opportunities to launder huge profits and 'legitimize' their business. They compose an additional centre of power, along with the constitutional establishments and justifiable pressure groups. One may even assert that laundered narcotics money in a way activates the political system. The Bank of Credit and Commerce International (BCCI), believed to have been charged with laundering drug money, financed the movement for the fall from power (1977) of the PPP government. Some drug barons, who supported party organizations and election campaigns, were themselves voted as MPs on the basis of the sheer power of the contraband money. Various lists of drug traffickers, occasionally seen in print,[24] include a number of active politicians, elected or not.

The Afridis, Khattaks and the Yusufzais are the major drug networks functioning in the NWFP. Pakistan's drug barons established a close trade nexus with other drug barons, including the Indian ones. Drug traffickers throughout the world resorted to destabilising especially the border regions. The drug-mafia was so powerful during the eleven years of General Zia-ul Haq's rule that it was running a parallel underground economy. Major Farooq Hameed, a pilot of General Zia and arrested for heroin smuggling, was the leader of a gang which operated through an elaborate network linking Dubai, Britain and Norway. Malik Saleem, another Pakistani drug prince, was extradited to the United States after a long legal battle. It is asserted that Malik Muhammed Ayub Khan Afridi (also known as Haji Ayub), one of the biggest barons in Pakistan, supported Nawaz Sharif's Islami Jamhoori Ittehad (IJI). Sohail Zia Butt, a Kashmiri and a cousin-in-law of Nawaz Sharif,[25] was known to be the controlling mastermind of one of the larger heroine gangs in Lahore. The election campaign (1988) of Malik Meraj Khalid, who served as a Speaker in the National Assembly, was reportedly financed by Haji Mirza Iqbal Beg, a Lahore landlord active in election campaigns. Although the U.S. Drug Enforcement Administration (DEA)[26] and the European Narcotics Police tried to put him behind bars several times, he was able to avoid arrest for two decades. When his political clout began to grow weaker, he initially hid in the tribal belt on the Afghan border and then surrendered to Pakistani police (1989). Another one, Haji Ali Muhammad Notezai, was twice elected to the Baluchistan Provincial Assembly. Another minister in charge of revenues in the Baluchistan Cabinet was a well-known smuggler. While Moeen Qureshi's caretaker government barred drug barons from contesting the 1993 elections, two renowned traffickers became members, nevertheless, in the provincial assemblies in Baluchistan and the NWFP.

While the drug money, laundered through a chain of investments before it returns to Pakistan, created a new billionaire class which became a major threat to Pakistan's ailing democracy as well as to the social fabric and economic development, some individuals who expressed their dismay over involvement in narcotics smuggling became prey to the drug barons' wrath. Dr. Sayed Majrooh, Director of the Afghan Information Center in Peshawar, was assassinated for objecting to clandestine drug operations, and Altaf Ali Khan, the regional chief of the Pakistan Narcotics Control Board, was found with a bullet in his chest the day after he supervised an anti-drug operation.

Some individuals in Pakistan's armed forces were either arrested for heroin smuggling or were reported for extensive links with the drug mafias. For instance, Swedish authorities discovered (1976) large amounts of hashish in two Pakistan Air Force (PAF) aircraft, which were in Sweden to collect spare parts. In the early 1980s, some officers, mostly majors, were accused of drug-related offences. Lieutenant General Fazle Haq, an ex-Chief Minister and Governor of NWFP, was believed to be a protector of the drug business. Some army vehicles that transported weapons and ammunition to the *Mujahideen* were also drug carriers. Profits from drug trafficking were partially used to finance the war in Afghanistan. The Turkish authorities seized (1993) ten tons of heroin dispatched from Peshawar via Karachi in army trucks. Groups in Pakistan's ISI are believed to have been involved in drug smuggling from the rebel-controlled poppy-producing areas of Afghanistan to Pakistan. Reportedly, Army Chief of Staff and the head of the ISI suggested[27] to the newly-elected Prime Minister Sharif that drug deals could be used to finance foreign covert operations. The army chiefs denied these claims.

There is also a link between illicit drug trafficking and Pakistan's funding of insurgents in Kashmir and in other parts of India.[28] The Kashmir insurgency as well as Sikh militancy were partly funded by heroin. Initially, the old city gangs formed the base of the "Kashmiri Heroin Syndicate". Sohail Zia Butt was the key figure linking the old city gangs with the men who regulated the flow of drugs and money. In a socio-cultural atmosphere wherein marriages are also alliances of wealth and influence, Butt's career prospered along with those of the Sharif brothers. Haji Iqbal Butt was a close advisor to the Sharifs, and Aslam Butt was the syndicate's "ambassador" to other drug mafias. He had good relations with Chaudhry Shaukat Bhatti, in charge of the Arain community network around Lahore. The Hizb-e Islami of Gulbuddin Hekmatyar, one of the strongest of the pro-Pakistani groups, and in the foreground of the Afghan *Mujahideen*, was not left out. Another pro-Pakistani group, the Hizb-ul Mujahideen, was supported by the ISI. Similarly, the Sikh rebels, assisted by Haji Mirza Iqbal Beg, from the Arain community and Pakistan's principal drug baron, carried heroin across the border for money and arms. Iqbal Beg, who had brought a specialist to see General Zia's retarded daughter, secured access to circles of power and privilege. Much of the profit from the drug trade is channelled into the purchase of arms, which end up in the hands of the local insurgents and imported mercenaries, who are among "the most determined zealots".[29] Easily accessible weapons fuelled violence on both sides of the Indo-Pakistan border. Pakistan's ISI and India's Research and Analysis Wing have waged a war against each other in Nepal, where Afghani-Pakistani networks of Wahabite Sunni persuasion have been working since the early 1980s. Sri Lanka is also increasingly used as a transit territory for narcotics, in which the Liberation Tigers of Tamil Eelam (LTTE) may be involved.

How to Combat?

The Government of Pakistan took a series of measures to combat some aspects of this multi-faceted drug problem.[30] A federal Narcotics Control Division sponsored a number of crop substitution development projects, and an Anti-Narcotics Task Force was set up with its headquarters in Islamabad and operational units in Peshawar and Karachi. The amendment of a relevant law provided for destruction of seized narcotics after retaining some samples under court supervision. A Drug Abuse Prevention Resource Centre actively supports efforts to reduce demands of drugs in the society and carries out a preventive education programme. Some chemicals which have potential use in the conversion of opium into heroin have been placed on a restricted list for the purpose of imports. India and Pakistan signed a bilateral agreement for exchange of information about drug trafficking and smuggling across the border.

However, the control and the ultimate elimination of the narcotics menace constitute a continuous process, and such a serious problem will not be solved in a short period of time. For example, the lands under poppy cultivation are essentially inaccessible areas along the Afghanistan-Pakistan border, and developmental infrastructure to provide alternative means of livelihood to the people is yet to be provided for the satisfaction of all concerned. The government has not been able to stop heroine cultivation. The heroin manufacturing laboratories are also largely located in inaccessible parts of the borders, and they can be easily shifted from one place to another when the authorities launch offensives. Some corrupted officials fail to act decisively against the drug lords. Moreover, since the tribal areas have preserved their autonomy even after partition, the tribal *jirga* in the NWFP described government action as interference in the "internal affairs" of their region.

Just as in the case of terrorism, the threats emanating from drug trafficking are international in terms of the unbounded sources of narcotics, the assortment of the routes employed, and multi-national cooperation as well as competition among the syndicates. Traffickers show particular tendency to abuse fragile societies, such as many Eastern European countries in the West or Kashmir in Asia, whose security as well as legislative and judiciary systems are rendered vulnerable by intense upheavals. In view of the heinous but excessive profits that the drug business delivers, the risk of the terrorist groups to seize new opportunities, especially after the disintegration of the Soviet Union, is no longer a matter of fiction. A momentous cost is the inescapable impact of drug trafficking on the quality of administration in terms of security, services and fair deal. All narco-terrorists corrupt various officials in their chain of contacts, undercutting in the process the trustworthiness of governments. Parts of the political body of some countries, the bureaucracy and even groups within the security services are permeated by narcotics-related decay.

The peril assumes an alarming appearance if there exists state sponsorship to narco-terrorists in the form of safe haven, training facilities and support of any kind. Some governments are accused of state sponsorship of terrorism and other crimes emanating from it. India is not the only country that frequently blames its neighbour Pakistan for some of the violence within its borders. For instance, Turkey repeatedly requested Syria, the adjacent state to its south, to close the terrorist bases of the self-styled "Kurdish Workers Party" (PKK), expel its narco-terrorist leader (Abdullah Öcalan), and terminate support for the narcotics industry in the Bekaa Valley of Eastern Lebanon. There are other instances of state sponsorship, some of them unusual and even fantastic. The United States apparently ran a secret war in Laos on opium profits.[31]

Narco-terrorism and money laundering are inter-related. In the process of converting profits collected from criminal activities into licit-looking financial power, the narco-terrorists disrupt the society's economic system. Since the sums involved exceed the annual gross national products of the majority of countries, colossal volumes of such dimensions possess the capacity of threatening democratic forms of governments, shake weak economies and destabilize global markets. While at times even stolen art objects are traded as part of drug deals, some accumulated capital is channelled into luxurious business, and portions of it pour into expensive weapons, bringing more bloodshed, more drugs, and more power.

No single country can win a war on drugs on its own. There has to be regional and global efforts. In the South Asian context, the SAARC countries should pool their resources by creating a joint anti-narcotics task force to check the flow of illegal produce and extridite traffickers. The task force, made up of representatives from all member states, must enjoy the powers to challenge the authority of the big fish. A treaty on extradition of smugglers may also help in setting up a regional anti-narcotics regime. No regional country should be regarded as a safe haven for drug traffickers. Pakistan and India especially should accord top priority to "drug education".

There have been international strategies to combat narco-terrorism.[32] The United Nations led multilateral initiatives including treaties, new organizational structures and congresses. To arrest the haphazard growth of the control system, the Convention of Narcotic Drugs (1961), amended by the 1972 Protocol, aimed to consolidate most of the earlier international instruments. Up to 1971, only narcotic drugs were subject to control, but growing concern over the harmful dependency effects of amphetamine-type drugs, sedative-hypnotic agents, hallucinogens, and other stimulants, led to the adoption of the Convention on Psychotropic Substances (1971). While the General Assembly Declaration on the Control of Drug Trafficking and Drug Abuse (1984) stated that its eradication was the responsibility of all states, the international conference in Vienna (1987), attended by the representatives of 138 states, about half of whom were ministers of cabinet rank, prepared the ground for a comprehensive convention.

Among a series of treaties dealing directly with narcotics, the United Nations Convention against Illicit Traffic in Narcotic Drugs and Psychotropic Substances (19

December 1988) obliges, among other provisions, the extradition of drug traffickers. During the same year (1990) that the 1988 Convention entered into force, the General Assembly adopted a Global Programme of Action to achieve the goal of an international society free of illicit drugs. A number of bodies have been created in the U.N. organizational structure to deal with the drugs control regime.[33] There have been nine congresses, held once every five years since 1955. The United Nations established (1991) the International Drug Control Program, which coordinates all U.N. control activities, promotes the implementation of the relevant treaties, and provides effective leadership in international control. It serves as the focal point for the U.N. Decade against Drug Abuse (1991–2000).[34] Some regional organizations are also committed to the struggle against narco-terrorism. The United Nations maintains working relationships with a number of interregional, intergovernmental and international organizations, not part of the U.N. family of organizations, but actively involved in drug control. The customs authorities of states belonging to the Customs Cooperation Council (CCC) work to harmonize customs laws and regulations, and advocate increased enforcement coordination. "Interpol" is the only international body, on the other hand, which can be requested to apprehend suspected criminals. Dozens of bilateral treaties that Britain signed, related to the confiscation of the assets of the narco-terrorists, may be a model for some other states to echo and repeat.

An intense international concern over the more insidious long-term effects of chronic drug use is evident today. The problem, which has reached epidemic proportions, has its main roots in the Golden Crescent and the Golden Triangle. It needs even more cooperative action. There have been some successes to date, but the usefulness of such international measures to contain or reduce narco-terrorism has been limited. Many more steps need to be taken especially to discourage state sponsorship of terrorism in all its manifestations. Some societies, notorious for their widespread corruption, are deeply involved in illicit economic activity. Agreements are needed on standardizing legislation, extradition, cooperation between law-enforcement agencies, and penalties.

Notes

1   Quite frequently, they are referred to as "empires". For instance: Richard Kunnes, *The American Heroin Empire: Power, Profits, and Politics*, New York, Dodd, Mead, 1972.
2   T. Judah, "Crime: the Biggest Business in the World", *The Sunday Telegraph*, London, 17 November 1996. Also: David W. Rasmussen and Bruce L. Benson, *The Economic Anatomy of a Drug War: Criminal Justice in the Commons*, London, Rowman and Littlefield Publishers, 1994.
3   R. Ehrenfeld, *Narco-Terrorism*, New York, Basic Books, 1990; David N. Nurco, Thomas E. Hanlon and Timothy W. Kinlock, "Recent Research on the Relationship Between Illicit Drug Use and Crime", *Behavioral Sciences and the Law*, (1991), pp. 221–249; David N. Nurco *et al.*, "The Criminality of Narcotic Addicts", *Journal of Nervous and Mental Diseases*, 173/2 (1985), pp. 94–102.

4   *The Times*, London, 17 February 1997.
5   Nicholas Hopkinson, *Fighting Drugs Trafficking in the Americas and Europe*, London, Wiston House, 1991, p. 1.
6   *Ibid.*, p. 11.
7   R. W. Dellow, *The Drugs Trade*, London, Sandhurst, Conflict Studies, 1995, p. 2.
8   Khalid Mahmood Malik, "Drug Menace in South Asia", *Regional Studies*, Islamabad, VIII/3 (Summer 1990), pp. 32–48.
9   Robert B. Oakley, "Pakistan and the United States", *Strategic Studies*, Islamabad, XII/3 (Spring 1989), p. 30.
10   Nisid Hajari, "Losing the Opium War", *Time*, New York, 22 March 1999, p. 22.
11   *The Pakistan Times*, Lahore, 27 May 1989.
12   U.S., Central Intelligence Agency, "Heroin in Pakistan: Sowing the Wind", reproduced in *The Friday Times*, Lahore, 3 September 1993. Also: "Opium War", *Sunday*, Calcutta, 21/13 (27 March–2 April 1994), pp. 27–29; "CIA Report on Heroin in Pakistan: Sowing the Wind", *Strategic Digest*, New Delhi, XXIII/10 (October 1993), pp. 1593–1628.
13   Also known as hashish, marijuana, and dope, it is a tobacco-like plant produced everywhere.
14   Also known as brown (when impure), junk, horse and others, it is generally a white powder procured mostly from the Golden Crescent and the Golden Triangle (Thailand, Myanmar, Laos).
15   Also called charlie, coke, foot, lady and snow, it is extracted from the coca plant, chopped up and usually sniffed through a tube.
16   It is a synthetic drug produced and exported from South Asia.
17   Sumita Kumar, "Drug Trafficking in the Golden Triangle", *Asian Strategic Review: 1997–98*, New Delhi, Institute for Defence Studies and Analysis, 1998, pp. 169f.
18   John Quigly, "The Legality of the United States Invasion of Panama", *Yale Journal of International Law*, 15 (1990), pp. 276–315.
19   R. W. Dellow, *Instabilities in Post-Communist Europe: the Drugs Trade*, London, U.K. Ministry of Defence Conflict Studies Research Centre, 1995, p. 2.
20   Sumita Kumar, "Drug Trafficking in Pakistan", *Asian Strategic Review: 1994–95*, New Delhi, Institute for Defence Studies and Analyses, 1995, pp. 194–222.
21   *The News*, Islamabad, 23 September 1994.
22   Türkkaya Ataöv, "Some Observations on Terrorism in India and Turkey", ed., Govind Narain Srivastava, *Democracy and Terrorism*, New Delhi, International Institute for Non-Aligned Studies, 1997, pp. 125–139.
23   Lawrence W. Sherman, *Controlling Police Corruption*, Washington, D.C., National Institute of Law Enforcement and Criminal Justice, 1978; Michel Girodo, "Drug Corruption of Underground Agents: Measuring the Risk", *Behavioral Sciences and the Law*, W. Sussex, 9 (1991), pp. 361–370.
24   *Pulse*, Islamabad, 21–27 May and 28 May–3 June 1993.
25   The CIA Report erroneously refers to S. Z. Butt as the brother-in-law of N. Sharif. It also erroneously refers to Momin Khan Afridi as a brother of Rehmat Shah Afridi, the owner of the *Frontier Post*. S. Z. Butt, S. Sharif and R. S. Afridi have denied involvement in drugs trafficking.
26   Rasmussen and Bensen, *op. cit.*, pp. 142–144.
27   *The News*, Islamabad, 13 September 1994.

28 The opium lobby is "very strong" in India as well, and a number of politicians are reportedly "involved in the business", according to some Indian sources. For instance: Avirook Son, "Money Plant", *Sunday*, *op. cit.*, p. 26.

29 K. D. Chadha, "Trans-National Threats to International Peace and Security: Terrorism and Drug Trafficking", *U. S. I. Journal*, New Delhi, CXXVIII/531 (January–March 1998), pp. 43–49.

30 The Government of Pakistan, *Pakistan Fights Narcotics Menace*, Islamabad, Ministry of Information and Broadcasting, n.d.; The Government of Pakistan, *Pakistan's Fight Against Narcotics*, Islamabad, Ministry of Information and Broadcasting, 1987.

31 John Quigly, *The Ruses for War*, Buffalo, N.Y., Prometheus Books, 1992, pp. 97–107.

32 International cooperation began in the early part of the 20th century. The first international conference to control the traffic in drugs was held in 1909 in Shanghai, near the source of the problem. The meeting led to the signing of the first drug control treaty (The Hague, 1912). The League of Nations established (1920) an Advisory Committee on Traffic in Opium and Other Dangerous Drugs, and the Permanent Central Narcotics Board introduced the second International Opium Convention (1925), to be followed by the 1931 and the 1936 Conventions. The last-mentioned was the first to call for the severe punishment of illicit drug traffickers.

33 For instance, the Commission on Narcotic Drugs (CND), one of ECOSOC's six functional commissions, is the central policy-making body within the United Nations system for dealing in depth with related questions. CND's subsidiary bodies coordinate enforcement at the regional level. The International Narcotics Control Board (INCB) was established to limit the cultivation, production, manufacture and utilization of drugs and, at the same time, to ensure their availability for medical and scientific purposes.

34 On the multi-faceted approach to drug control: United Nations, *The United Nations and the Drug Abuse Control*, New York, International Drug Control Program, 1992.

Chapter 9

Violence in Kashmir

It may be asserted that since 1947 there has always been some conflict and even hostilities in Jammu and Kashmir. Terrorism, now more than a decade old, on the other hand, is the product of recent years. Initially led by the youth of Srinagar, for what they called *azadi*, later largely usurped by Pakistan, and finally turned into a proxy war against India by the same neighbour, terrorism may be said to have moved through a number of phases.

As described earlier, interference blended with violence has a longer past. The tribal raiders and the invading Pakistani forces targeted, in late 1947, some minorities and indulged in devastation and looting in this piece of territory that belonged to a neighbour. Portraying Lal Shastri, who succeeded Nehru, as an ineffective and shaky leader, Pakistani commandos infiltrated into the same terrain a decade and a half later, only to find that they could not count on extensive support. It was the hijacking of an Indian Airlines plane by two Al-Fatah activists in early 1971 to help gain the release of two of their associates held in a Kashmir jail that signalled the start of terrorism there. The militant movement resulted in crystallizing the attitudes of groups of people towards a religious ideology, pushing the nationalistic component of the Kashmir identity into a phase of dormancy. The new ideology perceives of an Islamic state stretching from Kashmir and covering Pakistan, Afghanistan, Iran, and Central Asia. The weakening of the National Conference, the demise of Sheikh Abdullah, and the rising of Hindu fundamentalism in Jammu and Ladakh as well as in some other parts of India provided a fillip to the dissemination of such an Islamic orientation. Although Islamic ferver has not swept the entire Kashmir society, a new Caliphate movement "has great potential to come into conflict with the other [ethno-cultural] perception" in Kashmir.[1] Pakistan escalated its covert war in 1988 after it acquired nuclear weapons about a year before.[2] For years, the case of Kashmir presented the analyst with "an ideal study of proxy arming as an extension of policy by other means".[3] Although much reduced now, terrorism has not yet abandoned the region. What is called the "Islamic" component of the strife may not remain confined to Kashmir alone; it still has the potential to spill over to other countries.

The Long Insurgency

Violence in J&K commenced with the entry of Pakistani units into the land on the grounds that the place of this Muslim majority state ought not be in India. Although each census showed an overwhelming Hindu majority in the Indian provinces, the Muslim community within the same union constituted the largest minority. Not only India, but a good portion of world public opinion strongly suspects that Pakistan, which continues to keep about two-fifths of the state's territory, creates political instability in the rest of the state.

Sheikh Abdullah, who formally took over the government in early 1948, emphasized Hindu-Muslim unity from the very beginning of his political career, having been convinced that only Muslim-oriented slogans would bring misery for all. Nevertheless, he was dismissed, released and rearrested on account of his occasional but strong anti-India statements. Violence erupted after the disappearance in late 1963 of a strand of hair of the Muslim Prophet Muhammad at the Hazratbal Shrine. The mobs, which destroyed some Hindu property and condemned the Chief Minister Bakshi Ghulam Muhammad, shouted slogans for the release of Sheikh Abdullah. The latter, after discharge in early 1964, was invited both by the Pakistani President Ayub Khan and the Indian Prime Minister Nehru to find a solution to the Kashmir issue. Abdullah's role abruptly came to an end when Nehru suddenly died while Kashmir's veteran statesman, who did not trust any other Indian leader to the same extent, was still in Pakistan. His statements in support of Pakistan's demand for a plebiscite and his readiness to meet Chinese leaders led to his arrest a year after Lal Bahadur Shastri succeeded Nehru.

As briefly referred to above, Pakistan's President mistook the new Prime Minister's soft style to mean irresolution and embarked on Operation Gibraltar (and Operation Grand Slam) enabling 7,000 commandos to infiltrate into Kashmir. It was supposed to initiate a guerilla movement against the Indian Government. When the Indian security forces hit back by taking Haji Pir Pass to stop infiltration, Pakistan militant rebellion dispatched armoured units further provoking Indian response to cross the international border. A U.N.-sponsored ceasefire, accepted by both sides, ended the stalemate of the 1965 conflict. There seemed to be no reason for an insurgency by the Kashmiri Muslims. Mrs. Indira Gandhi, who came to power after Shastri's death (1965), showed more understanding towards Sheikh Abdullah who had always harboured secular views that brought him closer to Nehru before 1947. It was the act of two militants (Muhammad Ashraf and Muhammad Hashim Qureshi), who hijacked an Indian plane on 30 January 1971, and expected the release of their saboteur colleagues, thereby widely opening the chapter of terrorism in J&K. India banned the flights of Pakistani planes over its territory when the hijacked aircraft was burned in Lahore.

During the same year, Pakistan lost the Muslim population of East Bengal on account of the faults and misdeeds of its own armed forces, and not the intervention of the Indian army. The common denominator of religion was inadequate to preserve the union. Pakistan's Prime Minister Zulfikar Ali Bhutto, who, like the previous leaders of the country, backed the idea of Kashmir's secession and the equipping as well as the training of Muslim militants, had no option but to sign the Simla Agreement (1972), according to which the two neighbours contracted to resolve their differences through peaceful means and honour the Line of Actual Control (LOAC), previously known as the Line of Control (LOC).

In addition to Pakistan's continued interest in armed belligerency in parts of Kashmir, the ascent of hawkish activism in Punjab and the alienation of the Sikh community in response to Operation Blue Star inspired and buoyed up militancy in Kashmir. Muslim fundamentalists and the pro-Pakistani elements became more and more aggressive, and explosive devices started to go off more often and in more places. In the meantime, Mrs. Gandhi received a grandiose traditional welcome involving a procession of boats down the Jhelum River when Sheikh Abdullah took over as Chief Minister following the 1975 accord that came after three years of negotiations. Although India's new Prime Minister, who succeeded Mrs. Gandhi did not favour a Kashmiri government that would sympathise with the Congress Party which seemed to have lost the country-wide contest, the National Conference under Abdullah's leadership won the 1977 elections. Even after the death of the Lion of Kashmir in 1982, the National Conference, this time under Sheikh Abdullah's son Farooq, won another sweeping victory in the 1983 elections, the party showing strength mainly in the Valley, and the Congress getting most of the seats in Jammu. When Farooq Abdullah suspected his brother-in-law Ghulam Muhammad ('Gul') Shah of intriguing with the Congress to succeed him as Chief Minister, he was expelled from the National Conference but struck back by splitting it and forming the Asli (Real) National Conference to be headed by his wife Khalida.

While the Congress Party was searching for ways to remove Farooq Abdullah and to discipline him, some dissatisfied citizens waved Pakistani flags and shouted slogans against the Indian cricket team during a match (1983) with the West Indian team in Srinagar. At the time that Operation Blue Star furnished arguments for militancy in Punjab, the Kashmiri separatists labelled Farooq Abdullah as an "Indian agent". The latter argued with New Delhi, however, that to toe the Congress line could make Kashmir another Punjab. Farooq was dismissed, nevertheless, and his rival Shah was sworn in as the new Chief Minister only to be ousted in favour of an imposed Governor's rule. Farooq Abdullah would come back as the leader of the National Conference-Congress coalition government. This short experience should have illustrated that such interference from the federal capital promoted the cause of the militants, facilitated their publicity, and helped them to set up new formations. It is no surprise that the opposition groups favouring the Islamisation of the Valley and secession joined hands to forge ahead in support of the Muslim United Front, which painted both Farooq and his party as treacherous. The National Conference and Congress still won in the 1987 assembly elections, but there were charges of rigging at some polls.

The Valley Aflame

Peace and order in the state had radically deteriorated by mid-1988. There were bomb blasts in Srinagar (1 August)[4] and in the main bazaar of Jammu (12 August). While green flags were hoisted in downtown Srinagar on 14 August marking the anniversary of Pakistan's independence, the same people chose to jack up black flags the next day, the occasion of India's National Day.[5] The demonstrators shouting anti-Indian slogans the day after clashed with the police causing the death of one person and injury to about one hundred more, and attempted to set the Rishi Pir Temple on fire. Four persons were killed during the riots on18 August, and four more within a week. When a bomb exploded (31 August) in a bus killing one person, terrorism claimed this loss as the first casualty since the beginning of the new wave of violence in 1988. Eijaz Ahmad Dar, the first militant to lose his life in police action on 18 September, became a martyr. The day he died became another occasion for renewed protests. His loss meant more for the insurgents than the serious injuries suffered by eleven persons with the explosion in a van about a month later. By the beginning of 1989, the militants became brash and brazen enough to attack police stations in the state capital.

Shuddering at the prospect that violence would grow worse, many officials felt unfit to restrain the menace and welcomed the initially small contingent of the National Security Guard (NSG) commandos, stationed in Srinagar, to train J&K police officers in anti-terrorist tactics. This measure falling far short of meeting the growing peril, General K.V. Krishna Rao, the former Chief of the Army Staff and the Governor of Manipur and Nagaland, was appointed to replace Jagmohan as the new governor. Subsequent events amply revealed that what was needed to confront terrorism competently went beyond a change of governors. Such appointees, who exhibited little realistic vision to balance conflicting demands, were publicly criticized by high-ranking federal officials and quickly replaced by others.

This inconclusive official response to complex circumstances consequentially encouraged the militants in Kashmir. Under their coaching and intimidation, more and more people placed hopes on the path of violence to achieve certain aims. Acts of terrorism were better planned, daringly executed and created stronger roots. Terrorists successfully ambushed (13 July 1989) a Central Reserve Police Force (CRPF) bus killing two and wounding fourteen. While the so-called Jammu and Kashmir Liberation Front (JKLF) claimed responsibility for this bloodshed, a fundamentalist terrorist organization called the Hizbullah Islamia Jamhoria warned the "traitors" of further violence if found collaborating with the "enemy", that is, the government and its security forces. The Islamic extremists set in motion a fundamentalist campaign especially targeting women. An explosion (20 July)[6] in a ladies toilet in a cinema was followed by acid-throwing (29 July) on the faces of two young girls who had not worn veils. Pakistan Independence Day was observed (1989) with even more spirit and zeal than the year before. While green flags fluttered freely on the occasion all over Srinagar, some passionate groups burned the Indian colours trying to attach to their action an imposed air of solemnity. The police unable to carry out its conventional functions of check and control, the assertive activists engineered a series of bomb blasts that injured about sixty persons in one day. Feeling estranged and vulnerable, some members among the decision-making authorities found refuge in the thought that this was, after all, a "tolerable level of violence". Then, two Kashmiri secessionists hijacked a state transport bus and blew it up near Tangmarg (17 August).[7]

About 50 persons were injured in a series of incidents (18–21 August).[8] One of the leaders of the ruling National Conference (Muhammad Yusuf Halwai) was assassinated in daylight in the centre of the town, and the residence of the State Congress President (Shafi Muhammad Qureshi) was damaged by explosions. Even the effigies of Sheikh Abdullah were burnt for his association with India and attachment to the idea of secularism.

Terrorism threw the whole Valley into ferment. Starting with 14 September, Kashmiri Pandits became the next target. The Vice-President of the Baharatiya Janata Party (Tikka Lal Taploo) was killed for his belief that the accession of J&K to India was irrevocable.[9] Hand grenades injured eleven policemen and twenty others (18 September).[10] No police officer, including the Deputy Commissioners of Srinagar and Anantnag, could show enough courage to sign the detention warrant of Shabir Shah, the President of the People's League, who was arrested (27 September). In October 1989, 54 persons were injured, and the wife and daughter of Inspector Shabir Ahmed were killed. The judge (N. K. Ganjoo) who had sentenced a JKLF leader (Muhammad Maqbool Bhatt) was shot dead (4 November). There were 51 explosions the same month. The terrorists having scared away the voters during the elections to the *Lok Sabha* (22 November),[11] the average votes cast were no more than five per cent. About a week later (1 December), not only the Station House Officer of Maisooma (Saifullah Lone) was murdered, but his body, which lay in the street for hours, was finally taken by the militants and thrown in front of the police station. Practically no one had the courage to attend his funeral procession. The appointment of a Muslim Kashmiri (Mufti Muhammad Sayeed) as the Union Home Minister by V. P. Singh, who replaced Rajiv Gandhi as Prime Minister, soon proved to be a turn for the worse.

In late (8 December) 1989, Pakistani-trained JKLF activists abducted the Home Minister's daughter (Dr. Rubaiya Sayeed) and demanded the release of five militants (including Hamid Sheikh, one of the kingpins of the separatist movement) who were among the first to take to terrorism in J&K.[12] The Chief Minister being in London, not only the Council of Ministers accepted the demands of the kidnappers, but each mediator promised more to outbid his "competitor". When Farooq Abdullah returned from his lengthy trip abroad, he disclosed that he was not prepared to capitulate to the terrorists. Contrary to the earlier agreement, however, the five militants were released first, and the minister's daughter freed later. Kashmiri crowds, including some police officers in uniform, were jubilant on the streets not for the release of Rubaiya Sayeed but for the release of the militants.

The government proved incapable of controlling this state of affairs, and while the Chief Minister, who also held the Home portfolio, was in Jammu, there were daily disturbances in Srinagar. The Union Bank was looted (20 December), a guard of the Allahabad Bank was killed (21 December), two policemen were shot dead and seven others injured (24 December),[13] a bomb blast wounded seven persons (1 January 1990), two police officers were killed (9 January),[14] 13 more murdered, and over 100 injured (8 January). A police officer and an imam were killed and left hanging for display. The government, which for some time looked impatient to change the governor (General Rao), reappointed Jagmohan in his place, and Farooq Abdullah resigned. While the mobs took control of parts of the capital, the Kashmiri Pandits feared for their lives. The militants demanded the release of over a hundred suspects to the tune of broadcasts from the minarets that called for "death to Indian dogs!"

The new governor, whose second term of administration had opened in the worst possible circumstances, had no option but to ask the army to intervene. The army fire, not only killed some individuals and galvanized emotions, but it also led to rumours, spread by militants, that the police as well had erroneously suffered casualties. Although no such incident had taken place, an armed clash between policemen and the army could be staved off only after a few days of mediation. Some officers were removed from service, however, for their role in inciting their colleagues.

Increasing the level of their agitation, the terrorists adopted the "Punjab style" of assassinations while riding on motorcycles and shot at officers, other officials and Kashmiri Pandits. The armed activists were so much in control of the streets that even the governor could not attend the Republic Day Parade (26 January). When the director of the Srinagar TV and Radio Station (Lassa Kaul) was shot dead for refusing to adhere to the line of the terrorists, other functionaries declined to work until the station was moved to Jammu.

The hostility between Governor Jagmohan and Farooq Abdullah led to the dissolution (19 February) of the State Assembly, a move that could only block the political process even further. While selective murders continued, the police units, which proved to be inadequate in equipment and training to respond, were either passive bystanders or attackers of unarmed mobs, among whom even the National Conference supporters had become anti-government. The fire of the army near Rawalpura and Zakura caused the death of 17 Kashmiri civilians (1 March). Few acts other than police firing at unarmed citizens could kindle anti-government attitudes. The authority of the militants became so unquestionable that they could publicly hang one of their own (Mir Mustafa) for starting a dialogue with the government and get away with it.

Fanning the Flames

The circumstances in late 1989 and the beginning of 1990 transformed Kashmir into a dreamboat for Pakistan, which was interested in seeing political instability in these neighbouring lands since 1947. The mishandling of the situation by the Indian authorities, such as the stoppage of the democratic process in Kashmir and the police inability to respond by more peaceful means when necessary, created room for Pakistani interference. The militants changed the names of some roads, and reset their watches in accordance with Pakistan standard time. When the state of affairs were conducive to Pakistan's involvement, the pro-Pakistan fundamentalist leagues did not yet enjoy as much support as the JKLF, the leading separatist movement in the whole country.

The members of an all-party delegation, including the Deputy Prime Minister (Devi Lal), two cabinet ministers (George Fernandes and Dinesh Goswami) and a former Prime Minister (Rajiv Gandhi), visited Srinagar (9 March) with the best of intentions but were appalled to hear the sweeping slogans of *"azadi"* (freedom) and witness the widespread tension in the city. While the governor, who was not in Srinagar during these dramatic events, and could not meet the delegation at the airport, the staff of the hotel that hosted the leaders ironically joined the anti-Indian demonstrations. The delegation had to return to New Delhi the next morning leaving behind only George Fernandes who had just been appointed as the Cabinet Minister for Kashmir Affairs in addition to his portfolio for Railways. While there were more killings of the Indian Pandits and demonstrations, it was surprising that the governor could continue to stay in Jammu. Extensive demonstrations frightened the Pandits, who thought that the mobs expected them either to join them or quit the Valley. The imposing processions on the one hand, and the sluggishness of the government on the other seemed to register in the minds of many as though "independence" had really dawned.

Following Governor Jagmohan's participation in a meeting of the Cabinet Committee on Political Affairs (CCPA) in New Delhi, and the processions at Rawalpura and Zakura where the police had fired at the unarmed crowds, all parades and pickets, no matter what the occasion or source, were banned. The authorities had initially refrained from taking note of rallies that eventually gathered momentum, and now chose to prohibit them all when they seemed to have established roots. Both phases of official attitude offered opportunities to Pakistan to promote its political and material support to the terrorist-secessionist forces in Kashmir. The difficulties encountered in efforts to return to normality were in part created by this entrenched external dimension, explainable by successive ill-considered local policies as much as Pakistan's motives.

The whole Srinagar community suffered unreasonable hardship when Governor Jagmohan imposed an indefinite curfew immediately after the dead bodies of the General Manager of the Hindustan Machine Tools Factory (H. L. Khera) and the Vice-Chancellor of the Kashmir University (Musheer-ul Haq) were dumped somewhere near the Police Control Room (9 April). Although a decision for a curfew may at times show governmental sense of purpose and firmness, the people, whose homes were searched, felt nevertheless foreigners in their own land while the terrorists were still able to murder (1 May) an inspector of police (C. L. Shalla) and a prominent religious leader (Maulwi Farooq). When the police opened fire and killed many of the mourners, some of whom might have behaved in an unruly fashion during the funeral procession of the assassinated Islamic doyen who enjoyed a large following, an invaluable opportunity to alienate the people from the militants slipped out of the hands of the authorities. The panic and the overaction of the police offered the killers of the religious leader instead another chance to perpetuate and spread terrorism. Moreover, although this confrontation between the security forces and the public was no ordinary affair, the Police Control Room that received no report about it and the governor whose information came from the same source denied that the bloody tragedy had ever occurred. Nevertheless, the people blamed the governor, who was called to New Delhi and who never returned to Srinagar. Girish C. Saxena, an experienced bureaucrat who succeeded Jagmohan, believed in utmost secrecy to the extent of declining to share information even with his closest associates. Soon, senior civil servants publicly differed with the new governor, and the strike of the state government employees, supported even by the National Conference leaders, lasted for two-and-a-half months and was badly handled by the government. Moreover, every time the administration changed in New Delhi, the newcomers felt free to criticize the previous leadership and unintentionally encouraged anti-union forces. The Kashmir issue was skipping from one phase to another leaving behind slayings, hangings, firings, searches and arrests, whose culprits on both sides largely escaped punishment. In any case, with the removal of Jagmohan, it was no longer necessary to have a separate Cabinet Minister for Kashmir Affairs.

Under the circumstances, Pakistan continued to be the unmistakable "winner". The JKLF was the main "independence" movement in the initial period of the disturbances. There were other pro-independence groups such as the Ansar-ul Islam, Al-Fatah and Al-Harmzah. Pro-Pakistani groups were mostly later additions. Amanullah Khan, one of the leaders of the JKLF, was based in Pakistan from where he planned and handled the operations. Like all pro-independence groups who went along with Pakistan because India was the common enemy and the neighbouring Muslim state provided various kinds of material assistance, Amanullah Khan of the JKLF appreciated the value of correct relations with groups such as the Hizb-ul Mujahideen and the Jamaat-e Islami, both of which consistently championed accession to Pakistan. Hizbullah Islamia Jamhooria, which came into focus in 1989, stated that armed attacks on the security forces would continue until Kashmir abandoned the Indian Union.

In addition to the cliques and formations mentioned above, India's neighbour Pakistan curtailed its material support to the JKLF and channeled its subsidies to a number of Islamicist combative groups. In the mid-1990s, there were some forty terrorist organizations involved in intimidation, shock, and slaughter. Some of them, such as the People's League, upheld a merger with Pakistan but did not oppose independence. Their multiplicity enabled the organizers, local and foreign, to manipulate the surviving ones if some others proved to be inoperative on account of arrests or closures.

It is not surprising that the number of incidents in 1989 (2154) almost doubled in 1990 (3905)—only to decline in 1991 (3122). Terrorism was better organized and progressively funded and nourished from abroad, but the popular outcry began to wane. The terrorists now possessed sophisticated weapons and were better trained but were losing touch with the exhausted public. Only a year ago, the popular upsurge bordered on the maximum. The balance was now reversed. Forceful terrorist networks needed lively popular support to achieve the goal of secession. Pakistan had to revive what was now missing—the people's backing.

The year 1991 did not bring more popular support but disagreements and show-downs among the militants. For instance, a rival group killed a district (Balakot) chief (Muhammad Akbar Zargar) of the Muslim Mujahideen. Although the abduction of the daughter (Nahida Imtiaz) of the National Conference leader Professor Saifuddin Soz secured the release (8 March)[15] of a jailed militant, and the murder of two intellectuals (the veteran freedom-fighter A. S. Ranjoor and the Urdu daily *Al-Safa*'s editor M. S. Vakil) went unpunished, the Jammu and Kashmir Students' Liberation Front (JKSLF) appealed to the pro-Pakistani groups to cease illegal operations. While Islamabad diverted more funds and arms to pro-Pakistan factions, there were growing symptoms of disillusionment among the people, who now yearned for a return to normality; that is, an end to violence, and a flow of income from tourism.

When the Kashmiri authorities decided to reactivate tourism in the Valley, pro-Pakistani militants kidnapped two Swedish engineers employed at the Uri Hydro-Power Project, seven Israeli tourists and a Dutch citizen. With the angry crowds shouting anti-Pakistan slogans, the tide was turning against terrorism and foreign intervention for the first time since the year 1988. The JKLF had to also condemn the abduction of foreign visitors. This new trend did not restrain all of the hardliners, some of whom burnt to death (23 June) three Hindus and tied explosives to the bodies of two Muslims. Although the kidnapping (28 June) of a senior executive of the Indian Oil Corporation (K. Doraiswamy) by the Ikhwan-ul Muslimeen was unpopular with the masses, the militants secured the release of their colleagues including the terrorist (Javed Shalla) accused of the murder of an industrialist and a university administrator. The authorities could not capitalize on the acknowledged deception of the masses even when the Valley residents were weary of unending abductions and bloody rivalries between the militant groups. The successful rescue (18 October) of the Wakhloo couple, the wife being a former Tourism Minister in the J&K government, was a victory for the security forces.[16]

The predicament somewhat changed for the better when the 1991 elections brought the Narasimha Rao government to power in New Delhi, the slight switch becoming more visible towards the end of the year. The number of incidents declined considerably, and the security forces killed 17 and captured 31 militants in October 1991 alone. As it frequently happens with a change of government, the newcomers soon blamed their predecessors for failures and made repeated statements that things were improving rapidly. This charge and challenge once more helped the militants to make another comeback. Even the State Director of Police J. N. Saxena was among those injured when a bomb exploded (24 January 1992) in the main security office.[17] The militants were still able to kidnap 64 persons in the first three months of 1992. This temporary upward trend encouraged some Pakistani sponsors to suggest a mass crossing of the Line of Actual Control. Since Pakistan favoured Hizb-ul Mujahideen more than the other analogous organizations, the JKLF supported the idea to outbid its rivals. Lending an ear to arguments that such a move might cause war, the Government of Pakistan intervened and frustrated the border violation at the last moment.

With the year 1992 approaching its end, the demolition of the Babri Masjid at Ayodhya, which sent an exaggerated message all over the world that secularism in India was giving way to an extremist Hindu ideology, helped transform the semi-sleeping monster of communalism into an uncontrollable epidemic in the streets. The militants in Kashmir damaged a number of Hindu temples. The Rao government's partial response to strong criticism for its conduct during the riots in the aftermath of the Ayodhya affair was the appointment of a special Minister of Internal Security (Rajesh Pilot) to deal exclusively with Kashmir. Not only was this commissioning a repetition of the former superficial Fernandes experience, it corresponded to the reappointment of General K. V. Krishna Rao to governorship replacing G. C. Saxena. While these assignments were interpreted as part of a softer line policy, Dr. A. A. Guru, known for his close relations with the JKLF and also for his soft line, was kidnapped by the militants (31 March) and found dead the next day.

April 1993 was one of the worst months in the history of terrorism in Kashmir. Not only did 124 persons lose their lives in just three days, but a false rumour that a constable died in army custody caused an angry police procession, after which twenty officers were dismissed for their role in showing disobedience. April 1993 also witnessed waves of foreign Muslim mercenaries from Afghanistan, Morocco, Saudi Arabia and Sudan coming to the Valley and to the Doda district, where slightly over 40% of the population are Hindus. Reinforced by such well-trained people, the militants established "liberated areas" in parts of Srinagar, Anantnag and Baramulla, targeted checkposts and patrol units, and held some abducted persons (for instance, the former Bihar legislator P. K. Sinha) for almost a year.

Since 1993 the terrorists have been using more sophisticated weapons such as air-to-ground rockets, artillery shells, high-velocity grenades, long-range wireless sets, pen pistols, and telescope-fitted sniper rifles. Even the Secretariat building in Srinagar came under rocket attack. The militants laid siege to the Hazratbal Shrine in Srinagar, which lasted for thirty-two days (15 October–16 November),[18] and managed to hold a public exhibition of some of their sophisticated weaponry near a police picket. Both the terrorists and the officials had drawn lessons from the Golden Temple catastrophe in Punjab. The militants at Hazratbal surrendered in the end.

The year 1994 saw 85 rocket attacks, 370 kidnappings, 4,000 arrests, and 2,500 dead.[19] The great majority of the last mentioned were militants. The security forces successfully sealed the border along the LAC. New Delhi invited some foreign diplomats and the International Red Cross to visit the Valley. 1995 witnessed more frequent use of remote control devices to detonate explosives, one of which killed (20 March) a Brigade Commander of the Army (V. Gopal Sheridharan).[20] It also marked the possession (December 1994–May 1995) by the Harkat-ul Ansar militants of the shrine of the Sufi saint Nooruddin Noorani at Charar-e Sharif near Srinagar. Harkat-ul Ansar was born out of the merger of two Pakistani political activist movements, and financed mainly by Saudi Arabia and some other Arab Gulf countries. They all sought Kashmir's accession to Pakistan. Harkat-ul Ansar had several thousand armed men in the Pakistani-held part of Kashmir. The militants under Mast Gul, who killed two security officers for provocation, started a fire in the shrine of this exalted Kashmiri saint. While Mast Gul escaped to Pakistan to receive a hero's welcome there, it became obvious that, after the experience in Punjab, the militants preferred to use shrines to bring about confrontations with the authorities. The capture of a handful of militants not being worth the devastation of a shrine, it could be difficult to dislodge them. The rest of the year saw the kidnapping of four foreign tourists, four local journalists, sixteen forestry technicians and ten others, three of whom were killed.

The total number of incidents of terrorist violence in J&K in the last decade (1988–June 1999)[21] is 45,852 while about a quarter (11,240) of them are related to explosion and arson. The total number of killings in terrorist violence for the same period is no less than 21,039, about a third (7,672) being Muslims, the latter being more than the Hindus killed (958), some government officials (372), politicians (153) and top political leaders (15). There have been 3,179 cases of kidnappings, the whereabouts of 258 persons being still unknown but 1,222 put on file as killed. Kidnapped individuals include government officials (308), politicians (129), and foreigners (20). Although only a fraction of cases of extortion and lootings are reported to the authorities on account of fear, the number of registered incidents stand at 810, and the amount robbed adds up to 108,905,286 rupees. Total incidents of destruction of property by militants add up to 4,974. A great deal of weapons were recovered from militants, including grenades (35,163), grenade launchers (341), explosives (21,476 kg.), AK series rifles (20,476), snipers (305), pistols (8,179), mines (5,683), rockets (3,106), bombs (1,972), rocket boosters (1,577), rocket launchers (903), guns (1,603), machine guns (1,135), and mortars (127).

Violence perpetrated by terrorists included abductions and killings of targeted prominent personalities, brutalities inflicted on innocent persons, atrocities on women, children, Christian missionary institutions and foreign nationals, attacks on Hindus, Muslims, Sikhs and members of the press, robberies, extortions, destruction of property and looting. Torture followed kidnappings, with instances of gouging out of eyes, breaking of limbs, and slitting of throats until the victims bleed to death. In one incident a terrorist reportedly ate a bit of the victim's flesh. Extortions were as rampant as the rape of women. The lust turned lethal with the discovery of AIDS among some mercenaries. Such distressing stories are discernible in almost every corner of J&K embroiling all spheres and professions, in fact all walks of life, and modifying in the process the entire political life of the land. The incidents occurred in the towns and villages of Srinagar, Anantnag, Baramulla, Doda, Jammu, Kupwara, Poonch, Pulwana, and Rajouri. Instances of open public anger against militant actions have to be mentioned in this description of atrocities against different sections of society.

In the last decade, there have been close to 200 incidents in which prominent personalities were murdered or attacked. Among them were ex-ministers (Abd-ul Jabbar, Hissam-ud Din, Ghulam Hassan Shah), editors of daily newspapers, professors (Abd-ul Ahad Wani, Kundan Lal, Musheer-ul Haq), politicians, professionals, businessmen, human rights activists (H. N. Wanchoo), prominent writers, and poets

(Ahmed Din Mushtaq, Nazir Ahmed Hafiz). For instance, Dr. Rubaiya Sayeed, the daughter of the then Union Home Minister, was carried off at gun point. Professor Musheer-ul Haq was kidnapped from the Kashmir University campus and shot dead. Professor K. L. Ganjoo, from the Wadoora Agriculture College, was killed on the river bank. The principal of the (S.S.M.) Polytechnical College was abducted, and Professor M. A. Azhari from Kashmir University shot at. The mutilated body of Jalil Indrabi, the Chairman of the Kashmir Commission of Jurists, was recovered from the River Jhelum at Rajbagh. Professor Yusuf-ul Umar, the President of the Iqbal Memorial Trust, was shot at and injured. Even Dr. Farooq Abdullah, several times Chief Minister of J&K, was attacked (in Rajouri on 9 December 1995), and an explosion occurred in the building premises of Dr. A. M. Mattoo, the brother-in-law of Dr. Abdullah.

Innocent people were found hanging from trees, ailing men shot dead in hospitals where they were undergoing treatment, headless bodies with limbs chopped off recovered from rivers, and others dragged from their homes, tortured and slain. Some civilians lost thier lives in cross fire from rival militant groups. Many women children were not spared. While talking about virginity and the *purdah*,[22] the militants displayed no esteem for women. Many maidens and spouses, mostly Muslim, were carried off, tormented in various ways, decapitated, and sexually abused. Some were shot at work places or inside their own homes or burnt to death. Gunmen frequently intruded into private houses and liquidated the whole family including the womanfolk and infants. Thugs frequently looted household articles, and at times, entered private homes to open indiscriminate fire or hurl a grenade into the dwellings. The Muslim Kashmiri desperados sliced a woman's breast before shooting her (in Sajithana Mandi, Rajouri on 13 March 1998), and slit the throat of another (in Phagla Surankote, Poonch on 10 June 1998).

Some children were killed on a school compound, and others injured by anti-personnel mines. There were grenade attacks on school buses (in Pulwana on 5 January 1998). More than thirty youngsters were harmed in the Maulana Azad Stadium in Jammu (20 January 1998) when stormers caused three explosions during the Republic Day celebrations. Deranged cutthroats chopped the nose and ears of children before killing them (in Bhatadurian, Poonch on 2 March 1998). A brutal attack on a marriage party (in Doda on 19 June 1998) killed 26 Hindus.[23] The Lassa Sheikh family lost 19 of its members, the killers not moved to compassion even before minors (in Poonch on 3 August 1998).

Explosions were aimed at causing the closure of the Christian missionary schools in Srinagar. The hostel building of the Bisco Memorial School, among others, was set on fire, an attempt was made to set ablaze the Burn Hall School, affiliated with the local Catholic mission, and an explosion occurred near the Miss Melanson Girls' School. American, British, Dutch, French, German, Israeli, Norwegian, and Swedish tourists were abducted, and the bullet-ridden bodies of some of them were later recovered.

On several occasions, the hunters intruded into the J&K Bank, the Central Cooperative Bank, the Rural Development Bank and others to loot money. They attacked post offices and vanished with the cash. They ransacked shops, private homes and mosques and decamped with the contents of the money chests. They carried away, not only gold ornaments and jewellery, but even stone idols of Hindu deities from local temples. At times, armed militants cordoned off the village (in Sangra, Doda on 17 May 1995) and looted all Hindu houses or took away hundreds of sheep and goats (in Samber, Doda on 18 August 1995). They stole cars, jeeps, trucks, ambulances, oil tankers and scooters. Some of these vehicles were loaded with merchandise such as timber, cement, copper, steel rods, silk fabrics, and coal or food like rice, sugar, fruit and the like.

The Retreat of the Rebellion

For long years, the people of the Valley were afraid to condemn the militants. Quite often, the relatives could not even claim the body of the murdered person. They remained mute even after the militants moved beyond the symbols of the state, killing unarmed non-combatants. They were silent when the bodies of poet Sarwanand Koul and his son were found, their eyes gouged out and limbs broken. When Hindu Kashmiris or pandits were targetted, thousands of them had to be relocated in camps near Delhi. Although some city dwellers at times assisted fleeing militants willingly, many of the people in the countryside, who wanted to be left alone, had to provide food and shelter in exchange of security. Even some officials had to buy their peace with militants. The militants tortured or executed some individuals on grounds of mere suspicion that they were *mukhbirs* (informants). In some instances, the entire families were wiped out, including minors and babies.

Despite India's generally good past record in managing its minorities, some security personnel also resorted to unnecessary force and even brutality. The latter, however, should not be compared to what occurred in Bosnia or in Chechnya. But there are instances of personnel in uniform beating men with rifle butts, looting houses, stealing gold and jewellery, torching the dwellings in the poorer Muslim localities, indiscriminately firing from their positions, applying electric shock to the genitals of the interrogated person and inserting a rod into his rectum. Some of these personnel were severely reprimanded, but in some cases, nothing was done. Not all senior officers were like Lieut. Gen. M. A. Zaki, who did not tolerate any excesses. For some time, neither the Kashmiri officials, nor the Indian Government paid serious attention to the problems of the neglected security force, whose small-scale bunkers generally had no lighting or heating.

On the other hand, it is only natural that following the recovery of a burnt body, the ransacking of a local mosque or anguish over a murder, the local people should start putting up their shutters, holding anti-terrorist demonstrations, and registering their voices against violence. Gradually, people became emboldened to resist violence. Students boycotted classes (in Hazratbal, Srinagar on 11 October 1995) in protest against the attack on Professor Azhari, and members of the Bar Association did not attend the courts (in Srinagar on 17 October 1995) following the killing of a lawyer (G. Qadir Sailani). The local people reacted in various kinds of *hartals* (protests) against wholesale killings such as the murder of 15 Hindus in Barsala, Doda (on 6 January 1996),[24] 26 Hindus in Parankote, Bhakikote and Ladda villages (17–18 April 1996), 25 Hindus in Chapnari, Doda (19 June 1998) or 17 Hindus in Kishtwar (27–28 July 1998).

Militancy continued as the world entered the year 2000. On Christmas Eve, foreign militants struck the Jammu-Pathankot National Highway and gunned down three policemen near Vijaypur.[25] Four security men were killed and 13 others injured two days later.[26] In between the two events, an army camp became the target of rockets.[27] More dramatically, an Indian Airlines plane with 186 passangers was hijacked by a group of five extremists. Although Osama Bin Laden had reportedly left Kandahar shortly after the hijacked plane landed in a southern Afghan city,[28] he denied links to the event. The hijackers slipped undetected through remote mountain passes[29] after three hardcore militants were released in exchange for the hostages aboard the airbus.[30] While the Bharatiya Janata Party (BJP)-led National Democratic Alliance (NDA) government in New Delhi geared up for the political repercussions of such release, described by some analysts as a dangerous decision, senior police officers in Kashmir warned of a spate of enhanced terrorist activity following that move.[31] Although a local president of the ruling National Conference was shot at near Charar-e Sharif, and a policeman killed in Doda the same day, 11 militants were killed and 17 others surrendered during the same period.[32] Significantly, while the release of militants would have echoed with chants of *"azadi"* ten years ago, the same streets witnessed absolute silence now.[33] When a group of militant leaders were released in 1994, they were accorded a tumultuous reception. Prominent Kashmiri militant groups such as the Hizb-ul Mujahideen hastily denounced the hijacking in an effort to rule out any possibility of involvement in the act.

The massacre of a gathering attending a wedding party in a Doda village may mark the failure of the security forces, but it also shows the latter's success in pushing the militants to the hilly tracts where they attack unprotected rural people. In any case, the dream, injected a decade ago, that *azadi* was "around the corner"[34] was replaced by a rapid expansion of graveyards. About 20,000 persons have died, half of them being combatants.[35] Many were wounded, injured, and molested. At least some disillusionment was bound to dawn.[36]

Notes

1   Riyaz Punjabi, "The Concept of an Islamic Caliphate", *Journal of Peace Studies*, New Delhi, I/1 (November–December 1993), p. 48.

2   A seminal contribution to the study of terrorism in India, including some insights into the functioning of the government at the highest level, by someone who held important assignments in different states during his career spanning thirty-six years: Ved Marvah, *Uncivil Wars: Pathology of Terrorism in India*, New Delhi, HarperCollins, 1997. Another

account of the militant rebellion in Kashmir, especially since 1988: Manoj Joshi, *The Lost Rebellion: Kashmir in the Nineties*, New Delhi, Penguin Books, 1999.
3   Tara Kartha, *Tools of Terror: Light Weapons and India's Security*, New Delhi, Knowledge World in association with the Institute for Defence Studies and Analysis, 1999, p. 200.
4   *The Times of India*, New Delhi, 2 August 1988, p. 1.
5   *Ibid.*, 16–17 August 1988, p. 1. The Mirwaiz's fiery speech during the Friday prayers at Jama Masjid, which demanded the opening of the Srinagar-Rawalpindi road, apparently encouraged the support of the Awami Action Committee (AAC) to hoist Pakistan's national flag near Islamiya College, and they managed to raise black flags on some shops. The police opened fire when groups attacked the Khanyar police station. A ding-dong battle continued the whole day in the area considered AAC's stronghold.
6   *Ibid.*, 21 July 1989, p. 1.
7   *Ibid.*, 18 August 1989, p. 1.
8   *Ibid.*, 19 August 1989, pp. 1, 12.
9   *Ibid.*, 15 September 1989, pp. 1, 4.
10   *Ibid.*, 19 September 1989, p. 1.
11   *Ibid.*, 23 November 1989, p. 1.
12   Askari H. Zahidi, "Mufti's Daughter Kidnapped", *ibid.,* 9 December 1989, p. 1.
13   *Ibid.*, 25 December 1989, p. 1.
14   "Two IB Officials Shot", *ibid.*, 10 January 1990, p. 1. Editorial ("Long Haul in Kashmir"): "…The latest bout of violence comes in the wake of the decision by militants to organise rallies outside the United Nations military group headquarters to launch a 'Quit Kashmir' movement. By choosing the day (January 5) marking the arrival of U.N. troops following Pakistan's invasion of Kashmir in 1948, Kashmir's fundamentalist organisations cleverly wanted to stir up resentment over India's refusal to honour its now obsolete commitment to the U.N. to hold a plebiscite in the state…[O]ver a dozen people have died in the act of defying authority…" (p. 6).
15   *The Hindu*, Madras, 9 March 1991, p. 1.
16   *Ibid.*, 19 October 1991, p. 1.
17   *Ibid.*, 25 January 1992, p. 1.
18   "Hazratbal Siege Ends in Surrender", *The Times of India*, New Delhi, 17 November 1993, pp. 1, 11. Editorial ("Triumph of Patience"): "The peaceful end of the Hazratbal crisis is a matter of great relief, not only because of the militants' tame surrender, but also because of its long-term impact may well resemble that of the celebrated "Black Thunder" denouement in Punjab which severely demoralized the insurgents there. In Kashmir, too, it will obviously take some time for the terrorists and their patrons in Pakistan to overcome the effect of the supine manner in which the rebels trooped out of the shrine at the dead of night, belying all their dire threats including that of blowing it up…[T]he holy relic has not been harmed in any way…" *Ibid.*, p. 10.
19   A 16-year old Japanese boy, abducted by Harkat-ul Ansar, says the following in his reminiscences: "It was the fanaticism of my kidnappers that scared me. Their blind obedience to the commanders of the Islamic revolution made them capable of virtually anything. Waheed, a university-educated mercenary, would tell us, '…I have no fear of death, for Allah will protect me'…He would boast about how many soldiers, Russian and Indian, he had killed…" Kim Housego, "Hostage in Kashmir", *Peace Initiatives*, New Delhi, III/5 (September–October 1997), p. 35.

20 *The Hindu*, Madras, 21 March 1995, p. 13.
21 Government of India, Ministry of Home Affairs, *Profile of Terrorist Violence in Jammu and Kashmir: June 1999*, New Delhi, 1999, pp. 235–237.
22 A famous work on *purdah*, originally published in 1939 and reprinted several times: Maulana Abul A'la Maududi, *Purdah and the Status of Woman in Islam*, Lahore, Islamic Publications Ltd., 1979.
23 *The Hindu*, Madras, 20 June 1998, p. 1.
24 *Ibid.*, 29 July 1998, p. 1.
25 *The Kashmir Times*, Srinagar, 26 December 1999.
26 *Ibid.*, 28 December 1999.
27 *Ibid.*, 27 December 1999.
28 *The Asian Age*, 31 December 1999.
29 *Ibid.*, 3 January 2000.
30 *Ibid.*, 2 January 2000.
31 *Greater Kashmir*, Srinagar, 3 January 2000.
32 *The Kashmir Times*, Srinagar, 29 December 1999.
33 *The Hindustan Times*, 2 January 2000.
34 A former militant, Bashir Ahmad, stated even in 1992: "We thought that *azadi* was around the corner when the upsurge began". Dinesh Kumar, "Disillusion overtakes discontent in Kashmir", *The Times of India*, New Delhi, 9 July 1992.
35 Many people in Srinagar will tell an outsider that the number of the killed is as high as 50,000.
36 Public protests against atrocities occurred even in Trehgam, the native village of the JKLF founder Maqbool Bhatt. Dinesh Kumar, "Protests against militancy rising in J&K", *The Times of India*, New Delhi, 5 June 1994.

Chapter 10

Soldiers of Fortune

No state has the right to intervene in the domestic affairs of another state (United Nations Charter, Article 2/7), and all states should refrain from the threat or use of force (Article 2/4) except in self-defence (Article 51).[1] The recruitment and use of mercenaries in armed conflicts are forms of foreign intervention. They are described as soldiers of fortune, paid murderers or whores of war. Such activities constitute gross violations of maintenance of peace and security. It is only natural that the leading organs of the United Nations took several decisions condemning them. Mercenarism is, nevertheless, a widespread practice. With the passage of some Afghan veterans to Pakistan, it is now more frequently tried out in the Kashmir scene.

This point should bring us to mercenarism blended with terrorism in Kashmir. Indisputably, some neighbouring countries or individuals and formations in them make wide use of professional soldiers, castaways, traitors and expellees, quite a few of whom have criminal offences in their past, and even cases still pending on the books. These organizations, amalgamated with the ruling circles of a number of states, send their nationals and foreigners to this green valley, dotted with beautiful lakes and criss-crossed with streams, to engage in activities declared by considered international opinion to be illegitimate. The Afghan conflict produced a vast number of trained and battle-hardened war veterans "available for a sum of Pakistani Rs. 200,000 for one year" in Kashmir, their amount increasing to "Rs. 500,000 if they sign up for two years".[2]

Armed militants based in Pakistan, trained in Afghanistan or Pakistan, and motivated by pan-Islamism, wage war on behalf of a people within the frontiers of another state. Some of them work closely with Pakistan's Inter-Services Intelligence, over which that country's civilian authorities have only limited control. Pakistan asserts that its support is only moral and diplomatic, "but even on the streets of Lahore few believe it".[3] The Taliban is more of a Pakistani creation than an Afghan phenomenon. It is worth remembering that the Taliban was raised, armed, trained and led by Pakistan, with funding from other sources as well. Pakistan is now a nuclear-weapon state on the brink of economic collapse. A group of Talibanized Pakistani zealots handing over such weapons to militants with grandiose plans is a small possibility, but still a nightmare.

Mercenarism, an International Crime

Extensively used in ancient Rome and in the Middle Ages, mercenarism was understandably more widespread in the age of imperialism.[4] While the principal colonial powers of the last century noticeably institutionalized the employment of mercenaries in parts of Asia and Africa, its later application had to be more covert. While the founding fathers of the United States passed laws to monitor and discourage the recruitment of citizens of a state for service in the armed forces of another one, that country lost sight of its own well-defined regulations and practices when it allowed some American citizens of Jewish origin to be recruited for war by the Israeli Armed Forces. Although a Foreign Enlistment Act (1870) prohibited British subjects from participating in hostilities between two foreign parties in which the United Kingdom was not engaged, its citizens served in the racist army of Southern Rhodesia (now Zimbabwe) opposing the legitimate government of the People's Republic of Angola. Similarly, while French legislation laid down imprisonment and fine as penalties for its citizens if they served for money in foreign armies, many Frenchmen fought in Lebanon for the benefit of some local extremists. Swedish laws considering service in foreign armies as criminal, the Swedish authorities did not allow their nationals to participate either in the civil war in Finland or in Spain, but their nationals took part in the secessionist armed conflict in Nigeria. Likewise, the Belgian Penal Code promised imprisonment for those who served in a foreign army without permission. Many offered their services, nevertheless, in foreign forces in Katanga during the Congo crisis in the early 1960s. The first undertaking by mercenaries to undermine the legitimate authority in any African country occurred (1977) in Benin.

At times, mercenaries from a number of countries known for their legal opposition to participation in such armed conflicts assemble to fight in a foreign country for personal profit. Regular forces of South Africa and Zaire (the former Belgian Congo) were first thrown into action against Angola as early as 1976. Racist South Africa used mercenaries from the United States, Britain, France, Rhodesia, Portugal, Israel and some other countries to support its aggression (1980) against Angola. They were the former Vietnam "veterans", former Nazis, law-breakers of the *Légion Française*, former Rhodesian hangmen, Portuguese secret service agents, and the like. They engaged in hostilities against the civilians of Angola and Mozambique, the anti-*apartheid* members of the South-West African People's Organization (SWAPO), and also the new-born Republic of Seychelles.

Armed nationals from some of the states cited above attacked (1981) Mahé Island a little after oil was struck off the shores of the Seychelles. The attempt of the mercenaries to stage a coup having failed, they chose to hijack an Indian airliner and took it to Durban in South Africa. The then *apartheid*-government did not extradite them in spite of the expectations of the Seychelles. Some veteran mercenaries either bragged or confessed that they were involved in disruptive activities aimed at an independent African state. The application of the Seychelles Government to the United Nations to authorize an international commission of inquiry into the circumstances of the attack was followed by a decision of the U.N. Security Council condemning the aggression of the mercenaries against the Seychelles. It was in the same year that a group of Pretoria mercenaries, possibly endorsed by a Texas company called the Nordic Enterprises, Inc., ventured to bring down the legitimate government in the Republic of Dominica in the Caribbean.

The sources of international law, whether in treaties, custom, the general principles of law, decisions of courts or the teachings of prominent jurists, consider mercenaries as illegal entities in international relations. By forbidding the opening of recruiting agencies on the territory of a third party to assist the belligerents, the Hague Convention of 1907 banned mercenarism. The 1949 Geneva Conventions for the Protection of War Victims, which consider the status of prisoners of war, among other things, do not judge the mercenaries as legitimate combatants. Uplifting the relevant provisions of the U.N. Charter, the General Assembly confirmed the following principle in its special Declaration on Inadmissibility of Intervention in Domestic Affairs of States and Protection of Their Independence and Sovereignty: "No State has the right to intervene, directly or indirectly, for any reason whatever, in the internal or external affairs of any other State. Consequently, armed intervention and all other forms of interference...are condemned."

The U.N. General Assembly passed a series of resolutions censoring mercenarism and declaring that mercenaries were outlawed. A Declaration on the Granting of Independence to Colonial Countries and Peoples (1968) proclaimed that the practice of resorting to mercenarism was a criminal act, and called upon all countries to decree legislation considering the training, recruitment, and financing of mercenaries to be a punishable offence. Further resolutions in 1969 and 1970 reiterated the prohibition of allowing nationals from serving as mercenaries. The General Assembly Resolution on Basic Principles of the Legal Status of the Combatants Struggling against Colonial and Alien Domination and Racist Regimes (1973) states that mercenaries should be punished as criminals. There was a consensus in the Geneva conference (1975) related to the Draft Protocol Additional to the 1949 Geneva Conventions for the Protection of War Victims that the mercenaries should not be entitled to the status of combatants. Article 47 of the cited Protocol offers the following definition: "A mercenary is any person who: (a) is especially recruited locally or abroad in order to fight in an armed conflict; (b) does, in fact, take a direct part in the hostilities; (c) is motivated to take part in the hostilities essentially by the desire for private gain and, in fact, is promised, by or on behalf of a Party to the conflict, material compensation substantially in excess of that promised or paid to combatants of similar ranks and functions in the armed forces of that Party, (d) is neither a national of that Party to the conflict nor a resident of territory controlled by a Party to the conflict; (e) is not a member of the armed forces of a Party to the conflict; and (f) has not been sent by a State which is not a Party to the conflict on official duty as a member of its armed forces".

This definition makes a distinction between a mercenary and the participation of an individual citizen on a voluntary basis and without any material interest.[5]

Volunteers may be engaged in an armed conflict to promote the cause of a victim of aggression or of colonialism and to support the right of self-determination against foreign occupation. For instance, the Italian and German so-called "volunteers" who joined the insurgents during the Spanish Civil War (1936–39) should be regarded as illegitimate while the volunteers on the side of the Republicans may be judged as rightful and justifiable. Not only the insurgent generals, led by Francisco Franco who revolted in Melilla in Spanish Morocco, had at their disposal large Moorish contingents, but also the Italian Government came out more and more openly in support of Franco and ultimately had about 50–75,000 troops in Spain; in addition, the Germans had some 10,000 men serving there. While Britain and France continued their ban on supplies to the democratically elected government and only a group of *bona fide* volunteers such as the Lincoln Brigade aided the government forces, German and Italian "volunteers" aided Franco in transporting troops from Morocco and played a major role in later engagements.

Many sessions of the U.N. General Assembly debated a universal international convention to control mercenaries and to outlaw mercenarism in every shape. Nations supported the idea of concluding an international convention and proposed effective steps to ban the recruitment, training and employment of mercenaries. Considering that most of the mercenaries arrived in Africa from other continents, it is not surprising that the *ad hoc* committee pondered on the Nigerian draft (1981). While Mexico underlined the urgency of getting down to the task of working out a convention on the subject, that country also cited the events in Angola, Namibia, Rhodesia and Zaire.

The Human Rights Commission of the United Nations reaffirmed in its resolutions (1995/5 and 1996/113) that the recruitment, use, financing and training of mercenaries should be considered of grave concern and urged all states to prevent mercenaries from using any part of their territory to destabilize any sovereign state. States which had yet to accede to or ratify the International Convention against the Recruitment, Use, Financing and Training of Mercenaries (4 December 1989) were also urged to take action. To give effect to these resolutions, a special Report[6] emphasized that the stability of governments and international peace and security are seriously impaired by mercenary activities, which should be banned, and the existing international provisions relating to mercenaries must be enforced to ensure that these criminal acts are discontinued. The Special Rapporteur's analysis shows that this illicit activity takes a variety of forms and that they are recruited by state intelligence authorities or security forces, opposition groups, armed domestic resistance movements or criminal organizations to engage in illegal actions such as forming paramilitary forces for purposes of repression, organizing death squads or providing military protection for arms or drug trafficking. Mercenaries are "not a small number of individuals"; they are "professionals selling their skill in war and violence"; they are paid to "attack and kill" in a conflict alien to their nationality; they work for money although they may claim altruistic, ideological or religious motives "in order to disguise their true motives"; they use legal devices to "conceal the nature of their assignment"; their interest lies "not in peace and reconciliation but in war", since that is their business and livelihood, and therefore, the presence of mercenaries in armed conflicts tends to make them longer lasting.

It is only natural that the Organization of African Unity (OAU) should also be active in this issue. The condemnation of the OAU Council of Ministers in response to the mercenary threat to Guinea (1970) was followed by a timely resolution of the OAU Summit (1971) in Addis Ababa. The report of a committee of experts presented to the Council of Ministers in Rabat (1972) referred to the grave threat posed by mercenarism to the independence, sovereignty and territorial integrity of the member states. The African community of nations also share the view that a mercenary is anyone who, not a national of the state against which his actions are directed, is employed by or links himself to a group or an organization whose aim is to undermine the territorial integrity of the said state and to overthrow by force of arms or by any other means the government of that state. The trial (1976) of the British and American mercenaries in Luanda, Angola's capital, showed the criminal nature of their activity even in the wording of the defence of their lawyers who blamed their lack of education, unemployment and alienation for their inhumanity and sadism. That trial was a warning and message for the contemporary and future mercenaries to heed.[7]

Will mercenaries always be with us, or will they one day disappear?[8] Mercenaries must not only be declared outlaws, but should also be actually outlawed. The intruding governments should prevent their own nationals or foreigners living in their territory from committing the kind of offences enumerated in several U.N. decisions and other international texts. They should forbid the entry to their organization in, or their passage through their territory of any mercenary or equipment intended for use for such purpose. In the light of international consensus, they should ban the recruitment, training, equipping and financing of mercenaries. Not only should they refrain from interfering in the affairs of another country, but they should also take necessary legislative measures for the implementation of solely legal and legitimate activities. Not only laws in each country should clearly prohibit such acts, but also unequivocal political will should be exhibited to enforce them.[9]

Pakistan's Partisans

Where does Pakistan, India's neighbour, stand in terms of these judgements and expectations? Compiled evidence urges one to assert that Pakistan promoted militancy in Kashmir by providing training, arms and sanctuary to insurgents, some of whom are mercenaries. Apart from training leaders who could thereafter train others, Pakistan smuggled weapons into the Valley, supported militant pan-Islamic organizations, and ran training and transit camps. By inducting a large number of battle-hardened Muslim mercenaries, Pakistan's ISI also upgraded the level of violence. Some ISI personnel have also been identified for personally fomenting disturbances. Pakistan also took the side of terrorism in other parts of India. Most of these armed men want J&K to be ruled according to the *shari'a*. As expressed in the report of the

U.S. House Republican Research Committee, there was a "marked erosion of the secular Kashmiri personality", and a Muslim identity with fundamentalist overtones gave the struggle a "pan-Islamic character and extra-territorial dimension".[10] There has been an "intelligence war", not only between the military secret services and their civilian counterparts in Pakistan's interior ministry, but also within the ISI itself in the form of competition led by the fundamentalists versus the moderates. Inevitably, Pakistan came under increasing pressure from world public opinion for its role in sponsoring violence.[11]

During General Zia's regime, the energies of the youth, indoctrinated by the Jamaat-e Islami of Pakistan (JI),[12] were directed towards pursuing *jehad* in Afghanistan, and later in other areas such as J&K. Having failed to wrest Kashmir by means of direct armed conflicts, Pakistan helped raise the slogans of *jehad* and *Nizam-e Mustafa,* and opted for a low cost proxy war by sponsoring violence. Although the JI as an organization was never as popular in the Valley as it hoped to be mainly because Islam had come there through the *Sufi* influence, the Zia years may, nevertheless, be credited with laying the justification and groundwork for the later violence among the Muslim community. Beginning with Zia, and especially after the ouster of commanders like General Jahangir Karamat, the Pakistan Army itself, one of the leading components of power structure in the country, became more and more Islamicized. Fundamentalists like Lieut. General Javid Nasir, an ex-chief of the ISI, wielded a lot of influence.

While the JI-dominated Muslim United Front (MUF) secured 31.87% of the votes polled in the Valley (but achieving much less in the rest of the state) in the 1987 elections, the JI itself formed, in the same year, the Hizb-ul Mujahideen (HUM), or its military wing, which became the backbone of Pakistan's support of militancy. Again in those years, the number of JI-run schools and the students enrolled increased in the Valley.

Although the torch-bearer of fundamentalism in J&K has been the JI, there have also been other militant organizations. The Jammu and Kashmir Liberation Front (JKLF), among them, had its origin in Pakistani soil. Initially, it would be better to use the JKLF, rather than the obviously pro-Pakistani elements. When its leader, Amanullah Khan, was deported (1986) from the United Kingdom, he found a ready sanctuary in Pakistan, which promoted the armed movement under his command. He had few options but to accept whatever Pakistan had to offer. He was first led to capture the JKLF organization, removing Hashim Qureshi from the chairmanship. The date of the uprising (31 July 1988) also marks Pakistan's "capture" of the *azadi* movement. Since the JKLF seemed to be the initial vehicle for the uprising, it ran the early training camps. The ISI was involved in the training, and controlled the weapons.

Because Pakistan later became wary over the pro-independence stance of the JKLF, it shifted support to various pro-Pakistan groups such as the Al Jehad Force (AJF), Al Umar Mujahideen (UM), Allah Tigers (AT), and Muslim Mujahideen (MM). Some of them came into existence after splits or unions, such as the Muslim Janbaz Force (MJF) and the Kashmir Jehad Force (KJF) making up the AJF. A few

Maps

1. Kashmir and neighbours.

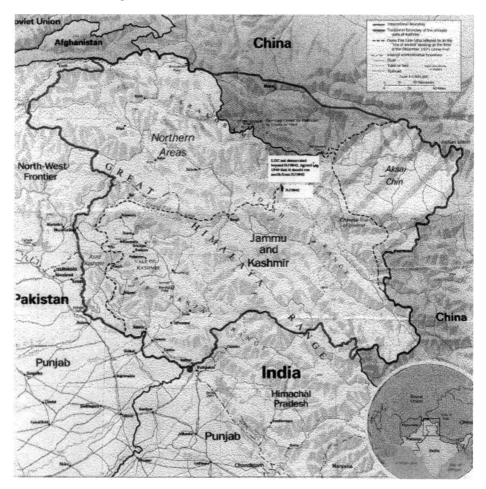

2. Jammu and Kashmir.

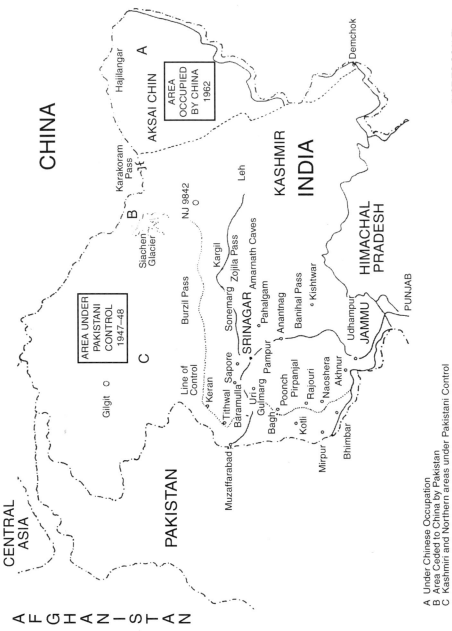

(NOT TO SCALE)

A Under Chinese Occupation
B Area Ceded to China by Pakistan
C Kashmiri and Northern areas under Pakistani Control

3. India: states and union territories..

4. Pakistan's deployment in Batalik.

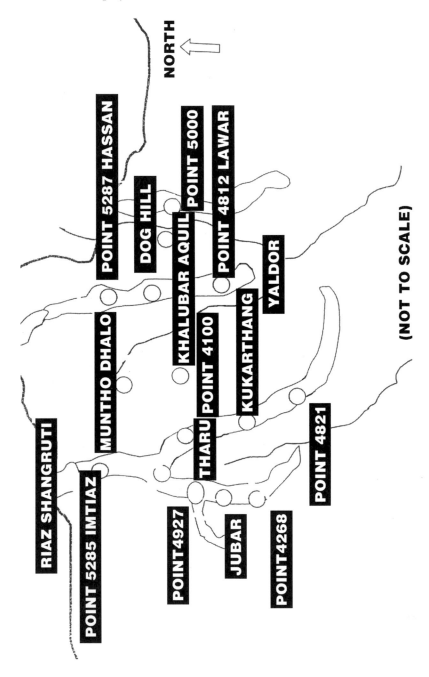

NORTH

POINT 5287 HASSAN

DOG HILL

KHALUBAR AQUIL

POINT 5000

POINT 4812 LAWAR

YALDOR

MUNTHO DHALO

POINT 4100

KUKARTHANG

THARU

POINT 4821

RIAZ SHANGRUTI

POINT 5285 IMTIAZ

POINT4927

JUBAR

POINT4268

(NOT TO SCALE)

Photographs

1. The author with Mrs. Gandhi.

2. Morarji Desai, Prime Minister of India, 1977–1979.

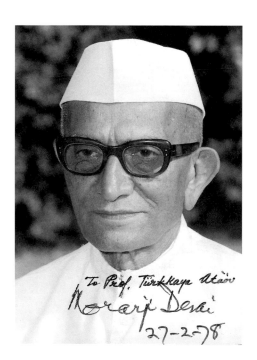

3. Rajiv Gandhi and the author, 1988.

4. Atal Bihari Vajpayee, Prime Minister of India, 1996, 1998–.

To

Mr. Türkkaya Ataöv

With Best Wishes

5. Benazir Bhutto.

To Prof Ataov,
Turkey and Pakistan are brothers
with many shared experiences.
May our friendship grow even stronger
with the passage of time. Benazir Bhutto

6. Kashmiri lake—photo taken
by the author.

7. Bunkers on Kashmiri city streets.

8. The author (middle) is shown with Dr. Mustafa Kamaal Pasha (right). Currently a member of the Kashmiri Cabinet, Dr. M. Kamaal was named by his secular-minded father, Sheikh Abdullah, after modern Turkey's founder.

9. The author interviewed by Mrs. Nayeema Ahmad at All India Radio, Srinagar.

10. Hazratbal Mosque on Lake Dal.

11. The author in front of the Shankaracharya Temple.

12. The author with Firdous Syed, an ex-guerilla.

13. The author (second from left) with Muhammad Yusuf Tang (third from left), the former personal secretary to Sheikh Abdullah.

of them, at times, operate under different names. For instance, Harkat-ul Ansar is also known as Al Hadith or Al Faran.

Some other active *tanzeems* (organizations) are: Al Mujahid Force (MF), Al Mustafa Liberation Fighters (MLF), Harkat-ul Ansar (HUA), Harkat-ul Jihad-e Islami (HJI), Islami Inqilab-e Mahaz (IIM), Islami Jamaat-e Tulba (IJT), Islamic Students League (ISL), Ikhwan-ul Mujahideen (IUM), J&K National Liberation Army (JKNLA), J&K Students Liberation Front (JKSLF), Lashkar-e Taiba (LT), Markaz-e Dawa-ul Arshad (MDA), Mahjaz-e Azadi (MA), Muttahida Jehad Council (MJC), Muslim Mujahideen (MM), People's League (PL), Tahrik-e Horriat-e Kashmir (THK), Tahrik-e Jehad-e Islami (TJI), Tahrik-e Nifaz-e Fiqar Jafaria (TNFJ), and Tahrik-ul Mujahideen (TM). Some of them Islamicized their names. For instance, the JKSLF became Ikhwan-ul Muslimeen.

In addition to personal biases and competition, these multiple groups came into existence to suit the faultlines of the Valley's polity. In spite of their dislike for Indian administration, these groups competed, and even fought, with each other. But the ISI had its own reasons to keep them divided. No single group or individual could, thus, become a force strong enough to assert its own authority over the whole of Kashmir, undermining Pakistan's influence. The reality of many groups was also a guarantee to ensure security in case a captured member would reveal the names and activities of his own organization.

Islamabad established (31 July 1988) 69 training camps (20 still active) on its soil and 80 more (30 active) on Pakistan-held Kashmir territory, in addition to 14 more (8 active) in Afghanistan.[13] There are 17 transit camps for the JKLF, 14 for the HUM and about one each for the rest.[14] Training seems to be handled by the Pakistan Army personnel and the ISI. Among the pro-Pakistan groups, the HUM received preferential treatment for a long time. The three schools in Gilgit offer a 15-day capsule course instead of the 21-day standard *dawra-e aam*, but the five higher training camps in Peshawar teach how to handle sophisticated weapons, such as the upgraded models of (Russian and Chinese) Kalashnikov rifles, (Soviet-made) Dragunov snipers, (Pakistani and Chinese) heavy machine guns, Krinkov sub-machine guns, (Japanese) solar-activated rockets, rocket launchers, (Chinese) surface-to-air missiles, (Pakistani-made) rocket-propelled grenade launchers, explosives, and (Italian) anti-tank mines with remote control devices. Some trainees are exposed to the anti-aircraft weapons. The Bannu and the Muridke bases, the largest operated by the Lashkar-e Taiba, give the three-months long specialized *dawra-e has* courses.

The recruited soldiers abandon their old names and adopt a *nom de guerre*, locally called a *kuniat* (registration name). For instance, a "supreme commander", Maulvi Yusuf Shah became known as Pir (saint) and Salah-ud Din (after the great Muslim commander who took Jerusalem from the Second Crusaders, 1187). Another leader, Mushtaq Ahmad Butt chose the more assertive Mushtaq-ul Islam and increasingly became a religious fanatic.

The Dera Ghazi Khan training centre also possesses an underground weapon and ammunition factory. Pakistan is believed to have raised three regular battalions of the

Kashmir Light Infantry comprising youth from Kashmir, Pakistan-held Kashmir and Afghanistan. Pakistan's overall involvement increased when it chose to support the Sikh terrorists as well. Although the Pakistanis cared little for the Sikhs (and vice versa), they created the K-2 organization under a certain Sajjad Ahmad Reza.

Pakistan's support was obviously not "only moral and political". It was a sponsorship in more ways than one. Pakistan initially backed the JKLF and a few other fundamentalist organizations. The fiction of a Kashmiri freedom struggle ended when the ISI began to support solely the pro-Pakistan groups. After the public refusal of the former to pursue a pro-Pakistan line, patronage was shifted to other outfits, mainly to HUM which recruited a few hundred foreign mercenaries, conveniently called the *mehmaan-e Mujahideen* (guest militants). Not being just "guests" or even foreigners, they actually helped to dangerously escalate the conflict. The latter included Pakistani nationals, Afghans, Sudanese, Bangladeshis, north African Arabs, Lebanese, Iranians, Tajiks, Chechens, plus a handful of people from the Gulf, Jordan, Myanmar, Nepal, Nigeria, Turkey, Uzbekistan, and Yemen. At times, there were attempts to create united fronts and emphasize the pan-Islamic aspect of the movements.

The Afghan War saw the arrival of thousands of such "guests" in Pakistan, through the *kafil* (sponsor) system supported by wealthy Arab circles or individuals interested in a *jehad*. The end of the war again left thousands of them jobless. Some signed for another *jehad* in Kashmir. Not all were poor and semi-literate. Some were educated and willing to take up arms against the "infidels". The "guests" enriched themselves while castrating, gouging out eyes, slitting throats, beheading, and peeling off skins.

The Taliban and Kashmir

Maulana Mohammad Farooq Kashmiri, *Ameer* (Commander) of the HUA stated that the "only solution" of the Kashmir issue lay in *jehad*, and that it was the duty of every Pakistani to take part in it.[15] The U.S. Secretary of State included this Pakistan-based Kashmiri activist group, along with Hamas, Hizbullah, the Japanese Red Army, the Kurdistan Workers Party (PKK), Tamil Tigers and others, among thirty major terrorist organizations.[16] Based in Muzaffarabad and with several thousand armed members in parts of Kashmir and the Doda regions of India, the HUA specifically included Afghans and Arab members of the Afghan war. With the toppling of the Najibullah government (1992), and the end of the *jehad* in Afghanistan,[17] recent years witnessed a change of command from Kashmiris to foreign mercenaries in the main pro-Pakistani militant outfits.[18]

Evidence accumulated indicating that Afghan training camps produced insurgents who infiltrated into Kashmir.[19] While the HUA owes its considerable arsenal, in large measure, to the generosity of the Pakistani Government, especially its intelligence service ISI, other sources are wealthy individual donors in Pakistan and the Gulf countries. The Taliban[20] may be better known as an Afghani movement, but they have a strong Pakistani component in the form of *madrassa* students from all over that country. In fact, the Pakistanis have been part of the Taliban ranks since this kind of student drive first appeared on the scene towards the end of 1994. Most youngsters in the *madrassas* receive some military training during their stay in any one of the 4,500 or so seminary schools across Pakistan.[21] Naseerullah Babar, a former Interior Minister, admitted that under his guidance the Taliban were trained in 1994.

The *madrassas* are growing pools of juveniles recruited to extremist causes. In addition to the registered religious schools, there are also unregistered institutions turning out students who go on to join militant groups. Babar, who was in charge of the national police as a former Interior Minister, views some of these schools as "hotbeds of terrorism".[22] The Dar-ul Uloom Haqqania among them is described as "the alma mater of the Taliban movement" that rules Afghanistan.[23] This school hails Osama Bin Laden, suspected of being one of the key men behind terrorism in the name of Islam and the mastermind of the U.S. Embassy bombings in Nairobi (Kenya) and Dar-es Salaam (Tanzania), as a "true believer". He was once the star recruiter by the CIA for the Afghan *jehad*. Ironically, the United States and Bin Laden had the common goals, about a decade or so ago, of the defeat of the Soviets and the demise of Communism. Now, he is the head of a new fundamentalist network. Some analysts are speculating whether he has acquired a suitcase nuclear bomb or chemical weapons from Russia.[24] Bin Laden returned to Saudi Arabia after the withdrawal (1988) of the Soviet forces. Three years later, he interpreted the arrival of the American troops in Saudi Arabia during the second Gulf War (1991) as occupation of Mecca and Madina, Islam's two most sacred cities.[25] He vowed to fight them and the royal Saudi family, which forced him to flee. Known as a multi-millionaire civil engineer stripped of his Saudi nationality, Bin Laden calls for attacks on American targets from his hideouts in Afghanistan, frequently changing his sanctuary from Jalalabad to Khandahar or from Khost to Nangarhar. Having generously distributed charities to Afghani orphans, refugees and widows, and having stood up against the world's only superpower, he is a popular man in Afghanistan and even a hero to groups of Muslims elsewhere.

Thanks to the Taliban and the various factions who rallied under the banner of Osama Bin Laden, Afghanistan has become a vast training camp for militant groups from across the Muslim world engaged in assorted *jehads*.[26] Militant Muslim groups from Pakistan and several other states found moral and material help as well as sanctuary in war-torn Afghanistan. After Bin Laden came to head the Al-Qaida organization, the supreme body of different militant outfits active in the Arab states, and announced the formation of the International Islamic Front, he had the support of the two sons of Sheikh Omar Abd-ur Rahman (the blind Egyptian cleric who was jailed on account of the bombing of the World Trade Center in New York), Aiman Al-Zawahiri (the leader of the Egyptian Jamaat-ul Jehad), Algerians representing the Islamic Salvation Front (FIS), supporters of the Ittehad-e Islami of Somalia and the Philippines' Abu Sayyaf organization. Pakistanis and Kashmiris also went to Afghanistan to strengthen Taliban ranks and receive military training. Along with the

Lashkar-e Taiba, the Harkat-ul Mujahideen, also a platform for anti-Shi'a elements on account of its Sunni base, is one of the two major Pakistani suppliers of manpower from both sides of the Line of Control for the battle in J&K. Most of them live and train in the Khost camps, which were initially established with the help of American and Pakistani secret agencies in the 1980s but hit by dozens of U.S. missiles in 1998.

The *Mujahideen* commandos in the Khost camps had been trained by American and Pakistani instructors, who followed the training books of the U.S. Marines. The camps were visited by William Casey, then director of the CIA, and the late General Akhtar Abd-ur Rahman, then in charge of the ISI.[27] Afghani, Pakistani and Kashmiri teachers now also train the militants in guerilla warfare on light and heavy weapons. An average of 250 people at a time go through training in each camp, the duration ranging from 40 days to six months. The day reportedly starts with morning prayers followed by military lessons and practical training after which come the *Dars-e Qur'an* or lessons on the Holy Book. The camps, called Al-Badr-1, Al-Badr-2, Abu Jindal, Al-Farooq, Khalid bin Waleed and Salman Farsi, constitute a complex in the Gurbaz district of Khost Province in southern Afghanistan, handed over to the Harkat-ul Ansar, which sends volunteers to fight in Afghanistan, Kashmir or to other parts of the world, all under the supervision of the Taliban administration. Subsequently, Abu Jindal came to be known as the "Arab camp", where the Saudi dissident, Osama Bin Laden, held his press conference in May 1998 to announce the launching the International Islamic Front for *jehad* against the United States and Israel.

Bin Laden's network is also being tapped by a number of fundamentalist groups in West Bengal.[28] Besides, other terrorist groups whose playground is J&K set up operation posts in Calcutta from where they can move into Nepal wherefrom men, material and money come. Such border districts, easily identifiable along the frontiers of Pakistan, Kashmir, Bangladesh, and India's North-East, virtually sit on a ticking bomb because of a combination of factors including the presence of terrorist groups and infiltration. The disciples of Bin Laden in Bangladesh have also planned to kill prominent intellectuals including writer Taslima Nasreen, "National Professor" Kabir Chowdory, and Islamic scholar Maulana Abd-ul Awal. They are believed to be responsible for an attempt on the life of the Bangladeshi poet Shams-ur Rahman in early 1999.[29] This senior poet is considered a symbol of Bangladesh's secular nationhood. The Bin Laden-aided armed cadres seek to create a *shari'a* society by murdering progressive intellectuals and waging a war against other temporal authorities. Terrorists in some of the training centres in Chittagong Hill Tracts identify themselves as "Bangladeshi Talibans", in whose activities the Pakistani ISI is believed to have a hand.

Bin Laden primarily and repeatedly called for attacks on the military and civilian American targets. The U.S. Government accused Harkat-ul Ansar and Bin Laden for planning the bombing (7 August 1998) of its embassies in Nairobi and Dar-es Salaam which killed 257 people, including 12 Americans. The American leadership further blamed his network for the deaths of Belgian, Pakistani and U.S. peacekeepers in Somalia, a plot to assassinate the Egyptian President, a bombing of the Egyptian Embassy in Islamabad, and the murders of German tourists in Egypt. Washington retaliated (20 August) by firing about 75 Tomahawk cruise missiles from ships close to Pakistani waters at the militant training camps in Afghanistan and a chemical factory in Sudan alleged to be manufacturing a component of nerve gas, a charge categorically denied in Khartoum. Bin Laden and his top aides were not present in the camps during the night attack, but some Pakistani, Kashmiri and Arab nationals perished. The attack destroyed two mosques, hostels and civilian houses. Seven missiles hit a pharmaceutical factory in Khartoum. The Taliban described the action as the terrorism of a superpower which let loose a reign of intimidation and destruction of Muslims all over the world. The next day, the Taliban held huge processions, blocked roads, delivered fiery speeches, attempted to storm the American Center and the British Council, and shot two United Nations officials, one of whom died. The Taliban intensified its verbal attacks on the United States asserting that the missile strikes were not against a Saudi dissident but proof of "enmity against Islam".[30] Two New York newspapers (*New York Post* and *New York Newsday*) reported that Bin Laden had directed his followers to assassinate Bill Clinton on two occasions, when the U.S. President visited (1994) the Philippines and when he planned (1998), later cancelled, a visit to South Asia.

Islamic mercenaries, partly funded by the exiled Osama Bin Laden, cross from Pakistan or Afghanistan and establish bases in the Kashmir Valley. They bring the *jehad* of the Saudi millionaire to Indian-controlled Kashmir. Apart from the fact that the Taliban were assisted by Pakistan's ISI partly to serve its purpose against India, some survivors of the U.S. missile attack admitted that they were trained in the use of weapons in Khost camps from where they expected to be sent to Kashmir.[31] The Afghan alliance opposed to the Taliban administration frequently reproved Pakistan for providing armed assistance to groups pledged to violence. The brute force greeted as the deeds of "holy warriors" in the eyes of many ordinary Pakistanis[32] is detested as disorder and savagery by the targeted or third parties.

It is not only that many Kashmiri Hindus abandoned their homes and land. Bloodshed, destruction, abductions, rapes, extortions, robberies, and inter-group armed encounters disillusioned the majority of the Muslim Kashmiris as well. Innocent citizens, including the Valley's large Hindu Brahman minority, are constantly under threat and attack. Especially the fear of rape, which the armed militants have used as a weapon to punish, intimidate, coerce, humiliate and degrade, was a factor in the flight of whole families, Hindu and Muslim.[33] The Kashmiris, on the whole, are exhausted and crave for a return to at least pre-1988 normality. Pakistan has not been able to wrest away the whole of J&K from India. But the Valley has become one of the most weaponized societies in that part of the world. While supporting violence there, Pakistan failed to control its spread into its own social fabric, and became more and more "Talibanized", as a result of the destabilizing export of Afghan-style radical Islam.[34]

Notes

1   Norman Bentwich and Andrew Martin, *Commentary on the Charter of the United Nations*, London, Routledge and Kegan Paul, 1950, pp. 9–10, 106–108; Bruno Simma, ed., *The Charter of the United Nations: a Commentary*, New York, Oxford University Press, 1994, pp. 141–154, 661–678.
2   Staff Report on "Mercenaries and the Criminilization of a People's Movement", *Peace Initiatives*, New Delhi, III/5 (September–October 1997), p. 3.
3   Jonah Blank, "Kashmir: Fundamentalism Takes Root", *Foreign Affairs*, New York, 78/ 6 (November–December 1999), p. 42.
4   A short history of mercenarism: Igor Blishchenko and Nikolai Zhdanov, *Terrorism and International Law (Terrorism i Mejdunarodnoye Pravo)*, Moscow, Progress, 1984, pp. 166–207.
5   Glyn Roberts, *Volunteers and Neo-Colonialism: an Inquiry into the Role of Foreign Volunteers in the Third World*, Cadishead, A. J. Wright, 1969. The Larousse definition (*'Soldat qui sert à prix d'argent un gouvernement étranger'*) is, therefore, inadequate. Anthony Mockler, *The Mercenaries*, New York, Macmillan, 1969, p. 17.
6   United Nations, High Commissioner for Human Rights, *Report on the Use of Mercenaries as a Means of Violating Human Rights and Impeding the Exercise of the Right of Peoples to Self-Determination*, Report No. E/CN.4/1997/24, dated 20 February 1997, presented to the U.N. Human Rights Commission by Enrique Bernales Ballestros, Special Rapporteur, Geneva, 1997.
7   The statements of the Assistant Secretary of State for African Affairs at the U.S. Department of State and the Deputy Assistant Attorney General, in response to questions like what is the extent of the enlistment of American citizens in foreign armies and how American citizens get involved in losing their lives in foreign lands: U.S., House of Representatives, *Mercenaries in Africa, Hearing Before the Special Subcommittee on Investigations of the Committee on International Relations, House of Representatives, Ninety-Fourth Congress, Second Session, August 9, 1976*, Washington, D.C., Government Printing Office, 1976.
8   Peter Tickler, *The Modern Mercenary: Dog of War, or Soldier of Honour?* Wellingborough, Northamptonshire, Patrick Stephens, 1987, pp. 216–220.
9   Wilfred Burchett and Derek Roebuck, *The Whores of War: Mercenaries Today*, Middlesex, Penguin Books, 1977, pp. 230f.
10 "Radical Islam, Mercenaries and the Proxy War", *Peace Initiatives*, New Delhi, III/5 (September–October 1997), p. 6. Although the Government of Pakistan, on the eve of the visit of the U.S. Under-Secretary of State (Thomas Pickering) to Islamabad, took the unprecedented action of raiding a HUA office in Rawalpindi, no similar action had been taken against it prior to this raid. Bansi Lal, "Harkat-ul Ansar among Groups Named as Terrorist Organisations by the United States Government", *ibid.*, p. 31.
11 Pakistan temporarily ceased direct support for Kashmiri insurgency when the United States threatened to add it to the list of countries backing terrorism. *The Washington Post*, 16 May 1994.
12 Kalim Bahadur, *The Jama'at-i-Islami of Pakistan*, New Delhi, Chetana Publications, 1977. Abul Ala Maududi's political philosophy was originally the ideology of the JI. Since all his ideas were admittedly deduced from the Holy Book and the Sunna, there could be nothing new in the JI on any issue. He defined Islam as an all comprehensive

system of life. Dissidents were treated as heretics. The state could only be an all-powerful monolithic one, upholding a definite religious ideology. Maududi advocated a *Nizam-e Mustafa*, a system (he thought) Prophet Muhammad would have wanted through the rigorous application of the tenets of the Holy Book. *Ibid.*, pp. 159–197. The JI, founded in 1941, is against democracy and secularism on which the Republic of India is established.

13   Sreedhar and Bhagat, *op. cit.*, pp. 100–102. The number of the active camps may change in time. For instance, pressure on Pakistan by the U.S. Deputy National Security Adviser Robert Gates (1990) caused the closure of 31 camps. Joshi, *op. cit.*, p. 45.

14   Sreedhar and Bhagat, *op. cit.,* pp. 108–112. For a list of camps, also see: K. Warikoo, "Islamist Mercenaries and Terrorism in Kashmir", *Himalayan and Central Asian Studies*, New Delhi, II/2 (April–June 1998), pp. 49–51.

15   *The Frontier Post*, Peshawar, 2 September 1997.

16   *Dawn*, Karachi, 9 October 1997.

17   The role of Islam in the political history of Afghanistan, including the fundamentalist movements of the previous centuries: Olivier Roy, *Islam and Resistance in Afghanistan*, Cambridge, U.K., Cambridge University Press, 1986.

18   Roger Howard, "Wrath of Islam: the Harkat-ul Islam", *Jane's Intelligence Review*, Surrey, U.K., 9/10 (October 1997).

19   *The Pakistan Times*, Lahore, 28 August 1998.

20   The word "Taliban" is derived from the Persian (and Pashto) plural of the Arabic "Talib", or seeker (of knowledge). Before 1947, Afghan students travelled to India to attend their favourite *madrassa*, the Dar-al 'Uloom of Deoband in Saharanpur (Utter Pradesh), which opposed the modernist policies of the Aligarh Muslim University, originally established by Sir Syed Ahmad Khan. Hafeez Malik, "Taliban's Islamic Emirate of Afghanistan: Its Impact on Eurasia", *Journal of South Asian and Middle Eastern Studies*, Villanova, PA, XXIII/1 (Fall 1999), pp. 66–67.

21   Rizwan Qureshi, "War Games", *The Herald*, Karachi, September 1998, p. 31.

22   Kathy Gannon, "Pak Islamic schools are 'hotbeds of terrorism'", *The Pakistan Times,* Lahore, 15 October 1998.

23   Uli Schmetzer, "Islamic School Trains the Taliban", *The Tribune*, Chandigarh, 5 October 1998.

24   An article which analyses Bin Laden's quest for weapons of mass destruction: G. D. Bakshi, "The Face of the Fifth Horseman: Osama Bin Laden's Global Terror Network", *Aakrosh*, New Delhi, II/5 (October 1999), pp. 17–32.

25   Rahimullah Yusufzai, "Myth and Man", *Newsline*, Karachi, September 1998, p. 43.

26   "Afghanistan's Nation of Islam", *ibid.*, September 1998, p. 37.

27   Behroz Khan, "Remains of the Day", *ibid.*, September 1998, p. 41.

28   Malabik Bhattacharya, "Osama network funding three groups in West Bengal", *The Hindu*, New Delhi, 4 April 1999.

29   Haroon Habib, "Osama spreads tentacles in Bangladesh", *ibid.*, 25 January 1999.

30   "Taliban pledge not to hand over Osama", *Dawn*, Karachi, 23 August 1998. Some Western sources also agree that the U.S.-led unipolar world runs the risk of declaring Islam as the "new enemy". For instance: Yvonne Yazbeck Haddad, "The 'New Enemy'? Islam and the Islamists after the Cold War", eds., Phyllis Bennis and Michel Moushabeck, *Altered States: a Reader in the New World Order*, New York, Olive Brench Press, 1993, pp. 83–94. A reply by an East-West team to Samuel P. Huntington's well-known thesis

on the "Clash of Civilizations": Hans Köchler and Gudrun Grabher, eds., *Civilizations: Conflict or Dialogue?* Vienna, International Progress Oreganization, 1999.

31 "Pakistan involved in terrorism", *The Pakistan Times*, Lahore, 25 August 1998.

32 "Osama hero to many Pakistanis", *Dawn*, Karachi, 25 August 1998.

33 "Kidnapping and Criminalization", *Peace Initiatives*, New Delhi, III/5 (September–October 1997), p. 13. Indian security force personnel have also been accused of raping Kashmiri women. Some resulted in court-martial proceedings and punishment. While the security personnel are accountable under Indian laws, militants and mercenaries are beyond that control.

34 Ahmed Rashid, "The Taliban: Exporting Extremism", *Foreign Affairs*, New York, 78/6 (November–December 1999), p. 22.

Chapter 11

Great Powers: Switch in Stances

Pakistan's leadership led its people to believe that their country was incomplete without Kashmir being a part of it, simply because the Muslims constituted the majority there. Consequently, Pakistan launched its fourth war, now known as the Kargil War, for this land in mid-1999. It was significant because it happened to be the first one fought with regular forces between India and Pakistan, both of whom had become overtly nuclear. India, which had demonstrated its ability to explode a nuclear device in mid-1974, carried out nuclear tests on 11 May 1998, and declared itself to be a state with nuclear weapons. The five tests in 1998 emphasized the continuity of this capacity over the years. Pakistan, which tested a nuclear device in 1983, reached successful nuclear weaponization by 1987, and fired a nuclear intermediate range ballistic missile (IRBM) a year later, immediately carried out six in response to India's five tests.[1]

When the American atomic bombs devastated Hiroshima and Nagasaki, Gandhi had characterized the bomb as the most "diabolical use of science".[2] Why did India require them more than four decades later?[3] For decades, its leaders pursued an independent and non-aligned foreign and defence policy. Simultaneously, India was critical of selective non-proliferation without disarmament. Permanent extension of the Non-Proliferation Treaty without commitment to disarmament exposed the recalcitrance of the nuclear weapon states to realize a global abolition of those weapons. The unwillingness of the great powers in the post-Cold War international order to institute reforms in the United Nations system forced countries, especially those outside the alliance system, to develop national capabilities more seriously than before. Iraq and North Korea pursued clandestine nuclear programmes. China, a nuclear power with a permanent seat in the U.N. Security Council, had territorial disputes with India. France, which had given assurances that it would exercise utmost restraint in nuclear testing, regressed from its earlier moratorium.

With the overt nuclearization of both India and Pakistan in 1998, a full-scale war between the two neighbours was unrealistic, but there was still some scope for limited war. This is what occurred in Kargil, which stood at the worst stand off between the two countries since 1971. Two important conclusions of the armed conflict were that a number of countries exhibited sympathy for the Indian position, and that Pakistan soon needed a face-saving device adding to the tensions in the domestic power structure that finally brought another military coup.

The Indian and the Pakistani bombs breached the monopoly of the five powers that monopolized the permanent seats in the U.N. Security Council. They also triggered a wave of sanctions in the United States, where not all influential people thought that these two Asian countries had no right to go nuclear. The Kargil War, fought against this background, caused shifts in the approaches of some leading states, principally the United States and China. American pressure on Pakistan, signifying a shift in approach, to pull back its forces to the Line of Control, the neutrality of China, to which Pakistan owed some of the significant transfers of nuclear weapons technologies, and even the reluctance of the Organization of the Islamic Conference (OIC) to endorse Pakistan's presence in Kargil boosted New Delhi's stand. Responses principally from Washington and Beijing hastened Pakistan's retreat perhaps earlier than expected.

Blunder in Kargil

In May 1999, Pakistani Army regulars and mercenaries belonging to at least four militant or terrorist organizations[4] crossed the LOC into the Drass-Kargil-Batalik sector of Ladakh.[5] The Indian press reported it as a "new dimension" of Pakistan's decade-old "proxy war" against India.[6] The LOC was established by mutual consent under the Simla Agreement. Since Pakistan, beginning with its creation, has made cross-border infiltration a pillar of its policy, what may now be termed as "Pakistan's fourth war for Kashmir"[7] was a military operation, the *Mujahideen* and other fighters playing a supportive role. It was, then, only in a limited sense that the Kargil episode was another manifestation of "medieval malevolence spilling over from Afghanistan".[8] It was foremost a military aggression, mainly led by Pakistan's army regulars across a wide stretch of a line, previously agreed upon to be the border. The intrusion into Indian air space of a Pakistani Navy maritime reconnaissance (Atlantique) aircraft and its shooting down added yet another dimension to the tension. Those who occupied Kargil heights were not *Mujahideen*, but were from Pakistan's Northern Light Infantry.[9] While the attacking side continued to fan the flames of "Islamic" militancy, India countered the surprise through the lethality of its response, and was generally praised for its restraint. Although the nature of the terrain may motivate a determined enemy to do the same all over again and, a few post-Kargil incidents such as the intrusion of a Pakistani aircraft do not help in returning to the table, there is no working alternative other than a meaningful dialogue if both parties are willing and ready to utilize the Simla Agreement as the basis.

Some Pakistanis expressed a doubt that the LOC in Kashmir, as indicated in the Simla Agreement, was vague. It was discussed, on the other hand, with meticulous care, maps giving detailed references and descriptions of land marks. They were checked and re-checked before the representatives of the two countries signed the documents. The members of the delegations were made up of highly respected individuals, who met no less than nine times at Suchengarh (India) and at Wagah (Pakistan) leaving nothing as uncertain.[10] The wording of the paragraph (4/ii) dealing with the sanctity of the LOC of the Simla Agreement is as follows: "…Neither side shall seek to alter it unilaterally, irrespective of mutual differences and legal interpretations. Both sides undertake to refrain from threat or use of force in violation of this Line". The invasion was also a violation of the United Nations Charter.

General Pervez Musharraf, then the Army Chief, admitted that his troops had captured 500 sq. km. of Indian territory across the LOC in the Kargil sector.[11] India's conventional military superiority hanging over Pakistan like a permanent Sword of Damocles, the Z. A. Bhutto government in Islamabad pursued a nuclear programme right after the 1971 defeat. India's conventional superiority was, thus, going to be neutralized. Pakistan manufactured a nuclear device and tested it in 1983. The year 1987 may be singled out as the date for the acquisition of nuclear weapons, followed by a new wave of extreme violence in Kashmir (1988). The years 1998 and 1999 witnessed more nuclear and IRBM tests. Both India and Pakistan declared themselves nuclear weapon states in May 1999. Pakistan assumed that the nuclear umbrella would allow action without risks. The chances of India's retaliation would be much lower on account of the hazard of escalation to a nuclear weapon exchange. Not only feelings of revenge for earlier defeats would be compensated and tensions in the domestic power structure lessened, but armed hostilities would be stopped by the international community anyway. While new waves of the *Mujahideen* might infiltrate into Kashmir, Pakistan would establish military bridge-heads across the LOC, dominating the Drass-Kargil road, which is the only link between Srinagar and Leh. Just as the Sino-Soviet border armed conflict on the River Ussuri (1969) did not bring nuclear weapons into the equation, the strategy of limited war[12] became a Pakistani scenario.

A previous (1987) Pakistani plan to occupy the strategic hilltops in and around Kargil had to be abandoned when former Lieut. General, and then, Foreign Minister Sahibzada Yaqub Khan explained, in the presence of General Zia, the reasons why he found the idea militarily inappropriate.[13] About a decade later, Pakistan's Army Chief General Jahangir Karamat was forced to resign when he made public talks, unusual under the circumstances, on the need for better decision-making in national security matters. General Musharraf, who had standing links with several Islamic fundamentalist organizations, had trained *Mujahideen* groups, and had experience in mountain warfare, was appointed (1998), superseding three officers senior to him, in Karamat's place. There is some evidence that Pakistan has been planning an invasion to acquire a bridgehead across the LOC.

Considering the necessarily large gaps in the deployment of guards and troops in particular sectors of the LOC, it is comparatively easy to set up initial positions on the Indian side of the line. India decided to launch Operation Vijay, and its prime minister described the situation as a "war-like" one.[14] Pakistan's action soon turned out to be a military disaster.[15] Prime Minister Sharif's meeting (4 July 1999) with President Clinton and the former's promise that he would appeal to the "Kashmiri freedom fighters" to pull out was a blueprint for a total defeat. Moreover, the Indian forces conducted themselves with predictable élan. For the first time, the world opinion seemed to endorse India's policy stance on the Kargil conflict.

Pakistan needs to repair the damage that it has done to trust through confidence-building deeds. Although Kargil does not compare with the previous wars in terms of forces or casualties involved, new Kargils have to be prevented.[16] One may remember that centuries ago Muhammad Ghauri attacked Prithviraj seventeen times before he achieved success. The geographical fact of Pakistan cannot be ignored. India recognizes the sovereign state of Pakistan, and this is final. But hand in hand with the use of the latest technology to enhance security goes a dialogue which can be productive only if the LOC is respected.

The U.S. Modifies Behaviour

The Kargil episode caused an unequivocal tilt in U.S. policy in favour of India, which virtually an international consensus designated as the victim. The initial American reaction of urging mutual restraint in this episode fast gave way to a conviction that fighting would end only if the intruders departed either voluntarily or by force. The Americans, more and more concerned over the export of rigid Islamic orthodoxy into Kashmir, persuaded the G-8 countries to demand full respect for the LOC. Supporting the Indian position on bilateralism, Washington now lays greater emphasis on Indo-Pakistan dialogue. The U.N. Security Council Resolution 1172 had already insisted a year before the Kargil episode that the two neighbours resolve their differences bilaterally, but international public opinion now backs the "Lahore process", which the Pakistani Army's actions in Kargil threatened to derail. The Indian Prime Minister Atal Bihari Vajpayee had dramatically driven across the border and met his counterpart on Pakistan's soil extolling hopes for future peace. The event was later labelled as "bus diplomacy". Vajpayee had affirmed the finality of partition by visiting the Minar-e Pakistan in Lahore.[17]

The United States had come a long way since the days of John Foster Dulles, later Secretary of State, who said that the Nehru-led interim government in India had allowed a strong Soviet influence.[18] Within the framework of global confrontation with the Soviet Union, Washington categorized Pakistan as a geostrategic ally in the "Northern Tier" of nations geographically under the nose of the Communist bloc. Dulles had considered India's non-alignment as "immoral".[19] American global interest *vis-à-vis* its competition with Communism influenced its stance on Kashmir rather than the merits of the issue itself. American partiality generated then official Indian reactions demanding the exclusion of Americans from the U.N. Commission on Kashmir. Only Chinese-Indian conflict in 1962 broke the ice slightly, Washington nevertheless pressuring Nehru to settle it on terms more favourable to Pakistan, its ally. The idea of a plebiscite, favoured by Pakistan, loomed behind the American suggestions for bilateral talks between the two countries in 1962–63. U.S. diplomacy supported Pakistan during the Bangladesh crisis, which was partly responsible for the subsequent Indo-Soviet Treaty (1971). After the Cold War, a new era appeared to have dawned, however, in Indo-American relations, which was reflected in the enhanced level of interactions among the high level officials, establishment of a "commercial alliance" and signing of a "defence cooperation" agreement. After the U.S. Commerce Department designated India as one of the new "Big Emerging Markets", the amount of American foreign investment in India during the first year of the Clinton Administration, although still a small amount in relative terms, exceeded the cumulative U.S. investment in India from 1947 to mid-1991.[20]

Although the United States at times exerted some influence to bring the two parties to the negotiating table, the pattern of interactions with India were fluctuating while misperceptions remained consisting of various elements.[21] For instance, U.S. acceptance of the workability of the Simla Agreement became evident as American intelligence gathered sufficient proof on Pakistan's inseparable involvement initially in training and arming of Kashmiri militants, and then in backing the Taliban. Cultivating some contacts with Pakistani-sponsored separatist groups in the United States, some American officials on occasion projected themselves as potential mediators within a trilateral frame of reference. Some American study groups or politicians, nevertheless, suggested the Simla option and the partition of J&K along the present LOC, perhaps with some minor adjustments.

The paradigmatic shift in U.S. policy towards India is more discernible after the Kargil experience. Apart from the merits of the incident as well as the broader Kashmir conflict, a writer portrayed the shift as a "Kargil Spring" emerging from the "Nuclear Winter" of 1998.[22] Besides being a democracy, India is a major player in Asia, destined to become a great power in a near future. Apparently, the United States, first of all, acknowledged the fact that the genesis of the Kargil crisis lay in Pakistan's adventurism, and refused to support a call for the internationalization of the issue in the wake of that crisis. It also rejected the Pakistani questioning of the legitimacy of the LOC. The change in the rules of military engagement on account of the introduction of nuclear weapons into the Sub-continent, made the United States deeply concerned on account of the danger of tensions escalating into a nuclear conflict. The Indian-American community, a wealthy minority in the U.S., has started to exert influence on the political process in that country. The U.S. did not even adopt merely a neutral position like China, whose departure from its former pro-Pakistan support is of value to India. The position of Washington, which played a crucial role in moderating the old OIC policies, has been unambiguous.

When I. K. Gujral, a former Indian Prime Minister, was talking to President Clinton in 1997, he was reminded of the Biblical saying that goes: "...delays are not denials".[23] Utilizing the opportunities that lie beyond Kargil, the two countries may agree, not only on a bilateral solution on the basis of partition along the LOC, but they may join forces against international terrorism, narcotics and small arms proliferation, and even seek to iron out differences on a range of other issues. In spite of a bitter conflict over Korea in the early 1950s, China and the U.S. found ways of confronting the Soviet Union together within a span of less than two decades. Similarly, India and the U.S. may be at the threshold of a more flexible approach towards each other. They now have an opportunity to build on the trust generated by the Kargil crisis.

China's Neutrality

The critical Clinton-Sharif deal (4 July 1999) expedited an honourable retreat for the Pakistani armed forces. But it was China's posture of neutrality that convinced the Pakistani leadership of the futility of insistence on armed intervention. China's new response was in contrast with its former policy of blessing and encouragement of Pakistan's actions. Known for taking a pro-Pakistan stand in all the earlier conflicts, China, this time, changed its strategic behaviour on the entire J&K question. Having supplied military hardware and sensitive technology to Pakistan for so many decades, China now advised its long-standing strategic partner to abide by the LOC and withdraw the intruders. This radical departure brings to mind the possibility that Kargil may also be the beginning of a new trend in Sino-Pakistan relations. If it indicates a changed context of Sino-U.S. stand off as well, new initiatives in Sino-U.S. and Sino-Indian ties will serve a mutually supplementing atmosphere of peace. Beijing's neutrality may bolster a new China-India-Pakistan security relationship.[24]

The Chinese Communists were still fighting in the Civil War when both India and Pakistan became independent. Official Peking (now Beijing) line after 1949 described Indian political life as bourgeois liberal democracy and Nehru as a stooge of Western interests. Following the Indo-Pakistan War of 1948 and the Indo-Chinese War of 1962, China and Pakistan built friendship against their common enemy. Pakistan even conceded some territory to China, which became its major supplier of military equipment and technologies. China provided the same kind of support during the 1971 War. As well put by an Indian writer,[25] one does not need to scratch too deep to discover the links between China's nuclear capability as well as its policy of assisting Pakistan's nuclear and missile programme and India's decision to keep the nuclear option open. India stationed five of its seven mountain divisions on its northern borders.[26] Pakistan facilitated Henry Kissinger's historic trip to Beijing, which made all three countries more suspicious in Indian eyes. In the 1970s, Pakistan emerged as the "number one recipient of Chinese supplies".[27] Although Pakistan made use of various contributions from other sources as well, Chinese help in transforming that country into a nuclear power was significant. Although China, from time to time, disappointed Pakistan, its frequent patronage, over the years, became the most central concern of India's security thinking. China was, thus, a critical factor in India's foreign policy, almost as problematic as Pakistan, but qualitatively different from that western neighbour.[28] On the other hand, since the signing of the Sino-Indian agreement (1993) on the maintenance of peace on the LOC, both China and India have been actively adjusting their policies towards each other, and their relationship has been improving at a faster pace than expected.[29]

China's recent posture of neutrality, however, may be singled out as the "most important factor" that greased the wheels of the Clinton-Sharif deal.[30] China remained neutral even after the visit of Pakistan's Prime Minister Sharif to Beijing. In the post-Cold War circumstances, Pakistan lost some standing in China's foreign policy calculations. Beijing has to adapt itself to the new realities. Pakistan is no longer the frontline state battling Soviet influence in Central and South Asia. A meeting of minds between the Chinese and the new Russian leadership replaced the former military threat along the western and southern borders. While a possible Western intervention in this region would bring new dangers closer to home, Pakistan's repeated nuclear and missile tests easily put China on the spot under the critical eyes of the United States, which also accused that country for "stealing" technologies from U.S. facilities. Neither did Pakistan restrict the domination and network of the Islamic militants, whose activities extended into the Muslim-Turkic (Uygur) province of Xinjiang (or Chinese Turkestan). Although China's leaders claim that Islamic extremism does not pose a threat to security, their country possessing a civilization with a long experience in dealing with multi-ethnic problems, Beijing is beginning to see, however, the emergence of fissiparous tendencies involving weapons and drugs.[31] Moreover, NATO's selective support of human rights of some minority ethnic groups would increase the probability of future interference in Tibet as well as in Xinjiang. For China, Pakistan's terrorist-mercenary linkage might prove to be a high risk in the long run. New China, critical of encouraging unilateralism in international relations, is bound to act like a great power of the 21st century with global interests rather than a mere regional balancer pursuing limited gains such as getting an ally off the hook.[32]

Notes

1   Relevant documents in chronological order on Pakistan's nuclear efforts: Sreedhar, *Pakistan's Bomb*, New Delhi, 1986. It does not include the China factor in Pakistan's nuclear program.

2   Muchkund Dubey, "India's Pursuit of a Minimum Nuclear Deterrence", *World Focus*, New Delhi, 222–223 (June–July 1998), p. 3.

3   Jasjit Singh, "India's Nuclear Policy: the Year After", *Strategic Analysis*, New Delhi, XXIII/4 (July 1999), pp. 509–530.

4   B. Raman, "Kargil: in Perspective", *U. S. I. Journal*, New Delhi, CXXIX/536 (April–June 1999), pp. 162–163.

5   Bidanda M. Chengappa, "Pakistan's Compulsions for the Kargil Misadventure", *Strategic Analysis*, New Delhi, XXIII/7 (October 1999), pp. 1071–1082.

6   For instance: Gurmeet Kanwal, "Kargil", *Seminar*, New Delhi, 479 (July 1999), p. 15.

7   Jasjit Singh, ed., *Kargil 1999: Pakistan's Fourth War for Kashmir*, New Delhi, Knowledge World, 1999.

8   Jaswant Singh, "Kargil and Beyond", *World Focus*, New Delhi, 234–235 (June–July 1999), p. 4.

9   The Indian Army recovered 249 dead bodies of Pakistan Army Regulars, together with identity cards, paybooks of soldiers, leave certificates and the like. Some responsible Pakistani generals acknowledged that the army has suffered more than forty officers killed. For instance: Aslam Beg, "Kargil-The Drop Scene", *The Nation*, Islamabad, 13 July 1999.

10   The Indian team captain was Lieut. General P. S. Bhagat and the Pakistani leader was Lieut. General Hameed Khan, both respected veterans, aided by trained survey personnel, who worked on the laborious mission with trust. The LOC was reproduced on two sets of maps prepared by each side, each set consisting of 27 map sheets formed into 19 mosaics. Each individual mosaic of all four sets of maps with the LOC marked on them has been signed by the representatives of the Chiefs of Army Staff of India and Pakistan, and each side has exchanged one set of signed mosaics as required under the joint statement by the representatives of India and Pakistan, signed on 29 August 1972. The Governments of India and Pakistan have accorded their approvals, and on 17 December 1972, the mutually agreed statement was released in New Delhi and Islamabad. Three days later, another joint statement was released regarding the withdrawal of troops to the international border.

11   Jasjit Singh, "The Fourth War", *Kargil 1999*, *op. cit.*, p. 119.

12   Swaran Singh, *Limited War*, New Delhi, Lancer Books, 1995.

13   Jasjit Singh, *op. cit.*, p. 133.

14   Vinod Anand, "India's Military Response to the Kargil Aggression", *Strategic Analysis*, New Delhi, XXIII/7 (October 1999), p. 1055.

15   Some Pakistani sources on Kargil: Lieut. General (retd.) Kamal Matinuddin stated that it was a "complete disaster and failure". *News,* Islamabad, 25 July 1999. Brigadier A. R. Siddiqi reminded of "the absence of a single word in support". *Nation*, Islamabad, 4 August 1999. M. P. Bandara described it as a "near disaster". *Dawn*, Karachi, 21 July 1999. According to Ayaz Amir, it was "ill-conceived, if not downright foolish". *Dawn*, Karachi, 9 July 1999.

16   Satish Nambiar, "Preventing New Kargils", *World Focus*, New Delhi, 234–235 (June– July 1999), pp. 11–13.

17   C. Raja Mohan, "The U.S. and Kargil", *World Focus*, New Delhi, 234–235 (June–July 1999), p. 29.

18   Harold A. Gould and Sumit Ganguli, eds., *The Hope and Reality: U.S.-Indian Relations from Roosevelt to Reagan*, New Delhi, Oxford, 1993, p. 5.

19   Many circles in India still seem to believe in the virtues of non-alignment. See the following three volumes by the International Institute for Non-aligned Studies (New Delhi): *50 Years of India's Foreign Policy: Retrospect and Prospects* (1997), *NAM in 21st Century* (1997), *NAM in the Ensuing Millenium* (1998).

20   Chintamani Mahapatra, "Indo-American Relations after the Cold War", *Asian Strategic Review: 1995–96*, New Delhi, Institute for Defence Studies and Analysis, 1996, pp. 237– 251.

21   Gopal J. Malviya, "An American Approach to India's Kashmir", *Strategic Analysis*, New Delhi, XVII/5 (August 1994), p. 633.

22   Kapil Kak, "International Responses", *Kargil: 1999, op. cit.*, p. 199.

23   I. K. Gujral, *A Foreign Policy for India*, New Delhi, Ministry of External Affairs, 1998, p. 144.

24   Swaran Singh, "The Kargil Conflict: Why and How of China's Neutrality", *Strategic Analysis*, New Delhi, XXIII/7 (October 1999), pp. 1083–1094.

25   Swaran Singh, "China Factor in India's Nuclear Policy", *Journal of Peace Studies*, New Delhi, 5/3 (May–June 1998), p. 23f.

26   Sahdev Vohra, "The North-Eastern Frontier of India and China's Claim", *Strategic Analysis*, New Delhi, XII (December 1989), pp. 931–948.

27 Jai Bhagwan, "Chinese Arms Transfers to the Third World: Emerging Patterns of Commercialisation", *Strategic Analysis*, New Delhi, XI/6 (September 1988), p. 641; Aabha Dixit, "Enduring Sino-Pak Relations: the Military Dimension", *Strategic Analysis*, New Delhi, XII (December 1989), pp. 981–990.

28 Sujit Dutta, "Sino-Indian Relations: Some Issues", *Strategic Analysis*, New Delhi, XI/11 (February 1988), pp. 1239–1264.

29 Mao Siwei, "China and the Kashmir Issue", *Strategic Analysis*, New Delhi, XVII/12 (March 1995), pp. 1573–1597.

30 Swaran Singh, "China's Posture of Neutrality", *World Focus*, New Delhi, 234–235 (June–July 1999), p. 32.

31 Surya Gangadharan, "The China-Taliban Equation", *Aakrosh*, New Delhi, 3/6 (January 2000), pp. 55–77.

32 Zhou Gang, "Sino-Indian Relations", *U. S. I. Journal*, New Delhi, CXXIX/536 (April–June 1999), pp. 171–178.

Chapter 12

The North-East

Some writers[1] assert, with good reason, that the strategic importance of the North-West Frontier Province adjoining Afghanistan and the then expanding Tsarist Russia during British times has been eclipsed by the growing relevance of India's North-East (NE), especially with the emergence of seven political units, and all having international borders. Moreover, the latter were involved in three wars (1962, 1965 and 1971). The Siliguri Corridor is the tenuous land link that connects the North-East, the least known corner of boundless India, with the rest of the country. This whole region of overwhelmingly Mongoloid India, bordering four countries (Bangladesh, Bhutan, China, and Myanmar), is virtually landlocked. With partition, the entrepot of Chittagong and the Brahmaputra waterway were lost to East Pakistan. Goods transported to Calcutta have to travel 1,600 kilometers now, instead of one-fourth of that distance before 1947. The North-East was, then, long secluded, to find itself reduced to a distant and landlocked appendage at partition, later overwhelmed by migrant waves. Some people of the region felt that they were fighting for the most fundamentral economic cause, namely, survival.

The region engulfs perhaps the most diverse communities of a most diverse country. Growing cultural consciousness threatened, therefore, to spill over into ethnic nationalism, and regional identity aspirations became somewhat of anathema to mainstream political parties in the North-Eastern[2] region of India, which remained the proverbial area of underdevelopment even after more than half a century of independence. At present, the region is made up of seven states (Arunachal Pradesh, Assam, Manipur, Meghalaya, Mizoram, Nagaland, and Tripura), each with its own governor. Some areas of that region were never a part of the Maurya, Gupta or the Moghul Empires, and the British, who incorporated this region rather late, used cultural diversities as well as dualistic composition such as hill people and plains people or tribals and non-tribals, as a trapdoor of divide and rule.[3] The colonial power pursued a policy of non-interference when the Naga National Council (NNC), the oldest movement of insurgency, raised the banner of independence in the mid-1940s.

Slippery Slope

The North-East has seen since then a number of insurgent groups whose tactics included intimidation, coercion, extortion, imposition of taxes, threats, kidnapping, hit and run raids, attacks on isolated posts, ambushes, explosions, assassinations, terrorising the population, and paralysing the government. Perhaps the best known insurgency is the Naga revolt. Various groups, among them the National Socialist Council of Nagaland (NSCN) having the best-trained cadre, either espouse secessionist rhetoric or demand a better deal. Insurgency is basically a reaction to years of economic neglect, political abuse, and prevalent corruption. All indicators of development such as capital formation, per capita income, communication network or irrigation facilities show that the North-East remained far behind the rest of India. The clichés on neglect of many militants project common aspirations for better living and generally hold the Central Government responsible for deprivations. The people witness that some political parties, with a minority support among the electorate, manage to grab power through a display of money and parliamentary horse-trading. Further, the continuing influx of neighbouring people changed the original essentials of demography in some states. In Tripura for instance, the indigenous people were reduced to a minority in their own land. In Assam, where the majority is engaged in subsistence agriculture, labour needs are met by considerably cheaper wages of the immigrants. But education outstrips, in the meantime, economic development. Only Arunachal Pradesh remained comparatively peaceful despite sharing a long international border with Bhutan, China, and Myanmar.

There is still another perpetrator among the seeds of insurgency. With the apparently continuing baptism of fire in J&K, Pakistan has an interest in exploiting the unsettled conditions in India's NE.[4] For one, the security forces involved in the latter region as well, the Indian Government's concentration will be diverted from J&K, consequently easing pressure on the militants. Moreover, if terrorist movements gain ascendancy in the NE, not only Pakistan's case of self-determination for Kashmir will look legitimate, but also the situation in the latter will seem to be less serious.

The Republic of India being one of the largest countries in the world, it is not surprising that the NE, sharing long frontiers with China, Nepal and Bhutan, is not a homogeneous area. In spite of some outward resemblances such as similarity of hilly terrains and jungle roads, the area and its peoples do not have common systems or problems. Manifold ethnic groups occupying these large tracts of land for many centuries evolved as separate *sui generis* peoples although they have some common denominators with the rest of India, which stretches from the highest Himalayan peaks to the tropical waters of the mighty ocean in the south.

Only Assam and parts of Tripura have some similarity with the remainder of the country. Even then, no two are cast in the same mold. The region's total population, slightly below thirty million, is diverse ethnically, linguistically, religiously and culturally. Apart from the non-tribal inhabitants of Assam and Tripura, 116 tribes, not counting several Kuki groups and considering all Naga tribes as one, remain settled in the NE. Of the 1,652 languages of India, one-fourth are spoken here.

The British, who designated some of these areas as "partially or totally excluded areas", demonstrated no effort to amalgamate them into the central administration, but left the tribal territories such as Nagaland, North-East Frontier Area (NEFA) and the Lushai Hills to be run according to their customs. Following independence (1947), the "totally excluded areas" became the NEFA, later renamed as Arunachal Pradesh, and supervised by the Governor of Assam.

In addition to the impression of seclusion and uncertainty, caused mainly by the disruption of the old communications system following British India's partition, incursions from neighbouring China in the early 1960s further inflamed these feelings. All links passing after 1947 through East Pakistan, almost the whole of the NE was land-locked. The original inhabitants were dependent on the outside for supplies and found the additional transport costs too much for their meagre budgets. The arrival of Hindus from East Pakistan, independent Bangladesh in 1971, increased the insecurity of the North-Eastern peoples who feared the competition of the newcomers for jobs and food. The threat that the aliens might grow to dominate the lands of the indigenous peoples whipped up secessionist movements. The slopy jungle setting was conducive to insurgency activities. In addition to the dire necessity of guarding the borders in that locality, a large force and the allocation of a huge budget were essential for internal security.

Thus, India has been trying to counter and restrain two major insurgencies, one in J&K and the other in the NE. Neighbouring Pakistan encourages terror in both regions where dissident sections among local inhabitants have genuine dissatisfaction but also yearn for tranquillity and peace. The tribal tendency to administer themselves first surfaced (1953) with the Nagas and later (1966) with the Mizos. Ultimately, very few of the North-Eastern peoples avoided resort to arms. Even the peoples of Arunachal Pradesh, the Garos and the Khasis may be included among them. When ethnic unrest turned into armed militancy, terrorist attacks on civilians were frequently accompanied by full-fledged guerilla war. Poor farmers in destitute conditions and the unemployed youth with diplomas supported the militants. Parts of funds to solve the growing enigma were absorbed by corrupt administrators. The area soon became a beehive of scores of mostly armed militant organizations, nearly seventy or more highly active cliques in revolt, some inspired or sustained by India's grudging neighbours, which attracted and engaged close to 200,000 Indian troops. Insurgent groups, often receiving incentives from Pakistan's ISI, hit banks, smuggled drugs, abducted people and killed off adversaries.

It should never be forgotten that insurgent movements received external support for about two decades. The almost secluded and land-locked region of the North-East shares most (98%) of its frontiers with four independent Asian countries, and less than 2% is with the rest of India. The partition of the country and the artificial creation of international borders negatively affected the economic links of this region.[5] The whole territory looks like a distant corner with a shrivelled neck linking it with the rest of the Indian Union. This isolation and the post-1947 disjunction encouraged neighbouring China and Pakistan, in the 1960s, to keep the Mizo and Naga insurgencies on foot. Pakistan's toehold had to melt away, however, with its frustration in the 1971 War. The support of the Kachin Independent Army, which had provided weapons and training to some Assamese, as well as Manipur and Naga groups, likewise underwent an eclipse in the late 1980s.

The National Socialist Council of Nagaland (NSCN) tried to establish some support among the Lanchpo and Nocte tribes in eastern Arunachal Pradesh and the Moriani sector of Assam. A number of insurgent groups, ostensibly to oppose the 'Indianization' campaign of the Central Government by allowing an inflow of Indians, joined hands to form a joint organization, styling themselves as the "Self-Defence United Front of the South-East Himalayan Region".

The insurgents especially favoured the routes including two junctions, one connecting Assam, Manipur and Nagaland, and the other tying Mizoram with the Chittagong Hill Tracts of Bangladesh and the Chin Hills of Myanmar some of which are sparsely populated and offer the needed vegetation. Although the Indian army has been able to seal these routes, at least partially, by surprise attacks, as well as some synchronizing with the Myanmar authorities which have launched operations against the Chins, Kachins, Karens and Shans, the lasting solution is in the further recognition of their identities and more economic opportunities. There have been some accords with local groups; the key to peace, however, lies not in merely signing them, but in rapid economic development, and in understanding tribal psychology.

Some communities in India's NE often enough express the belief that the rulers in the Centre have not been sufficiently caring or even fair to them. There have been times when some entertained the idea of leaving India. The feelings of inequity on the part of various ethnic groups and the rising expectations fanned the flames of autonomy. While the Naga insurgency remained for the greater part the most volatile one in the whole region, the neighbouring Khasis and the Garos carved the state of Meghalaya out of Assam. The Bodos too wished a separate state on part of Assamese land. The Mizos in the south as well rose against the Indian state. The Dimasa Halong Dogou and the Karbi National Volunteers, in links with counterparts in Nagaland, expect separate homes for the Dimasa and the Karbi peoples. In spite of such agitation and convulsions, secession is not the unbroken and dominant trend.

Isolation being a geographical fact, several states such Assam, Meghalaya and Tripura carry on nearly all of their border trade with Bangladesh. Manipur, Mizoram and Nagaland have barter trading relations with Myanmar. Mizoram among them exchange some products with Bangladesh as well. All had stopped trade with China following the frontier clash in 1962. India proceeded to sign a Border Trade Agreement with Bangladesh (1972) and with Myanmar (1994). As part of a drive to put a minimum infrastructure in place, the first trade route between India and Myanmar was opened (1995) at the frontier post of Moreh in Manipur and Tamu in Myanmar. Taking a second step, the Union Ministry of Commerce proposed to establish a Regional Trade Promotion Council to plan a trade guidance and branches of the Agricultural Production Export Development Association. The airport at Guwahati, where a Trade Fair Exhibition was set up, underwent upgrading. All these new departures, however, may be no more than thin ends of the wedge. The products offered to world markets have to be of high quality at competitive prices.

Nightmare in Nagaland

Twenty-six tribes and several other sub-tribes, whose members belong to the Indo-Mongoloid ethnic group,[6] inhabit the narrow strip of mountainous territory, now called Nagaland,[7] between the Brahmaputra Valley of Assam and Myanmar, virtually a *terra incognita* until the 19th century.[8] The Nagas are an indigenous hill people numbering 700,000 inhabiting this remote mountainous country flanked by Assam and Myanmar. There exist sixteen main tribal Naga groups,[9] each with its own language or dialect.[10] Since this area was formed (1881) into the Naga Hills District within Assam, Assamese was used as the administrative language for a long time. Nagas also live in the neighbouring states of Arunachal Pradesh, Assam, Manipur, and along the border with Myanmar. The question of the Naga Hills District to be "independent" did not rise during the colonial rule, except when the Nagas made a plea to the Simon Commission (1929) for autonomy stating that Nagaland had never been a part of India. The Nagas, who had remained loyal to the British during the Second World War, were utilised as a guerilla force against the Japanese. The dumps of arms left by both sides when the war ended became sources of supply for some Nagas who resorted to violence later. Thus, Nagaland spearheaded insurgency in this region.

A Naga National Council (NNC) submitted (1947) a memorandum to Gandhi in New Delhi stating that they would declare their independence on 14 August 1947. When Nehru refused the demand, a Nine-Point Agreement between the governor of Assam (Sir Akbar Hydari) and the secessionist leaders recognized the right of the Nagas to develop themselves according to their wishes. The latter interpreted the provision of this accord which introduced the idea that the NNC would be asked, at the end of ten years, whether a new agreement was needed to determine the future of the people, meaning to confer on them the right to quit the Indian Union after a decade.[11]

The Naga leader, Angami Zau Sapu Phizo,[12] had started fighting for independence before India became free. The Assamese State Government could not agree to a special status for the Nagas because if this option was conceded, other tribes, such as the Mizos, diverging much more from the mainstream, would raise similar demands. The Naga conference at Kohima passed a unanimous decision in favour of a plebiscite, on the basis of which Phizo, elected NNC's President in 1950, moved from village to village "holding" a plebiscite. He declared that over 99% of his people demanded an "independent Naga State".[13] Under his leadership, the NNC and groups of Naga people boycotted the first general elections in the same year, ostensibly because their land was not a part of the Indian Union. In late 1952, Phizo went underground, left for Burma, was intercepted there, returned to Nagaland, and went underground again. In early 1953, the Prime Ministers of India and Burma decided to visit their Naga territories together. A few minutes before Nehru, accompanied by U Nu, ascended the rostrum, three to four thousand Nagas left the place of meeting protesting that their delegation was not allowed to read a statement to the public there. Phizo started preaching the unity of the Nagas of Tuensang near the Burmese border with those of the Naga Hills District and the independence of Tuensang. It may be asserted that the war with the Nagas started in late 1955 when Indian troops moved into that border area before the trouble extended to other parts. It was about the same time that Phizo set up an independent "Naga Government" (*Khunak Kautang Ngeukhum*, People's Sovereign Republic of Free Nagaland) under some fictitious "Hongkin" issuing orders and collecting taxes. By early 1956, Phizo extended his violent operations to the Naga Hills District and formally set up a Naga Federal Government and a Naga Federal Army (NFA). That the initial infantry brigade had to be supplemented later by about a force 20 times bigger than itself speaks of the extraordinary conditions that developed.[14]

Charismatic but authoritarian Phizo, who did not allow dissent in the NNC,[15] was believed to have links with the Chinese and Pakistani intelligence agencies. It was under his direction that the armed wing of the NNC exploited the hilly terrain and the forest area, both suited for guerilla warfare. He established bases in the Arakan Hills in Burma and in the Chittagong Hills in East Pakistan. Not only some neighbouring peoples, but also the British had sympathies for the Nagas who had fought on their side during the Second World War. Repeating the strategy in Malaya to cut off the rebels from the civilian population and thereby breaking their supply and intelligence system, it was planned to group the villages and keep them under the protection of strong security forces. A Naga People's Convention (NPC) of all the tribes (22 August 1957) was called again at Kohima, and on the basis of their unanimous decision, a Sixteen-Point Agreement (1960) between the NPC and the Union Government, the Naga Hills District, along with Tuensang, was separated from Assam (1 December 1957). Now, there were two Naga demands before the Indian Government, one by the NNC for complete independence, and the other asking for statehood within the Union. President Radhakrishnan inaugurated (1963) the separate State of Nagaland. Phizo eventually slipped into East Pakistan, then to Britain where he died (1990).

It was when schism split the secessionist groups that some former insurgents supported the Indian State of the Nagas which had already materialized. Some others continued the violence with a small group of rebels stationed in East Pakistan. There was some joint effort by Pakistan and China to train the Naga belligerents, especially in the year 1962. But after the inauguration of the Naga State within the Indian Union, theoretically there was little cause for the Nagas to persist with their fight. Although Nehru did not live to see the cessation of hostilities, a Peace Mission[16] was able to bring about a cease-fire (late 1964), which continued for some years during which there was off-and-on fighting. For instance, better trained and equipped new terrorist groups blew up railway lines and key road bridges. After the 1971 War, however, the underground groups lost the support of Pakistan, but continued to benefit from Chinese backing. While some NNC guerillas took refuge on Myanmar soil, the bulk was defeated.[17] Some weapons were surrendered in accordance with the Shillong Accord (1975) between the governor and the FGN representatives.

The hope that peace would return to Nagaland after 1975 did not fully materialize. While the majority of the hard-core terrorists, that is, the old generation of Naga insurgents returned to settled life and reconciled to integration with the country, a fresh group of insurgents arose, denouncing the Shillong Accord as a "sell out" and describing their movement as the "mother of all insurgency" in the North-East.[18] There have been a series of agreements in the past, and every time an adjustment is made, a breakaway faction announces that it does not accept the accord. The security forces have to be prepared for any sudden resort to large-scale violence by the insurgents.

Some Nagas continued to blame New Delhi for political bickerings after elections, fall of governments and even corruption. The number of terrorist acts soon increased. Although insurgency in Nagaland has experienced a number of ups and downs, it may be said that terrorism there showed some upswing even after the Shillong Agreement. Does this mean that efforts of reconciliation have gone in vain? First of all, no more sudden deaths in the hands of silent enemies! The wheel may not have come full circle, but, not only opposition party candidates came out victorious in free and fair elections, but the face of Nagaland has also changed.[19] While the Naga people showed that they can make and unmake governments, some schools and factories appeared in various corners of the country. The belief that the strength of the terrorists radically declined following a split (1988) among the Nagas of Indian and Myanmarese origin hardly was borne out, however, by the further insurgence of violence. With the support that it gets from Pakistan's ISI and even from the Bangladesh Government, those who indulge in terrorism still collect "taxes", acquire an arsenal of sophisticated weapons, and state their objective to be a "greater Naga state" comprising all the Naga inhabited areas in the region. Like the terrorists in J&K and in Punjab, those who put in operation a parallel government under the name of "the Government of the People's Republic of Nagaland" banned some "immoral" practices to gain more public backing. However, the democratic conscience of contemporary Indian elite does not look at the Naga issue only as a problem of law and order. For the Indians, the Nagas are not mere "headhunters",[20] as they appeared to the British. They are awakened to the anguish of the Naga people and understand the complexity behind resentment and hurt.[21]

Assam—Agitation and Accord

Assam is a part of the NE that controls the eastern end of the neck that links this region with India.[22] A former governor of Assam says that the loss of this state would mean the dispossession of the entire land mass in the North-East with its rich natural resources.[23] It is the core state of that region. Although once undivided Assam was later balkanized into various political units, its preeminence prevails. Its population is more than twice the total number of citizens of the remaining six states, and the ratio in terms of economic resources is also in its favour.

Like the other neighbouring states, Assam's feelings of neglect were partially ignored as *ad hoc* policies little by little were offered to deal with violence.

Assam's borders kept changing during the colonial era.[24] Following Britain's conquest (1826) of Assam, the Cachar and the Jaintia Hills were added to it but with Lord Curzon's partition of Bengal (1905), Assam was altogether joined to the new entity of East Bengal. The Assamese were thus reduced to a minority in that new province until their land was elevated to the status of a governor's province in less than two decades. Bengali clerks and professionals came with the British, who owned the tea gardens. While the labourers in them were mostly from the neighbouring areas, the middlemen were all Marwaris from Rajasthan. The settlement of Bengali Muslims on large tracts of state land with the intention of "growing more food" during the Second World War, was motivated by political reasons, and actually grew more Muslims in Assam.

During the partition of India, the predominantly Muslim Sylhet joined with East Pakistan, and later (1951) Dewangiri was ceded to Bhutan. Four tribal districts of Assam, namely, the Garo Hills, the Lushai Hills, the Khasi and Jaintia Hills, and the Naga Hills were elevated to the status of autonomous states of Nagaland (1963), Meghalaya (1972) and Mizoram (1986). All being created as full-fledged states out of Assam, that state experienced considerable shrinkage of its area.[25] Assam became a state with a very high percentage of Muslims in India. Bangladesh being a Malthusian nightmare, the illegal influx of Muslim migrants continue. The Assamese will soon be a minority in their own state. They have produced, nevertheless, several persons who have made their mark at the national level.[26]

Assam always had a fertile land and sparse population. Although rich in natural resources and having a favourable population-land ratio, Assam is behind the Indian Union average in respect to power supply, health facilities, education and communications. The state of the whole infrastructure is poor. Stagnation in both the industrial and agricultural sectors has resulted in about 12% unemployed or underemployed. Close to half of the population lives on or below the poverty line. Illiteracy is growing; hospitals are ill-equipped; much of the land is inaccessible. The village economy is still at a subsistence level. Floods adversely affect one-third of the agricultural land. The consumer goods are brought from outside, so whatever wealth there is, produced mainly from the oil sector, flows outside. Otherwise, Assam possesses many ingredients such as oil, coal, hydro-power potential, fertile land (tea) and cheap labour. With a population increasing and economic expectations shrinking, the Assamese identity is also threatened by outsiders who take control over trade and industry.[27]

Assamese nationality is plagued by massive and unceasing immigration. Newcomers from Bengal, Bhutan, Bihar, Nepal and Tripura swarmed into Assam. Bengali Hindus were forcibly evicted, and Bengali Muslims came for economic reasons. Since settlers from the neighbouring countries and parts of India make up a sizable portions of Assamese society, the middle class especially feels threatened culturally as well as economically and politically, and the Assamese consequently ask for job reservations and seats in electoral politics. In addition, tribal ethnic groups such as the Bodos and even the Karbis underline their separateness from the mainstream community.[28]

The deportation of illegal Hindu immigrants who rushed out of the Sylhet area of East Pakistan as well as the alleged neglect of the Bodo language coupled with the demand for a separate state of "Bodoland" within the Indian Union were the main issues behind terrorism in Assam. The Hindus had abandoned their original places of residence in East Bengal for economic reasons as much as in response to the Islamization drive of the Government of Pakistan. Large-scale immigration persisted after the secession of the eastern wing of that Islamic state. Assam now has a total of 269 km. of border with Bangladesh.

Although ethnic divisions surfaced more and more in the 1990s, Assam has experienced turmoil since 1979.[29] It was in late 1978 that the All-Assam Students' Union (AASU) started agitation against the infiltration of outsiders. This group of Assamese students especially resented the inclusion of the foreigners in the voters' list. "It needed only a spark for a popular agitation to begin in 1979."[30] The objective of the "Asom" movement, initiated (1979) by the All-Assam Gana Sangram Parishad (AAGSP), was to deport all foreigners. The year 1980 witnessed the launching of a serious drive to deport illegal immigrants. The government's refusal to drop the name of those immigrants from the electoral rolls, in contradiction to the demands of the AASU which insisted on the rejections, further magnified fears of the indigenous peoples that the authorities were capitulating to alien preferences for political reasons. The AASU and AAGSP intensified their agitation when their demands could not be met in full. Initially the backing and later the championship of the energetic student leaders of this movement finally bred the Lalonga tribal attacks (1983) on Muslim villages at Nellie involving the hell of plunder and butchery of over 1,700 persons. Mrs. Gandhi decided to forge ahead with state elections, which was boycotted by the AASU leadership and which attracted a very small percentage of the electorate.

Although the new Chief Minister (Hiteshwar Saikia) convinced the student leaders to give up the expulsion of the immigrants who had come to Assam before 1971, the United Liberation Front of Assam (ULFA), organized in 1979 with some backing from Pakistan's ISI and links with the Kachin and Naga insurgents, indulged in a series of killings and attacks on communications to create terror. It also helped the poor, acquiring at times a Robin Hood image. With no cutback in terrorist acts and no progress in secret talks with the AASU leaders, elections were renewed, and the dynamic student group came to power. After the AASU leaders resigned from the student organizations, and the AAGSP was voluntarily dissolved, the Asom Gana Parishad (AGP), formed by the leadership of these movements, came to power on a towering tide of Assamese sub-nationalism. The man on the street shared the view that everything would be well since youth power took control of the land. Although the new government immediately generated optimism, confidence in it was shortlived as the young politicians soon succumbed to corrupt practices and quickly wasted their initial support. Representing frustrations in the Assamese society, the youth leaders raised hopes for a better future but lacked the know-how and the direct support of the Centre necessary to clear up the complex puzzles of this isolated state. Cold water was poured on the electorate when practically nothing was done to remove the difficulties.

V. P. Singh's government in New Delhi had to dismiss the administration, and the President's rule was established (1990) in Assam. The new administration, which degenerated into army supremacy, thus harboured another explosive predicament.

Response of the government to agitation between the years 1979–85 further motivated the militant organizations to enforce a blockade on the export of crude oil, jute and some other products. Some student groups may have made an issue out of the establishment of an oil refinery, but it was the sober reality of ever increasing foreign nationals which seemed to threaten the identity of the Assamese and kept the Assam movement alive. A movement against the Barauni Refinery, connected with the pumping of crude oil out of Assam and the construction of a pipeline to take the commodity to the refinery in the neighbouring state of Bihar, further alienated groups to each other. The oil pipelines have served as target symbols for terrorist groups. But it was actually the ceaseless influx of immigrants that fanned disorder in the society as much as disarranging the economic set up of the province. "The Assam Disturbed Areas Act" went into operation during the same period. The report (1984) of the Central Government Commission recommended that Assam may be granted "special protection as in Kashmir" where no electorate can be bought by or sold to an outsider. Just about simultaneous with the fall of the local government, Operation Bajrang started assaults on the ULFA camps near the border or in the forest areas. Although the army operation was not a great success in some camps such as at Lakhipather, it nevertheless created the conviction that the government, and not ULFA, controlled Assam. Some terrorists at Saraipung were taken by surprise, but many escaped at Tinsukhja. The myth of their impregnability vanished, however.

After the Assam Accord (1985) between Rajiv Gandhi's government and the AASU, new elections were held, and the Asom Gana Parishad, the newly-created party, achieved a landslide victory. The Accord, officially known as the Memorandum of Settlement, could not be interpreted in full, however. The number of immigrants did not decrease after the Assam Accord. The local chapters of the political parties needed the votes of these additional residents, who were illegal settlers from abroad, and therefore, non-citizens. India had passed a single 'Foreigners Act' for the whole of the country except Assam, and the special Illegal Migrants (Determination by Tribunals) Act (1983) was put into operation for Assam only. Neither the poor application of the Act, nor the cosmetic changes (1988) to it met the requirements of the day.

Although groups in revolt continued to enjoy the support of likeminded cliques in Bangladesh, and certainly of Pakistan's ISI, India's agreement with Bangladesh on challenging the terrorists discouraged some of them who previously benefited from logistics and training facilities in Chittagong and Sylhet. In 1992, a group of ULFA leaders issued statements in favour of giving up and ending violence and, at the same time, denouncing the Bangladesh-based leaders who had links with the ISI. Pradeep Gogoi, vice-chairman of ULFA, according to his admission, was an official guest in Pakistan in most of 1991.[31] Although the ULFA statements opted for a peaceful solution within legal means, some of their members continued terrorism in Assam and still others stayed in the Cox's Bazaar and Mymensingh camps of Bangladesh.

Various Assamese groups harbour a sense of neglect but do not seek a separate sovereign entity based on the principles of self-determination. They cherish feelings of affinity with the remainder of India, and expect the Centre to help them develop. Probably, ULFA remains the largest underground organization with a front-runner place in militancy. Militant camps, formerly in Assam, moved into the jungles of neighbouring Bhutan. Although many ULFA militants surrendered with their weapons, operating from sanctuaries across the border, their potential for hit and run remains. During the *Lok Sabha* elections of 1998, Assam was one of the few states where polling was completely peaceful, and the voter turn-out was 62% as against the national average of 54%.[32] There are also fundamentalist groups such as the United Muslim Liberation Front of Asom and the Muslim Liberation Tigers, engrossed mainly in retaliations against militant Assamese groups.

A demand for a separate state of Bodoland within the Indian Union is widespread in the northern part of the Brahmaputra, where the Bodos complain of neglect of their language and feel exploited but where they do not constitute the majority in any area. In fact, they are no more than 4% of the population of Assam. They claim, however, the entire north bank of the Brahmaputra. The Bodos, early immigrants of Mongoloid stock from China, constitute the eighth largest tribe in India. They are scattered on the pasture lands of north Bengal as well as south Assam. They have strong bases in Kokrajhar and parts of Goalpara as well as in the Manas sanctuary bordering Bhutan.

Alienated from the majority community (the Assamese), the Bodo tribes felt disturbed that their own culture might leave no trace in some future date. Enjoying very little constitutional guarantees among all the Scheduled Tribes of India, their initial demand was limited to the inclusion of the Bodo language as the medium of instruction in schools and the adoption of the Latin script. The Bodo Sahitya Sabha (BSS) was formed (1952) to unite the Bodo people on the language issue. When the BSS suggested the use of the Latin script for the Bodo language, the Central Government insisted on the Devanagari letters of Hindi, which soon proved to be incompatible for that tribal tongue. The Bodos finally adopted the Latin script.

There was much more than that to the Bodo grievance and the Assamese response to it. The underlying conflict came to the surface when the life of the landless peasants worsened, and when the Assamese felt that the Bodo desire to administer their own community could further divide Assam, which had already lost Meghalaya, Mizoram and Nagaland. Other related issues seemed to be playing a role when the All-Bodo Students' Union (ABSU) joined hands with others to stop the flow of crude oil from north Assam to a refinery in Bihar.

Dreading the power and oppression of the non-Bodo majority, the Bodos, previously trained in arms by the Special Security Bureau (SSB) as a rear-line of defence, have committed acts of terrorism since the 1980s. The demands for a separate homeland for the Bodos, first launched resolutely in 1984, were confined basically to a full-fledged Bodoland on the north bank of the Brahmaputra and autonomous districts in the south of the same river. Until 1987, they were satisfied with the demand for an autonomous council, as enjoyed by the other Assamese hill tribes. The Memorandum of Settlement, or the Bodo Accord, signed (1993) between the leaders of the Bodo movement on the one hand, and the central and state governments on the other, granted considerable autonomy to these tribal people living in about 2,000 villages. Some of the Accord's cardinal parts could not be implemented owing to government half-heartedness as much as infighting among the resurgent factions. Moreover, insisting on the inclusion of an additional 2,000 villages plus the forests near the Bhutan border, the Bodo leaders gave the impression that they were gradually but progressively enlarging the frontiers of a separate 'Bodoland'. Apparently, conditions were not ripe for the success of an agreement. A number of Bodo leaders categorically rejected the Bodoland Autonomous Council, created by this agreement and comprising certain districts and villages. They suspected that some other villages were not included because the latter were situated near the international border.

Several militant groups such as the National Democratic Front for Bodoland (NDFB) and the Bodoland Liberation Tiger Front (BLTF) compete for leadership. There are other tribal organizations like the Bodoland Statehood Movement Council (BSMC), the People's Democratic Front (PDF), the All-Bodo Students' Union (ABSU), and the United Tribal Nationalist Liberation Front (UTNLF) that have laid claim to legitimate representation of the people. The Bodo Security Force, a militant organization operating on the side, persisted in terrorist activities.

Efforts for a political settlement have borne no fruit so far. While New Delhi recently set up a working group to assess the Bodoland issue once more, the Bodos continue to feel that their culture is being swallowed up by the Assamese dominance. It may be asserted that the struggle of the Bodos, since 1966, has been more for a separate political identity than a separate state on the north bank of the Brahmaputra, as well as local autonomy for the districts of Rabha and Tiwa in the south. Although Bodo terrorism has not underscored separatism, the ISI and the NSCN interference may feed secessionist tendencies, not entirely non-existent, for an "independent Udaychal state".

The Bodo militants proved to be more ready than the ULFA leaders to negotiate to end the bloodshed. Nevertheless, various terrorist organizations do not shrink from occasional killings among themselves in order to win the support of the entire Bodo nation. Further, keen to attain numerical majorities in areas where they are less than half of the population, the Bodos are also prone to evict especially the land-owning immigrant Muslim Bengalis and the Santhals. It should be added that when hundreds died and many more became homeless, some Santhal groups founded several armed organizations such as the Adiulfa, the Birsa Commando Force and the Cobra Force to withstand the Bodo attacks. In view of such off-and-on carnage, New Delhi insisted on the inclusion of safety devices in the Bodo Autonomous Council areas.

Manipur, Mizoram, Tripura

Manipur, a former princely state[33] with a hilly terrain, is sandwiched between Myanmar on the east and Assam on the west with Mizoram and Nagaland on the south and the north. Manipur seems to be remote, inaccessible and therefore largely isolated. The Manipur River Valley extends from the north to the south, and the hill ranges include the Naga hills in the north, and the Chin and Mizo hills in the south. Manipur has a long (350 km.) border with Myanmar.[34] Although granted statehood in 1972,[35] the lands are surrounded by the Mizo and Naga separatists, in the southern and northern districts respectively. While some Manipur groups went to East Pakistan, others sought the assistance of China, in both cases to fight against the Indian Government. Insurgency in Manipur has been no less intense than in Nagaland. Besides the National Socialist Council of Nagaland (NSCN), operating from Manipur, the People's Liberation Army (PLA) and the People's Revolutionary Party of Kangleipak (PREPAK) are based in the Manipur Valley, and have at times played havoc with the people.

The Kukis[36] and the Nagas are the two main tribes[37] who live in the Manipur Hills, and the Meiteis dwell in the valley. The Kukis, who are the ethnic cousins of the Mizos, congregate in the southern hills, where they are active in drug smuggling, a profitable business they do not want to share with the Tangkhul Nagas. The latter generally support a faction (Muivah-Isak group) of the National Socialist Council of Nagaland. Thuengaling Muivah, who is a Tangkhul, is responsible for a series of terrorist acts in Manipur. The Meiteis, who have repudiated Hinduism which they had embraced about three-hundred years ago, now stress their pre-Hindu past.

Some years such as 1979–81 may be summed up as the peak of terrorist activities, but Manipur still goes through political instability. While the NSCN(M) is active in the hill districts, and the ethnic war with the Kukis take heavy toll of innocent lives, politicians of practically all schools cultivate underground groups, eroding democratic institutions in the process. Some politicians use communal terror to serve their purposes, and most of the funds New Delhi provides find their way into the private accounts of corrupt bureaucrats.

Formerly the Mizo Hill district of Assam, Mizoram,[38] originally inhabited by small Tibeto-Burman stock,[39] became a state of India in 1972.[40] While the Mizo Union, a political party founded in the late 1940s, did not resist becoming a part of Assam, a secessionist group demanded that the people living in the hills of Mizoram should join the tribes of upper Burma where their kin congregated.[41] When the Mizo[42] Union (which emerged to fight for the vested interests of the chiefs) carried all the seats, except the two won by the United Mizo Freedom Organization (UMFO), the latter sought support for the formation of a separate hill state bringing together some parts of Assam, Manipur, Tripura and NEFA, the present Arunachal Pradesh. One of the worst famines (1959) in the history of the country led to the Mizo National Front (MNF), which formed an armed wing called the Mizo National Army (MNA) and which demanded independence for Mizoram.

Insurgency[43] started in 1966 when armed MNF militants attacked some government installations, followed by an announcement declaring independence from the Indian Union. The MNF, with Pakistani and Chinese help, set up training camps in the Chittagong Hills, and later a provisional government in East Pakistan. The regrouping of some villages for economic development reasons or because the security forces find it difficult to penetrate alienated the local peoples. In the year 1971, when East Pakistan could no longer welcome the insurgents, the Indian Government gave "Union Territory Status" to the Mizo district, and a North-Eastern Council was organized to plan the integrated development of the whole region. The assassination of high-ranking police officers, nevertheless, continued until Lal Denga, the leader of the terrorists, who was staying in Pakistan, wrote to Prime Minister Indira Gandhi expressing a preference for peaceful settlement and accepting Mizoram as an integral part of India.

Prime Minister Morarji Desai, who succeeded Mrs. Gandhi after the latter's defeat in the 1977 elections, expected Lal Denga first to surrender his arms before negotiations could proceed. There were frequent elections, new governments, recurring President's rule, surrender of terrorist leaders, and the emergence of new factions. Some politicians, sweeping the polls, fell only to come back with a comfortable majority. Prime Minister Morarji Desai, who was given a very warm welcome by the people when he set foot on Mizoram soil for a two-day visit in late 1978, displayed extreme insensitivity to the sentiments of the local inhabitants and went back without the cheers of the crowd. Desai's remarks having neutralized whatever constructive work had been done for some months, President Sanjiva Reddy, who visited the territory later, was also received in total silence.

A new wave of insurgency was perhaps inevitable, although unpopular on the part of the Mizoram people, who were fed up with violence. Terrorist acts continued even after Indira Gandhi returned to power in 1980. Following a series of events involving ambushes, attacks, killings, and setting of fires, the MNF leader Lal Denga met the newly elected prime minister and issued a statement repudiating terrorism. Although Lal Denga acknowledged that Mizoram was an integral part of India, he urged, in a 26-point memorandum submitted to the prime minister, for "Greater Mizoram" to comprise all the Mizo-inhabited parts of the neighbouring states. One may note here that a small group, the Hmar People's Convention (HPC), raised a demand for a state separate from Mizoram. In spite of the eruption of violence once again, the negotiations between New Delhi and the MNF leader were proceeding satisfactorily when Mrs. Gandhi was assassinated in late 1984.

The new Prime Minister Rajiv Gandhi met Lal Denga, who signed the Mizoram Accord (1986) with the Union Home Secretary. Mizoram was granted statehood, and Lal Denga was sworn in as the new Chief Minister. The relative peace in Mizoram may be explained by the later moderate attitudes of the Mizo leaders as well as the Central Government in New Delhi.

Tripura is a formerly princely state situated in the southwest of Assam, and surrounded by Bangladesh on three sides. It is linked with the Indian Union through the Cachar district of Assam. The cause of terrorism in Tripura[44] is the response of some tribal organizations[45] to the massive migration first from East Pakistan and then from independent Bangladesh. Consequently, the indigenous peoples have been reduced to a smaller percentage in their own native land. Tripura insurgents, particularly the Sengkrak in the 1960s and the Tripura National Volunteers (TNV, formerly Tripura Sena) in the 1970s, also resorted to secessionist rhetoric but mainly to secure a better deal, and insurgents emerged as a reaction to the tribals' growing marginalization. The successive waves of migration from the Chittagong, Comilla and Sylhet districts of Bangladesh polarized the Tripura polity.[46] Those groups, like the Tripura Upajati Juba Samiti (TUJS), formed in 1967, or the Amra Bangali (AB) that most feared that they would lose their identity as well as their land, formed militant organizations ostensibly to protect their rights. While the Tripura tribals were alienated from the political and the economic process, the extremist movements thrived basically on poverty. Many joined the TUJS since it had a platform to protect the tribal interests in the state. Radicalism, preached by Bijoy Harangkhawl, led to the split of the TUJS, and the radicals, who styled themselves as the Tripura National Volunteers (TNV), formed (1977) their own organization and benefited from a training camp in the Chittagong Hill Tracts. Maintaining close links with the Mizo underground, they committed a series of terrorist acts causing the death of more than a thousand non-tribals. Another one thousand lost their lives in the notorious Mandai massacre (1980). After the arrest of its leader (Harangkhawl), the TNV was succeeded (1980) by the All-Tripura People's Liberation Organization (ATPLO), which also surrendered after a year.

But the violence during the 1988 Assembly elections left no alternative except to extend the Disturbed Area Act to Tripura. In spite of the accord between New Delhi and Harangkhawl in the same year, the attempt to manipulate the fact of terrorism and its consequences on the part of politicians for their narrow interests prevented the application of a long-term strategy and eventual peace. The militants who lost the support of the members of the tribes in the process now indulge in other criminal activities for personal gain. There is no separatist movement but violence for its own sake.

Insurgency in the NE thrived because the local peoples felt a separate ethnic identity combined with a suspicion of neglect. As elsewhere, outside support from across the borders added fuel to fire. The insurgents in the NE received some support from Bangladesh, China and Pakistan. Agitators set up operational bases or received training in safer localities in East Pakistan, later in Bangladesh. For instance, both Phizo and Lal Denga, Naga and Mizo leaders, crossed over to East Pakistan where they were welcomed with open arms. The former's three-year stay in Dacca was a prolonged one, and the latter's uprising started (1966) after consignments of arms were dispatched from Chittagong. A few thousand insurgents were trained in camps close to the Indian border. For instance, the group led by Kaito Sema went (1962) to East Pakistan through the North Cachar Hills, and returned to Nagaland to blow up the railway track near Rangapahar (1963).[47] Several other groups under Dusoi

Chakhesang or Zuheto Sema trekked to Pakistan and infiltrated back to Nagaland. The liaison officer of Lal Denga, the Mizo chief, was reportedly General Ershad, then a captain. After the temporary loss of rebel sanctuaries during the 1971 War, even the Tripura Volunteer Force found some patronage in Bangladesh. ULFA of Assam also established contact with Pakistan's ISI circles and the Afghan *Mujahideen*. It is believed, however, that the Government of Bangladesh freezed all help to the NE insurgents after the victory of the Awami League in the 1995 elections.

Active Chinese support to the Naga, Mizo, Meitei and Kuki rebels started in 1966, mainly in the form of instruction at the guerilla training centres in East Pakistan. China terminated material support in 1978.[48] ULFA had camps in the jungles of southern Bhutan. The rebels could use Myanmar territory for their own purposes on account of the inability of the government to effectively administer the hilly areas along India's border.[49]

Although the time of troubles has not completely ended in the North-East, there have been constitutional and political adjustments some of which may be seen in Article 371 and onwards as well as through other dispensations such as the creation of sub-states, autonomous districts, and the North-Eastern Council, all giving some expression to new demands. Recent settlements caused many armed cadres to surrender their arms. The expansion of the economy, however, is a vital part of their rehabilitation. "Relative deprivation"[50] needs to be eliminated by attacking the roots of insurgency.[51] This can happen only if necessary conditions are created, coupled with education, entrepreneurship and market links. Waterways, hydro-power, varied plantation and tourist appeal may transform the lives of the North-Eastern peoples, who want and need peace. The whole region had been a part of a larger Brahmaputra-Yangtze-Mekong economic unit. A dynamic vision may be realized only if the interested governments take steps to re-establish the transit routes and markets disrupted by partition. Given Indo-Bangladesh settlement and improving relations with Myanmar, insurgency, gun-running, narcotics, and sanctuary will be replaced by market opportunities stimulating infrastructure development, trade, investments, joint ventures, and employment.

Notes

1   For instance: S. K. Chaube, *Hill Politics in Northeast India*, Hyderabad, Orient Longman, 1999, p. 217.

2   Sajal Nag, *Roots of Ethnic Conflict: Nationality Question in North-East India*, New Delhi, Manohar Publications, 1990; H. K. Barpujari, *Problem of the Hill Tribes: North-East Frontier*, 3 vols., Gauhati, Lawyer's Book Stall, 1970; United Publishers, 1976; Spectrum Publishers, 1981; Nirmal Nibedon, *North-East India: the Ethnic Explosion*, New Delhi, Lancers, 1981; Mahitosh Purkayastha, *The Anatomy of North-East: Its Problems and Solutions*, Silchar, Puthighar, 1980; V. I. K. Sarin, *India's North-East in Flames*, New Delhi, Vikas, 1980. A broad-brush macro view of the "Greater North-East": B. G. Verghese, *India's Northeast Resurgent: Ethnicity, Insurgency, Governance,*

Development, New Delhi, Konark Publishers, 1997. From the pen of a former governor of Manipur, Mizoram, Nagaland and Tripura, and later of J&K: K. V. Krishna Rao, "Insurgency in the North-East: Part 1", *U. S. I., Journal*, New Delhi, CXXVIII/531 (January–March 1998), pp. 10–25.

3   Ash Narain Roy, "Insurgency Movements in North-Eastern India", *Journal of Peace Studies*, New Delhi, II/11 (July–August 1995), pp. 25–32.

4   V. K. Madhok, "Pakistan's Gamble in India's North East: Will It Succeed?", *U. S. I. Journal*, New Delhi, CXXIV/515 (January–March 1994), pp. 78–81.

5   Sanjoy Hazarika, *Strangers of the Mist: Tales of War and Peace from India's Northeast*, New Delhi, Viking, 1994, pp. 257–260; B. N. Mukherjee, *External Trade of Early North-Eastern India*, New Delhi, Har Ananad Publications, 1992.

6   Suniti Kumar Chatterji, "Kirata-Jana-Kriti, the Indo-Mongoloids: Their Contribution to the History and Culture of India", *Journal of the Royal Asiatic Society of Bengal*, Calcutta, XVI/2 (1950).

7   Prakash Singh, *Nagaland*, New Delhi, National Book Trust, 1977; M. Alemchiba, *A Brief Historical Account of Nagaland*, Kohima, Naga Institute of Culture, 1970.

8   A. W. Davis, "Naga Tribes", *Assam Census Report: 1891*, Part 1, Shillong, 1892, pp. 237–251.

9   The leading tribes are the Angamis, Aos, Chakesangs, Changs, Konyaks, Lhotas, Sangtams and the like. Sipra Sen, *Tribes of Nagaland*, New Delhi, Mittal Publications, 1987.

10   Sometimes, a dialect is different within a tribe itself.

11   Vijay Kumar Anand, *Conflict in Nagaland: a Study of Insurgency and Counter-Insurgency*, New Delhi, Chanakya Publications, 1980; M. Horam, *Naga Insurgency: the Last Thirty Years*, New Delhi, Cosmo Publications, 1988.

12   Many individuals get part of their names from their tribes: Angami, Ao, Chakasang, Konyak, Ziliang. Y. D. Gundevia, *War and Peace in Nagaland*, New Delhi, Palit and Palit, 1975, p. 213.

13   Mullick, *op. cit.*, p. 302.

14   K. P. Kandeth, "Insurgency in Nagaland", *Indian Express*, New Delhi, 19 April 1978.

15   He had a dissident leader (T. K. Sakrie, Secretary of the Naga National Council) kidnapped from his house, tied to a tree and tortured to death to strike terror into the hearts of other would-be defectors.

16   Formed by Sri Jayaprakash Narayan, Rev. Scott and Sri Chaliha, the Chief Minister of Assam.

17   An overstatement: International Work Group for Indigenous Affairs, *The Naga Nation and Its Struggle against Genocide*, Copenhagen, 1986.

18   Roy, *op. cit.*, p. 29.

19   M. Aram, *Peace in Nagaland: Eight Year Story, 1964–72*, New Delhi, Arnold-Heinemann, 1974, pp. 315–316.

20   J. P. Miller, "The Naga Head-Hunters of Assam", *Journal of the Royal Central Asian Society*, XXII (July 1935), pp. 418–424.

21   Luingam Luithui and Nandita Haksar, *Nagaland File: a Question of Human Rights*, New Delhi, Lancer International, 1984.

22   Iscot Marbaniang, *Assam in a Nutshell*, Shillong, Chapala Book Stall, 1970.

23   S. K. Sinha, "Insurgency in Assam", *U. S. I. Journal*, New Delhi, CXXVIII/533 (July–September 1998), p. 425.

24   Nari Rustomji, *Enchanted Frontiers: Sikkim, Bhutan and India's North-Eastern Border-lands*, Calcutta, Oxford University Press, 1971; _____, *Imperilled Frontiers*, Bombay, Oxford University Press, 1983.
25   Shekhar Gupta, *Assam: a Valley Divided*, New Delhi, Vikas, 1984.
26   For instance, F. A. Ahmad (former President of India) and D. K. Barooah (former President of the Congress Party). T. S. Murty, *Assam, the Difficult Years: a Study of Political Developments in 1979–83*, New Delhi, Himalayan Books, 1983, p. x.
27   Amiya Kumar Das, *Assam's Agony: a Socio-Economic and Political Analysis*, New Delhi, Lancers Publications, 1982.
28   P. S. Datta, ed., *Ethnic Movements in Poly-Cultural Assam*, New Delhi, Har-Anand Publications in association with Vikas, 1990.
29   Mahesh Joshi, *Assam: the Indian Conflict*, New Delhi, Prachi Prakashan, 1981; Hamid Naseem Rafiabadi, *Assam from Agitation to Accord*, New Delhi, Genuine Publications, 1988.
30   Shailesh K. Singh, "Background to the Insurgencies", *Peace Initiatives: Assam Today, Can the Fires be Put Out?*, New Delhi, IV/1–2 (January–April 1998), p. 7.
31   Karan R. Sawhny, "Insurgency and Counter-insurgency: Ending Two Decades of Deadly Conflict in a Fracturing Polity", *ibid.*, p. 89.
32   Sinha, *op. cit.*, p. 436.
33   Arun Kumar Sharma, *Manipur: the Glorious Past*, New Delhi, Aryan Books International, 1994.
34   Leishangthem Chandramani Singh, *The Boundaries of Manipur*, Imphal, Pan Manipuri Youth League, 1970.
35   M. Ibohal Singh, *Constitutional and Legal History of Manipur*, Samurou, Samurou Lakpa Mayai Lambi Law College, 1986.
36   Thangkhomang S. Gangte, *The Kukis of Manipur: a Historical Analysis*, New Delhi, Gyan Publishing House, 1993.
37   Sipra Sen, *Tribes and Castes of Manipur*, New Delhi, Mittal Publications, 1992.
38   Animesh Chandra Ray, *Mizoram*, New Delhi, Ministry of Information and Broadcasting, 1972.
39   Lalrimawia, *Mizoram: History and Cultural Identity, 1890–1947*, Guwahati, Spectrum Publications, 1995.
40   C. G. Verghese, *A History of the Mizos*, 2 vols., New Delhi, Vikas, 1997.
41   Sipra Sen, *Tribes of Mizoram*, New Delhi, Gian Publishing House, 1992.
42   The new name Mizo (*mi* meaning man, *zo* meaning hill) used in preference to Lushai.
43   R. N. Prasad, ed., *Autonomy Movements in Mizoram*, New Delhi, Vikas, 1994.
44   Sambhuti Ranjan Bhattacharjee, *Tribal Insurgency in Tripura: a Study in Exploration of Causes*, New Delhi, Inter-India Publications, 1989.
45   Description of tribes: Sipra Sen, *Tribes of Tripura*, New Delhi, Gyan Publishing House, 1993.
46   Gayatri Bhattacharyya, *Refugee Rehabilitation and Its Impact on Tripura's Economy*, New Delhi, Omsons Publications, 1988.
47   S. P. Sinha, "Insurgency in North-East India: the External Factor", *U. S. I. Journal*, New Delhi, CXXVIII/533 (July–September 1998), p. 440. Also: Singh, *Nagaland, op. cit.*, pp. 118–145.
48   For the China connection: Nibedon, *op. cit.*, pp. 50–53, 68.

49　Some Indian writers occasionally criticize the Indian Minister of Defence (George Fernandes), whose sympathy for the pro-democracy movement in Myanmar is no secret, for not taking action against illegal gun-running operations while the government frequently blames the unrest on "foreign hands". For instance, Nitin A. Gokhale, "Route to Suicide", *Outlook*, New Delhi, 1 February 1999, pp. 39–44.

50　W. C. Runciman, *Relative Deprivation and Social Justice*, London, Routledge and Kegan Paul, 1986.

51　P. S. Datta, "Roots of Insurgency", *Seminar*, New Delhi, 366 (February 1990), pp. 46–49.

Chapter 13

Punjab, Bengal and the Tamils

Terrorism in Punjab[1] is linked with the politics of some members of the Sikh religious minority which forms the majority in that state. About 80% of the 15 million Sikhs live in India. There are over a million of them seeking their livelihood outside the mother country. The Sikhs, who object to the headlines that link them with terrorist acts, are not terrorists. One may reserve the term "Khalistani" to describe the groups that favour a separate Khalistan, or an unborn "land of the pure" for Sikhs. *Khalsa* means the "pure" or the militants of the faithful. The "Naxalites", who had resorted to terrorist methods but who did not have separatist aims, however, focused their efforts ostensibly on their "class enemies" and tried to keep up a bloody vendetta against them. The hoped-for nation wide uprising failed to occur, but the Naxalite strategy of agrarian mass revolution, coupled with urban terror, profoundly shook the Indian political system between 1967 and 1972. Terrorism of the Liberation Tigers of Tamil Eelam (LTTE) in Sri Lanka, lying in the southern tip of India, spilled over in Tamil Nadu, an Indian state.

Punjab—Plenty and Panic

Punjab, the bountiful heart of Khalistan (or Sikhistan), is India's frontier state. Although the present-day Indian Punjab is about the size of a Central American republic, the maps of Khalistan envisage a "Sikh empire" engulfing all the lands between the Himalayas to the Arabian Sea. All Khalistanis are Sikhs, but not all Sikhs are Khalistanis. The causes of the problem in Punjab, posed by the Khalistanis, are complex, comprising history, misperceptions, changing trends, political and economic dynamics, and "foreign hand".[2] Between the years 1947–66, a minority became a majority in Punjab.[3] The majority of the Sikhs entertain the notion, however, that all of India is their home, and that Khalistan is a medieval farce. They marry with the Hindus, who also worship at the Sikh *gurdwara* (temple).

Dissatisfied with Hinduism and Islam, Guru Nanak (1469–1539)[4] had founded the Sikh religion in his quest for a doctrine egalitarian according to his conception.[5] He wrote: "Make Love thy mosque, Sincerity thy prayer-carpet, Justice thy Koran, Modesty thy circumcision, Courtesy thy kaaba, Truth thy guru, Charity thy creed and prayer…"[6] By the time of the sixth Guru, who started the habit of wearing two swords (*piri* and *miri*) representing the spiritual and worldly authority, militancy was institutionalized in it.[7] Sikh males are generally recognized by their colourful turbans and beards. Their other distinguishing marks are a comb in the hair, a dagger, a steel bracelet and short outer pants. Collectively, they are known as the "five Ks", for the first letter of the Punjabi word for each of them. They have "Singh" (lion) as a middle or a family name, but Singh is also a common Hindu name. The females take the word *"Kaur"*, which means "princess".

The Sikhs have experienced two massacres, in 1746 and in 1762, during which the attackers tried to sack their leading city Amritsar and attempted to tarnish and dishonour their Golden Temple. The period of Ranjit Singh, who ruled as the Maharajah of Punjab for four decades (1799–1839) is a source of inspiration for Sikh militancy.[8] The militants now overlook the fact that the Sikh Maharajah's rule necessarily encompassed Punjab's total social diversity including Hindus and Muslims.

The British came to control the whole of Punjab after two Anglo-Sikh Wars (1845–46, 1848–49),[9] following which the Sikhs gained a favoured position in the British army, and some of them emigrated to other colonies in East Africa and elsewhere.[10] At times, they revolted. There was a powerful peasant movement against a new colonization bill (1905–07), a Ghaddar movement (1913–18), and the Jajjaianwala Bagh tragedy (1919) involving bloodshed. Expecting independence for India, the Sikhs proposed changes in Punjab's boundaries to guarantee more representation in future parliaments. When partition seemed to be inescapable, and some Muslims attained Pakistan,[11] some Sikhs urged for an independent Khalistan.[12]

Ever since partition,[13] many Sikhs felt that its consequences have been unfair to their community. Pakistan, a Muslim state, had taken the larger portion causing the flight of some 2.5 million or 40% of the Sikhs to the Indian part, the majority of whom resettled in east Punjab. They had lost in the western section the rich and productive land which had belonged to their forefathers for some centuries. The British exit had also taken away their privileges such as reserved legislative seats and their selective place in the armed forces. Accounting for a high share of the country's export trade, what had remained of the former united Punjab was still the granary of independent India situated, nevertheless, alongside the nation's leading competitor in the west, thus occupying a key position in defence as well.[14]

Alarmed that their identity might be lost in the mergers and blending, the Sikhs, on the other hand, underlined that they should possess separate institutions and distinct legal guarantees.[15] If they have later resorted to violence in pursuit of these aims, there was a basis for this movement going back to the Sikh Gurdwara Act (1925) and the guiding role of the Akali Dal which controlled the committees set up under it. Although the story of terrorism in Punjab started much later (1978),[16] there were agitations to bring about changes in its boundaries to give the Sikhs a majority. The Nehru-Tara Singh agreement (1955) could not prevent Sant (Saint) Fateh Singh's long fast in the Golden Temple (1960) or Master Tara Singh's[17] fast, which started on Independence Day (1961), just as the division (1971) of Punjab[18] into Haryana, Mimachal Pradesh and a reduced Punjab did not satisfy the Akali Dal[19] whose hopes were centred on coming to power.

Even after the creation of the new Sikh-majority state of Punjab, a considerable Sikh minority had to stay in Haryana while the Hindus made up the majority in the urban areas of Punjab. The Sikhs were also not satisfied when the capital city of Chandigarh doubled as the capital of Haryana as well. Further, the Sikhs deemed the way the waters of the Punjab rivers[20] were divided to be unjust. While some Sikh leaders like Darshan Singh Pheruman went on fast unto death and became martyrs, Prime Minister Indira Gandhi, to pacify the Sikhs, presented Chandigarh to Punjab in exchange for two Hindi-speaking areas (Abhor and Fazilka) to Haryana. The Sikhs now constituted the majority in Punjab, but this transformation did not prevent the Akali Dal from becoming more militant. Especially after the latter's historic resolution (1973) which underscored Sikh separateness, politics in Punjab deteriorated into terrorism, based on demands for greater autonomy and a further alteration of frontiers now to incorporate the Punjabi-speaking portions of Haryana and Rajasthan in the south. The frustration of the ambitious Akali leadership, which could not come to power, enabled the unemployed but educated Sikh youngsters to come to the forefront of state politics with an eye on terrorism.

Terrorism first appeared (1978) with a collision between the fundamentalist Akhanda Kirtani Jatha and the opposing Nirankaris. In response to the loss of eighteen Jatha demonstrators, the fundamentalist leaders swore vengeance against their adverseries including the government. The Akali leaders, on the other hand, in competition with the other extremists, pressed for the announcement of Amritsar as a holy city and the renaming of the express train to that city as the Golden Temple Express. What was originally a clash between the Jatha and the Nirankaris evolved into a separate state for the Sikhs. Some writers argued that Sikh militancy was actually the result of socio-economic factors rather than purely religious ones, and that the shrinking base of the Punjabi economy, coupled with unemployed educated youth, contributed to militancy.[21]

Agriculture was no longer able to absorb the growing populace, and people were forced to search for employment elsewhere. The central authority in New Delhi, which misused Article 356 of the Constitution to topple the democratically elected local goverments, further disenchanted the Punjabi people. The Akalis, who were entrusted with the mandate to administer after no less than four elections (1967, 1969, 1977, 1985) resorted to agitation only in 1980 when their government was toppled for the third time. The opposition parties became active only after thousands of people were jailed.

Sant (Saint) Jarnail Singh Bhindranwala(e),[22] who was also arrested and then released and thus became a martyr and also a charismatic leader in the eyes of the Sikh youth, publicly advocated violence.[23] When those whose names appeared in the hit lists printed in newspapers were actually assassinated, some Hindus of Punjab started migrating to other states. Not only were several Nirankaris murdered, but the proprietor of the Samachar group of newspapers was also killed, and an Indian Airlines Boeing was hijacked (1981).[24]

The diffusion of violence in the fertile and the strategically important state of Punjab gave Pakistan a chance to influence events. Many Indians believed, at that time, that some Pakistanis harboured a "K-2" (Kashmir-Khalistan) plan. Pakistan's support of the Punjabi terrorists in providing sanctuaries, operational bases, weapons and training facilities would promote Hindu-Sikh alienation, keep the Sword of Damocles hanging over India's head, discredit that country's secular credentials, and keep its security forces tied down within its borders. When that neighbouring state, now a local ally of the United States in support of the *Mujahideen* in Afghanistan, was ready to pass on weapons into Punjab, as well as J&K, the Sikh terrorists had already cultivated links with the smugglers at the common border. Much of the coordination of links with the J&K militants and the NE insurgents was being done by Pakistan, which was facilitating terrorism if not directly aiding and abetting it. Another web of external involvement ran through the Sikh communities abroad.

Sant Bhindranwala,[25] who had ordered his flock to disrupt the 1982 Asian Games in Delhi,[26] chose to move his headquarters to the Golden Temple, where he immediately started to amass arms, ammunition and explosives. Assault rifles, procured partially with Pakistan's help, replaced the smaller weapons. A large number of followers from the rural areas congregated in the same complex. Their leaders made a call for *Dharma Yudh*, or mass agitation. On a number of occasions, solution acceptable to both sides was in the offing. At a crucial stage during one of those negotiations, an aircraft was ready to fly Akali's Sant Longowal to the capital but the flight did not take off since the Congress Party seemed to take advantage of the situation in the 1985 elections.

The militants targeted, not only a number of Hindu temples, but also the Punjab police officers twenty of whom were killed in 1983. The President's rule replaced the elected Darbara Singh government in Punjab when a terrorist group hijacked a bus in Amritsar and murdered six Hindu passangers. With the popularly elected government gone, the number of terrorist acts dramatically rose. The political arena was now widely opened to Bhindranwala and his followers, whose challenge of authority would be met only by rushing large paramilitary forces to Punjab. Such forces lacked, however, pertinent information related to the locality. The militants felt free to display the sophisticated weapons acquired, thanks in part to Pakistan's interest in the conflict.

The Golden Temple turned into a fortified castle in public view. The government should have shown a determined but toned down reaction when the developing crisis could have been contained without shedding blood or as little as possible. Indira Gandhi was not disposed to risk a military adventure. Some army advisors assured her that it would be a brief operation. One should not ignore the fact that the extremists showed no regard for the sanctity of the temple. Although it was true that the terrorists were taking advantage of a famed religious shrine no less than the Golden Temple for their own purposes, it was a sacred place where a full-fledged armed clash should not take place. It was too late for the people to support the government in such a conflict, especially when it involved severe damage to the shrine. Apart from the Akal Takht (Throne)[27] of historical fame and the Harmindir Sahib in the middle of the holy tank, the Golden Temple is a huge complex with a number of buildings, Guru Nanak Niwas, workshops, several entrances and pathways. All of its buildings, even the gates with majestic domes, were heavily fortified and had holes to fire on the army. Every opening was a firing position. Fortifications were visible everywhere. With bunkers and fire trenches, the whole complex seemed to be an impregnable bastion. Not only the passages underneath, but also the buildings around the complex were in the control of the extremists. Starving them and forcing them out was impossible because there was a huge amount of foodgrain stock.

According to some Indian writers, the army was simply given the task of ending the defilement of the Golden Temple, a symbol of Indian secularism as much as the holiest shrine of the Sikhs, by a "bunch of terrorists and criminals".[28] Operation Blue Star,[29] which gave the army, not well informed about the complexities of the problem, the assignment to empty the Golden Temple of the terrorists, proved to be a mistake with fatal consequences. The operation, launched on the night of 5 June 1984, used tanks to silence fortifications. Lieut.-Gen. K. S. Brar, a top-ranking officer responsible for the military action on the Golden Temple, and whose observations endorse the findings of the Indian Government, justified the intervention in the following words: "[T]he ultimate decision to use the army was taken most reluctantly when every other avenue for a peaceful settlement had been exhausted and the integrity of the country stood seriously threatened and endangered".[30] The rolling tanks and thundering artillery shattered walls, crushed stairs and knocked down monumental relics such as the Akal Takht. Troop movement from any direction came under heavy fire from the Akal Takht, which had a machine-gun bunker. Any plan to clear the extremists out of it without causing damage to it seemed impossible. Attempts by the army to throw non-lethal gas into the Akal Takht building failed. The sound of the rocket launchers, mortars, machine-guns, and hand-grenades still echo in the minds and the hearts of those who witnessed the traumatic scenes. In addition to the 4,712 killed, about 10,000 were arrested. The army suffered 84 dead and 262 wounded.[31]

Almost the entire Sikh community, not only in Punjab or in the whole of India, but also in the diaspora, judged the massive army intervention as an attack on their religion as well. The misuse of a holy shrine should have been an incredible shock for an average Sikh. It is asserted that "thousands of youth crossed over the borders to Pakistan for training in arms".[32] While the Sikhs swore vengeance, the foreign-based militants urged for an independent "Republic of Khalistan". One solid effect of Operation Blue Star was the rise of terrorism in Punjab for years to come. Pakistan took advantage of the situation for its own purposes, channelling more arms and financial aid to some militants.[33] One dramatic consequence was the assassination (31 October 1985) of Prime Minister Indira Gandhi by two of her Sikh bodyguards, resulting in another tragic response, the anti-Sikh riots during which at least 2,150 Sikhs were killed in New Delhi and more than 600 in other parts of India.[34] The key stumbling block in Hindu-Sikh relations was not so much the transfer of Chandigarh, or the equitable sharing of waters, or even local autonomy, and finally Operation Blue Star, but the massacre of Sikhs in Delhi and elsewhere.

The large-scale anti-Sikh riots, the gruesome murder of thousands of Sikhs and horrendous scenes in the presence of kith and kin threatened to tear apart the secular edifice of the country besides delivering still one more cruel blow to the Sikh psyche.

Another consequence of Operation Blue Star was the growth of rivalry between the leaders of Sikh factions. After the death of Bhindranwala, the new Prime Minister Rajiv Gandhi ordered the release of Akali Dal leaders, announced an economic package for Punjab, and realized the Rajiv-Longowal (Punjab) Accord (1985).[35] The people of the country, particularly the Punjabis, heaved a sigh of relief when ultimately an accord was signed after paying a heavy price. Sant Longowal was killed by Sikh extremists who considered it a sell-out. This murder did not stop the Longowal Akali Dal faction winning a large majority, for the first time in the state's history, in the 1985 State Assembly elections.

Neither did this triumph prevent the Punjabi terrorists from sabotaging an Air India jumbo jet, which exploded (1985) over the Atlantic. A bomb went off in the baggage hold of the aircraft, bound for New Delhi and Bombay from Toronto and Montreal. A certain "M. Singh", who later did not board the flight, had persuaded the officials in Vancouver to put his bag on board, for transfer to the Air India flight leaving Toronto. The death toll of 329 stands as the worst at-sea air crash of all time. As a terrorist act, it is the bloodiest in the modern era. The case against a Vancouver-based Sikh extremist cell was very strong, and the call for justice of the bereaved families was bitter and loud. The lives lost were unpayable except in shared remorse.[36] Once more, groups of Sikhs housed themselves in the Golden Temple complex. But this time, the public sentiment and the terrorists were mismatched. There was hardly any tension in the city. The militants, who realized that they were in a hopeless situation, surrendered without the army firing a single shot. The so-called Operation Black Thunder was one of the most successful anti-terrorist operations anywhere in the world. There were no casualties, and no damage. Sikh sensitivities were not hurt. Even the Sikh masses supported the operation.

An extraordinary success story like Operation Black Thunder fell short of signifying an end for terrorism in Punjab. Some youngsters introduced remote control timed devices and land mines in addition to the AK-47s and other sophisticated weapons imported from Pakistan. There are documents, such as letters about arms supplies or suggestions for organizational changes, establishing Pakistan's active involvement.[37] Punjab is not only a border state with a long (550 km.) frontier with Pakistan, but it also adjoins J&K, whose lifeline it always was. Barbed wire fencing with observation posts were erected along the whole Indo-Pakistan border. Every situation in Punjab had its impact on J&K. By the same token, the state of affairs in Punjab affected the country as a whole, including its economic life. Punjab is still the granary of India, and its food production traditionally contributed to reducing dependence on imports. It is one of the sources of raw materials like cotton, sugarcane and other crops.

When terrorism hit high spots, Punjab's economy was in bad shape. As there were cases of railway track sabotage and random firing at crowds, trade virtually reached a standstill, and there was an outflow of capital. Most educational institutions were communalized and became centres of extremist activities. About half of the new generation terrorists came from the urban middle class and the rich peasant families. Some were engaged in illicit drug trade. Their avowed aim was to control Khalistan through violent action. The Khalistan Commando Force (KCF),[38] on record for smuggling arms from Pakistan, and the Khalistan Liberation Force (KLF), hoped to incite passion by killing Hindus. The Khalistan Liberation Organization (KLO) set off a number of explosions in the past. Some Babbar Khalsa activists, who received training in Pakistan, made more use of explosives than the other groups.

The situation went precipitously downhill between 1986 and 1989 with murders becoming more and more common. The killings started to consume those very people on whose behalf the activities were supposed to have been carried out. In two years (1989–90), the militants issued 31 codes of conduct for academics, bureaucrats, farmers, journalists, policemen, school children, shopkeepers, and others. The people found these codes more oppressive than anything the government had done.[39] It was those depredations against some Sikhs that eventually led to the collapse of support for the militancy. While the veneer of religion grew thinner and thinner, the terrorists killed more Sikhs than Hindus, attacked women and extorted money. Finally, the Sikh-dominated Punjab Police defeated the Khalistani terrorists. The Babbar Khalsa and the KCF leaders escaped to Pakistan, and some fled to North America. The remaining ones still have the capacity, however, to commit terrorist acts.[40] In any case, time may heal the wounds inflicted by the extremists.

Punjab terrorism, which grew out of a number of Sikh grievances, real and imaginary, and which briefly spilled over to a limited Western corner of the neighbouring state of Uttar Pradesh, eventually declined because of a general abhorrance of violence and lack of public support. The success of Operation Black Thunder buried, at least partly, the disastrous memory of Operation Blue Star. Most Indian sources seem convinced that terrorism will not revive in Punjab. But developments partly caused by the failures of the political-administrative system that has allowed problems to fester, in the past, creating a base of grievances upon which terrorist movements, later encouraged by Pakistan's ISI, were built. However, the speech (27 March 1985) of Khushwant Singh in the Upper House (*Rajya Sabha*) of the Indian Parliament may still be remembered: "We are now concerned with one issue. It is the dignity and the self-respect of a community of about 15 million people whose susceptibilities have been deeply hurt. You have to learn how to assuage those feelings and win this community back into the community that comprises India".[41]

Two important root causes lie in the economic situation and the shape of the political map of the state. For instance, it is very difficult to fight extremism if the Punjabi peasants are deprived of water. Every government has to tackle the problems of poverty and unemployment. Further, the political parties should abandon the use of communal divisions with the hope of winning the next elections. The Akali party, in power and out of power, played different roles. When removed from power, it pursued the Anandpur Sahib Resolution (1973), which contained the seeds of separatism, but when in power (1973–81) the same Resolution was put in cold storage. The people of Punjab, who want peace, are against the separatist slogans and extremism. The implementation of the essence of the Punjab Accord will restore harmony and isolate the militants.

The Naxalites

Inspired by an incident (1967) of agrarian agitation in the town of Naxalbari (hence, their name) in West Bengal, the Naxalite movement was an uprising of armed revolutionaries, aggressively opposing what they termed to be exploitation. It "radically challenged the premises of established morality".[42] Targeting landlords, moneylenders, and police, the practice of terrorism was typical of this movement as well.[43] Although it was crushed within a few months, perhaps nothing was quite the same afterwards in the Indian countryside. If contained in one place, it erupted in another corner of the land. Naxalbari was followed by Srikakulam, Debra-Gopiballavpur, Birbhum, Bhoipur, and the like. It may be described as a part of a worldwide impulse among the radicals in the late1960s. In the Indian context, it took the form of appealing to the peasantry,[44] which had been a source of change in China but also meant in India ignoring other important layers of society.[45]

Since the initial bloodshed in the late-1960s, groups of radicals organized into "*dalams*" and intensified the armed struggle. The Indian society witnessed the Naxalite model for the first time (1968) in North Bihar, violence reaching stormy proportions in the Communist-dominated districts of Uttar Pradesh, and in Madhya Pradesh as well as in the tribal areas of Orissa. Even before the Communist Party of India (CPI-ML) put into shape a People's Liberation Army in early 1971, the Naxalites attacked the police, whom they saw as the guardian of the existing order.

Although several Naxalite groups now exist in various parts of India, most of them are concentrated in Andhara Pradesh and Bihar. The People's War Group in the former was the most active. It sought to gain popularity with the people by insisting on an ethical code such as a ban on alchohol, and introduced (1989) the use of the AK-47 assault rifles. The Maoist Communist Centre (MCC), which came into existence in 1975, spread to Bihar's central districts. Starting in Bastar, the Naxalite movement in Madhya Pradesh broadened to include some other districts and became more brutal involving the burning alive of a police platoon commander.

The people's support to the Naxalite movement has declined in West Bengal. The reason for this loss should be sought in the local government's execution of some land reform projects rather than restraining police action. But the CPI (ML) Liberation, based in central and south Bihar,[46] and recognized as a legitimate party in 1994, engaged in murderous acts while at the same time conducting an open political campaign. Party unity, with followings among the Harijans,[47] Adivasis[48] and similar backward communities, functions covertly since its inception (1982) and indulges in caste violence. The MCC operates through armed squads which assassinate rural landlords, the so-called people's courts which metes out quick justice, and the peasants' committees which constitute the root structure of the movement. Opting for illegal activities, the MCC burnt down election vehicles and threatened the electorate to keep away from the polls. The Shanti Pal Group of the CPI (ML) also defied parliamentary struggle and chose armed agrarian revolution, in pursuit of which, it not only tries to mobilize peasants, but also enrolls criminals. Some of these groups such as the Santosh Rana team, which took part in the 1995 Assembly elections, occasionally relies on the votes of the electorate. Some others, like the Yatindra faction, frequently clash with other gangs. Occasionally, the Andra Pradesh Government set 30-day limits for suspension of police operations against the Naxalites, and some extremists surrendered during that period.[49]

The Naxalite movement, which grew on account of socio-economic exploitation but which also enjoyed some external support, now lost, is fragmented but still active. While none of these groups favours secession from the country, their violence will probably continue as long as the root causes are not eradicated.

The Sri Lankan Tamils

Although separated from the pear-shaped island of Sri Lanka by a strip of narrow sea, India is affected by the Tamils of neighbouring Sri Lanka.[50] The British planters, unable to convert the Sinhalese subsistence farmer into a wage-labourer, chose to draw on the vast reservoir of manpower in what is now Tamil Nadu. Thus, the British planted, not only tea and coffee, but also the seeds of antagonism between the Sinhalese farmer and the Tamil worker, both dark-skinned labourers. The Tamils had come to the Jaffna Peninsula and much of the east coast since the 2nd century A.D. While the Sinhalese already entertained concerns over Tamil dominance, the two Tamil groups could not stand together in the way the Sinhalese believe that they do. The LTTE, or the terrorist organization of some Tamil groups already involved in a kind of a civil war with the Sri Lankan Army, executed a number of savage acts, the most dramatic being the former Indian Prime Minister Rajiv Gandhi's assassination (1991).

For the question of sorting out the rights of minorities, the Tamils in particular, prevailed and dominated Sri Lankan politics. The basic conflict was between the majority Sinhalese (13.4 million, 74%) and the minority Tamils. Almost every Sri Lankan government, starting with that of the first Prime Minister, Stephen Senanayake, strove to harmonize the interests of the main ethnic groups. While the majority Sinhalese, originally from Bengal, are mainly (90%) Buddhist, and speak Sinhala,[51] the Tamils are predominantly Hindu and have their own tongue.[52] Two groups constitute the latter, however, one known as "Sri Lankan" (Ceylon or Jaffna) Tamils (2.2 m., 12%) and the other "Up Country" (Indian or Estate) Tamils (1.1 m., 6%).[53] The first category constitutes of the descendants of immigrants who came centuries ago from south India. The second category is made up of the sons and daughters of the Tamils brought by the British in the last century or the beginning of the 1900s to work on the tea and rubber plantations. Most of the Up Country Tamils were stateless when the country became independent, and many of them were the most disadvantaged among the population. According to an agreement (1964) between Sri Lanka and India, 975,000 Tamils were to be repatriated,[54] and the rest would be given Sri Lankan citizenship.

The LTTE, among the several extremist groups formed after the new Sri Lankan Republican Constitution that did away with some protective articles of the minorities, started to entertain the idea of a separate state for the Tamils. The Up Country Tamils came under the attack of the militant Sinhalese as secession became dominant with the minority groups who sought refuge in the safer north-eastern areas. While not all Indian Tamils became militants, the government project (1981) offering some autonomy to the Tamils, in spite of opposition from the Sinhalese hardliners, was too little and too late.

No Indian government could overlook the ethnic strife between the majority and the minority in Sri Lanka. It came increasingly under pressure to intervene for the Sri Lankan Tamils. An Indian-Sri Lankan Agreement (1987)[55] provided for a largely autonomous provincial council and an equal status between Tamil, Sinhala and English. An Indian Peace-Keeping Force (IPKF), some 3,000 Indian troops, were sent to the north-eastern part of the island. While the LTTE renounced the agreement, the Indian troops were increased twenty-five fold. There was no improvement of the situation when the Indian troops withdrew in early 1990. The well-intentioned agreement satisfied neither the Sinhalese, nor the Tamils and resulted in the assassination of Rajiv Gandhi for sending the Indian troops to Sri Lanka.

The IPKF was at first assigned the thorny duty of interposing between the Sri Lankan army and the LTTE and shouldering the difficult burden of removing the mines and booby traps in the Jaffna region. The Indian troops could not achieve these objectives. They failed to end the intervention within a reasonably short time as some decision-makers initially envisaged, and the military involvement led to loss of Indian lives and money. Dragged more and more into an overseas ethnic conflict, the Indian soldiers turned into a party taking direct action against the LTTE militants, whose exploits may only be termed as illegal in impartial opinion as well as in the judgement of the Sri Lankan authorities. During the 967 days of its stay, intended to be peace-keeping, the Indian army's losses reached 1,155 deaths by the time the V. P. Singh government withdrew the forces. While a new build-up of the LTTE in Tamil Nadu has been underway in recent years, this militant organization seems committed to terrorist acts in India. It is regrettable that an aggressive group seeks to make south India a hinterland of covert activities related to ethnic violence in a neighbouring state.

Notes

1 An effort to analyse the long-term forces which have produced the Punjab crisis: Pramod Kunar *et al., Punjab Crisis: Context and Trends*, Chandigarh, Centre for Research in Rural and Industrial Development, 1984. This study defines three kinds of communalism-the conformist, the secessionist and the incremental-concessionist (pp. 17–30). While taking note that communalism may express discontent, the authors point out that it fails to provide viable remedies to socio-economic conditions that generate it, and becomes an instrument of vested interests to maintain their dominant position (pp. 92–100). A short (130 pp.) general reference: H. R. Khanna *et al., Terrorism in Punjab: Cause and Cure*, Chandigarh, Panchnad Research Institute, 1987.

2 Pakistan is meant by "foreign hand". For a criticism of the image of "design to destabilize India", see the chapter entitled "The 'Foreign Hand'" in: Ghani Jafar, *The Sikh Volcano*, Lahore, Vanguard Books, 1987, pp. 193–201.

3 Devinder Pal Sandhu, *Sikhs in Indian Politics: Study of a Minority*, New Delhi, Patriot Publishers, 1992, pp. 84–108.

4 On the attitude of the first *guru* towards the Muslims: N. D. Ahuja, *The Great Guru Nanak and the Muslims*, Chandigarh, Kirti Publishing House, 1971. Also: S. S. Bal, *Guru Nanak in the Eyes of the Non-Sikhs*, Chandigarh, Punjab University, 1975.

5 The first five volumes on the ten Gurus: Max Arthur Macauliffe, *The Sikh Religion*, Vols. I–VI, Oxford, Clarendon Press, 1909. The Sikhs on the basis of original records, partially unpublished: S. Gopal Singh, *A History of the Sikh People: 1469–1978*, New Delhi, World Sikh University Press, 1979. A comprehensive view of the growth of Sikh thought and action based on original English and Indian sources: Hari Ram Gupta, *History of the Sikhs*, Vols. I–VIII, New Delhi, Munshiram Manoharlal Publishers, 1973.

6 H. G. Rawlinson, *A Concise History of the Indian People*, Delhi, Low Price Publications, 1994, p. 137.

7 On how a monotheistic faith became political in aims and military in methods: Indu Bhushan Banerjee, *Evolution of the Khalsa*, Vols. I–II, Calcutta, A. Mukherjee and Co., 1979. For the Sikh struggle for survival as a separate community against Muslim domination, British expansionism, and absorption by renascent Hinduism: Khuswant Singh, *A History of the Sikhs*, Vols. I–II, Princeton, New Jersey, Princeton University Press, 1966. Just before Govind Singh died, he told his followers that he was the last of the true Gurus and that they should afterwards look upon the holy book for constant guidance. Singh, *op. cit.*, Vol. I, p. 95.

8 The following source describes the evolution of the Sikh community from its relationship with the parent Hindu society towards a Khalsa identity: Rajiv A. Kapur, *Sikh Separatism: the Politics of Faith*, London, Allen and Unwin, 1986.

9 Patrick Turnbull, "Ferozeshehr and the Sikh War, December 1845", *History Today*, London, XXVII/1 (January 1977), pp. 31–40; Hugh C. B. Cook, *The Sikh Wars*, Delhi, Tomson Press, 1975.

10 One of the very first works as a comprehensive history of Sikhs from their origin to their war with the British in 1845–46: J. D. Cunningham, *A History of the Sikhs: from the Origin of the Nation to the Battles of the Sutlej*, Delhi, S. Chand, 1966. Author Fox argues that the British superimposed a separate identity on the Sikhs as a requirement of their "divide and rule" policy: Richard G. Fox, *Lions of the Punjab: Culture in the Making*, Berkeley, University of California Press, 1985.

11 The following author argues that although Sikh history is centred in Punjab, the Sikhs did not appear to have claimed a separate homeland until the creation of Pakistan: Harjot S. Oberoi, "From Punjab to 'Khalistan': Territoriality and Metacommentary", *Pacific Affairs*, Vancouver, 60/1 (1987), pp. 26–41.

12 Satinder Singh, *Khalistan: an Academic Analysis*, New Delhi, Amar Prakashan, 1982. The beginnings of the Khalsa movement: Arjan Dass Malik, *An Indian Guerilla War: the Sikh People's War, 1699–1769*, New Delhi, Wiley Eastern Limited, 1975. Descriptions of early expressions for an independent Sikh homeland: Sahdu Swarup Singh, *The Sikhs Demand Their Homeland*, Lahore, Lahore Bookshop, 1946; G. S. Dillon, "Evolution of the Demand for a Sikh Homeland", *Indian Journal of Political Science*, Guntar, A.P., 35/4 (1974), pp. 362–373.

13 For a compilation of official documents: Mian Muhammad Sadullah, ed., *The Partition of the Punjab*, Vols. I–IV, Lahore, National Documentation Centre, 1983. On the after-effects of partition on Punjab: Satya M. Rai, *Partition of the Punjab*, New Delhi, Asia Publishing House, 1965.

14 A prominent Punjabi writer's polemic addressed to the former Indian Prime Minister, requesting him to do justice to Punjab's legitimate demands: Jaswant Singh Kanwal, *The Other Zafarnamah: an Open Letter to Rajiv Gandhi*, Sirhind, India, Lokgeet Parkashan, 1987. Emphasizing Punjab's contribution to the country's defence and economy, the author asserts that the Central Government discriminated against the Punjabis, which have no heavy industry and whose foodgrain was drained away at low prices.

15 Rajiv A. Kapur deals with the contemporary Sikh communal consciousness: *Sikh Separatism: the Politics of Faith*, London, Allen and Unwin, 1986. More on the politics of the Congress Party and its relations with the Sikhs: K. L. Tuteja, *Sikh Politics: 1920–40*, Kurukshetra, Vishal Publishers, 1984.

16 On the rise of religious and political consciousness among the Sikhs: Ajit Singh Sarhadi, *Punjabi Suba: the Story of the Struggle*, Delhi, U. C. Kapoor, 1970.

17 Durlab Singh, *The Valiant Fighter: a Biographical Study of Master Tara Singh*, Lahore, Hero Publications, 1972.

18 The Sikhs as a minority in the pre-1966 Punjab: Baldev Raj Nayar, *Minority Politics in the Punjab*, Princeton, New Jersey, Princeton University Press, 1966.

19 For the birth and development of the Akali Party: Kailash Chander Gulati, *The Akalis: Past and Present*, New Delhi, Ashajanak Publications, 1974. For a reevaluation of the Akali movement and its contribution to India's independence: Mohinder Singh, *The Akali Movement*, Delhi, Macmillan, 1976.

20 An official view on the waters of Ravi and Beas: Punjab Government, *Ravi-Beas Agreement: White Paper*, Chandigarh, Information and Public Relations Department, 1982. By the Council of Sikh Affairs: *The Punjab River-Water Dispute: Amended Copy, the Truth*, Chandigarh, 1982. A third work chronicling the dispute between Haryana and Punjab: Paul Singh Dhillon, *A Tale of Two Rivers*, Chandigarh, Dhillon Publishers, 1983.

21 Hamish Telford, "The Political Economy of Punjab: Creating Space for Sikh Militancy", *Asian Survey*, Berkeley, 32/11 (November 1982), pp. 969–987.

22 B. M. Sinha, "Sant Jarnail Singh Bhindranwale: the Man Who Set Punjab Aflame", *Illustrated Weekly of India*, Bombay, 103/38 (24 October 1882), pp. 9, 22.

23 An interesting interpretation of the "humane" nature of young Sikh terrorists, whose amateurishness reveals the influence of the low-brow commercial films: Ashish Nandy,

"The Discreet Charms of Indian Terrorism", *Journal of Commonwealth and Comparative Politics*, Essex, U. K., 28/1 (1990), pp. 25–43.

24 Excerpts from statements: "...[A]rm yourselves and prepare for a war...Every Sikh boy should keep 200 grenades with him...A Sikh without arms is naked..." Balraj Madhok, *Punjab Problem: the Muslim Connection*, New Delhi, Vision Books, 1985, pp. 169–170.

25 A sensationalist depiction of Sant Bhindranwala and his followers: Chand Joshi, *Bhindranwale: Myth and Reality*, New Delhi, Vikas, 1984. In contrast: Surjeet Jalandhry, *Sant Bhindranwale*, Jalandhar, Punjab Pocket Books, 1984.

26 Arun Shourie, "Growth of Sikh Separatism", *Secular Democracy*, New Delhi, 5 (May 1982), pp. 16–32.

27 H. S. Dilgir, *The Akal Takht*, Jullundur, Punjabi Book Company, 1980.

28 V. D. Chopra, R. K. Mishra and Nirmal Singh, *Agony of Punjab*, New Delhi, Patriot Publishers, 1984, p. 18.

29 For the narration of the event: Harminder Kaur, *Blue Star over Amritsar*, New Delhi, Ajanta Publications, 1990. The official report on the chronology of meetings between the Central Government and Akali leaders and including a diary of the violence in Punjab: Government of India, *White Paper on the Punjab Agitation*, New Delhi, Department of Information and Broadcasting, 1984.

30 K. S. Brar, *Operation Blue Star: the True Story*, New Delhi, UBS Publications, 1993, p. 169. Three more eye-witness accounts: Kuldip Nayar and Khuswant Singh, *Tragedy of Punjab: Operation Blue Star and After*, New Delhi, Vision Books, 1981, pp. 160–166; Subhash Kirpekar, "Operation Bluestar: an Eyewitness Account", ed., Amarit Kaul *et al*, *The Punjab Story*, New Delhi, Roli Books International, 1984, pp. 76–89.

31 A guide to the casualties: Mark Tully and S. Jacob, *Amritsar: Mrs. Gandhi's Last Battle*, London, Jonathan Cape, 1985, pp. 192f.

32 A veteran Communist leader: Harkishan Singh Surjeet, *Deepening Punjab Crisis: a Democratic Solution*, New Delhi, Patriot Publishers, 1992, p. 3.

33 A former Jan Sangh leader claims that Pakistan is intimately connected with the Punjab issue: Madhok, *Punjab Problem: the Muslim Connection*, op. cit. An appendix (pp. 171–172) reproduces the interview of the Akali leader Sant Longowal with the Indian magazine *Sunday,* 31 March 1985. Two other sources which assert Pakistani interference: Attar Chand, *Pakistan Terrorism in Punjab and Kashmir*, New Delhi, Amer Prakashan, 1991; Afsir Karim, *Counter-Terrorism: the Pakistan Factor*, New Delhi, Lancer International, 1991.

34 Description of the riots: People's Union for Civil Liberties, *Who Are the Guilty? Report of a Joint Inquiry into the Causes and Impact of the Riots in Delhi from 31 October to 10 November*, Delhi, 1984. The narratives of victims who survived and/or their relatives: Uma Chakravarti and Nandita Haksar, *The Delhi Riots: Three Days in the Life of a Nation*, New Delhi, Lancer International, 1987. The report of the Mishra Commission, mandated to look into the anti-Sikh riots, was not officially published. Some of its excerpts in: Harish Jain, ed., *Mishra Commission Report*, Sirhind Mandi, India, Takshila Publications, n.d.

35 The Sikh question and the signing of the Rajiv-Longowal Accord, 1985: Ghani Jafer, *The Sikh Volcano*, New Delhi, Atlantic Publishers, 1988.

36 These were the years when India did not want its communal violence to gain international spotlight, and Canada did not welcome scrutiny of its communal difficulties. Clair Blaise

and Bharati Mukherjee, *The Sorrow and the Terror: the Haunting Legacy of the Air India Tragedy*, Markham, Canada, Viking, 1987.

37   V. N. Narayanan, *Tryst with Terror: Punjab's Turbulent Decade*, Ajanta, 1996, p. 44. Prime Minister Rajiv Gandhi repeatedly warned Pakistan against helping the terrorists in Punjab. For front-page statements: *The Times of India*, New Delhi, 16 August 1988, 17 July 1989, etc.

38   The history and workings of the Khalistan Commando Force for an independent Sikh state: Joyce Pettigrew, *The Sikhs of the Punjab: Unheard Voices of State and Guerilla Violence*, London, Zed Books, 1995.

39   Narayanan, *op. cit.*, pp. 56–57.

40   For the new shocks that made several people to ask whether Punjab was back in the days of terror: *Frontline*, Madras, X/20 (25 September–8 October 1993), pp. 17–28.

41   Kushwant Singh, *My Bleeding Punjab*, New Delhi, UBS Publishers, 1992, pp. 105f.

42   Rabindra Ray, *The Naxalites and Their Ideology*, Delhi, Oxford University Press, 1988, pp. 3, 82-120.

43   Sumanta Banerjee, *India's Simmering Revolution: the Naxalite Uprising*, London, Zed Books, 1984. For a history of the Santals, tribals of south Bihar: Edward Duyker, *Tribal Guerillas: the Santals of West Bengal and the Naxalite Movement*, New Delhi, Oxford University Press, 1987.

44   A. Gosh and K. Dutt, *Development of Capitalist Relations in Agriculture: a Case Study of West Bengal, 1793–1971*, New Delhi, People's Publishing House, 1977.

45   Sankar Ghosh, *The Naxalite Movement: a Maoist Experiment*, Calcutta, K. L. Mukhopadhyay, 1974.

46   In spite of the all-embracing title of the book, the revolutionary movement in Bihar from 1902 to 1935: Shaileshwar Nath, *Terrorism in India*, New Delhi, National Publishing House, 1980.

47   Suresh Narain Srivastava, *Harijans in Indian Society: a Cultural Study of the Status of Harijans and Other Backward Classes from the Earliest Times to the Present Day*, Lucknow, Upper India Publishing House, 1980. What it means to be an Untouchable (Harijan) in contemporary India: Barbara R. Joshi, *Untouchable! Voices of the Dalit Liberation Movement*, London, Zed Books, 1986. A field work among the Chamar community: Ravindra S. Khare, *The Untouchable as Himself*, Cambridge, Cambridge University Press, 1984.

48   Government of India, Ministry of Information and Broadcasting, *The Adivasis*, Faridabad, 1960; V[asant] D[attatraya] Deshpande, *Adivasis of Thane*, Pune, Dastane, 1985; Godari Parulekar, *Adivasi's Revolt*, Calcutta, National Book Agency, 1975; Prafulla Ch. Mahapatro and Daityari Panda, eds., *Adivasis: their Problems and Remedies*, Koraput, Dayanand Anglo-Vedic College, 1972.

49   For instance: *The Times of India*, New Delhi, 16 July 1989, p. 8.

50   E. Nissan, *Sri Lanka: a Bitter Harvest*, London, Minority Rights Group (MRG), 1996; W. Schwarz, *The Tamils of Sri Lanka*, London, MRG, 1988; M. Vije, *Where Serfdom Thrives: the Plantation Tamils of Sri Lanka*, London, Tamil Information Centre, 1987; S. W. R. de A. Samarasinghe and Vidyamali Samarasinghe, *Historical Dictionary of Sri Lanka*, Lanham, Md. and London, The Scarecrow Press, 1998, pp. 5–31.

51   K. N. O. Dharmadasa, "Language and Sinhalese Nationalism", *Modern Ceylon Studies*, III/2 (1972), pp. 125–143.

52   K. N. O. Dharmadasa, "Language Conflict in Sri Lanka", *Sri Lanka Journal of the Social Sciences*, IV/2 (December 1981), pp. 47–70.

53   M. D. Raghavan, *Tamil Culture in Ceylon*, Colombo, Kalai Nilayan Ltd., 1972. Also: A. S. Abraham, "Indian Tamils of Sri Lanka", *The Other India: the Overseas Indians and their Relationship with India*, ed., I. J. Bahadur Singh, New Delhi, India International Centre, 1979, pp. 70–79.

54   M. Vamadevan, *Sri Lankan Repatriates in Tamil Nadu: Rehabilitation and Integration*, Madras, Zen Publishers, 1989.

55   H. L. de Silva, "The Indo-Sri Lanka Agreement (1987) in the Perspective of Inter-State Relations", *Ethnic Studies Report*, Kandy, Sri Lanka, X/2 (July 1992), pp. 10-17.

Chapter 14

Conclusions

A prominent Indian states that "there is an urgent need for India to look at its tradition or rather its traditions".[1] What are the Indian values that have survived till our day?[2] Mulk Raj Anand indicates "universalism" as the first value. In spite of social compartments based primarily on the caste system, the universalist outlook, fed by constant intermixture, has been the dominant traditional trend. There have even been successful attempts to transform this all-embracing perspective into religions. It is natural that the value of tolerance, at times co-existing with intolerance, should accompany universalism. The Hindu god Krishna says in the *Bhagavadgita*: "I give to everyone according to his worship". And the Islam's Holy Book states: "Unto you your religion and unto me my religion". But there is also the bitter history of Hindu-Muslim rivalry and atrocities during the partition of the Sub-continent. Moreover, India has gone through macabre phases of terrorism, not only in J&K, but also in the NE, Punjab and various other corners of India.

Much of the violence stems from the retreat of both neighbours from the standards visualized by their founding fathers. As recently admitted by Pakistan's leading paper,[3] Quaid-e Azam's landmark speech while inaugurating the Constitutional Assembly (1947), has been unrepentantly abandoned over the years. There is almost nothing that his successors have not done to destroy that dream. The Pakistanis have indeed buried deep the ideal on which Jinnah had founded their state. More depressingly, as conceded by Pakistan's army commanders or presidents who terminated parliamentary regimes, links between politics and crime are often structurally complementary elements.

Likewise, Nehru had voiced with conviction, in a statement in the Indian Parliament (1956), that the strongest bonds that linked people were not the armies or even the Constitution, but those of love, affection and understanding.[4] Since the cadres may well be replaced, it is not rewarding to rationalize, as did K. P. S. Gill, a veteran member of the National Security Advisory Board, that the security forces liquidated many terrorists every month and that it will take a little over a year to put the lid on the whole problem.[5] A great deal of political skill is needed, not just strong armies and tough police forces, to communicate a transcendent vision to meet the needs of the people. Unless the public policy of secularism is rendered capable of ensuring for people so different in worldviews, including religious affiliations, access to all opportunities without their self-identification becoming a negative factor against them, there will be more communalism and less secularism.

The Muslims and Co-existence

The Muslims are the single most numerous minority in the contemporary federal all-India polity. They also constitute the majority in J&K, albeit in the Valley which forms about a tenth of that state. The Muslim minority in India, in numerical strength, constitutes one of the biggest Muslim populations in the world. Although it is more numerous, even several times, than at least two-thirds of the other states, it is still a minority in the Indian national context, and moreover, a minority in all the federative states on account of the wide dispersal all over India.

One crucial question is how can the Muslims of India, the Kashmiri Muslims included, harmonize their sense of belonging with the over-all change in the larger Indian community.[6] When some Muslim leaders propagated the two-nations theory and took the field for an exclusive Muslim state, most of those who remained in India, who had stayed there more on account of the dictates of geography and the compelling economic links, could not modernize sufficiently to compete with the Hindus. The question, however, is also a part of the wider political confrontation with the whole of India in respect to its policies of democracy and secularism.

Remembering that centuries of Muslim rule in India has come to an end, or worse, the Muslims of Spain, were either exterminated, forcibly Christianized or expelled after more than seven hundred years of governance, the adherents of the Islamic faith, like many other groups, are caught in the whirlpool of inevitable breaks and alterations in the Indian society. A general Muslim response to these winds of change was even greater awareness of its minority status, mistrust of "Hindu domination" and more adherence to traditional Islamic views. As a tool of defence against the British and the Hindus, the religious leaders had not developed the Muslim laws even during the decay of the Moghul Empire. The Muslims also agreed, then, however, that British rule, though not *Dar-al Salam* (Land of Peace), was neither *Dar-al Harb* (Land of War), but was *Dar-al Aman* (Land of Basic Liberties). Why cannot contemporary India, neither ruled by Muslims nor hostile to Islam, but a new republic based on the diffusion of democracy and secularism, be another *Dar-al Aman*?

Instead of feeling like co-rulers, they continue to harbour the minority psychology and hence communal consciousness. The population ratio most unlikely to change in the foreseeable future, the "in-group" feeling based on religion is bound to persist. One can understand the sub-nationalism of a minority in a democracy. If some Hindu circles suggest a *Ekta Yatra* or a journey for national unity, starting at Kanya Kumari and ending in embattled Srinagar, thus covering the entire length of the country, such a move awakens new fears among the Muslims of a "Hindu" India. The communalism of a minority may be a reaction to the fear, real or imaginary, of the communalism of the majority. Conversely, the communalism of the latter may also be a response to the creation of Pakistan. Neither Hinduism, ideologically and historically free of the "inquisition" mania, aims to annihilate Islam in India, nor may all the Muslims, who have traditionally shown abilities to conform to new environments, be described as fundamentalists. But a minority as numerous as the Muslims of India and with a long and an impressive history, especially living basically in a secular democracy, may be expected to make a much more creative contribution to society at large.

The Hindus and the Muslims stood on unequal levels of growth during the British rule. The well-to-do Muslims could afford to leave for Pakistan after partition. Those landlords who stayed were hit hard by the land reforms of independent India. There still exist differences between the two communities on account of the disparities among the educated middle class members and the consequent benefits or losses that accompany such unevenness. But new elites are coming up from the rural areas inhabited both by the Hindus and Muslims. This evolution gives the Muslims a chance to integrate better with the mainstream, contribute to modernization, and play a new role in the building of secularism. Whether in the wider framework of the Indian Union or in J&K, it is possible to be a Muslim and an Indian at the same time and help create a closer unity in an obviously plural society. More democracy, the promotion of secularism and faster industrialization will diminish or destroy the obsolete relationships based on caste and religious differences. The Muslims of India have a chance to play such a constructive role in a country in whose history their contribution has been outstanding.

Terminus to Terrorism

Those Muslims, Hindus or Sikhs who welcome brute force and destructiveness fall outside this route to harmony. No matter what their motives are, the terrorists everywhere, including India and Pakistan, undermine the democratic process. Seeing a 'Rambo inside Hamlet' in the mind's eye, violence based on some kind of vengeance may be understood, even when deplored. But their activities should be described as assaults on the democratic traditions. Openness, pluralism, peaceful evolution and compromise are the tenets of democracy. One assumes that groups learn during the democratic process to value forbearance, moderation and consensus. Although much truth may be found in this assumption, the democratic system may also cause conflict, since each compromise may be used by groups for new demands through violence.

Assuming that the world was becoming more rationally modern, some analysts hoped that the problems caused by nationalism, ethnicity and secessionism would be left behind, and that the world would commit itself to common interest and shared values. The relative absence of ethnic strife during the Cold War was treated as an evidence of the stability of the existing states. In the so-called New World Order, however, these suppositions taken for granted proved to be incorrect, and ethno-nationalism served as a motivation for a number of groups. Armed conflicts immediately occurred with the dissolution of the Soviet Union and Federal Yugoslavia. The fracturing of Iraq and Somalia indicated dangers for some other states.

Great Powers, which for centuries interfered in the events of Afghanistan, treated that country as a minor player in the game of international politics, but never in human terms.

On account of the upward trend visible in the instances mentioned above, even the democratic societies remain under a threat that is growing. They need to establish how best to conduct their counter-terrorism while maintaining democratic values. These societies, in which there is a strong trend to respect the democratic rights of the citizens, believe that failure to follow these principles causes a slide towards authoritarian rule. The brutality of terrorist attacks, however, caused some reservations about this rule of law approach. Some circles assert that terrorism is a form of covert warfare, and that it should be treated as such. Consequently, at least in some cases, the rules of the game may be changed, and democratic rights may be temporarily curtailed. Some governments declared virtual 'war' on terrorism and engaged in repression at a human and political cost. But, on the other hand, this approach may well be counterproductive since it will generate additional support for terrorist groups, which will reappear as soon as repression comes to an end. Moreover, "declaring war" on terrorists may give them some "legitimacy", taking them out of the classification of common criminals. Further, a number of liberal societies do not wish to throw out the baby with the bath water; they stress the need to deal with terrorism only within the confines set by respect for democratic values.

As another alternative, some circles argue that the laws may be legitimately altered to meet the new terrorist threats. Some advocate regional police forces, others suggest an international court to try terrorists. Almost all concerned underline that possible terrorist access to weapons of mass destruction must be prevented. There is, indeed, a long tradition of states combining their efforts in the battle against types of crime which affect many countries. There is also sufficient basis in international law for cooperation among states to combat terrorism. For instance, the U.N. General Assembly Resolutions of 1994 (49/185) and of 1995 (50/186) and the Security Council Resolution of 1999 (1269) reiterate great concern over gross violations of human rights perpetrated by terrorist groups. They call upon states to take all necessary and effective measures to prevent acts of terrorism wherever committed. In order to raise the effectiveness of the agreements already made, all states must strictly fulfil their obligations and must not apply different yardsticks to the various acts of international terrorism. All states must take appropriate measures at the national level, harmonize their domestic legislation with international conventions, perform their international obligations, and prevent the preparation in their territory of acts directed against other states.

Believing in the values that lie at the very base of modern India, one has no other alternative but to uphold secular democracy. One's determination should be all the more forceful when terrorism challenges it. In spite of violence, India succeeded so far in protecting its democratic system. The country's federal structure continues to offer a framework within which national and state parties share power. Politicians should not instigate the feelings of hatred of their followers by reminding them, for electoral or other purposes, of certain previous conflicts. Instead of retreating to the golden age of Rama, no matter how glorious it may be, and demanding from others to purge the country from the so-called "foreign impurities", a constructive way of rediscovery is to emphasize India's rich cultural, philosophical, religious and artistic traditions that include Islamic contributions as well.

Although there are many different situations in various corners of the world where ethnic groups are concerned, each case has to be assessed in the light of its particular circumstances. Some general observations, applicable also to India, may be made. First, the protection of persons belonging to such groups has to be seen essentially in the interest of the state and of the majority. If the state exhibits care and loyalty to its citizens, it can expect loyalty in return by those who will have an interest in the stability of the country. Secondly, solutions should be sought within the framework of the state. The self-realization as an ethnic group within the frontiers of the existing state being quite possible, secession is not necessarily an answer to the problems and aspirations of the minorities. In most cases, secession is neither necessary, nor helpful, and changing borders is neither feasible, nor desirable. Moreover, it is almost impossible to find a government willing to cede even a small section of its territory. Even the mere mentioning of such an option motivates a greater rigidity on the part of the central authorities.

While human rights organizations are recurrently occupied by "state-sponsored terrorism", it is too simple to reason that all state actions against terrorist groups necessarily fall under this category. Sometimes, they are taken when all democratic avenues fail. What is more, they are often taken against unbridled terrorist outfits who by the sheer violence they practice cow the silent majority with the aim of disrupting law and order and destabilizing established institutions and national structures and who hardly represent the people in whose name they purport to fight. The golden rule still seems to be a recognition of the fact that the questions relating to minorities may be resolved in a democratic framework, and also that self-determination and secession are not the one and the same thing.

Although Pakistan has repeatedly denied any involvement in aiding and abetting cross-border terrorism, it is appropriate to remind here that its record of sponsoring terrorist infiltration commenced as early as 1947. Kashmir was then invaded under the guise of tribal raiders, ostensibly to liberate their Muslim brethren. There was another armed incursion in Rann of Kutch in 1965, allowing hundreds of infiltrators to move deep into Kashmir territory. The people in the Valley reported the presence of the infiltrators to the security personnel right at the beginning of the operation. Pakistan denied links in the insurgency that wreaked havoc in Punjab. Pakistan even denied connections with cross-border terrorism in Afghanistan, but the idea of raising a fanatical group called Taliban basically originated from Islamabad. Militancy in Kashmir may not be out, but it has lost a great deal of popular support.

Association with Drugs

In spite of improved international coordination, drug trafficking in South Asia as well as worldwide continues to grow. A global, integrated and multi-disciplinary approach to fighting drugs seems indispensable. Such a pursuit should include improving information exchange, global coordination, treaty implementation, crop substitution, adequate funding of development programmes, controlling precursor chemicals, restraining arms transactions, widening educational programmes and discouraging money laundering.

The International Criminal Police Organization (ICPO, Interpol) and other agencies, in an effort to catch up with the latest array of smuggling methods and routes, should complete their information about known and suspected traffickers, contacts, routes and all kinds of vehicles. A pragmatic as well as an integrated approach requires an understanding of interaction of factors and the avoidance of isolated strategies. Instead of various national policies moving in different directions, all anti-drug activities should be part of the agreed strategy to be coordinated by the United Nations International Drug Control Programme (UNDCP). The treaties which already exist, foremost among them being the U.N. Convention against Illicit Traffic in Narcotic Drugs and Psychotropic Substances (1988), are enough to put into shape a comprehensive body of international legislation. What is needed is their implementation rather than new treaties. Gradual crop substitution, instead of crop eradication, accompanied by persuasion and aid, may return peasants to their original occupation. The UNDCP's experience in Latin America, which has shown that much can be achieved, may be repeated in parts of Asia as well. However, the farmers should be persuaded to plant other crops, encouraged to form producers' associations to organize the purchasing of implements and the marketing of produce, and there should be a strict surveillance to eliminate new plantation of narcotic drugs.

There should be an international pressure for the control of precursor chemicals and weapons exports. Although the Chemical Action Task Force (CATF), established by the Houston G–7 Summit (1990) with a mandate based on a technical text in the 1988 U.N. Convention, formed three working groups and identified five basic measures to implement control diversion, most nations are preoccupied with the export of high technology weapons to developing countries. A balanced approach must reduce both demand and supply.[7] To reduce a demand, not only socio-economic living conditions have to be ameliorated, there must also be renewed emphasis in education. An all-embracing warfare against drug trafficking should also include a concerted policy of identification, trace, seizure and confiscation of the financial assets of the traffickers or the eradication of money laundering. The Financial Action Task Force on Money Laundering (FATF), convened by the Paris Summit (1989), published forty recommendations designed to permit rapid and tough actions. While FATF-2 was created at the Houston G–7 Summit (1990) to assess the implementation of the recommendations, it should be asserted that control of money laundering alone will not end drug trafficking. The solution lies more with the consumer nations who should reduce their demand for drugs and provide substantial aid to development programmes in producing countries. The old adage, "an ounce of prevention is worth a pound of cure", is also true here. Prevention reaching every community, school, and business, a drug-free society, although far off, is possible.

Peace with Pakistan

Engaging India in one war after another, Pakistan took plausible risks while coming close to Srinagar in 1947 and making a breakthrough near Amritsar in 1965, but splitting itself into two in 1971. The "covert war" since the 1980s, which began with the battles for Siachen, still continues. The Kargil War in 1999 was the first one fought with regular forces after both Pakistan and India had become overtly nuclear. Except the one in 1971, all the others were specifically linked with Kashmir. Although Pakistan's expectations of success turned out to be miscalculated ventures, the present power equation between the two countries, based on nuclear capabilities, leaves only one alternative for them: the pursuit of peace.

In spite of the initial success of Pakistan to win the sympathy and support of many Muslim countries and communities over Kashmir, the "Muslim bloc" is no longer the cohesive cartel on this issue that it used to be. Pakistan, which had hosted gatherings of the OIC, grabbed the chance of serving as the frontline state during much of Afghanistan's civil war. The *jehad*, supported by General Zia and the CIA, finally led to Muslims killing Muslims. Pakistan has burnt its fingers in Afghanistan, as the armed Taliban are now beyond the control of Islamabad. The United States, an ally of Pakistan since the Baghdad Pact days and its long-time supporter on the Kashmir issue, seems to have accepted, apart from occasional suggestions of Washington's mediation, India's primary responsibility in Kashmir's future and basically advocates a solution through direct negotiations with the people concerned and with Pakistan, even after the defeat of Soviet influence in Afghanistan, the collapse of Communism in Central Asia, and the change of regime in Russia itself. Similarly, China, another friend of Pakistan, recommended, since 1980, negotiations only between India and Pakistan. Some of Pakistan's links with the Muslim world, the United States, and China dried up.

It is in the best interest of India and Pakistan to co-exist peacefully.[8] Even undeclared low-intensity hostilities may erupt into a full-scale war in which the most lethal weapons are employed. Hot pursuit of terrorists may be a *casus belli* inviting counter-measures. Pakistan aimed to overcome its inferiority in conventional weapons by going nuclear. The acquisition of nuclear weapons has not increased Pakistan's military capabilities against India, however, because the latter is also a nuclear power. If continued fighting over Kashmir leads to an atomic war between the two neighbours, who possess nuclear explosives with developed delivery systems, the consequence can only be mutual annihilation. Thus, the choice is either friendship or destruction.[9] Nuclear weapons actually prevent war because of their deterrent effect. Each country can gain more from cooperative than from antagonistic relations. Both can agree to extend to the nuclear field what the Simla Agreement put on paper regarding conventional weapons. Trust has its own risks, but more so perpetual mistrust. The chances of friendship are better now than in the past. The peoples of India and Pakistan, who have the capacity to elect rulers dedicated to peace through negotiations, may ask themselves whether the whole Sub-continent should perish for a comparatively small piece of land, even if it happens to be the divinely beautiful Kashmir.

Options for Kashmir

The key to resolving tensions between India and Pakistan lies in a settlement of the Kashmir issue. Both New Delhi and Islamabad recognize the need for a way out of the deadlock. Options may be summarized as joining India or Pakistan, becoming independent or turning the Line of Control into an international border. The two countries can accept only solutions that will not cause severe domestic repercussions. Therefore, the possibility of the whole undivided state joining India or Pakistan is almost nil. Some Kashmiris may welcome independence but this alternative cannot be accepted by India and Pakistan. A plebiscite is unacceptable not only to India, but also to Pakistan. To approve the creation of an independent state out of India would pose a danger to the country's territorial integrity. Nehru's Interim Government back in 1947 had conveyed to Lord Mountbatten and to the Maharaja that J&K could accede to India or Pakistan but that it must not attempt to stay independent. It had been an independent state between 15 August and 26 October 1947. Even then, India had not approved of a Standstill Agreement which would maintain that status quo. The independence option would have balkanized India, even it had been adopted by a handful of states. For Pakistan, it would also be another failure for the two-nations theory. Moreover, it may further partition J&K into three units, Hindu and Buddhist, as well as Muslim.

The last option is to formalize the status quo leaving with India the portion it now administers and allowing Pakistan to hold to whatever it has. This alternative is closer to India's solution of the issue. It may be said that this line of reasoning was pursued from the time of Nehru, who had agreed to a ceasefire in 1948. Between the years 1949–72, the Indo-Pakistan border in Kashmir had been defined by this ceasefire line. Even a victorious India pushed for that kind of a partition during the Simla talks. The latter agreement accepted the same as a LOC, designed to lay the basis for conversion into an international border. As the initial phase of an eventual solution, an end to Pakistan's military aid to the Kashmiri militants goes hand in hand with India's support of elections that would choose Kashmir's representatives.[10] Those Kashmiris who had fled may return home and vote in free and fair elections to be monitored by a team of experts. Both regions, administered separately by the two neighbours, may enjoy maximum autonomy with soft borders. A harmonious balance may be struck between the need to integrate J&K within the national mainstream and the installation of autonomous self-governance. What is meant by the last concept is good governance or accountable political machinery, stable economic infrastructure and even-handed as well as effective judiciary. To paraphrase Tennyson a bit, one may conclude: "Let us not lose ourselves in light!"

Notes

1   Sitakant Mahapatra, "Redefining Indian Tradition(s)", *The Divine Peacock: Understanding Contemporary India*, eds., K. Satchidananda Murty and Amit Dasgupta, New Delhi, Indian Council for Cultural Relations, 1995, p. 91.

2   Mulk Raj Anand, *Is There a Contemporary Indian Civilisation?* Bombay, etc., Asia Publishing House, 1963, pp. 80f.

3   M. H. Askari, "Quaid's Forgotten Legacy", *Dawn*, Karachi, 25 December 1996.

4   Prem Nath Bazaz, "The Much Abused Article 370", *op. cit.*, p. 2.

5   Narayanan, *op. cit.*, p. 34.

6   Rasheeduddin Khan, "Modernization of the Muslim Community in India", reprinted from *Seminar*, New Delhi, June 1968, pp. 25–31.

7   Two opinions on whether or not to legalize drugs: Ethan A. Nadelmann, "Should We Legalize Drugs? History Answers Yes", *American Heritage*, New York, February–March 1993, pp. 42–48; James Q. Wilson, "Against the Legalization of Drugs", *Commentary*, New York, 89 (1990), pp. 21–28.

8   Pran Chopra, "Prospects for Peace with Pakistan", *Securing India's Future in the New Millennium*, ed., Brahma Chellaney, New Delhi, The Centre for Policy Research, 1999, pp. 467–505.

9   Birbal Nash, *Kashmir: the Nuclear Flashpoint*, New Delhi, Manas Publications, 1998, pp. 213–225.

10 David Cortright, ed., *The Price of Peace: Incentives and International Conflict Prevention*, New York, Carnegie Commission on Preventing Deadly Conflict, 1997, pp. 145–153. The authors suggest debt relief and additional credits for Pakistan and the possibility of a permanent seat in the U.N. Security Council for India.

Documents

Kashmir's Accession to India, 26–27 October 1947

Whereas the Indian Independence Act, 1947, provides that as from the fifteenth day of August, 1947, there shall be set up an independent Dominion known as INDIA, and that the government of India Act, 1935, shall, with such omissions, additions, adaptations and modifications as the Governor-General may by order specify be applicable to the Dominion on India;

And whereas the Government of India Act, 1935, as so adapted by the Governor-General provides that an Indian State may accede to the Dominion of India by an Instrument of Accession executed by the Ruler thereof:

Now therefore I Shriman Indar Mahandar Rajrajeshwar Maharajadhiraj Shri Hari Singhji Jammu Kashmir Naresh Tatha Tibbet adi Deshadhipathi Ruler of JAMMU AND KASHMIR State in the exercise of my sovereignty in and over my said State Do hereby execute this my Instrument of Accession and

1. I hereby declare that I accede to the Dominion of India with the intent that the Governor-General of India, the Dominion Legislature, the Federal Court and any other Dominion authority established for the purpose of the Dominion shall, by virtue of this my Instrument of Accession but subject always to the terms thereof, and for the purposes only of the Dominion, exercise in relation to the State of Jammu and Kashmir (hereinafter referred to as "this State") such functions as may be vested in them by or under the Government of India Act, 1935, as in force in the Dominion of India, on the 15th day of August 1947, (which act as so in force is hereafter referred to as "the Act").

2. I hereby assume the obligation of ensuring that due effect is given to the provisions of the Act within this State so far as they are applicable therein by virtue of this my Instrument of Accession.

3. I accept the matters specified in the Schedule hereto as the matters with respect to which the Dominion Legislature may make laws for this State.

4. I hereby declare that I accede to the Dominion of India on the assurance that if an agreement is made between the Governor-General and the Ruler of this State whereby any functions in relation to the administration in this State of any law of the Dominion Legislature shall be exercised by the ruler of this State, then any such agreement shall

be deemed to form part of this Instrument and shall be construed and have effect accordingly.

5. The terms of this my Instrument of Accession shall not be varied by any amendment of the Act or of the Indian Independence Act, 1947, unless such amendment is accepted by me by an Instrument supplementary to this Instrument.

6. Nothing in this Instrument shall empower the Dominion Legislature to make any law for this State authorising the compulsory acquisition of land for any purpose, but I hereby undertake that should the Dominion for the purposes of a Dominion law which applies in this State deem it necessary to acquire any land, I will at their request acquire the land at their expense or if the land belongs to me transfer it to them on such terms as may be agreed, or, in default of agreement, determined by an arbitrator to be appointed by the Chief Justice of India.

7. Nothing in this Instrument shall be deemed to commit me in any way to acceptance of any future constitution of India or to fetter my discretion to enter into arrangements with the Government of India under any such future constitution.

8. Nothing in this Instrument affects the continuance of my sovereignty in and over this State, or, save as provided by or under this Instrument, the exercise of any powers, authority and rights now enjoyed by me as Ruler of this State or the validity of any law at present in force in this State.

9. I hereby declare that I execute this Instrument on behalf of this State and that any reference in this Instrument to me or to the Ruler of the State is to be construed as including a reference to my heirs and successors.

Given under my hand this 26th day of October nineteen hundred and forty-seven.

(Sd.) Hari Singh
Maharajadhiraj of
Jammu and Kashmir State

**Acceptance of Instrument of Accession of Jammu and Kashmir State
by the Governor-General of India**

I do hereby accept this Instrument of Accession.
Dated this twenty-seventh day of October, nineteen hundred and forty-seven.

(Sd.) Mountbatten of Burma
Governor-General of India

UNCIP Resolution, 13 August 1948

The United Nations Commission for India and Pakistan, having given careful consideration to the points of view expressed by the Representatives of India and Pakistan regarding the situation in the State of Jammu and Kashmir, and

Being of the opinion that the prompt cessation of hostilities and the correction of conditions the continuance of which is likely to endanger international peace and security are essential to implementation of its endeavours to assist the Governments of India and Pakistan in effecting a final settlement of the situation,

Resolves to submit simultaneously to the Governments of India and Pakistan the following proposal:

Part I
Cease-fire Order

A. The Governments of India and Pakistan agree that their respective High Commands will issue separately and simultaneously a cease-fire order to apply to all forces under their control in the State of Jammu and Kashmir as of the earliest practicable date or dates to be mutually agreed upon within four days after these proposals have been accepted by both Governments.

B. The High Commands of the Indian and Pakistani forces agree to refrain from taking any measures that might augment the military potential of the forces under their control in the State of Jammu and Kashmir.
(For the purpose of these proposals "forces under their control" shall be considered to include all forces, organised and unorganised, fighting or participating in hostilities on their respective sides.)

C. The Commanders-in-Chief of the forces of India and Pakistan shall promptly confer regarding any necessary local changes in present dispositions which may facilitate the cease-fire.

D. In its discretion and as the Commission may find practicable, the Commission will appoint military observers who, under the authority of the Commission and with the co-operation of both Commands, will supervise the observance of the cease-fire order.

E. The Government of India and the Government of Pakistan agree to appeal to their respective peoples to assist in creating and maintaining an atmosphere favourable to the promotion of further negotiations.

Part II
Truce Agreement

Simultaneously with the acceptance of the proposal for the immediate cessation of hostilities as outlined in Part I, both Governments accept the following principles as a basis for the formulation of a truce agreement, the details of which shall be worked out in discussions between their Representatives and the Commission.

A. 1. As the presence of troops of Pakistan in the territory of the State of Jammu and Kashmir constitutes a material change in the situation since it was represented by the Government of Pakistan before the Security Council, the Government of Pakistan agrees to withdraw its troops from that State.

2. The Government of Pakistan will use its best endeavour to secure the withdrawal from the State of Jammu and Kashmir of tribesmen and Pakistan nationals not normally resident therein who have entered the State for the purpose of fighting.

3. Pending a final solution, the territory evacuated by the Pakistan troops will be administered by the local authorities under the surveillance of the Commission.

*B.*1. When the Commission shall have notified the Government of India that the tribesmen and Pakistani nationals referred to in Part II A-2 hereof have withdrawn, thereby terminating the situation which was represented by the Government of India to the Security Council as having occasioned the presence of Indian forces in the State of Jammu and Kashmir, and further, that the Pakistan forces are being withdrawn from the State of Jammu and Kashmir, the Government of India agrees to begin to withdraw the bulk of its forces from that State in stages to be agreed upon with the Commission.

2. Pending the acceptance of the conditions for a final settlement of the situation in the State of Jammu and Kashmir, the Indian Government will maintain within the lines existing at the moment of the cease-fire the minimum strength of its forces which in agreement with the Commission are considered necessary to assist local authorities in the observance of law and order. The Commission will have observers stationed where it deems necessary.

3. The Government of India will undertake to ensure that the Government of India will undertake to ensure that the Government of the State of Jammu and Kashmir will take all measures within its power to make it publicly known that peace, law and order will be safeguarded and that all human and political rights will be guaranteed.

*C.*1. Upon signature, the full text of the Truce Agreement or a communiqué containing the principles thereof as agreed upon between the two Governments and the Commission will be made public.

Part III

The Government of India and the Government of Pakistan reaffirm their wish that the future status of the State of Jammu and Kashmir shall be determined in accordance with the will of the people and to that end, upon acceptance of the truce agreement, both Governments agree to enter into consultations with the Commission to determine fair and equitable conditions whereby such free expression will be assured.

Article 370 of the Constitution of India

(1) Notwithstanding anything in this Constitution:

(a) the provisions of Article 238 shall not apply in relation to the State of Jammu and Kashmir;

(b) the power of Parliament to make laws for the said State shall be limited to

(i) those matters in the Union List and the Concurrent List which in consultation with the Government of the State, are declared by the President to correspond to matters specified in the Instrument of Accession governing the accession of the State to the Dominion of India as the matters with respect to which the Dominion Legislature may make laws for that State; and

(ii) such other matters in the said Lists as, with the concurrency of the Government of the State, the President may by order specify.

1. *Explanation:* For the purposes of this Article, the Government of the State means the person for the time being recognised by the President as the Maharaja of Jammu and Kashmir acting on the advice of the Council of Ministers for the time being in office under the Maharaja's Proclamation dated the fifth day of March, 1948.

(c) the provisions of Article (1) and of this Article shall apply in relation to this State;

(d) Such of the other provisions of this Constitution shall apply in relation to that State subject to such exceptions and modifications as the President may by order specify:

Provided that no such order which related to the matters specified in the Instrument of Accession of the State referred to in paragraph (i) of sub-clause (b) shall be issued except in consultation with the Government of the State;

Provided further that no such order which relates to matters other than those referred to in the last preceding proviso shall be issued except with the concurrency of the Government.

(2) If the concurrency of the Government of the State referred to in paragraph (ii) of sub-clause (b) of clause (1) or in the second proviso to sub-clause (d) of that clause be given before the Constituent Assembly for the purpose of framing the Constitution of the State is convened, it shall be placed before such Assembly for such decision as it may take thereon.

(3) Notwithstanding anything in the foregoing provisions of the Article, the President may, by public notification, declare that this Article shall cease to be operative or shall be operative only with such exceptions and modifications and from such date as he may notify.

Provided that the recommendation of the Constituent Assembly of the State referred to in clause (2) shall be necessary before the President issues such a notification.

Tashkent Declaration, 10 January 1966

The Prime Minister of India and the President of Pakistan, having met at Tashkent and having discussed the existing relations between India and Pakistan, hereby declare their firm resolve to restore normal and peaceful relations between their countries and to promote understanding and friendly relations between their peoples. They consider the attainment of these objectives of vital importance for the welfare of the 600 million people of India and Pakistan.

(i) The Prime Minister of India and the President of Pakistan agree that both sides will exert all efforts to create good neighbourly relations between India and Pakistan in accordance with the United Nations Charter. They reaffirm their obligation under the Charter not to have recourse to force and to settle their disputes through peaceful means. They considered that the interests of peace in their region and particularly in the Indo-Pakistan subcontinent and indeed, the interests of the peoples of India and Pakistan were not served by the continuance of tension between the two countries. It was against this background that Jammu and Kashmir was discussed, and each of the sides set forth its respective position.

(ii) The Prime Minister of India and the President of Pakistan have agreed that all armed personnel of the two countries shall be withdrawn not later than 25 February 1966 to the positions they held prior to 5 August 1965, and both sides shall observe the cease-fire terms on the cease-fire line.

(iii) The Prime Minister of India and the President of Pakistan have agreed that relations between India and Pakistan shall be based on the principle of non-interference in the internal affairs of each other.

(iv) The Prime Minister of India and the President of Pakistan have agreed that both sides will discourage any propaganda directed against the other country and will encourage propaganda which promotes the development of friendly relations between the two countries.

(v) The Prime Minister of India and the President of Pakistan have agreed that the High Commissioner of India to Pakistan and the High Commissioner of Pakistan to India will return to their posts and that the normal functioning of diplomatic missions of both countries will be restored. Both Governments shall observe the Vienna Convention of 1961 on Diplomatic Intercourse.

(vi) The Prime Minister of India and the President of Pakistan have agreed to consider measures towards the restoration of economic and trade relations, communications as well as cultural exchanges between India and Pakistan, and to take measures to implement the existing agreements between India and Pakistan.

(vii) The Prime Minister of India and the President of Pakistan have agreed that they will give instructions to their respective authorities to carry out the repatriation of the prisoners of war.

(viii) The Prime Minister of India and the President of Pakistan have agreed that the two sides will continue the discussions of questions relating to the problems of refugees and evictions/illegal immigrations. They also agreed that both sides will create conditions which will prevent the exodus of people. They further agree to discuss the return of the property and assets taken over by either side in connection with the conflict.

(ix) The Prime Minister of India and the President of Pakistan have agreed that the two sides will continue meetings both at highest and at other levels of matters of direct concern to both countries. Both sides have recognised the need to set up joint Indian-Pakistani bodies which will report to their Governments in order to decide what further steps should be taken.

The Prime Minister of India and the President of Pakistan record their feelings, deep appreciation and gratitude to the leaders of the Soviet Union, the Soviet Government and personally to the Chairman of the Council of Ministers of the USSR for their constructive, friendly and noble part in bringing about the present meeting which has resulted in mutually satisfactory results. They also express to the Government and friendly people of Uzbekistan their sincere thankfulness for their overwhelming reception and generous hospitality.

They invite the Chairman of the Council of Ministers of the USSR to witness this declaration.

Lal Bahadur Shastri   Mohammad Ayub Khan
Prime Minister of India   President of Pakistan

Tashkent, 10 January 1966

Simla Agreement, 3 July 1972

The Government of India and the Government of Pakistan are resolved that the two countries put an end to the conflict and confrontation that have hitherto marred their relations and work for the promotion of a friendly and harmonious relationship and the establishment of durable peace in the sub-continent, so that both countries may henceforth devote their resources and energies to the pressing task of advancing the welfare of their people.

In order to achieve this objective, the Government of India and the Government of Pakistan have agreed as follows:

(i) That the principles and purposes of the Charter of the United Nations shall govern the relations between the two countries.

(ii) That the two countries are resolved to settle their differences by peaceful means through bilateral negotiations or by any other peaceful means mutually agreed upon between them. Pending the final settlement of any of the problems between the two countries, neither side shall unilaterally alter the situation and both shall prevent the organisation, assistance or encouragement of any acts detrimental to the maintenance of peaceful and harmonious relations.

(iii) That the prerequisite for reconciliation, good neighbourliness and durable peace between them is a commitment by both the countries to peaceful co-existence, respect for each other's territorial integrity and sovereignty and non-interference in each other's internal affairs, on the basis of equality and mutual benefit.

(iv) That the basic issues and causes of conflict which have bedevilled the relations between the two countries for the last 25 years shall be resolved by peaceful means;

(v) That they shall always respect each other's national unity, territorial integrity, political independence and sovereign equality;

(vi) That in accordance with the Charter of the United Nations, they will refrain from the threat or use of force against the territorial integrity or political independence of each other.

Both Governments will take all steps within their power to prevent hostile propaganda directed against each other. Both countries will encourage the dissemination of such informations as would promote the development of friendly relations between them. In order progressively to restore and normalise relations between the two countries step by step, it was agreed that:

(i) Steps shall be taken to resume communications, postal, telegraphic, sea, land including border, posts and air links including over-flights.

(ii) Appropriate steps shall be taken to promote travel facilities for the nationals of the other country.

(iii) Trade and co-operation in economic and other agreed fields will be resumed as far as possible.

(iv) Exchange in the fields of science and culture will be promoted.

In this connection delegations from the two countries will meet from time to time to work out the necessary details.

In order to initiate the process of the establishment of durable peace, both the Governments agree that:

(i) Indian and Pakistani forces shall be withdrawn to their side of the international border.

(ii) In Jammu and Kashmir, the line of control, resulting from the cease-fire of December 17, 1971, shall be respected by both sides without prejudice to the recognised position of either side. Neither side shall seek to alter it unilaterally, irrespective of mutual differences and legal interpretations. Both sides further undertake to refrain from the threat or the use of force in violation of this line.

(iii) The withdrawals shall commence upon entry into force of this agreement and shall be completed within a period of 30 days thereof.

This agreement will be subject to ratification by both countries in accordance with their respective constitutional procedures, and will come into force with effect from the date on which the instruments of ratification are exchanged.

Both Governments agree that their respective heads will meet again at a mutually convenient time in the future and that, in the meanwhile the representatives of the two sides will meet to discuss further the modalities and arrangements for the establishment of durable peace and normalisation of relations including the questions of repatriation of prisoners of war and civilian internees, a final settlement of Jammu and Kashmir and the resumption of diplomatic relations.

Indira Gandhi   Zulfikar Ali Bhutto
Prime Minister, Republic of India   President, Islamic Republic of Pakistan

Kashmir Accord, 1975

1. The State of Jammu and Kashmir, which is a constituent unit of the Union of India, shall in its relations with the Union, continue to be governed by Article 370 of the Constitution of India.

2. The residuary powers of legislation shall remain with the State; however, Parliament will continue to have power to make laws relating to the prevention of activities directed towards disclaiming, questioning or disrupting the sovereignty and territorial integrity of India or bringing about cession of a part of the territory of India or secession of a part of the territory of India from the Union or causing insult to the Indian national flag, the Indian national anthem and the Constitution.

3. Where any provision of the Constitution of India had been applied to the State of Jammu and Kashmir with adaptations and modifications, such adaptations and modifications can be altered or repealed by an order of the President under Article 370, each individual proposal in this behalf being considered on its merits; but provisions of the Constitution of India already applied to the State of Jammu and Kashmir without adaptation or modification are unalterable.

4. With a view to assuring freedom to the State of Jammu and Kashmir, to have its own legislation on matters like welfare measures, cultural matters, social security, personal law and procedural laws, in a manner suited to the special conditions in the State, it is agreed that the State Government can review the laws made by Parliament or extended to the State after 1953 on any matter relatable to the Concurrent List and may decide which of them, in its opinion. needs amendment or repeal. Thereafter, appropriate steps may be taken under Article 254 of the Constitution of India. The grant of the President's assent to such legislation would be sympathetically considered. The same approach would be adopted in regard to the laws to be made by Parliament in future under the proviso to clause 2 of that Article; the State Government shall be consulted regarding the application of any such law to the State and views of the State shall receive the fullest consideration.

5. As an arrangement reciprocal to what has been provided under Article 368, suitable modification of the Articles applied to the State should be made by Presidential order to the effect that no laws made by the legislature of the State of Jammu and Kashmir, seeking to make any change in or in the effect of any provision of the Constitution of the State of Jammu and Kashmir relating to any of the under-mentioned matters shall take effect unless the bill having been reserved for the consideration of the President receives his assent. The matters are:

(a) the appointment powers, functions, duties, privileges and immunities of the Governor; and,

(b) the following matters relating to elections, namely the superintendence, direction and control of elections by the Election Commission of India, eligibility for inclusion in the electoral rolls without discrimination, adult suffrage, and composition of the Legislative Council, being matters specified in Sections 138, 139, 140 and 150 of the Constitution of the State of Jammu and Kashmir.

6. No agreement was possible on the question of nomenclature of the Governor and the Chief Minister and the matter is, therefore, remitted to the Principals.

Mirza Mohammad Afzal Beg   G. Parthasarathi
New Delhi, 13 November 1974

The United Nations Convention against Illicit Traffic in Narcotic Drugs and Psychotropic Substances, 19 December 1988

The Parties to this Convention,

Deeply concerned by the magnitude of and rising trend in the illicit production of, demand for and traffic in narcotic drugs and psychotropic substances, which pose a serious threat to the health and welfare of human beings and adversely affect the economic, cultural and political foundations of society,...

Recognizing the links between illicit traffic and other related organized criminal activities which undermine the legitimate economies and threaten the stability, security and sovereignty of States,...

Recognizing that eradication of illicit traffic is a collective responsibility of all States and that, to that end, co-ordinated action within the framework of international co-operation is necessary,...

Article 2
Scope of the Convention

1. The purpose of this Convention is to promote co-operation among the Parties so that they may address more effectively the various aspects of illicit traffic in narcotic drugs and psychotropic substances having an international dimension...

Article 3
Offences and Sanctions

1. Each Party shall adopt such measures as may be necessary to establish as criminal offences under its domestic law, when committed intentionally:

(a) (i) The production, manufacture, extraction, preparation, offering, offering for sale, distribution, sale, delivery on any terms whatsoever, brokerage, dispatch, dispatch in transit, transport, importation or exportation of any narcotic drug or any psychotropic substance...;
(ii) The cultivation of opium poppy, coca bush or cannabis plant for...;
(iii) The possession or purchase of any narcotic drug or psychotropic substance...;

2. Subject to its constitutional principles and the basic concepts of its legal system, each Party shall adopt such measures as may be necessary to establish as a criminal offence under its domestic law, when committed intentionally, the possession, purchase or cultivation of narcotic drugs or psychotropic substances for personal consumption...

Article 6
Extradition

2. ...The Parties undertake to include such offences as extraditable offences in every extradition treaty to be concluded between them...

Article 7
Mutual Legal Assistance

1. The Parties shall afford one another, pursuant to this article, the widest measure of mutual legal assistance in investigations, prosecutions and judicial proceedings...

Article 10
International Co-operation and Assistance for Transit States

1. The Parties shall co-operate, directly or through competent international or regional organizations, to assist and support transit States and, in particular, developing countries in need of such assistance and support, to the extent possible, through programmes of technical co-operation on interdiction and other related activities...

Article 12
Substances Frequently Used in the Illicit Manufacture of
Narcotic Drugs or Psychotropic Substances

5. The Commission, taking into account the comments submitted by the Parties and the comments and recommendations of the Board, whose assessment shall be determinative as to scientific matters, and also taking into due consideration any other relevant factors, may decide by a two-thirds majority of its members to place a substance in Table I or Table II...

Article 14
Measures to Eradicate Illicit Cultivation of Narcotic
Plants and to Eliminate Illicit Demand for
Narcotic Drugs and Psychotropic Substances

2. Each Party shall take appropriate measures to prevent illicit cultivation of and to eradicate plants containing narcotic or psychotropic substances, such as opium poppy, coca bush and cannabis plants, cultivated illicitly in its territory...

Article 17
Illicit Traffic by Sea

1. The Parties shall co-operate to the fullest extent possible to suppress illicit traffic by sea, in conformity with the international law of the sea...

Article 20
Information to be Furnished by the Parties

1. The Parties shall furnish, through the Secretary-General, information to the Commission on the working of this Convention in their territories...

Article 21
Functions of the Commission

The Commission is authorized to consider all matters pertaining to the aims of this Convention...

Article 23
Reports of the Board

1. The Board shall prepare an annual report on its work...

International Convention against the Recruitment, Use, Financing and Training of Mercenaries, 4 December 1989

The General Assembly,

Considering that the progressive development of international law and its codification contribute to the implementation of the purposes and principles set forth in Articles 1 and 2 of the Charter of the United Nations...

Adopts and opens for signature and ratification or for accession the International Convention against the Recruitment, Use, Financing and Training of Mercenaries, the text of which is annexed to the present resolution...

Affirming that the recruitment, use, financing and training of mercenaries should be considered as offences of grave concern to all States and that any person committing any of these offences should be either prosecuted or extradited,

Expressing concern at new unlawful international activities linking drug traffickers and mercenaries in the perpetration of violent actions which undermine the constitutional order of States...

Have agreed as follows:

Article 1

For the purposes of the present Convention,

1. A mercenary is any person who:

(a) Is specially recruited locally or abroad in order to fight in an armed conflict;

(b) Is motivated to take part in the hostilities essentially by the desire for private gain and, in fact, is promised, by or on behalf of a party to the conflict, material compensation substantially in excess of that promised or paid to combatants of similar rank and functions in the armed forces of that party;

(c) Is neither a national of a party to the conflict nor a resident of territory controlled by a party to the conflict;

(d) Is not a member of the armed forces of a party to the conflict; and

(e) Has not been sent by a State which is not a party to the conflict on official duty as a member of its armed forces...

Article 5

1. States Parties shall not recruit, use, finance or train mercenaries and shall prohibit such activities in accordance with the provisions of the present Convention...

3. They shall make the offences set forth in the present Convention punishable by appropriate penalties which take into account the grave nature of those offences.

Article 6

States Parties shall co-operate in the prevention of the offences set forth in the present Convention, particularly by:

(a) Taking all practicable measures to prevent preparations in their respective territories for the commission of those offences within or outside their territories, including the prohibition of illegal activities of persons, groups and organizations that encourage, instigate, organize or engage in the perpetration of such offences;...

Article 8

Any State Party having reason to believe that one of the offences set forth in the present Convention has been, is being or will be committed shall, in accordance with its national law, communicate the relevant information, as soon as it comes to its knowledge, directly or through the Secretary-General of the United Nations, to the States Parties affected...

Article 10

1. Upon being satisfied that the circumstances so warrant, any State Party in whose territory the alleged offender is present shall, in accordance with its laws, take him into custody or take such other measures to ensure his presence for such time as is necessary to enable any criminal or extradition proceedings to be instituted...

Article 12

The State Party in whose territory the alleged offender is found shall, if it does not extradite him, be obliged, without exception whatsoever and whether or not the offence was committed in its territory, to submit the case to its competent authorities for the purpose of prosecution, through proceedings in accordance with the laws of that State...

The United Nations Security Council Resolution 1269 (1999) related to all acts of terrorism, 19 October 1999

The Security Council,

Deeply concerned by the increase in acts of international terrorism which endangers the lives and well-being of individuals worldwide as well as the peace and security of all States,

Condemning all acts of terrorism, irrespective of motive, wherever and by whomever committed,

Mindful of all relevant resolutions of the General Assembly, including resolution 49/60 of 9 December 1994, by which it adopted the Declaration on Measures to Eliminate International Terrorism,...

1. *Unequivocally condemns* all acts, methods and practices of terrorism as criminal and unjustifiable, regardless of their motivation, in all their forms and manifestations, wherever and by whomever committed, in particular those which could threaten international peace and security;

2. *Calls upon* all States to implement fully the international anti-terrorist conventions to which they are parties,...;

4. *Calls upon* all States to take, *inter alia*, in the context of such cooperation and coordination, appropriate steps to:

   - cooperate with each other...to prevent and suppress terrorist acts...;
   - prevent and suppress in their territories through all lawful means the preparation and financing of any acts of terrorism;
   - deny those who plan, finance or commit terrorist acts safe havens by ensuring their apprehension and prosecution or extradition;
   - take appropriate measures...before granting refugee status, for the purpose of ensuring that the asylum-seeker has not participated in terrorist acts;
   - exchange information...to prevent the commission of terrorist acts;

5. *Requests* the Secretary-General, in his reports to the General Assembly...to pay special attention to the need to prevent and fight the threat to international peace and security as a result of terrorist activities;...

7. *Decides* to remain seized of this matter.

Bibliographic Notes

Sources on Kashmir are abundant if one can find the occasion to visit the printed collections in India, Pakistan and Kashmir and utilize the sources in the outstanding libraries of the world. I had recourse to some of these opportunities. Since this book already made references to some published material on the subject, there is no need to reproduce a long list of books and articles. The reader may consult the bibliographical pages of a number of works, such as Sisir Gupta's *Kashmir* (pp. 483–502), A. R. Desai's now classic *Social Background of Indian Nationalism* (pp. 443–451) and its sequel, *Recent Trends...* (pp. 139–144), as well as Yu. V. Gankovskiy-L. R. Gordon-Polonskaia's *Istoriia Pakistana* (pp. 358–374), M. T. Stepanyants's *Pakistan* (pp. 119–128), and the like. Desai's two volumes are perhaps the best account by an Indian scholar of the qualitative structural transformation that took place under the impact of British rule. John Garrett's *A Classical Dictionary of India* is "illustrative of the mythology, philosophy, literature, antiquities, arts, manners, customs" and the like of the Hindus.

It is not difficult to trace political and polemical information about Kashmir. Reports on Kashmir are stacked in several rooms in the United Nations Headquarters in New York. The U.N. itself printed documents and arguments, and the Governments of India and Pakistan have published more. For instance, Verinder Grover's *The Story of Kashmir* (3 vols.) and P. L. Lakhanpal's (ed.) *Essential Documents and Notes on Kashmir Dispute* on the Indian side, as well as *The Kashmir Question* by Pakistan's Institute of International Relations and *White Paper on the Jammu and Kashmir Dispute* by the Ministry of Foreign Affairs in Islamabad. In addition to the published *Jammu and Kashmir Official Reports, Acts and Gazettes,* the unpublished primary sources in the National Archives in New Delhi include the "Foreign Department Proceedings" of the Government of India. The "Old English Records" of His Highness' Government may be found in the Jammu and Kashmir State Archives (Jammu). For some selected primary sources, one may see R. K. K. Bhatt's bibliography in his *Political and Constitutional Development of the Jammu and Kashmir State* (Delhi, Seema, 1984, pp. 269–282). There are also unpublished private papers, such as the Halifax Collection at the Nehru Memorial Museum and Library in New Delhi, or the Private Papers of Lord Minton on microfilm, or the Private Records of Maharaja Pratap Singh.

The broad category on Kashmir's history may be based on indigenous records, foreign chronicles, memoirs of travellers and contemporary works. There are references to Kashmir in early Greek, Chinese and Muslim records. The initial Indian chroniclers were poets as well as historians who utilized Sanskrit, the language for official business. Perhaps the oldest reliable writer is Kalhana (A.D. 12th century), who consulted even earlier informants to compose his own *Rajatarangini* in eight cantos of Sanskrit verse, translated into Persian (15th century) and English (1935). Being the history of various dynasties, Kalhana, not only consulted older works, but also first-hand sources not hiding the errors of kings in whose time he wrote. Jonaraja brought the chronicle of events to the reign of Sultan Zain-ul Abidin, his pupil Srivara adding four more chapters. Prajyabhatta's *Rajavalipataka* ends with the year 1514, his work completed by his pupil Suka following Emperor Akbar's conquest of Kashmir. Malik Haider Chaudura wrote a history of Kashmir in Persian down to his time in 1617. Khwaja Muhammad Azam Kaul's *Wuquat-e Kashmir* (1735–46) was enriched by his son Muhammad Aslam. Maulvi Ghulam Hasan's (1832–98) *Tawarikh-e Kashmir* (3 vols.) is on the geography, political history and the arts of the country. Pandit Anand Koul's *Geography of Jammu and Kashmir* is in English. Ghulam Mohi-ud Din Sufi's *Kashir* (so spelled by the local people) deals with the land after the entry of Islam.

Some of the first Europeans to visit Kashmir were Gerome Xavier who accompanied Akbar to the famine-stricken Valley, François Bernier who described life during the rule of the Moghuls, Desideri who passed to Ladakh after Srinagar, George Forster who witnessed the harsh Afghan rule, and Frederick Drew and Sir Walter Lawrence who both gave detailed accounts of the physical features of the country.

The Cambridge and Oxford histories of India are considered to be relevant and distinguished. The original Oxford history by V. A. Smith (1848–1920) has been rewritten by Percival Spear. The new Cambridge history, under the general editorship of Gordon Johnson, is to cover the centuries from the Moghul era to the present day in twenty-eight volumes (1988–). Unlike the previous series (1922–53), each volume of the present series deals with a separate theme, written by a single author.

Leonard Mosley in *The Last Days of the British Raj* wrote that the official documents dealing with the transfer of power in India would not be released until 1999, but that in the interim period his book would throw some light on events hitherto obscured. The British side of the story, however, was unfolded soon, and twelve volumes of documents, under the general editorship of Nicholas Mansergh, entitled *Constitutional Relations between Britain and India: the Transfer of Power, 1942–47*, were published (1970–83).

Apart from Gandhi's and Nehru's several books, some prominent witnesses, inseparable from events, wrote or spoke on crucial developments: Lord Mountbatten *(Time Only to Look Forward)*, Jinnah *(Speeches;* also: Muhammad Anwar's *Quaid-e-Azam Jinnah: a Selected Bibliography)*, Sheikh Abdullah *(Flames of Chinar)*, Liaquat Ali Khan *(Pakistan)*, Joseph Korbel *(Danger in Kashmir)*, M. C. Mahajan *(Looking Backward)*, V. P. Menon *(The Story of the Integration of the Indian States)*, Sir Francis Tucker *(While Memory Serves)*, and the like. Among the biographies, Sir Penderel Moon's *Wavell: the Viceroy's Journal* contains some almost day-to-day accounts. Ziegler's *(Mountbatten: an Official Biography)* and Campbell-Johnson's *(Mission with Mountbatten)* books throw some more light on that crucial period (23

March-15 August 1947). Ayub Khan's *(Friends, Not Masters)*, Zulfikar Ali Bhutto's *(The Myth of Independence)*, and Benazir Bhutto's *(Daughter of the East)* chronicles are semi-memoirs.

Many books by researchers contain valuable accounts: For instance, Michael Brecher *(Nehru: a Political Biography)*, Hector Bolitho *(Jinnah: Creator of Pakistan)*, H. V. Hodson *(The Great Divide)*, Tara Chand *(History of the Freedom Movement*, New Delhi*)*, Mahmud Hussain *et al. (A History of the Freedom Movement,* Karachi*)*, etc. Rasheeduddin Khan's *Bewildered India* as a treatment of "identity, pluralism and discord", and Prem Shankar Jha's India as "a political economy of stagnation" as well as Chaudri Muhammad Ali's (a former secretary of the Partition Council and later Prime Minister of Pakistan) *The Emergence of Pakistan,* Sreedhar-Nilesh Bhagat's *Pakistan: a Withering State?* and Tahir Amin's *Ethno-National Movements of Pakistan,* all authoritative accounts, may be added.

Some of the books especially on Kashmir are: Shaheen Akhtar *(Uprising in Indian-held Jammu and Kashmir),* Prem Nath Bazaz *(Azad Kashmir),* Lord Birdwood *(Two Nations and Kashmir),* Pran Chopra *(India, Pakistan and the Kashmir Tangle),* Vernon Hewitt *(Reclaiming the Past? The Search for Political and Cultural Unity in Contemporary Jammu and Kashmir),* Prem Shankar Jha *(Kashmir 1947: Rival Versions of History),* M. Anwar Khan *(The Partition of India and the Kashmir Problem),* Rahmatullah Khan *(Kashmir and the United Nations),* M. L. Kotru *(The Kashmir Story),* Alastair Lamb *(Birth of a Tragedy: Kashmir 1947; Kashmir: a Disputed Legacy, 1846–1990),* Arjun Ray *(Kashmir Diary: Psychology of Militancy),* B. L. Sharma *(The Kashmir Story),* Shafi Shauq, Qazi Zahoor and Shoukat Farooqi *(Europeans on Kashmir),* Tavlen Singh *(Kashmir: Tragedy of Errors),* Robert G. Wirsing *(ed., Kashmir: Resolving Regional Conflict; India, Pakistan and the Kashmir Dispute),* and Lars Blinkenberg *(India-Pakistan: the History of Unsolved Conflicts).* The last mentioned recent study consists of a re-edition of the original single volume and a new analytical volume containing an evaluation of many structural factors.

Terrorism continues to pose a serious threat to India's security. The volatile situation in Kashmir has been discussed in a number of publications. The Indian Ministry of Home Affairs brings out periodic volumes on *Profile of Terrorist Violence in Jammu and Kashmir,* which contain descriptions of atrocities by militants. Ved Marwah, a former member of the Indian Police Service who held many important assignments in different states in India, traced the genesis of terrorist movements and analysed how extremist violence has taken deep roots, in his book entitled *Uncivil Wars: Pathology of Terrorism in India.* Manoj Joshi's *The Lost Rebellion: Kashmir in the Nineties* is a riveting account of the human drama in Kashmir. Tara Kartha's *Tools of Terror* examines the connection between light weapons and India's security. *Beyond Terrorism* by Salman Hurshid, the Indian Minister of State for External Affairs, provides a graphic account of the suffering in Kashmir and also looks beyond terrorism to a more peaceful future. Two new Indian periodicals, *Aakrosh* and *Faultlines,* concentrate on conflict, terrorism, and resolution. The former is published by the Forum for Strategic and Security Studies, and the latter by the Institute for Conflict Management, both in New Delhi. The founder of the Institute is K. P. S. Gill, who served in a number of theatres of civil strife and low intensity warfare and led a successful campaign against terrorism in Punjab. *Strategic Analysis,* a monthly journal of the Institute for Defence Studies and Analyses (IDSA), frequently carries articles on Kashmir and terrorism. IDSA, led by Air Commodore Jasjit Singh, also brings out books, a recent one entitled *Kargil 1999,* which may be described as Pakistan's fourth war for Kashmir. The *Kashmir Trends* is a digest of news and views from J&K media files as well as international and Indian national press on Kashmir. Several other periodicals *(Asian Affairs, Asian Strategic Review, BIISS Journal, Islamic Order, Kashmir Today, Kashmir Watch, Journal of Peace Studies, Pakistan Defence Review, Pakistan Horizon, Pakistan Journal of History and Culture, Pakistan Perspectives, Peace Initiatives, Regional Studies, Secular Democracy, Seminar, South Asian Studies, Strategic Bulletin, Strategic Studies, U.S.I. Journal, World Focus)* are also useful. The past issues of some Indian daily papers are available at the main library of the Jawaharlal Nehru University (New Delhi).

Index